Crisis,
Absolutism,
Revolution:
Europe, 1648–1789/91

Crisis,
Absolutism,
Revolution:
Europe, 1648–1789/91

Raymond Birn
University of Oregon

The Dryden Press
Hinsdale, Illinois

For Randi, Eric, and Laila

Preface

More adeptly than ever before historians are interpreting the political, economic, and intellectual past within the framework of their subject's social environment. Imaginative new hypotheses link familiar themes such as the development of absolutism, decline of religious authority, and even international rivalries to the lives of groups hitherto treated condescendingly or ignored altogether. Furthermore, in their attempts at evaluating the force of popular culture, population development, and sources of economic productivity, historians are employing original measurement devices and quantitative techniques. Few periods have been more receptive to such examination and reinterpretation than the century and a half preceding the French Revolution.

This book about the peoples of Europe from 1648 to 1789 is indebted to the work of contemporary scholars sensitive to social history. Each of the two sections of the book begins with an analytical essay dealing with "the people, the land, and the state." The remaining chapters try to strike a balance between chronological narrative and comparative analysis. Because the book is primarily an introduction to the period for undergraduates, I have virtually ignored footnotes and other scholarly apparatus. By no means, however, should this be taken as a mark of an author's ingratitude towards his predecessors. On the contrary, the appended bibliography should not only lead students towards a deeper appreciation of the period but also reveal to them and their instructors a number of works that have influenced my thinking.

Individuals closer to home certainly have influenced it. They include my colleagues at the University of Oregon—particularly Robert M. Berdahl, Thomas A. Brady, and Robert G. Lang; my friends Robert and Patricia Patterson, who read every word of the manuscript with devoted critical attention; and, most especially, my wife and children, who shared with me the development of my ideas as well as the joys and tribulations of expressing them. Dedicating this book to Randi, Eric, and Laila is the least I can do in recompense.

Raymond Birn

Contents

Part One

An Age of Crisis and Discovery: 1648–1715/26

Chapter One

The People, the Land, and the State

POPULATION

From 1620 until 1720, the population of the world rose from about 460 million to about 520 million. During this same period, Europe's share of humanity rose from about 100 million to about 120 million. To a modern observer, painfully aware of contemporary overpopulation crises, Europe's increase of approximately 7 percent per generation seems like a model of demographic restraint. To the historian, however, acutely aware that Europe's population doubled in the sixteenth century, and that from 1750 to 1850 it doubled again, the interim period of 1620 to 1720 looks exceedingly strange because the reproductive habits of people in preindustrial society did not counsel restraint.

It is doubly surprising that during this hundred-year period, when Europeans exercised an unprecedented dominion over nature, thanks to their scientific and technological achievements, and over the non-European world, thanks to their military and commercial prowess, their demographic vigor failed to keep pace with what had gone before and with what came later. About 1620, the trend of the sixteenth century abruptly halted, and for the next three generations, the traditionally high birthrate was overwhelmed by an exceptionally high death rate. Even economically advanced England, France, and the United Provinces of the Netherlands barely held their own. After 1720, the pattern changed. By 1750, births outnumbered deaths in a spectacular fashion, with twice as many infants surviving their first year; those who reached adolescence lived ten years longer than their parents had.

The nagging question remains: Why was there such an upsurge in mortality between 1620 and 1720? We still are far from the answers. However, by studying regional conditions in England and Germany, historians may confirm hypotheses and apply their findings to other places on the continent. One fact is certain. What used to be called the "splendid century"—an age dazzled by the achievements of Louis XIV, Peter the Great, Descartes, and Newton—is now seen as a hard and difficult time of brutal warfare, economic recession, and political instability. The consequences can be measured in sheer human losses.

For the overwhelming number of Europeans, the vagaries of war, climate, famine, and epidemic overshadowed the intellectual and material achievements of the period. The second half of the seventeenth century literally rings out with the litany of misery: *A peste, fame et bello libera nos Domine* ("Free us, O God, from plague, famine, and war"). The condition of the harvest wielded absolute power over the rhythm of life. In preindustrial Europe, where two-fifths of the land under cultivation had to lie fallow each year, two consecutive poor harvests, a paucity of available cereals, and the conversion of producers into purchasers could create a vicious pattern: In town, prices would spiral dizzily, and unemployment would become endemic. The authorities then might requisition bread from another province, but interminable delays in transport, toll charges at practically every turn in the road, and a general psychological incapacity of officialdom to cope with crisis would delay help until it was too late.

The distinguished French historian Pierre Goubert vividly describes the effects of poor harvests upon a cloth worker and his family in the town of Beauvais, northwest of Paris. Jean Cocu has a wife and three daughters, the youngest nine years of age. The wife and girls all work at home as spinners. The family earns 108 *sols* per week, and their staple diet is heavy rye bread. They consume nearly ten pounds of it per day! With bread at one-half *sol* per pound, existence is normal. But with the poor harvests of 1693 and 1694, the price of bread rises to 2 and then 3 *sols* per pound. Piecework for the women declines drastically; Cocu is laid off. He spends his savings; then he borrows. The family must replace bread with items they scavenge: bark, cooked nettles, the entrails of slaughtered animals. Others are in competition with them for survival. Their dignity as artisans shattered, the Cocus are inscribed in the Bureau of the Poor for Beauvais. But the town officials are no more adept than they at obtaining food. The youngest is the first to succumb to malnutrition in March 1694. In May the father and eldest daughter follow. The mother and a single child are left, beggars now. The harvest of 1695 brings relief, and the pair apparently live on for a few more years. But as a productive economic unit, the Cocus are destroyed.[1]

Like Jean and his daughters, tens of thousands of "producers" in seventeenth-century society were annihilated, and their survivors converted into drones. The human waste was enormous but tolerated. Famines usually were localized calamities. There were enough of them, however, to slow the economic development of nearly every state in Europe.

At least once per decade, famines ignited genuine regional catastrophes in the form of bubonic and pulmonary plague. Customarily, the towns,

---

[1]Pierre Goubert, *Cent mille Provinciaux au xviie siècle* (Paris, 1968).

overflowing with starving refugees from the countryside, suffered epidemics in the extreme. From 1649 to 1654, the plague repeatedly struck the cities of the entire Mediterranean basin. In 1657, it returned to southern Italy. In 1665, London and its region felt it, and from 1676 to 1685, most of Spain's urban centers could not escape it. Early in the eighteenth century, improvements in sanitation and housing construction gradually rescued the west European city dweller. The rat that carried the mortal plague-producing flea found brick walls less congenial than timbered ones, tile roofs less penetrable than thatched ones. In England, the Netherlands, and France, townsmen dispensed with pigstys in their streets. As the eighteenth century opened, Scandinavia and central and eastern Europe still felt the effects of plague. In 1720, an epidemic returned to France's Mediterranean coast, but it was the last major one to strike Europe. In its prime, the plague had exacted enormous tolls. The three great seventeenth-century epidemics had taken over a million Spanish lives.

Certain important regions suffered from depopulation in such absolute terms that the consequences contributed to national disaster. The three most striking regions were Germany, Poland, and Spain.

In 1648, Germany was the most publicized region of human loss. After three decades of nearly continuous warfare, Germany sank into the peace of exhaustion. In a rough line running from Strasbourg in the southwest to Stralsund in the northeast, 50 to 70 percent of the civilian population had either died or disappeared along the refugee highways in the direction of new and strange lands. In Brandenburg—counted among the war's winners —half the farms were destroyed. At the other end of Germany, in Württemburg, forty thousand homes and farms had vanished. Cities that had begun to stagnate in the sixteenth century were finished. The Thirty Years' War cost Germany seven to eight million lives. A population that probably had reached twenty million in 1600 was under thirteen million by 1648.

Because Germany suffered depopulation on such a catastrophic scale, most of the three-hundred-odd princes thoroughly understood the dictum that the Elector of Brandenburg coined: "People are the greatest wealth of a country." In their bid to reconstruct their principalities, Frederick William of Brandenburg and his fellow sovereigns in Hesse-Kassel, the Palatinate, and Nassau avidly sought immigrants. So did the patricians of north coastal towns like Hamburg, Bremen, Lübeck, and Danzig, where refugees had settled during the war. Even the sensitive issue of religious affiliation became secondary. Princes courted foreign settlers, especially French Huguenots, Swiss, Dutch, Scandinavians, and Scots, to reclaim what now were frontier lands. As a result of immigration and resettlement, Germany held its own during the second half of the century. By 1700, there were fourteen million Germans. This was one-third fewer than at the outbreak of the Thirty Years' War, but it also was a million more than during the bleakest year, 1648.

Poland was not so fortunate. What Germans had known from 1618 to

1648 Poles were to learn from 1648 to the 1720s. The failure of Polish institutions to create a political order of sufficient resilience to withstand the incursions of rapacious neighbors turned wide swaths of Poland into battlegrounds. Overwhelmingly agrarian, Poland was the chief exporter of grain to northwestern Europe. For more than two generations, Swedes, Russians, Austrians, Saxons, and Prussians would fight over Poland's sources of production and ports of exit. When its aristocracy failed to defend it, Poland's peasantry paid the price. Areas of tillage were reduced drastically and exports fell. A midcentury population of ten million was down to eight at the end of the Great Northern War (1721). By this time, Poland's surviving peasantry was Europe's most depressed, its political life was paralyzed by a landowning class unwilling to grant central government the semblance of national authority, and its fate as an independent state was in the hands of rulers in St. Petersburg, Vienna, and even Versailles.

Spain also suffered a population collapse in the seventeenth century, and it dragged its southern Italian possessions into its decline. The province of Castile had been the primary force of the sixteenth-century Spanish empire. Castile had possessed more than six of the nine million inhabitants of the Iberian peninsula. A densely settled, arid region, Castile's population was concentrated in towns that fed on the countryside, without being developed sufficiently in an industrial or commercial sense. Furthermore, rural Castile leaned towards sheep herding rather than tillage, and raw wool was Spain's leading export. The expulsion of 300,000 Moriscos and the neglect of agriculture at a time when population was increasing and Spanish military expenditures were outdistancing income from the New World's silver mines, had jarring consequences for future generations. From 1620 on, Spanish agriculture was unable to feed the Spanish people. The demands of the tax collector and recruiting sergeant drove peasants to the towns, where high prices for scarce bread proved the rule and where epidemic took its toll.

After the 1680s, Spain's catalogue of misfortunes seemed endless: it was beset with a dynastic crisis, its neighbors plotted the dismemberment of its empire, and from 1702 to 1713, war was fought on its soil. Peasant proprietorships covered scarcely 5 percent of the tilled land. Over 250,000 Spaniards belonged to an unproductive clergy. In Castile, the peasant, shepherd, and artisan gave way to the beggar, bandit, and vagabond. By 1715, even the towns of Castile were emptying as populations drifted to the coastal regions or secured passage on boats headed for America. This era, the darkest page in Spanish history, marked a population loss of one-fourth to under seven million. Castile alone lost half its people.

From 1648 to 1715, the most densely populated region in Europe was Italy, and the most densely populated state was France. The dominant territorial states were France and the Hapsburg empire, and the dominant commercial ones were the Netherlands and England. Except for Italy, these places were spared the experience of regular, repeated epidemics, and none knew the excesses of perpetually marauding armies. Yet their population growth was slight and in some cases nonexistent. At the close of the period, Italy's population was 14 million, down a million from what it had been at the beginning. Despite the acquisition of new lands, France's population hovered between 18 and 19 million. The population of the Hapsburgs' German possessions did not rise above six million. The United Provinces and England enjoyed slight population increases: the former went from 1.5 to 1.8 million, and the latter from 5 to 5.4 million. Of all the nations of Europe, only the least known and least European, Russia, experienced a sizable population growth, from 11 to 18 million. It was at this time that the lands leading to the Black Sea, Ukraine, and Lower Volga, the breadbasket of the emerging empire, were settled. But the bulk of Europeans lived in the west—within the radius of an oval drawn from Amsterdam to the Pyrenees, veering westward to include London and southeastern England, eastward to include the Rhine Valley and Switzerland, and southward to incorporate Spanish Catalonia and Italy. The region contained twenty-five people per square mile, whereas the European average was ten.

TOWN AND COUNTRYSIDE

The overwhelming majority of Europeans lived off the land, and famine, rather than the search for opportunity, drew them to the cities. What the refugees found in towns was not free bread but soaring prices, made all the higher by the increased competition for limited stocks. Faced with unemployment as a result of decreasing demand for the products they made, town dwellers despised the new immigrants. Their arrival aggravated problems over fuel, garbage disposal, housing, and water supply. They augmented the chance of epidemic. Late seventeenth-century urban society was a human pressure cooker. Periodic crowd-related diseases might reduce the populations, but the megalopolises—Istanbul with its 750,000, Paris and London with their 300,000 each, Naples with its 250,000—made up their losses with new influxes. On the other hand, smaller cities in commercial decline, particularly those that dotted the Mediterranean, could hardly be expected to recoup their vigor with infusions of the rural poor. Throughout the century, the populations of Venice, Rome, Palermo, and Seville declined steadily. By 1700, each had fewer than 150,000 inhabitants. Valencia, Granada, and Genoa sank to below 100,000. Lyons and Vienna stagnated at 100,000.

Of Europe's cities, Amsterdam alone experienced large-scale commercial growth. Like other European cities, Amsterdam may have drawn the miserable and infected, but it also attracted the persecuted and ambitious. It prospered as it grew. Its population of 200,000 in 1700 was double what it had been a century earlier.

In town and countryside alike, the shadow of death hovered over most human activities. Only recently have historians managed to lay to rest the myth of the peasant or artisan child-marriage which bore fruit in the form of half a dozen sturdy offspring. Had this actually occurred, a crisis of overpopulation would have stricken Europe four generations earlier. In reality, the limits of agricultural technology braked everything else. It took the labor of eight to feed ten. In rural France, peasant females rarely married before they were twenty-five, males rarely before they were twenty-seven. Female fertility ceased at forty-five, and interbirth periods averaged no fewer than two years. Statistically, this meant seven births per couple. But such conditions never existed. In the first two years of marriage, particularly during the first pregnancy and first birth, female mortality was exceedingly high. Moreover, famine, accident, and most often simply worn-out bodies terminated marriages before fifteen years had elapsed.

The aristocracy and wealthy bourgeoisie married earlier, and these women were the sheltered, childbearing matrons of the age, living from pregnancy to pregnancy, turning each infant over to a wet nurse, and then repeating the process. The upper classes married in their teens. They averaged a dozen conceptions, eight to ten live births. It is safe to assume that sheer reproductive vitality assured the leadership of the dominant social groups, so long as they could exploit the labor of the suppressed groups for their own maintenance.

For the peasant or artisan family, matters were different. One child in three died at birth or before reaching the age of ten. Only half of those born ever reached twenty. During periods of dearth, there always was a corresponding drop in marriages, conceptions, and births. Despite the threats of priest and pastor, couples practiced elementary forms of birth control. Nowhere did median life expectancy exceed the age of forty. In France it was thirty-three, in north Italy, twenty-six. Everywhere, those over sixty were worshiped as village Methuselahs. Indeed, what they had survived did make them exceptional. They comprised fewer than 5 percent of the population. Europe was filled with individuals young in years, but old in body.

Eight of ten lived off the land. Except for rare experimental outposts in southeastern England, parts of Holland, and the Spanish Netherlands—where attempts at crop rotation were made and where root crops and clover were introduced to restore soil fertility—the time-worn field-strip system of agriculture, which was dependent upon cereals, dominated. On each estate, plots of arable land were divided into three fields (two in southern Europe) that most often alternated annually among wheat, oats, and fallow. Corn and potatoes were as yet undeveloped. Dairy products, leaf vegetables, and (except for south Italy and Spain) fruit were rare. Because cattle raising was nearly unknown, fertilizer was insufficient. The techniques of plowing and harvesting had not changed in over five hundred years. The water-driven mill and wooden plow were basic equipment. Primitive technology helps to explain why in France, continental Europe's most highly developed agricultural state, only half the potentially arable farmland was actually exploited at any one time. In the Mediterranean, perhaps one-fourth was put to use. East of the Elbe River, it was about 10 percent. The limitations upon agricultural productivity held back everything else.

On the continent, the village community provided the social basis for agricultural activity; field-strip farming was a communal enterprise. The village was recognized in law as a corporate body, woven together by custom, common ownership of equipment and goods, and the parish church. The peasants knew that they had to work together or starve alone. Generally not even possessing surnames, their individuality was subordinated to their collective obligations, and their social superiors saw them as an undifferentiated mass to be treated at best condescendingly but more frequently with simple contempt. A Prussian pastor in 1684 summarized the patrician's view of the peasantry:

> The peasants are indeed human beings, but somewhat more churlish and uncouth than the others. . . . In his movements [the peasant] would only seldom think of his hat and take it off, . . . but if he does so he turns it round like a potter's wheel, or spits into his hand and polishes it. . . . When they eat they do not use a fork, but they dip their five fingers into the pot. . . . If soldiers steal they do it out of extreme need; but most peasants who help themselves do it out of malice. . . . It is also well-known that those who keep on good terms with the vicar are maltreated by the other peasants, for they give them all kinds of bad names, call them traitors, lickspittles, toadies, talebearers. . . . The peasants have that in common with the stockfish: these are best when beaten well and soft. The dear peasants too are only well-behaved when fully burdened with work; then they remain well under control and timid.[2]

The pastor reveals not merely his own prejudices, based upon the peasants' lack of social polish, but he shows us something of the peasants' own consciousness of identity. The image of subservience displayed for their betters was one that they despised. In contact with their superiors, they conformed to roles others had written for them. The psychological tension produced must have been very great. Cheating the lord or his bailiff might have offered some relief—this was the "malice" to which our pastor refers—and genuine revolt, accompanied by looting, murder, and arson, might provide the ultimate release. This latter possibility existed within the framework of the most stable peasant-lord relationships. We may well assume that fear of it helped convince the higher orders to recommend beating the peasants "well and soft" through hard labor and economic dependence.

For those with funds to spare, land was the century's most attractive investment. Wars, social unrest, sluggish demand, and monetary devalua-

---

[2]Cited in F. L. Carsten, "The Empire after the Thirty Years' War," *The New Cambridge Modern History*, vol V (Cambridge, England, 1961), p. 438.

tions turned all but the Dutch—and the English at the end of the century—away from commerce. Moreover, for the heirs of sixteenth-century families who had grown wealthy through trade or the liberal professions, the ownership of land represented, on the continent, the surest route towards ennoblement and tax exemption. The gift of land was the sovereign's means of rewarding military or administrative service. In the late seventeenth century, landowners pushed hard to increase the size of their estates and to raise cereals not merely for village subsistence but also for sale to urban markets or even export abroad, but the prevalence of unrelieved regional famines reveals the difficulties producers had sending their grain to the places that needed it. In England, merchants and gentry, investing in the reclamation of marshes and swamps and in the exploitation of common lands, woods, and wastes, were ahead of their contemporaries on the continent in the art of estate building. In eastern Europe, magnates in Poland, Hungary, and Russia gained control over tens of thousands of acres.

Though a trend clearly existed toward larger estates in the hands of fewer owners, land in seventeenth-century Europe was exploited in a large variety of forms. By 1700, even as wealthy Englishmen evicted renters and enclosed common lands, nearly half the rural population consisted of yeomen who owned or had long-term leases on farmland of up to two hundred acres or grazing land of up to six hundred acres. Nevertheless, the yeomanry was a declining element in English agriculture.

France provided the model for ownership and tenure for most of western Europe. The estate owner held the right of eminent domain over his property, and this was translated into the expectation of homage and dues from those who occupied it. The estate owner might lease out an entire estate on long-term rates to a single party, who customarily held a rank in society similar to his own. The lessee could exploit the estate as he saw fit and even sell the lease rights to a third party.

Far more widespread, however, was the leasing system called the *fief roturier* in which a peasant village assumed collective responsibility over a stipulated portion of the proprietor's estate. In return, the proprietor held certain rights and privileges over the village and its inhabitants. He controlled village justice; he held a monopoly over the estate's oven, mill, and wine press, charging the peasants a use fee; he retained absolute rights over hunting on estate lands or fishing in estate waters; he controlled and charged fees for the utilization of streams and rivers that might flow through the estate; and he could market his own products before the peasants were allowed to market theirs. The individual peasant was responsible for paying his percentage of the village's lease fee to the landlord. The peasant also had to pay the landlord a set of stipulated dues, plus additional taxes on production. Whenever the village renegotiated an expired lease with the landlord, the latter would attempt to dig up new dues and charges that, of course, were passed on to the peasant. The peasant hated these fees with a vengeance. They were paid in kind and represented from one-tenth to one-third of his crop yield. He had to pay them in bad times and good, and the landlord insisted that the peasant pay the seigneurial dues before paying his taxes to the state.

On the surface it would seem that the peasant was a helpless renter, saddled with a collection of exploitative dues and taxes that held him in perpetual bondage to the seigneur. In reality, however, the existence and payment of these dues and taxes were what kept him from slipping down the rungs of peasant society to a sharecropper or day laborer. The fees guaranteed him the right of tenancy, and in the seventeenth and eighteenth centuries, the legal concept of tenancy had a vigor and distinctiveness that are no longer apparent today. The tenant held title to his plot, and he could even bequeath or sell it. Once the landlord—a nobleman, churchman, or bourgeois—accepted rents, dues, and taxes for a piece of the eminent domain, he turned usufruct (the legal right to make a profit) over to the tenant. The landlord was entitled to additional dues whenever the tenant sold or willed the property to someone other than his eldest son. But all agreed that the rights of tenancy were as inviolable as the dues and taxes that the peasant paid to the seigneur, however large the estate might be, however powerful the landlord, however humble the tenant.

For an estate owner content with a fixed income, the tenancy system provided a means of security that was woven tightly into the structure of west European rural society. But those who purchased estates as a growth investment were not likely to be content with an arrangement that had emerged in conjunction with the economically self-sufficient manorial units of the Middle Ages. Modern-minded landlords wanted to keep the social, economic, and juridical privileges they held over the peasant village, but they also wished to convert the estate into an agricultural factory that supplied grain to distant cities and even foreign states. To accomplish this, they had to get their tenant's plot while keeping his labor. Landlords grew reluctant to renew long-term tenancies, and new estate owners grew reluctant about abiding by tenancy arrangements agreed to by predecessors. They were willing to try their luck in the courts, where magistrates with social views similar to their own might give them a sympathetic hearing. Their aim, and the aim of estate managers whom they often hired in their absence, was to regain the plots of the *fief roturier* and then rent them to former tenants on short-term leases unencumbered by the dues, taxes, and guarantees inherent in the old system. The new rental terms would be simple: 50 to 70 percent of the crop. The estate owner preferred to rent large plots on these terms to the wealthiest peasants of the village, who themselves would hire poverty-stricken day laborers—most likely dispossessed former tenants—to work them. Or estate managers might be responsible for finding their own day laborers to work the repossessed plots. Whatever the method employed, the goal of the modern-minded estate owner was the same—to reduce the medieval forms of land tenancy, based upon complex arrangements with inhabitants of the peasant village who were stubborn about reciprocal rights and obligations, and to increase the landlord's direct exploitation of and profits from the arable area. The increased cash income then could be reinvested.

In France, Sweden, the Netherlands, north Italy, and Germany west of the Elbe—those parts of Europe with a rich heritage of village tenancy—the *fief roturier* arrangement declined considerably in the second half of the seventeenth century. Village chiefs, those literate enough to handle the contractual details between community and landlord over justice, dues, and taxes, rose to newly privileged positions in peasant society. They did so because they took the risk of renting important blocks of the estate's reserve and hiring their own agricultural laborers.

On the other hand, the mass of villagers found themselves slipping in the opposite direction. They might become small renters—sharecroppers really —dependent on an estate manager or wealthy peasant for their plot, seed, plow, and beasts and obligated to give him more than half of what they harvested. Subject to possible eviction each year, they lost the security the old tenancy arrangement offered. The old village tie of responsibility for communal well-being and the well-being of widows and orphans loosened, since the village chiefs had become their economic oppressors. Worst of all, during the period of recession that marked virtually the entire second half of the century, they might fall clear to the bottom, becoming hired hands, vagabonds, or errants wandering from estate to estate in search of work, dragging along their miserable women and bedraggled offspring. They were at the mercy of any potential employer, but even more so of nature, for they were the most likely victims of famine, epidemic, or plague.

The west European peasant, however depressed in social status, at least negotiated his labor. The new forms of exploitative agriculture assumed the existence of a mobile work force. East of the Elbe River, where the work force was much smaller than in the west, estate owners wanted to fix a permanent labor force to estate lands, and they secured legislation from governments that prohibited the movement of agricultural workers. In Denmark, much of northeastern Germany, Bohemia, the Hapsburgs' Austrian lands, Hungary, Poland, the Baltic provinces, and Russia, tenants on estates saw the dues and taxes owed to the seigneur converted largely into labor services on the landlord's own reserve. Such services might come to four or five days of the total workweek. They so overwhelmed all other tenancy responsibilities of the peasantry that historians call the seventeenth and eighteenth centuries in eastern Europe the age of a new serfdom. It was a particularly insidious kind, written into the king's law and protected by the king's troops. In order to succeed, it had to keep peasants tied to the estate. In 1649, the new Russian law code expressly fixed every family chief and his dependents to an estate, and no statute of limitation was placed upon the landlord in hunting down workers who might flee. After 1682, the concept of a free peasantry had become so alien to Russian thinking that landlords short of funds were allowed to take peasants from the estate and sell them like cattle to other landlords. In 1650, the Saxon peasant lost the right to leave his estate without the explicit authorization of the proprietor. Three years later, Frederick William of Brandenburg confirmed that every peasant in his electorate was a serf unless a specific title or the landlord's goodwill could prove otherwise. Estate owners in Brandenburg obtained virtual government authorization to evict peasants from their plots and then add the plots to the reserve.

Throughout eastern Europe, an inexorable process deprived the peasant of his liberty, property, and security. The estate owner needed peasant labor, not peasant rents. Agriculturally deprived regions, such as Holland and Spain, were crying for grain, timber, beer, and wine. So were the new armies and princely courts. The seigneur therefore gobbled up peasant land and added it to his own. He compelled serfs to purchase from him the grain, drinks, and cheese needed for their own sustenance. He served the state as its tax collector. He was delegated control over justice. He ran the village tavern, mill, and store. After 1648, the entire economy of eastern Europe was tilted in favor of the estate owner, and the regime of subjugation and privilege was engraved into the law.

THE STRUCTURE OF SOCIETY

In today's world, an individual's contribution to the economic life of the state and the material benefits derived from it are crucial determinants of his status in society. Sources and sizes of income generally unite people within a "class" and are the primary factors determining lifestyles and attitudes. In the seventeenth and eighteenth centuries, people were grouped not according to their productive role in the nation's economy but rather according to the esteem, honor, or dignity attached to their person—an esteem, honor, or dignity that was tangentially rather than directly related to their material well-being.

Society in the old regime was compartmentalized in accordance with a formula of orders and ranks that conformed to the hierarchy God had created in nature. Each rank was conceived of as a distinct biological entity, with observable standards of dress, decorum, eating habits, and forms of address. Each rank defined the education and the tolerated occupations of its membership. As it was unnatural for a pig to climb a tree and munch acorns, so too was it unnatural for a nobleman to dream of directing a woollens mill. Of course, the social body did contain its mutants, and by 1750, money was purchasing places in the hierarchy to an extent that was unknown a century before. But until the dissatisfaction of the moneyed and ambitious became such that only replacement of a "society of orders" by a "society of classes" would satisfy them, wealth was respected as a *consequence* of rank, not as a *cause* for it; and by no means was it a necessary consequence.

Three general categories, each divided into a welter of subcategories, distinguished the members of society. The great categories, known as the Estates, were based upon the medieval distinction that had been made among those who prayed, those who fought, and those who worked. The First Estate, the clergy, had the most important duty of temporal existence, the care for human souls. The Second Estate, the aristocracy, bore the responsibility of defending the lives of everyone else. The Third Estate, containing the overwhelming majority, had to feed, clothe, and shelter society.

Within each Estate distinctions were enormous. In Catholic countries, bishops and parish priests stood worlds apart from each other, and even the monastic orders had their own ranks of prestige. In Protestant countries, the smaller size of the clergy produced a social order that was somewhat more homogeneous. The typology of aristocracy set court nobles apart from country gentry, and in a state such as France, important judges and magistrates formed yet another distinct aristocratic group. Nowhere, however, were ranks so distinctive, subgroups so conscious of their unique corporate characteristics, as in the Third Estate. Middle- and lower-ranked government officials, attorneys, men of letters, merchants, and master craftsmen—self-proclaimed "honorable men"—distinguished themselves from one another. A physician's wife enjoyed a form of address that was more exalted than a surgeon's. In the innumerable processions that celebrated a holiday or the visit of some dignitary to town, cloth merchants would cede their habitual place in rank to no others. But all the "honorable men" kept themselves apart from shopkeepers, craftsmen, and tenant farmers, not to mention the masses of the *bas peuple*—mechanics, laborers, sharecroppers, and itinerant workers. In the framework of the law, the subgroups had corporate personalities, and the members of each possessed specific fiscal responsibilities. In the Third Estate, one's occupation was an obvious determinant of social station, but it was not the exclusive determinant. The geographical region of the country in which one lived, one's religion, property qualifications, and sex helped shape one's place.

Though a static, compartmentalized hierarchy built upon privilege, esteem, and responsibility was the idealized structure for European society, the aspirations of individuals always threatened to create imbalance in the edifice. The sole possession of money could not transport an individual from an Estate or rank with few privileges and many burdens into one with many privileges and fewer burdens, but the judicious use of money might help. Because rank was associated with a whole code of behavior that included one's dress, language, eating habits, and even posture, it was rare for a single individual west of Muscovy to make a large leap upwards—say, from the ranks of the peasantry to a professional or mercantile group. If a merchant acquired some landed property or a government office, however, within three or four generations his descendants might learn the art of "living nobly." Exercising seigneurial rights over a peasant village, they might withdraw from retail commerce and invest discreetly in an overseas company, the slave trade, or state loans. Or they might sink everything into the estate, exploiting it in modern fashion. By now well-known in his neighborhood, the family chief might marry off a daughter to a titled clan, petition the king for his own armorial bearing, and doctor a few genealogical charts to show an aristocratic ancestor. Distinguished service in the king's administration or, especially, his army could speed up the process. Warfare accelerates social turmoil, too, resulting in personnel changes in the dominating group. In the Thirty Years' War, German conquerors assumed the land and titles of nearly the entire native Czech nobility; the English Protestant conquerors of Ireland did the same to the Catholic aristocracy there.

Old aristocrats constantly complained about the passage of land and titles into the hands of parvenus. By the end of the seventeenth century, the pace of property transfers, very rapid during the social crises from the 1640s through 1670s, had slowed down demonstrably. Nobles, especially newly arrived ones, pressured sovereigns into being more stingy with titles. Furthermore, Europe's emergence from recession by 1720 renewed the pleasures of urban life and the attractiveness of commerce and manufacturing. In France and England especially, but also in western Germany and even Russia, a bourgeois consciousness emerged that no longer needed to ape the aristocratic lifestyle. Until this occurred, however, it was the nobleman's world.

For the largest of society's subgroups, the peasantry, matters were very different. Despite the fact that money alone could not dictate one's social status, the gulf between rich and poor widened considerably during the seventeenth century. West of the Elbe, peasant society was highly complex. The sharecropper had a rude hut and perhaps a scrawny cow and a couple of chickens. The day laborer had even less. On the other hand, the village chief owned a comfortable cottage and rented out hovels to his hired workers. He might control seventy or eighty acres. He possessed half a dozen horses and pigs, twice as many cows, and fifty chickens. He loaned money and rented equipment to his fellow villagers. He purchased their grain and took his chances on the open market. The remaining villagers fit into two or three categories, depending upon the comfort of their houses, the number of acres held as tenants, amount of livestock possessed, and nonagricultural jobs pursued. Generally, sharecroppers and the poorer tenants had to supplement their field work by taking in weaving or spinning. Diet helped determine peasant status as well. Most likely the peasant and his family ate less nourishing and less varied food than his grandfather had. Certainly he ate less meat, and the caloric content of his porridge and bread was below sixteenth-century standards. However, variations were great from country to country and region to region. English renters ate better than French sharecroppers, but a Polish serf or Sicilian day laborer would have considered the diet of a Dutch truck farmer as positively princely.

The urban counterpart of the peasant—the artisan, shopkeeper, or mechanic—had a more precarious existence than those on the land. During a steady recession, his rigid wages might be expected to increase in real value. But the 1648–1715 period was a recession punctuated with disastrous crop failures, famines, and plagues. The moment prices rose, demand for items other than food collapsed, and men like Jean Cocu faced disaster. In town during a bad year, high bread prices correlated with low pewter prices, which meant that workers were trying to sell their household possessions, and the Jean Cocus of Europe fell into ruin.

It appears that a shift away from the middle took place during the late seventeenth century in all the orders. Within the upper reaches of nearly all ranks, individuals consolidated their positions. A village chief became a little tyrant over his community and on occasion might even transform himself into an estate manager or owner. A comfortable merchant might invest in landed property and redirect the social aspirations and status of future generations of his family. A bishop might accumulate for his diocese and for himself. But tenured peasants, urban artisans, petty gentlemen, and parish priests were sinking. While Jean Cocu starved to death, half a dozen of the elite in his home town of Beauvais had incomes, mostly in land, that could have fed him and a hundred like him for a normal year.

POLITICAL INSTITUTIONS

As an institution wielding effective political authority over a large geographical region, the seventeenth-century state lay midway between the feudal monarchies of medieval Europe and the centralized, bureaucratic leviathans that emerged in the western world just before the French Revolution of 1789. Anomaly and contradiction seemed to govern its structure and administration. The glorified idea of divine right and a Roman tradition of absolute power confronted the reality of a political society where corporate privileged groups had negotiated individual contracts and agreements with the sovereign that circumscribed his authority. Chief among the agencies were the political Estates, representing the orders of society. But towns, provinces, professional bodies, and even individuals also had contracted for their "liberties" with a sovereign, and his successors were legally obliged to honor the agreement. There were other hindrances to uniformity and centralization. Within a single state, laws, dialects, weights, and measures might change so frequently that a traveler might feel he was crossing a new frontier at every hitching post. For that matter, the actual borders *between* states were ill-defined, vague, and always in dispute. They often were formed when a ruler simply constituted a frontier by building fortresses at strategic points.

In order to collect taxes, raise armies, and dispense justice, generations of governments had divided their states into administrative units. Nearly always, however, these divisions deferred to historical realities and respected another type of regionalization created by custom, a shared past, language, or simply domination by a single great family. In all of the states of the seventeenth and eighteenth centuries, what first strikes the eye are the "historic regions"—unequal in size and diverse in statutory law, each claiming a unique set of judicial rights and fiscal responsibilities. These states-within-states represented perpetual challenges to the centralizing efforts of the sovereign. Spain and the Hapsburg empire contained "historic regions" that caused rulers particular difficulty in the seventeenth century. However, even in a relatively centralized kingdom such as France, provincial governments quarreled with one another to a point barely short of war. The king tried to arbitrate.

Nevertheless, pulling against the guarantees of regional and corporate privilege was a powerful idea—that of a hierarchical political order, at the helm of which rested the sovereign. It was exceptionally rare, even in periods of social unrest and outright civil war, for rebels to dispense with the principle of monarchical or quasi-monarchical authority. Evil advisers might dupe the king, or the sovereign himself might be a wretch. Nevertheless, standing in the wings was a hope, an heir, a successor, legitimized through birth or election, who would set matters straight again. The French philosopher Blaise Pascal was no friend of absolutism. Nonetheless, he understood that necessity dictated the existence of a hierarchical political order based on the principle of male hereditary succession:

> Because of the disorderly nature of mankind, the most unreasonable things of this world become the most acceptable. What could be less reasonable than choosing the first son of a king or queen to govern the state? We do not select for a ship's captain the passenger who happens to come from the best family. The principle of hereditary monarchy seems absurd and unjust, but habit makes it reasonable and just. Moreover, just who should be chosen to rule? The most virtuous and most skillful? How do we recognize him? Everyone pretends to be the most virtuous and most skillful. Let us therefore add something beyond dispute. That is the principle of the ruler's eldest son. It is clear-cut. It is incontestable. Reason itself is powerless to do better, for civil war is the greatest of misfortunes.[3]

The overwhelming number of Pascal's contemporaries shared his position. Only England from 1649 to 1660 and the Dutch Netherlands from 1650 to 1672 tried to adopt a form of government that dispensed with a

---

[3]Blaise Pascal, *Pensées*, ed. L. Lafuma (Paris, 1952), p. 158. (Author's translation.)

monarch or superaristocrat at the helm; on each occasion the experiment failed. Religion, the Roman legal tradition, and popular legitimization sanctioned the pyramidlike hierarchy. A divine autocrat commanded the universe. He delegated control over men's secular interests to an agent. Catholic priests and Protestant pastors alike, believing that it was in the interests of the Church to maintain those of the king, never tired of citing scriptural bases for royal authority. The office of kingship was shrouded in mystical religious fervor. The coronation ceremony was a magnificent spectacle built upon miracle. Once rightly anointed, the ruler was supposed to possess the touch that cured the lame and healed the sick. Christ himself had passed on to sovereigns certain of his divine powers. Principles derived from the law of the late Roman empire held that the maintenance of efficiency and social peace necessitated placing kings and their delegated officials above the compartmentalized segments of society. In the end, however, even religion and the law provided incomplete bases for maintaining—or extending—a sovereign's power. He needed the acquiescence of his people. When Louis XIV sent royal agents to the remote province of Auvergne in 1662 to prosecute a group of landlords who were terrorizing their tenants, he was successful because Auvergne's townsmen, clerics, and peasants supported him. Twenty-five years later, when James II tried to use *his* agents to enforce an unpopular royal authority over England, he invited his dethronement.

In the second half of the seventeenth century, the major problems of government were to create a working administration in the interests of the state itself and to organize the resources of the state for exploiting opportunities in Europe and overseas. Representative Estates on the national and regional levels were highly suspicious of the methods used by sovereigns and their servants to resolve the problems of government, since this usually meant restricted privileges and increased taxation. Though their function was less to legislate than to petition the sovereign or ratify his decisions, Estates in England, the Dutch Netherlands, and Poland resisted the centralizing tendencies of their sovereigns with a good measure of success. Elsewhere, Estates maintained their nuisance value. Spain never had developed an Estates General for the entire kingdom, and that of France failed to meet until 1789. Yet regional parliaments in Catalonia, Aragon, Valencia, and Navarre made it impossible for the Spanish Hapsburgs to establish good government. In 1648, France's provincial Estates and its twelve great regional law courts helped provoke the worst civil war in the kingdom's history. The Estates of Hungary made life miserable for the Austrian Hapsburgs, and regional parliaments in Scotland and Ireland could cause the Stuarts nearly as much difficulty as that met at Westminster.

Nevertheless, by 1715, Estates in most places were on the decline. During his long reign, Louis XIV successfully impressed a unitary ideal upon France, while Philip V of Spain and Leopold I of Austria used the excuse of war emergency to neutralize the effectiveness of regional Estates in Catalonia and Hungary, respectively. The princes of the Holy Roman Empire constructed their minor absolutisms upon the wreckage of both imperial and Estate authority. In Denmark a royalist coup d'état established the king's unchallenged supremacy, while in Russia, Estates paralleling those in the west—that is, built into the constitutional framework of the state—never really developed at any level.

The groups customarily represented by the national Estates were the most highly esteemed elements in the clergy, aristocracy, and urban bourgeoisie. Almost never did the peasants, town craftsmen, or country priests have a voice. The Swedish Estates were unique in that the more prosperous tenant farmers had their own House. In England, the middling gentry had representation in the House of Commons, but elsewhere in Europe, smaller landlords had to be content with having their spokesmen in regional or provincial assemblies. In Poland and the Dutch Netherlands, the provincial Estates were more important than the national one. A member of the Diet or States General could vote only in accordance with instructions sent him from home.

In order to extend their authority into the economic, political, and spiritual lives of their subjects, governments had to create instruments of coercion. Bureaucracies had to be formed to whom the ruler delegated areas of power and responsibility, especially in financial, judicial, and military matters. In the international arena, sovereigns theoretically possessed a plenitude of power. At home, their claims as the source of justice, their leadership of the state's Church, and their right to assess contributions from districts, households, and consumers depended upon the existence of loyal servants possessing the will and means to translate wishes into fact. For most governments, however, the supreme irony was that the sovereign's chief officers wished to restrain his authority rather than extend it.

The court, or royal household, was technically the ceremonial wing of government. The ambulatory monarch, trudging the dusty roads of his kingdom nine months out of twelve, was a thing of the past. By 1648, every sovereign in Europe had a royal residence in a royal capital. Now the landowners came to him. The reasons behind this unending procession are not hard to find: it had grown too costly to maintain a magnificent lifestyle in a provincial chateau; the sovereign wanted a potentially rebellious noble where he could keep an eye on him; and the court was the right place to be for the favor seeker. It also was where the sovereign could establish and preside over the most privileged society in the realm, a society governed by unswerving rules of etiquette and precedence and a steady round of festivities and ceremonies. In Sweden, England, Spain, and Austria, members of the royal household doubled as government officials. In contrast, Louis XIV tried to distinguish the court from the working bureaucracy. He was successful only in part. Wherever a court existed, it insinuated itself into the structure of the regime. Because courtiers existed within a universe of sinecure, favor, and bitter personal rivalry, they hindered the development of disinterested government.

The rulers' persistent need for cash created a far more pernicious hindrance. In the seventeenth century, newly enriched bourgeois subjects craved an elevated social status, but not even the king could sell them prestige willy-nilly. Estate ownership was a path that led to nobility only after several generations. A second path was office ownership. An office was a government post that could be purchased and inherited, like a piece of property. But it also was a public function. In return for specific obligations and periodic financial contributions, the aspiring officeholder obtained a public power from the sovereign. Some officeholders, like judges in the French sovereign courts, collectors of royal taxes, or managers of state finances, labored long and hard at posts they were proud to own. They even forged a corporate identity, a kind of guild, with holders of similar posts. A type of aristocracy accompanied certain important offices. In France, it was called the *noblesse de robe.* For some posts, like a royal chancellorship, presidency over a sovereign court, or headship over the customs collectors, one had to be born noble.

Most individuals invested in offices not to serve the king but to obtain privileges. An officeholder won exemption from most direct taxes and military service. He was subject to a special jurisdiction reserved for members of his group, and he was expected to use his office to earn an income. Tax collectors retained a percentage of their take, judges and their officeholding clerks collected all manner of fees from litigants, and petty officials practiced what today we would call graft in return for a permit or stamp. Therefore, alongside the dignity of function assumed by the great responsible officers of state was the sordid embezzlement of an army of lesser functionaries.

The royal need for funds merged with the hopes of those with some sums to spend, creating an industry that glutted the state with officials while failing to respond to its need for servants. In France or Spain, individuals and groups worked as stockjobbers in offices, purchasing dozens of posts from the crown and auctioning them off at a profit. Conversely, two or three individuals might hold the same post, splitting income and fees. While places like England and Brandenburg escaped the worst calamities of officeholding, people in Italy, Austria, most of the smaller German principalities, France, Spain, and even the Dutch Netherlands complained about grasping "agents" of the sovereign. Public opinion was expressed in the aphorism: "Each time the king creates an office, God creates a fool to buy it."

The multiplication of offices was antithetical to effective government. And sovereigns knew it. They therefore tried to develop another track of officials more likely to be responsive to the state's interests than the self-serving, corporate-minded officer corps that often worked hand in glove with regional and provincial Estates. This second track of government agents comprised the commissioners. Like officers, they were socially ambitious, but unlike officers, their positions were awarded, not sold, posts at the sovereign's discretion. Their tenure never was guaranteed, and disgrace was a daily possibility. But their power and responsibilities were large. The king tried to make them his closest advisers, and he sent them into the countryside to investigate, cajole, and browbeat Estates and officers alike. Point by point the duties of commissioners were established in opposition to those of the officers. They were inspectors and controllers, watchdogs for the sovereign. They supervised local police, exercised control over the domestic militia, investigated the tax rolls, and were constantly looking for new ways to increase royal revenues. They were responsible for developing the economic potential of a region. They proposed land reclamation projects and requested funds for canal and bridge construction.

The number of commissioners was kept within limits, and the state tried to educate them for their jobs. Their social origins probably were not very different from most of the officers. Wherever possible, they were the middling bourgeoisie or, in overwhelmingly rural states, the country nobility. Some, like the French *intendants*, emerged from the junior ranks of the law officer corps. The Elector of Brandenburg recruited his from the Estates themselves. Peter the Great of Russia went abroad to find servants for his state. By the early eighteenth century, every state in Europe had its commissioners. In places like Brandenburg, Denmark, and Russia, they overwhelmed the older forms of officialdom. In France and Spain, they carried on a struggle with officers. In places like the Hapsburg empire or Poland, where governments were too poor or too weak and aristocracies or Estates were well-entrenched, the commissioner corps was very feeble.

One group of commissioners was particularly important—the state servants charged with the responsibility of raising, feeding, clothing, and equipping the sovereign's army. Noble retinues, town militias, and mercenary bands hired for a limited campaign no longer sufficed for rulers worried about internal revolt and external threats. The second half of the seventeenth century witnessed the rapid evolution of the large standing army. Philip II had been content to send 40,000 troops into war. Louis XIV needed half a million. Commissioners had to advise kings on how to raise the productive capacity of the state in a time of recession, so that the military machine could be supported. They had to devise tax schemes on consumer goods that would allow few or no exemptions. They had to haggle with uniform makers, munitions makers, and regimental colonels who hunted down potential troops. They had to make certain that soldiers were adequately trained, drilled, and paid.

Thus, from the middle of the seventeenth century on, governments tried to devise means of creating effective administrations through which they could wield effective authority. But the modern state did not emerge over-night. The financial poverty of regimes, the shortage of trained and loyal personnel, the inherent difficulties built into a society that tolerated the concept of corporate privilege, the idea that a government post was a piece of exploitative property—all of these factors slowed the development of the impersonal, centralized state as we know it. Well into the eighteenth cen-tury, court favorites and cliques of royal cousins might topple an able, disinterested minister of state. Government agencies still had to be systema-tized according to function. The incessant "special cases" of administrative jurisdiction—entire countries like Ireland or Hungary, provinces like Britta-ny or Cleves, cities like Barcelona or London, countless villages, not to mention socioprofessional groups like clerics, nobles, guilds, landowners, and magistrates—all of these frustrated the extension of the state's control over people's lives. The centralizing sovereigns were the wave of the future in most places. But time and again their efforts were frustrated by de-pendence upon the habits and institutions of the past.

Chapter Two

The Age of Mercantilism

THE INDICATORS OF RECESSION

Except when famine-provoked scarcities made agricultural necessities inordinately expensive, the period from 1648 to 1715 was one of low demand and falling prices. This contrasted enormously with the sixteenth century, when a powerful inflationary spiral gripped Europe, prices soared, and wages lagged behind. The influx of bullion from Spanish America with the consequent increase in the supply of money, the attempts of traditional agriculture to feed a rapidly increasing population, and the rising costs of governmental administration and military needs had contributed to the sixteenth-century inflation. After 1620, however, the boom was over. The Mediterranean was the first region to sink into recession. Spain's bullion imports fell off, war disrupted commerce, and famine and plague struck hard. By 1648, even distant Poland and Russia felt the shock waves.

The most common economic indicator of the seventeenth-century recession, which was not shaken off until the 1730s, was falling prices. Cereals experienced the worst slump. From 1650 to 1700, prices in France fell off by 25 percent; in Spain, by 30 percent; in Poland, by as much as 40 percent. Only scarcities caused by poor harvests would temporarily redirect the trend; for a short interval, prices would soar out of control, and the results would be calamitous. Except for such occurrences, however, agricultural sales were sluggish. It is no wonder that west European tenant farmers experienced increasing difficulty in meeting the costs of their rents and dues from the income derived from their produce sales.

A scarcity in money accompanied the lag in prices. From 1610 to 1660, Spanish bullion imports from America plummeted nearly 90 percent below midsixteenth-century levels. Colonial populations fell, and the silver mines of Potosí and Mexico lay nearly abandoned. Throughout the sixteenth century, the commercially vigorous continent had greedily swallowed imports of precious metals. After 1620, this vigor continued only in isolated spots, such as the ports of the Dutch Netherlands and, to a lesser extent, London and Hamburg. In the seventeenth century, over a third of Europe's reduced stocks of bullion drained off to Asia. Because of a lack of widely shared commercial exchange within Europe, these stocks were not replenished. One major state, Sweden, for a time reverted to a natural economy. The government took its taxes in grain, meat, and iron. Soldiers were paid in farm produce. Professors at the University of Lund received their salaries in oats.

The indicators of seaborne commerce support the conclusions drawn from the price-money factor. The first set concerns the Spanish port of Seville, focal point for West Indian commerce during most of the century. From 1600 to 1604, an average of fifty-five ships per year carrying nearly 20,000 tons left Seville for the New World; from 1670 to 1680, the average annual departures were down to seventeen ships carrying only 4,650 tons; by 1701 to 1710, an average of eight ships per year left Seville, carrying a mere 2,600 tons. Arrivals followed a similar pattern. There is, of course, a danger in collating commerce in slaves and luxury products with general economic trends, and north European smugglers—who left no written records—took over a good share of Seville's commerce during the century. But a second set of statistics, the toll accounts of the "Sound," that narrow strip of water at the entrance to the Baltic, confirms the trend suggested by Seville's figures. Through the Sound came ships laden with Polish and German cereals, Swedish iron, Russian naval stores, and timber from Scandinavia and the Baltic. First the Danish and then the Swedish government used the Sound's toll charges as important sources of state revenue. Compared to the base year of 1650, there were half as many average annual passages through the Sound from 1655 to 1675 and 40 percent fewer from 1700 to 1720. These forty years were heavily punctuated by warfare, it is true; yet for only eight of the years between 1651 and 1730 did the number of ships passing through the Sound reach or exceed the number for 1650.

A psychology of recession gripped most of Europe. Attempts at land reclamation stopped altogether in Italy and slowed down appreciably in France and England. Theoretical works on agricultural improvements were as rare as agricultural inventions. Spanish industry, like Spanish agriculture, was in an advanced state of decay. Toledo silks and Segovia woollens virtually disappeared from the market. The Spanish government tried to vitalize overseas commerce by opening up Cadiz as an *entrepôt*, but foreigners immediately took over its port trade. Italy, the sixteenth century's most highly industrialized region, had become an agricultural backwater. Of her cities, Venice, whose textiles had clothed sultans and kings, showed the most spectacular decline. In the 1680s, her output was one-tenth of what it had been a century before. She kept up a good front by becoming an aristocratic tourist resort, but Milan, Florence, Genoa, and Naples—to say nothing of Sicily's teeming slums of Palermo and Messina—collapsed with less grace. The entire western Mediterranean was in a state of transition. The old economy had been built upon a carrying trade in wheat, wines, olives, woollens, textiles, and glassware. The Barbary Coast, Sicily, and the Near East supplied the goods; Spain and southern France, the market; and Italy, the carriers. After the 1620s, however, the routes of supply had shifted, and the carriers had changed as well. Now Dutchmen brought Polish cereals and North Sea herrings to Spain and Italy. What was left of the trans-Mediterranean commerce fell into the hands of the French and Dutch.

The south German towns and old Hanseatic League ports on the Baltic–North Sea coast declined, too. Of the few German coastal towns that were active, the northeastern grain export centers of Memel and Danzig were controlled by middleman shippers from the Dutch Netherlands and England. The south German towns were in the sinking orbit of Italy. The princes of the Holy Roman Empire, whose political triumph was consolidated by the Peace of Westphalia, exercised an especially nefarious influence upon German trade through haphazard prohibitions of the export of raw materials. They also charged tolls for river traffic at every turn. The emergence of Hamburg as an important financial and shipping center was virtually the only bright spot on the German commercial scene. The shortsighted tariff practices of the princes, the conservatism of the urban guilds, and a distinct shortage of capital, manpower, and national markets conspired to maintain and even accelerate a decline that had already begun on the eve of the Thirty Years' War.

THE COMMERCIAL LEADERSHIP OF THE DUTCH

By 1648, European industrial and commercial leadership had concentrated in new hands. The fastest growing source of copper and iron, as well as timber and tar, was Sweden. England was bidding for supremacy in the manufacture of woollens and worsteds. Its coal and metal industries were growing. In the 1670s, it began exporting grain, and it *reexported* nearly everything else, including tobacco and sugar from America and calicoes and silks from Asia. After 1661, France reorganized its commercial and industrial life. Louis XIV's great controller-general of finances from 1661 to 1683, Jean-Baptiste Colbert, laid out the ground rules for French development: direct government investment followed by encouragement and regulation of very selective heavy industries, such as shipbuilding, and luxury goods, such as quality cloth, mirrors, and tapestries; government pressure to export more manufactured goods than were imported and to import more raw materials than were exported; heroic attempts to force provinces and towns to abolish or reduce internal tolls; and the construction of an overseas empire through trade and colonization.

But for the half-century after 1648, the real masters of Europe's economic life were the Dutch. Even by seventeenth-century standards, the Dutch political system looked genuinely medieval, incapable of sustaining commercial leadership. Sovereignty was carved out of a successful rebellion that had taken eighty years to settle, and the chosen form of government was a halfway house between royal and republican. This resulted in a persistent constitutional tension. Moreover, Dutch fears of centralization were as powerful as their fears of absolutism. The basis of their government was a loose federation of provinces and free towns. Nowhere in western Europe did regionalism have such a strong bearing upon a state's politics and society. Through town and provincial assemblies, a thousand citizens directed the decisions of the States General meeting in The Hague. But the Orange family, its legitimacy enshrined in Dutch life because of its leadership in the revolt against Spain, prevented a more thoroughgoing republicanism. Its leading male member, the stadholder, held patronage power over the central offices of state, especially the military ones. He headed an aristocratic political party, and he was very popular with the Calvinist clergy, shopkeepers, peasantry, and urban workers. It was no secret that his constitutional propensities veered towards monarchy rather than republicanism.

Despite tensions in Dutch political life, the great burghers of the coastal province of Holland created a trading-banking empire that knew no peer in the century. Commercial fishing and shipbuilding formed its basis. A merchant marine was constructed that exceeded in total tonnage all rivals combined. A pair of international trading companies and the bank of Amsterdam capped the empire. How can one explain this unparalleled energy for gain in a small, insecure, politically unstable nation of fewer than two million?

In part it was due to the persistence, courage, and sobriety that one tends to find among a small people aware that nothing in this world comes easily. The provinces of Holland and Zeeland always had nourished themselves upon the herring off their shore. Sometime in the sixteenth century, the spawning grounds of Baltic herring shifted southward, creating a surplus catch to be sold all over Europe. By the middle of the seventeenth century, two thousand Dutch fishing vessels plied the North Sea and English Channel up to the Thames itself. The Scania shoals and Norwegian Sea were within their orbit. The ships were of good size, up to thirty tons apiece. Each was manned with a crew of ten to fifteen and rigged so ingeniously that the fish could be salted and kept onboard until the catch was complete. A full fifth of the Dutch population lived off the herring industry. The catch averaged well over a quarter million tons per year.

As shipbuilders, the Dutch were so far ahead of their rivals that as late as 1700 one-fourth of the English fleet was made in Holland's yards. The piers of Amsterdam contained a welter of wind-driven sawmills, winches, and cranes. The "flute" was the most celebrated vessel built in Dutch yards. It was a stout, sturdy ship meant to bear heavy and bulky commodities such as the salt, grain, naval stores, and packed fish that were the chief items passing between the eastern Baltic and Mediterranean. Wholly utilitarian, the flute doomed the costly armed merchantman. Everything was sacrificed for the cargo. The hold was enormous, the cabin space miniscule, the crew of minimal size. It weighed from two to five hundred tons and could be modified for specialty transport, such as timber or whale carrying. The Dutch could build a flute 50 percent more cheaply than their competitors. They passed savings in construction and crew costs on to carriers. In their turn, the carriers could offer merchants the best prices in Europe.

Geographical good fortune offered the Dutch an opportunity to exploit rivers and sea lanes. Holland and Zeeland contained the mouths of the Scheldt, Maas, and Rhine. The coastal towns of these provinces faced out upon the convergence of the Baltic, North Sea, English Channel, and Atlantic routes. At the quays of Amsterdam, Rotterdam, and Schiedam, as well as dozens of smaller ports, native ships containing Polish and east German grain, Scandinavian timber, and Baltic naval stores jostled against trawlers reeking of North Sea herring and Arctic cod. Beside the ships, burghers scurried back and forth arranging sales and exchanges. By 1648, the Dutch gained control of the Baltic's grain trade, and their agents exercised almost complete command over the German export centers of Danzig and Memel.

Price determined the success of the Dutch shippers. They made large-scale purchases, offered liberal credit terms, provided cheap transport, and relentlessly exploited their sources of supply. They might purchase Finnish and Norwegian forests outright. They invested in Swedish mines and cornered the production of Tuscan marble. They were busy in south-to-north commerce. Three-fourths of the salt sent from Portugal and France to the Baltic was transported on Dutch ships. Half the west European cloth intended for Scandinavia and eastern Europe was made or finished in Leyden and its suburbs. In the course of the century, the Dutch added new products. Sugar, tobacco, and cotton from the West and East Indies were processed in Dutch towns and then sold to foreign merchants. All of this activity stood in marked contrast to the passion for land investment that tied up capital elsewhere on the continent.

Fundamental to Dutch prosperity was the maintenance of open seas and open ports. No people abhorred war at sea more than the Dutch. No people in Europe feared more the development of economic nationalism, as defined by import and export tariffs and the closing of foreign ports to nonnative shipping. From 1648 until 1721, however, wars tested Dutch ingenuity to the utmost—in the Baltic from 1655 to 1660, 1674 to 1679, and 1700 to 1721; in the North Sea and Atlantic from 1652 to 1654, 1665 to 1667, 1672 to 1678, 1689 to 1697, and 1702 to 1713; and sporadically in the Mediterranean. The wars carried to both Indies as well. After the 1670s, the

Dutch became major participants and investors in the wars against Louis XIV. The wars strained their resources while forcing rivals and enemies to develop their own. By 1715, the Dutch still were carrying half of the Baltic's grain and up to 40 percent of the region's timber and naval stores. But the French and English were manufacturing their own flutes now. Moreover, these larger states were beginning to understand a concept that the Dutch had failed to grasp adequately—that fishing, shipping, and investment abroad were not sufficient bases upon which to establish a nation's lasting economic strength. The Dutch still controlled the *transport* of Swedish iron in 1715, but the fact that two-thirds of it eventually wound up in England was most prophetic of all.

Nevertheless, contemporary observers in the Netherlands did not understand the significance of the first faint signs of industrialization. To them a more obvious sign of economic health remained the carrying trade, and Holland's mastery over non-European sources of supply was the sharpest indicator of all. It may seem exceedingly strange to us that Malabar pepper, Yemenese coffee, and Bengali silks—in short, luxury items enjoyed by fewer than 1 percent of Europe's population—should weigh so important. But an age of economic stagnation, when the gulf increases between the whisper-thin layer of the very rich and everyone else, is not one to recognize the long-term advantages of creating a market of consumers. Few in the seventeenth century conceived of the market as anything more than war materiel for kings, subsistence articles for the majority, and luxury items for the wealthy. The boom in the new, inexpensive printed calicoes that the English brought from India around 1700 caught everyone by surprise. A state's economic strength was supposed to be measured by its share of control over the luxury trade, and it was difficult to shift one's mentality.

The Dutch never really did. Their handling of overseas commerce, particularly in the East Indies, which they considered their major enterprise, contrasts markedly with their price-cutting techniques in handling the Baltic and North Sea trade. They controlled so completely European imports of pepper from Malabar, Sumatra, and Java, as well as the more exotic Indonesian cloves, nutmeg, cinnamon, and mace, that they might well have experimented with lower prices in order to influence habits of consumption. Indeed, in the eighteenth century, this is what the English and French did do for sugar, tea, and coffee. But the Dutch were very cautious. Even if it meant destroying the stocks already in Amsterdam's warehouses, they kept the price of spices at consistently high levels. A privileged company possessing exclusive rights to overseas commerce from the Cape of Good Hope clear across the Pacific to the Straits of Magellan ran the East Indies. Directed by seventeen of Amsterdam's greatest merchants and bankers, the Dutch East India Company possessed a spirit of independence that was legion. It could wage war, make treaties, command military units, and supervise conversion of the heathen.

The half-century after 1648 was the company's golden age. It was the most important European institution in Asia. Its sphere of interest radiated out from its headquarters on the island of Java to control the spice trade of Malaya and Ceylon, dominate the coastal traffic of India, and ply the Persian Gulf. The company's ships had a major share of Asia's own carrying trade, particularly between India and Japan, and between China and the Philippines. But the spice trade between Indonesia and Europe remained its primary interest, and its guiding philosophy never parted from maintaining enforced scarcities. Such techniques proved costly. Toward the close of the seventeenth century, the company introduced the Arabian coffee bean into Java. The newly established plantations raised the crop according to the principles established for spice production. While the rivals of the Dutch never challenged the company's monopoly over spices, coffee was another matter. The French and English in the Antilles and the Portuguese in Brazil experimented with methods of increasing productivity. By the 1730s, west Europeans were becoming accustomed to coffee, but it was coffee from America, not the East Indies. The Dutch had allowed the market to slip out of their hands.

Dutch commerce in the West Indies was built upon less solid foundations than the cautious techniques that brought the dignified East India Company such prestige. In the late seventeenth century, two million Spanish speaking inhabitants in the New World needed textiles, tools, and manufactured goods that their declining motherland was unable to supply. In the West Indies, English and French planters were creating a vast new sugar, tobacco, and coffee culture, but they desperately needed cheap labor and cheap food for their workers. The Dutch had the ships. It was logical for them to supply the goods. They brought manufactured goods to New Spain and black slaves to the Caribbean. They brought New England grain, beef, and fish to the planters and carried back to Europe rum, molasses, and sugar. Nearly all of this commerce was accomplished in defiance of trading restrictions that the Spanish, English, and French governments had placed upon their colonists. Much of it occurred during times of war. Rival states called these activities smuggling, and on occasion such activities degenerated into piracy —such as raids upon Spanish galleons suspected of containing bullion. For the Dutch, America was a riskier adventure than the East Indies. They depended upon the cooperation of producers and their own ingenuity, bypassing the barriers that governments set up in their way.

The fishing industry, shipbuilding, and the carrying trade inside and outside Europe helped make Dutch fortunes in the seventeenth century. But they were not all the Dutch accomplished. Amsterdam's insurance house dated from 1598, its stock exchange from 1608, and its exchange bank from 1609. Private Dutchmen loaned funds to chronically impecunious states such as Denmark, Austria, and Spain. One Dutchman, Louis De Geer, ran Sweden's munitions industry. Others held export monopolies in

Russian ports and were behind the one truly important land reclamation project of the century, the draining of the Cambridge fens in southern England. When the Bank of England was founded, Dutchmen bought a major interest. While the Dutch state strained its resources beyond repair in forty years of hot and cold war against Louis XIV, individual Dutchmen were investing in French textiles, sugar refining, and shipbuilding, and their flutes were carrying powder, matches, and lead to French ports. They were not overly scrupulous about whom they supplied, and the government of tradesmen and bankers understood. One of the happiest investments for Dutchmen remained at home, however, in the exchange bank of Amsterdam. An account in the bank was a mark of true prestige. In the seventeenth century, it was Europe's most secure financial institution. From 1611 to 1701, deposits rose from under a million florins to sixteen million. Money placed into the bank could be withdrawn anywhere in the world.

The canvasses of de Hooch and Vermeer may not show it, but there actually were poor people in the Dutch Netherlands in the seventeenth century. Amsterdam had slums that could rival those of Naples and Madrid. Still, the Dutch never starved, and in this fact they were alone among the continent's people. Buying in low season, their merchants stored goods until it became a seller's market. The warehouses of the ports were stocked with munitions, brandy, tobacco, dried herrings, spices, and—most important— grain. As an importing nation, the Netherlands was always prepared for a domestic food crisis, and they were always ready to seize the advantage in case of a foreign one. In 1672, on the eve of the war with France, the Dutch had a twelve-year supply of cereals stored away. Twenty years later, when famine hit Europe, Amsterdam made a fortune.

By 1715, however, the undisputed commercial leadership of the Dutch was in jeopardy. During the War of the Spanish Succession (1702–13) Amsterdam's customs receipts declined. They never returned to prewar levels. Conversely, the war created a boom in English shipbuilding. Back in 1663, the English merchant fleet came to 90,000 tons. Fifty years later, it had grown more than threefold. The Dutch state had exhausted itself financing the allied coalition, and most importantly, native merchants and bankers were looking outside the Netherlands for investment opportunities. They remained loyal enough to Amsterdam's exchange bank, but they were losing faith in their country's commercial future. They grew impatient waiting for famine to make their grain investments materialize. Leyden's textile industry, mired in the habits of a guild system and scorning technological innovation, looked less attractive than the newly developing woollens manufactures of England. The trading habits of the East India Company hardly seemed geared for the modern world. Short on people, lacking natural and agricultural resources, unable to develop new domestic channels for investment, the Dutch Netherlands was slipping as an economic power. For other countries, however, emerging from a period of stagnation, Dutchmen with funds were a godsend. Austrian mining, Swedish munitions, French sugar refining, the Bank of England—all owed their eighteenth-century prosperity to the prescience of Dutch investors. This dispersion of resources, costly to the Netherlands, heralded better days for Europe as a whole.

THE BREAKTHROUGH OF THE ENGLISH

The Dutch had consolidated their commercial triumphs within the confines of a traditional seventeenth-century economy. They carried what others needed, provided the essentials of survival for those who could pay, and brought prestige items to the leisured groups. It was left up to others to work out the idea of an expanding market—one in which a modest peasant or craftsman might desire some sugar to sweeten his coffee or an extra calico shirt to place on his back. Around the 1680s, the English merchants began to exploit this market. Why it occurred in England is hard to say. England's towns and villages had been spared the ravages of war, small industries never had to rebuild from rubble, river transport was easy and customs-free, the land was unforested but contained sufficient ore and abundant coal, and the guild structure was weak. Moreover, both landed and merchant groups shared an interest in commerce, industry, and investment. With its export of woollen cloth, England always had done well enough in Europe's subsistence economy. Late in the seventeenth century, England began sending its grain surplus abroad.

But it was neither the export of familiar products, nor the expansion of commonplace industries, such as buttons or cutlery, that turned it into the most formidable rival of the Dutch. England's new economic strength derived from obtaining control over the reexport of products coming from the New World or Asia. London became a major *entrepôt* for sugar, tobacco, cod, cottons, and calicoes. Merchants, carriers, and the government became convinced that not only their countrymen but also the Dutch, French, Germans—and perhaps one day Spaniards and Italians—would want new products. Even the age of recession offered hopeful signs. From just over a million pounds in the 1630s, Maryland and Virginia tobacco exports rose to twenty-two million in the years from 1699 to 1701. Prior to the 1640s, West Indian sugar was practically unknown in Europe, but from 1699 to 1701, nearly four million pounds of it entered English ports. In 1660, calicoes from India were rare and feared by all of Europe's cloth interests. From 1699 to 1701, over 860,000 pieces reached England. Particularly encouraging was the fact that two-thirds of the tobacco and calicoes and one-third of the sugar that arrived in England from 1650 to 1700 were reexported to other parts of Europe.

Such a windfall led English governments to make certain that it was

English merchants and carriers who would be profiting from the overseas trade. From 1651 to 1673, Parliament passed six sets of protective legislation, called the Navigation Acts, that were aimed at the Dutch. Essentially, the acts were intended to restrict commerce between English colonies and England to ships bearing the English flag and manned by English crews. This restriction was extended to English trade with Asia, Africa, and the non-English colonies of the New World. To assure English ports of customs receipts and ensure the prosperity of the reexport trade, certain "enumerated articles" produced in the colonies—generally tobacco, sugar, indigo, and dyewoods—were forbidden from going directly to ports other than those in England, Ireland, or an English possession. European exporters to England might use their own ships, but merchants sending goods to British North America usually had to pass through an English port first, pay tolls there, and then reload their cargoes on an English ship that would make the Atlantic crossing. Imports from the continent to England had to come directly from the producing country or country of normal first shipment, never through another port such as Amsterdam. Trade along the English coast was to be limited to English vessels.

The restrictive element of the Navigation Acts is obvious—to cut into the Dutch carrying trade, especially that part of it destined for England and the English colonies in the New World. The acts succeeded gradually. From 1660 to 1700, the amount of colonial commerce reexported to Europe through English ports rose fourfold over the previous half-century. Tobacco, sugar, and calicoes alone formed two-thirds of this reexport trade. After 1688, the idea of privileged trading companies gave way to unfettered expansion in England's trans-Atlantic commerce. The African slave trade opened up. Thanks largely to the acts, the English government began to view the parts of the empire as interdependent units of production and consumption. Merchants and shippers in the motherland controlled the machinery. Thus, the Devon fishing fleet picked up the Newfoundland cod and transported it to Spain and Portugal, returning with wine and olive oil. English slavers dumped their human cargo into the West Indies or mainland southern colonies and picked up raw sugar, tobacco, or cotton for shipment home. In England the colonial products were refined, used domestically, and sold to the continent. From England the slavers took arms to West Africa in exchange for more blacks. Newfoundland and New England sent fish to feed the cane workers in the West Indies; the islands returned molasses, sugar, and rum to the northern colonies. All the while, England supplied its colonial markets with a stream of textiles, guns, tools, and machinery at prices favorable to producers and suppliers.

The Dutch, against whom the Navigation Acts were mainly directed, tried to circumvent them as best they could. They smuggled textiles and machinery into New England and the West Indies, and their fishermen insisted on pursuing their catch off the English coast. In 1652, war erupted between the Netherlands and Oliver Cromwell's Protestant republic. Observers were astonished by the struggle between the two European states most alike in religion and political ideology. The Anglo-Dutch War was the first in modern times to be fought almost exclusively for commercial motives. The English were the aggressors, the Dutch on the defensive. Thirteen years later, a second war broke out when the English fleet attacked Dutch shipping off the coasts of West Africa and North America. On this occasion, the Dutch proved that their commercial triumphs had not softened them, and Admiral De Ruyter conducted one of the boldest maneuvers in the history of modern naval warfare. In 1667, he led his fleet straight up the Thames and Medway, destroyed most of the English navy resting in drydock, and returned home with a prize warship in tow. Though the Dutch relinquished New Netherlands at the Treaty of Breda (1667), the English recognized Germany and the Spanish Netherlands as Holland's economic sphere of influence. The Navigation Acts were modified to permit Dutch vessels to carry goods to England from this enlarged trading area. In 1672, a third Anglo-Dutch war erupted, ending in stalemate two years later. For the remainder of the century, England and the Dutch Netherlands kept at peace with one another because the two countries shared a common interest of survival against Louis XIV's France. But the Navigation Acts stood. Through the eighteenth century and well into the nineteenth, they represented the cornerstone of British trade and imperial policy.

In the late seventeenth century, England's technological development did not yet measure up to the ambitions of its merchants and shippers for serving an expanding market. A hundred years earlier, it had experienced what has been called, with some exaggeration, "the first industrial revolution." New factories opened in England—paper and gunpowder mills, cannon foundries, saltpeter works. By the 1640s, England and its dependents already produced three times as much coal as the entire continent, but the failure to devise a workable process of smelting with coal prevented Britain from becoming preeminent in metallurgy. At length, in 1709 the first genuinely successful smelting of iron with coal took place as Abraham Darby discovered that by "precooking" his coal he was able to remove most of the impurities that had rendered the ore hopelessly brittle. But even Darby's breakthrough failed to surmount all the obstacles between invention and its full use in manufacturing.

Textiles comprised England's chief industry from 1648 to 1715. Perhaps it was the greatest industry of any kind in Europe. However, the basis for preparation, spinning, and weaving remained but slightly mechanized. Carding and combing of the fibers were hand processes. Weaving looms were exceedingly simple mills that pounded cloth either with vertically moving pestles or angle-set hammers. Production was decentralized. The merchant-employer bought the raw materials and distributed them to rural laborers, who worked them on ancient family looms during their spare moments away from the fields. Since the jobs were performed on farms and in cottages, the employer was unable to supervise the efforts of the worker, and the quality of the products varied. Without a technological revolution, the factory was unable to develop. The wholesale change from wood to coal as fuel, the mastery of heavy machinery, and the organization of urban-based centers of complete and supervised manufacture had to await the mid-eighteenth century. From 1648 to 1715, England was far from becoming an industrial giant. Nevertheless, it was in the age of recession that its investors and merchants began to display a commercial optimism out of step with the times, and this new conception of a market created an environment for invention and eventual technological breakthrough.

In one final respect the English moved ahead of their commercial rivals: in the creation of a financially solvent state—a government that balanced its books and to which subjects and foreigners loaned funds with confidence. The Dutch had provided the model. They were the first seventeenth-century Europeans to invest safely in government enterprise. During the war against France from 1672 to 1678, the States General borrowed without difficulty at 4 percent, while the overcommitted Louis XIV could barely find takers willing to finance him at 10 or even 15 percent. Still, when it came to questions of taxation, the Dutch were backward. The provinces possessed the right to bargain over the contribution the States General assessed them, and this customarily meant the reduction or even removal of quotas. The Dutch state did not have a central agency to supervise the collection of its taxes, and the government had to depend upon excises on consumer items. These indirect taxes usually were farmed out to individuals who advanced the government a lump sum and then kept for themselves most of what they subsequently collected.

When it came to taxation, the English were only slightly ahead of the Dutch. In fact, until 1692, England's tax revenue probably was the smallest per capita in Europe. It was one-fifth the size of France's. It derived from surcharges on certain consumer goods, customs dues, and direct taxes agreed to by Parliament. Under James II (1685–88), some reforms were tried. For example, tax farming came to an end, and by 1710, a single agency, the Royal Treasury, controlled all accounts of collection and expenditure. The costs of the major European wars in which England found itself after 1689 called for a reevaluation of the public's tax-paying responsibilities. To raise revenue, characteristic nuisance taxes were levied, such as duties on window panes and houses. The major direct tax—on land rentals—was raised to 20 percent, so that those who could best afford to pay, the great property owners, were the ones who paid. However, taxes still accounted for only half of the state's revenue. The remainder had to come from loans contracted with the public and chartered companies. Through the Bank of England, founded in 1694, the English developed the most efficient system of state borrowing to date. Individuals would deposit funds into the bank and receive its notes, plus interest ranging from 4.5 to 7.5 percent. The bank proved to be a safe, solid investment. Businessmen in Parliament underwrote it, and Dutch capital sustained it. By 1715, England attained a financial equilibrium that avoided overtaxing the poor and under-taxing the rich. Investors showed a confidence in the financial future of the government that paralleled their confidence in the commercial future of the nation.

FRANCE: MERCANTILISM IN THEORY AND PRACTICE

The Anglo-Dutch trade wars represented the culmination of ideas of com-merce that were common in the late seventeenth century. The basic idea held that the amount of international trade was fixed and that every state must therefore acquire a slice of the pie at the expense of every other state. Governments were supposed to formulate economic programs assuring the outward flow of finished products and the inward flow of precious metals or raw materials. These ideas postulated a stagnant consumer demand. Even after English merchants and manufacturers began disproving this, they continued to cherish the Navigation Acts, which represented its fruit. The old theories had a good deal of staying power. Late in the eighteenth century, critics placed them under the umbrella of the disparaging title of mercantilism.

Mercantilist theory and practice should be placed within the context of the age—a time of excessive international warfare, defective consumption, inefficient distribution, and depressed prices alternating with scarcity-pro-voked hikes. Governments felt obliged to intervene in the economic life of the nation in order to find ways of combatting the gloomy prospects. Jean-Baptiste Colbert, Louis XIV's controller-general of France, was the most energetic of the experimenters. He persuaded his king to raise tariffs, regu-late manufactures, establish and underwrite commercial companies, and encourage the immigration of foreign craftsmen. He also convinced his king to attempt more drastic measures in order to push aside commercial rivals. Louis XIV needed little encouragement to merge his dream of dynastic glory with Colbert's mercantilist vision, and in 1672, king and minister dragged France into war with the Dutch Netherlands. This was intended to be much more than the relatively limited struggles on the high seas that had occupied the English and Dutch in 1652 and 1665. It was planned as a total war, one that would destroy Holland's economic capacity. French intervention thus converted the third Anglo-Dutch war into a crusade aimed at annihilating the Netherlands. The plan was for Louis's army to occupy Amsterdam, Rotterdam, and Leyden. In the end, the French failed to accomplish their aim, the Dutch survived, and Colbert had to channel his energies into dredging up war revenues for his marching king.

War was the crudest weapon of the mercantilists. It promised the quickest solution but entailed the gravest risks. Tariff barriers against the manufactured goods of others offered a more subtle approach. Colbert directed French duties primarily at Dutch and English textiles, but he also prohibited Venetian glass and lace from entering the country. Indiscriminately applied tariffs have a boomerang effect, however. The French lists of 1664 and 1667 were so long and the duties so high that the plan amounted to a virtual exclusion of imported manufactures. French merchants who depended upon foreign articles howled in protest. The Dutch reciprocated with their own discriminatory tariff. In 1678, England refused to import French products. Colbert's bludgeons thus produced a counterattack. To change the metaphor, instead of increasing France's share in the pie, he seemed to be reducing the very size of the pie itself.

Tariffs are defensive measures, intended to keep capital at home for investment in domestic production. But Colbert believed that the state alone possessed the will to undertake industrial experimentation. In France, where recession merged with the thirst of moneyed individuals for the prestige of estate or office ownership, the controller-general probably was correct. The government underwrote an entire series of international trading ventures—the French East and West Indies Companies (1664), Baltic Company (1669), Levant Company (1670), and Senegal Company (1673). It established luxury workshops that trained artists and artisans in the manufacture of laces, lavish mirrors, and tapestries. It built cannon and munitions foundries, as well as the great dockyard at Toulon. It paid for navigation improvements for France's great rivers, and it financed construction of a canal in the southern province of Languedoc, connecting the Atlantic and Mediterranean for ships up to two hundred tons.

Through such projects Colbert hoped to lure private investment. He could not award titles of nobility to budding capitalists, but he did offer bounties, tax breaks, and control over labor to those who would invest in French shipbuilding, silk production, or sugar refineries. Foreigners, especially the ubiquitous Dutch, accepted the offers. The most celebrated of them, Josse van Robais, came to France to build the country's first important textile factory. Bounties and fiscal privileges were used to tempt foreign artisans as well. Shipwrights, silkworkers, glassblowers, leatherworkers, dyers, and papermakers were recruited from all over. Of course, the individual or corporate privileges they received only served to fragment yet further a society that represented a welter of divided groups.

Colbert believed that the state must not only encourage commerce and industry but must also regulate it. The controller-general attacked local toll charges within each of the three great customs districts of the country. He was fairly successful with the inner ring, called the Five Great Farms, but in the outer districts, Parlements, Estates, and tax farmers successfully resisted him. He did better—or thought he was doing better—with town industries. First, he revised France's industrial guilds, but not as autonomous organizations. Masters were to serve as government inspectors to make certain that rigorous standards of manufacture were maintained. When a regime decrees that fabrics made in one place must contain 1408 threads per cloth, while those made in another must contain 1216, it stifles individual initiative—particularly among the manufacturers of the first place, who may wish to sell cheap cloth. The privileges that Colbert awarded to the publishing guild of Paris, which could not hope to supply the needs of the country, had the twin effect of nearly destroying the legitimate publishing industry in the provinces and of turning illicit book production into big business. In the long run, Colbert's regulations over French industry worked against his desire for its development. Nevertheless, wherever he could enforce the regulations of his Council of Commerce, Colbert succeeded in establishing a social discipline and regional specialization unmatched in any other country. The glass of Saint Gobain, silks of Lyons, tapestries of Beauvais, Chaillot, and the Paris-based Gobelins factory, the embroidered cloths of Arras and Carcassonne—all became bywords for quality and beauty among the leisured groups of Europe. France became a workshop for the aristocracy. Colbert could conceive of no other kind of market. He set the tone of *luxe* for French production that haunts its industry to this day.

Custom and, ultimately, royal policies that conflicted with his own undercut Colbert. Village spinners and weavers hired out by small-time merchants frustrated his dream of establishing an urban work force under quasi-military discipline. Aware of the strengths of the seigneurial system and the resistance of regional custom, Colbert practically ignored attempts to reform agriculture. After 1672, he paid the supreme price for having pushed his king along the path of martial glory. Increasingly, until his death eleven years later, Colbert had to track down money lenders and office purchasers to meet the state's needs for quick military funds. The government could no longer subsidize the trading companies, and they collapsed. The controller-general even had to ease up on his attack of local toll officials so that the government might be assured of its share in the take. Against his better judgment, Colbert had to tolerate the persecution of the French Protestant community, the mainstay of a host of industries ranging from silks to hats, jewelry, and shipbuilding. The great Huguenot exodus occurred in 1685–86, after Colbert's death. By the end of the century, the restrictive legislation seemed to represent his major legacy.

Some contemporary theorists already saw the shortcomings of mercantilism. The great French marshal Sébastien le Prestre de Vauban pleaded for a system of priorities that would place the welfare of the laboring poor ahead of a favorable balance of trade. In his *Dixme royale* (1707) and other writings, Vauban advocated state responsibility for full employment even if it meant giving away exports, and he called for a graduated tax based upon income, not rank. In *Détail de la France* (1695), the legal officer Pierre le Pesant de Boisguilbert pointed out mercantilism's failure to grapple with the issue of maldistribution. Money, he believed, had become the master instead of the servant of commerce. He wrote that as a first priority the state ought to direct itself to increasing agricultural productivity. Sturdy peasant proprietors thus would form a market for manufacturers. As might be imagined, Colbert's theories found severe critics across the English Channel. In 1691, in *Discourses Upon Trade*, Englishman Dudley North wrote that a nation's true economic interest rested upon free individual enterprise, not upon state regulation of production. In the enormously popular *Fable of the Bees* (1714–28), Bernard de Mandeville rejected such regulation outright. Even the excesses of unrestricted individualism led to the betterment of society, wrote Mandeville: "Private vices, public virtues." This was the obverse of Colbertism.

In the eighteenth century, Europe's neomercantilist states were its most underdeveloped ones—Spain, Prussia, the Hapsburg empire—where the energies of the state were put to work to subsidize industry and reduce dependence upon imported manufactures. England's prosperity appeared to be centered on unrestricted production and commerce regulated by the Navigation Acts. France edged cautiously away from controls. All eighteenth-century governments, however, placed into the forefront an intention that Colbert would have considered unattainable: full employment. This tended to put into the background Colbert's corollary that a nation's prosperity was fundamentally dependent upon its neighbor's poverty. But this neomercantilism also was based upon a hope for a better material life for the majority, something Colbert also would have considered unattainable. The controller-general's theories and reforms were the product of a time of pessimism. They were the alternative to despair.

Chapter Three

Crisis and Resolution: The West

THE MIDCENTURY CRISES

In 1648, the three great treaties incorporated into the Peace of Westphalia
ended a generation of war in Germany. The armies of Spain, Austria,
Sweden, and France withdrew, leaving vast areas of central Europe in ruin.
Wars shortly flared up elsewhere—in Poland, along the eastern Baltic, on
the Spanish and French frontiers, and on the high seas. But for the overwhelming number of Europe's statesmen, townspeople, and peasants, 1648
was the year of peace among nations.

Within states themselves, however, matters were far different. While
most of Germany sank into the peace of exhaustion, elsewhere civil turmoil
either erupted or passed into a new and critical stage. The 1640s and 1650s
were decades of rebellion against constituted governments that would know
no parallel for another century and a half: revolts of social orders, of regions,
of corporate groups, revolts in large measure determined by local conditions, yet somehow feeding upon one another, even in an era of parochial-
ism and poor communications. Some historians have interpreted the
uprisings as desperate protests of the poor against high taxes in a period of
bad harvests. Others have seen the rebellions as motivated by the capitalist-
minded bourgeoisie turning against governments committed to a regressive
agrarian-based economy and social structure. Still other historians have
considered the revolts to have been the response of an exploited, bitter
"country" alliance of landowners, townsmen, and peasants against an exploiting group of court nobles, churchmen, and officers. Finally, some scholars have viewed the last gasps of the Thirty Years' War, the unrelieved
conflict between France and Spain, and the struggles in Poland and the
Baltic as driving corporate groups to rebellion.

The outbreaks were widespread. No state and few capitals seemed immune. In 1648, riots erupted in Paris and Moscow. In Istanbul, the Royal
Guard murdered the sultan, and a few months later, the English executed

their king. During much of 1649, it appeared that the French monarchy itself was going to be dismantled. The following year, armed troops and burghers faced each other in the streets of Amsterdam. In Spain's tottering empire, conflict spread to Naples, Palermo, and Barcelona. In the North, Stockholm and Berlin were scenes of unrest. While major revolt was nothing new to Europe, the almost universal character of the midcentury uprisings was.

THE CROMWELLIAN EXPERIMENT

In 1648, England was in the midst of revolution. An awakening of political consciousness among urban artisans and craftsmen, Protestant sectarian preachers, and small property owners in town and countryside had created a situation unique in English history. Even more dangerous was the articulation of a political and social ideology within the people's New Model Army that had crushed the forces of Charles I two years previously. Simple soldiers seized upon the revolutionary situation to call for representative government and universal male suffrage. Civilian counterparts, particularly in London, erected a pragmatic political program based upon broadened suffrage, a written constitution, and a sovereign House of Commons. Other small groups formed: some advocated the people's occupation of common grazing land; others, a religious terror unleashed against the "non-elect," approximately 99 percent of the country's population. The great Civil War had given birth to as volatile a social and political atmosphere as England had ever known.

The army leadership, behind Oliver Cromwell and his son-in-law Henry Ireton, was deeply troubled by the rising tide of radicalism among the troops and in the cities. Cromwell and Ireton identified themselves with small property holders, an elite that had brought revolution to England, but an elite nonetheless. They believed in parliamentary sovereignty and a franchise extended to men like themselves, but more radical programs appeared dangerous to them. Cromwell and Ireton believed that those with a "fixed interest" in the nation–the propertied–were the only ones responsible enough to govern. Thus they abolished the soldiers' councils in the army and arrested the leadership of the civilian radicals. When the king tried to take advantage of the revolutionaries' problems by staging a countercoup along with some Scottish troops and Cromwell's most lukewarm followers in Parliament, the pitiful uprising was easily crushed. A detachment of Cromwell's troops surrounded the Parliament building. Colonel Pride, leader of the force, permitted entry only to those members who swore fidelity to the army. Sixty did so. The remainder were sent home. The generals had erased opposition of both the left and right.

Cromwell, Ireton, the generals, and "Rump" parliamentarians were convinced now of the unredeeming rottenness of the Stuart court, Church, and institutions of government. They decided to bring the Civil War to its logical consummation. Already the House of Lords had been abolished and the privileged role of the Anglican Church dropped. In January 1649, the Rump established itself as a court of law to try Charles I for crimes of high treason. Cromwell directed the scenario, and the issue never was in doubt. Charles was executed as king, and with him, the regicides hoped, would perish all the trappings of the English monarchy.

Thus the country became a republic, and its new leadership searched for a workable alternative to the old regime. There was unfinished business to settle in Ireland and Scotland, where a residue of Stuart sympathy remained. Ireland was conquered savagely, leaving a legacy of religious hatred. Along with the troops, Protestant immigrants flowed into the country, dispossessing both native and Anglo-Irish landlords and seizing control over Irish trade. In Scotland, feudal land tenures were abolished, reforms were instituted in law and local government, and toleration was granted to Baptists and other small Protestant sectarian groups. In England itself, large transfers of land occurred. Crown lands, Anglican Church lands, and lands of suspected Royalists were seized and sold. Troops received plots in lieu of wages. While some whose property was expropriated paid large fines and received their lands back, the revolution did produce a new landholding class of London merchants, lawyers, speculators, and army officers. The shippers and important tradesmen of the ports now had a government that sympathized with their interests. In 1651, the first Navigation Acts were passed and the Anglo–Dutch War erupted. Within a few months, English sea victories netted seven hundred prizes.

But the outward successes of the Republic were deceptive and only concealed very real difficulties. Chief of these was the impatience of military leaders like Cromwell with the agonizing search for a workable political settlement. An obscure country squire in 1640, Cromwell had entered the Long Parliament and eventually made his career among the warriors of the New Model Army. In 1649, as head of the army he became head of state. He believed in parliamentary government, but he was even more convinced of the holy self-righteousness of military leadership. The army had destroyed the old monarchy and Church. Then it nipped the radical menace. To Cromwell, it was more than a cold military machine. It was a moral force, "a lawful power," whose duty was to recreate politics and society according to the wishes of God. On the other hand, from 1649 to 1658, in its desire to control use of taxation and reduce military commitments, Parliament became a focal point of opposition to both Cromwell and his army. Exasperated, Cromwell prorogued the Rump Parliament in 1653, and by 1658 three successor Parliaments met the same fate. The Instrument of Government, the only written constitution England ever had, proved ineffective, and at the local level the rift widened between civilian officials and the military. Unrepentant Royalists became active, and plots were uncovered to effect a Stuart restoration. Merchants complained about customs taxes, landlords complained about property taxes, and those with administrative experience refused to hold local office.

Finally, Cromwell gave up on civilian rule. To maintain internal security, he divided the country into eleven districts, each under the control of a major general. The military regime was not meant to be permanent, and the major generals were not supposed to be petty tyrants. They were efficient in extorting tax grants, but their interference in nearly all aspects of civilian life and their prudish opposition to taverns, sports, and popular pastimes exacerbated an already tense situation. Many who had supported the idealistic programs of the 1640s now beheld the fruits—a grim military dictatorship. As late as 1656, Cromwell might have saved the revolution had he presented the nation with a constitutional monarchy with himself as king. But his religious and political principles made him shudder at royalism in any form, and his chief military supporters vigorously opposed a solution that failed to give the army a central place in government. By 1658, it was evident that the republican experiment had failed. Far from laying the foundation of the new Jerusalem, the 50,000-man army had become an inordinately expensive agency of repression. Each day, the major generals created more sympathizers for a Stuart restoration. In exile on the continent, the son of Charles I was ready. The crisis broke when the Lord Protector took ill and died.

Almost immediately the Cromwellian regime fell apart. Troops were unpaid, and the courts were not functioning. Without Cromwell there to patch together differences, the army itself split into factions. Late in 1659, General George Monck, commander-in-chief in Scotland, concluded that the only way to restore order to public life was to reestablish continuity with the monarchical past. Having decided to recall the son of Charles I from exile in Holland, Monck moved his troops southward and entered London unopposed. Monck leaned towards the political solution Cromwell had rejected earlier—a disbanded army and a government that would work out its own balance between king and Parliament. Monck restored the survivors of Pride's Purge to Commons, and those moderate Royalists disclaimed their right to vote in the absence of the House of Lords. A new election was held. It returned a heavily Royalist Commons. The Lords took their seats in the Upper Chamber. On April 25, 1660, the Convention Parliament declared the government of England to be invested in King, Lords, and Commons. A month later, Charles II returned from his travels to take up what he called the twelfth year of his reign. Parliament imposed no new restrictions upon the king. He was granted an annual subsidy of over a million pounds to pay for the upkeep of his estates, the navy, royal judges, and diplomatic corps. This was far more than his unfortunate father had ever gotten.

Much of the onus for the failure of republicanism must fall on Cromwell himself. He never was able to extricate himself from the military frame of mind that had produced such a resounding victory over the forces of Charles I. His religious tolerance was his most endearing trait. His Puritanism tried to comprehend Protestant points of view from Presbyterian to Quaker, and it was he who took back the Jews after three centuries of exile from England. But even here, his dependence upon military men for whom success was sufficient proof of God's will turned him against religious groups which, to his mind, were frustrating that will—first Roman Catholics and High Church Anglicans, and eventually Presbyterians and Quakers. Cromwell earnestly wished to be a "healer and settler," and during the Republican interlude much was achieved. Many laws were made intelligible, and all men were declared equal before justice. Many medieval monopolies over production and trade collapsed, and the market rather than the guild came to determine the laws of supply and demand. England emerged as a commercial power. Ireland and Scotland became the fundamental components of the empire. Judges learned to depend upon salaries, not litigants' fees, for their income. Finally, though the vicissitudes of Parliament were many and great under Cromwell, the fact that he summoned it time and again, in one form or other, assured its survival as the essential repository of the interests of the nation. Cromwell erred in trying to build the Republic upon a military foundation, and he never could dispense with the military's arch-adversary, Parliament, for very long. In the end it was Parliament, speaking for England, that restored Charles II.

THE STUART RESTORATION

The immediate problem of the Restoration concerned the religious, political, and civil rights of the so-called Dissenting Protestants—the Presbyterians, Congregationalists, Baptists, and Quakers, who had dropped out of the Anglican Church's narrowly defined community of true Englishmen in the first half of the century. The reestablished state Church rejected any theological or institutional concession to the Dissenters. It offered nonconforming Protestants a begrudging, minimal amount of religious toleration but prohibited them from worshiping in public and barred them from local political office. Meanwhile, complacent and devoid of much spiritual infusion, Anglicanism came to represent a certain social order under the command of the bishops and landed oligarchs who controlled both houses of Parliament.

Most members of the Cavalier Parliament that sat from 1661 to 1678 wanted a Stuart king, for he embodied legitimacy and was a sacred barrier to republicanism. But they also wished to keep the king in tow, out of local government that they themselves ran and out of foreign adventures that cost money and threatened to enhance royal prestige. The most effective way to curb royal influence was by controlling its income, so Parliament exercised the power of subsidy over Charles II. It granted him revenue from customs receipts and half the income derived from a sales tax on certain consumer items. It withheld supplementary grants without a royal accounting of how the funds would be spent. While Charles won larger subsidies than his father, his royal income from 1660 to 1673 was half of what Cromwell had controlled from 1649 to 1659. The Cavalier Parliament made certain that the tax burden fell on the landless through charges placed on consumer goods and individual hearths. Large rural properties escaped taxation. Whenever possible, Royalists whose lands had been sold or expropriated in the Civil War instituted legal action to get their property back. Only the wealthiest were successful, and those who had borrowed in order to pay fines under the Commonwealth and Protectorate discovered that they still were debtors. Thus, in questions of land ownership and debt responsibility, the Restoration Parliament trod very cautiously. Its members were not committed to an ideology of vengeance. A loose coalition of courtiers, officeholders, country gentlemen, and merchants, they wished to steer a course that avoided the shoals of both revived republicanism and Stuart tyranny.

The king was a pragmatist. An intelligent, witty, cynical sensualist who took much more naturally to bribes and intrigue than to direct confrontation, Charles II had not enjoyed exile, and he had little desire to risk being sent abroad again. He hoped, however, to construct a personal following in Parliament and therefore plied the strongly Royalist members with gifts, bribes, and favors. For the first six years of the Restoration, his chief adviser and minister was the earl of Clarendon, a dour conservative holdover from the prerevolutionary years. Victimized by a series of events beyond his power to control—the plague of 1665, the London fire of 1666, De Ruyter's destruction of the English fleet in 1667—Clarendon was suspected of wishing to increase the king's authority beyond proper limits. Impeached, Clarendon fled to France, where he wrote both an autobiography justifying his career and a great history of the Civil War. Clarendon was replaced by five politicians known as the "Cabal," forming a ministerial group around the king. They advised Charles to reduce his financial dependence upon Parliament, and two of them helped concoct the Secret Treaty of Dover with Louis XIV (1670). By its terms, Louis granted Charles subsidies. In return, Charles promised support in any future French war with the Dutch. Furthermore, Charles, who was a closet Catholic, was to declare his religion openly at the first convenient opportunity, and Louis offered him help in re-Catholicizing England.

The Secret Treaty of Dover was a dreadful blunder. Rumors about it leaked out, and fears mounted in Parliament that a re-Catholicized England, the pawn of Louis XIV, was a distinct possibility. In 1672, without parliamentary consent, Charles and Louis made war on the Dutch. In addition,

Charles issued the Declaration of Indulgence, which offered religious liberty to Catholics and Protestant Dissenters alike. Caught between fear and anger, Parliament in 1673 passed the Test Act, a direct challenge to the king's Declaration of Indulgence. The act stated emphatically that all civil and military posts must be reserved for Anglicans. Charles's younger brother James, an open Roman Catholic since 1670, promptly resigned as Lord Admiral of the Fleet.

The king knew when to retreat. He revoked the Declaration of Indulgence and withdrew from the Dutch war. The Cabal broke apart, and Charles selected as chief minister Lord Danby, an experienced man convinced that effective royal leadership depended more upon the manipulation of institutions than upon foreign policy adventures or confrontations with Commons. Danby courted whatever sympathizers he could find in Parliament. To hold onto Anglican squires in the Commons and bishops in the House of Lords, he enforced the Test Act to the letter. This aroused Dissenter sympathizers; clubs and coffeehouses in London seethed with political activity. A one-time member of the Cabal, Anthony Ashley–Cooper, sought support for a program that would counter Danby's. He called for new elections; though fewer than half the original members remained, the Cavalier Parliament of 1661 was still in session.

While Danby courted a parliamentary following for the king and opposition took root, a single crucial issue began to assume ominous form. In 1678, Charles was nearly fifty. He had no legitimate offspring, and his brother James, next in line to the throne, was a devout convert to Catholicism. Moreover, James had a young Italian wife. By a first marriage, James had two Protestant daughters, Mary and Anne. Should he sire a son, the boy would have precedence and guarantee England a Catholic sovereign for the next generation. The Parliament and country might accept James, but they would not tolerate the continuation of a Catholic royal line. Charles would not hear of divorcing a barren wife toward whom he had been persistently unfaithful all his life, and there was no sentiment behind legitimizing the king's eldest male bastard, the Protestant duke of Monmouth. So the succession issue began to overwhelm all others, and England was seized by a climate of fear for the future. People asked how Parliament could exclude Catholics from public office and allow James Stuart the highest one of all. On the other hand, if James were denied the throne, would there not be political chaos and perhaps civil war?

The crisis came to a head in 1679. Taking advantage of the climate of fear, a defrocked priest named Titus Oates, along with a core of associates, claimed knowledge of a great "Popish Plot," in which the king would be murdered and James put on the throne. A massacre of Protestants would follow, and James would turn a re-Catholicized England into a French satellite. Oates's accusations had no basis in fact. However, hysteria swept through Parliament, London, and England. No one near the king was above suspicion. Even Danby fell. A second Test Act excluded Catholics from the House of Lords. Exasperated, Charles was forced at last to prorogue the Cavalier Parliament that had sat for eighteen years.

The Popish Plot fizzled out, but the air of constitutional crisis remained. The election of 1679 returned a majority hostile to the possible succession of James. Ashley-Cooper (Lord Shaftesbury) organized a political group called the "Exclusionists," and their bill to deny James the throne passed in Commons. Meanwhile, Royalist members claimed that no parliamentary body could tamper with the fundamental laws of succession, accused the Exclusionists of treason, and labeled them "Whigs" after a particularly savage gang of Scottish cattle thieves. The Whigs responded by calling their adversaries "Tories," after an Irish Catholic guerrilla band. The epithets stuck and gained respectability. Shaftesbury tried to mold a positive program for the Whigs. They were more anti-Catholic and pro-Dissenter than the Tories, were more inclined to define limits to the royal prerogative, opposed a standing army, and liked the idea of frequent parliamentary elections. They also seemed more sensitive than Tories to questions of civil liberties. Two weeks after the vote on the Exclusion Bill, the Whig-dominated Commons passed the Habeas Corpus Act, whereby a judge could force release of a prisoner if the jailer failed to show cause for imprisonment. Charles accepted the Habeas Corpus Act but would have nothing to do with the Exclusion Bill. He dissolved Parliament.

For two additional years the country was deadlocked over the succession. Whig-dominated Parliaments would present exclusion bills to Charles, and the king would prorogue the assemblies rather than submit. At length an extremist Whig faction laid plans for a popular uprising that would force the king to accept an exclusion bill. But the plot backfired. Shaftesbury's involvement led to a charge of treason against him, and he fled the country. In 1683, the Rye House Plot, a scheme to coordinate a series of urban riots with the assassination of both Charles and James, was uncovered. Monmouth was to assume the throne. Several Whigs were implicated. They were arrested, accused of high treason, and executed. By now the Whigs were disgraced, and exclusionism thoroughly discredited. Sick of plot hysteria, the peerage, older gentry, and mercantile-financial elite turned to Charles as the sole harbinger of stability. Still collecting his French subsidy, he determined to live on his own rather than call for another parliamentary election. Tories submitted to royal leadership, while chastened Whigs were deprived of their soapbox in Commons. Charles kept a small army ready, suppressed the corporate charters for London and sixty-five other cities, and filled judgeships and other administrative posts with certain allies. On his deathbed in 1685, he formally converted to Catholicism. When his brother James succeeded him, the opportunity never looked better for the monarchy to dominate the nation's constitution.

THE GLORIOUS REVOLUTION

Argyll's uprising in west Scotland and Monmouth's in Cornwall accompanied the succession of James but were easily subdued. At first, James showed every indication of being moderate and conciliatory. He allowed himself to be crowned according to the Anglican rite and graciously called a new Parliament. The country responded with one that was heavily Tory. Only the most diehard Whigs and Republicans seemed beyond James's reach. The Parliament of 1685 gave James the largest peacetime budget ever enjoyed by an English king. A wave of euphoria and relief swept across England.

Two months after his accession, however, James showed his true face. Argyll and Monmouth were executed. A royal commission rounded up suspected collaborators. Drumhead courts sentenced dozens to death, long imprisonment, or deportation. Increasingly, these "Bloody Assizes" began to look like a convenient way of getting rid of potential opposition, not actual rebels. James started to look less like a transitional monarch than a royal revolutionary bent upon remaking England into a Catholic absolutism. He replaced Anglican advisers with Catholics. He demanded that Parliament revoke both the Test and Habeas Corpus acts. In 1686, he decided to do without Parliament altogether. He kept the army on a permanent war footing and surrounded the gates of London with 30,000 troops. He personally urged conversions to Catholicism and authorized Anglican priests who did so to keep their incomes. He heaped honors upon the papal nuncio and kneeled ostentatiously in his presence. Even Louis XIV advised him to go more slowly.

By 1687, the national unity that had accompanied James's accession was in shreds. Tories and Whigs, Anglicans and non-Conformists, country gentlemen and merchants—all viewed him as a menace. The leading alternative was his elder daughter Mary. She was married to Stadholder William III of the Netherlands, himself a grandson of Charles I. Meanwhile, James was attacking Anglicanism on all fronts. His Declaration of Indulgence repealed the Test Act and reopened public office to Catholics and Dissenters. A new royal court, the Ecclesiastical Commission, dismissed Anglicans from public posts. In the spring of 1688, the queen became pregnant and seven Anglican bishops, including the archbishop of Canterbury, rejected James's demand that they approve of his Declaration of Indulgence. Their reasoning was that no king of England had the right to overturn an act of Parliament, namely the Test Act. James had the churchmen arrested and tried for seditious libel. A jury acquitted them, the first major legal decision in modern English history to go against the wishes of a reigning monarch. Not even the news of the birth of James's son could dampen the exultation in London produced by the acquittal of the seven bishops. A showdown was inevitable. Wavering Tories hastened to oppose the king. Even some

Catholics saw the writing on the wall and withdrew support from James.

During the autumn of 1688, a secret committee representing Parliament, the military, and the Anglican Church opened negotiations with William and Mary. At The Hague, exiled Whigs were convenient intermediaries. The stadholder and James's daughter were asked to cross over to England and rescue Protestantism. Though the secret committee was divided over whether William and Mary should simply compel James to change his ways, establish a regency for the baby prince, or assume the throne themselves, the stadholder was clear in his purpose: to become king of England. In November 1688, he and Mary sailed for England with fifteen thousand Dutch troops. As his fleet approached the English coast, an east wind bottled up James's navy in the Thames estuary and kept it from confronting the Dutch flotilla on the open sea. William's force sailed down the channel, landing on the southern coast. The invaders met no opposition, and James's army retreated to London and disbanded. His younger daughter Anne went over to the other side. Then the king lost his nerve. Turning authority over to no one, he sent his wife and infant son to France, destroyed the writs summoning Parliament, threw the Great Seal of Justice into the Thames, and joined his wife at Louis XIV's court. William and Mary entered London in triumph.

England had no king in residence, but government had to continue. The House of Lords took the initiative to keep the revolution bloodless. The peers called together a convention drawn from the membership of the last Parliament, and negotiations reopened with William and Mary. Ever obstinate and calculating, the stadholder wished above all to get England into the Grand Alliance he was molding against Louis XIV. He therefore consented to nothing less than joint rule with his wife. This was the point the Convention Parliament debated and ultimately accepted. A legal fiction declared James to have abdicated. The Whigs and a handful of Tories maintained Parliament's right to offer the throne to the most legitimate claimant. They judged the claims of William and Mary equally valid, adding that Parliament possessed the authority to define the scope of royal prerogative powers, and it set down a declaration of civil rights for all Englishmen.

Such was the basis of the revolutionary settlement. By the terms of the Bill of Rights, the monarch was enjoined from suspending the laws, and the prerogative of royal pardon in particular cases was severely restricted. In all criminal cases, jury trials were made the right of the accused, and special prerogative courts like James's Ecclesiastical Commission were prohibited. The sovereign had to take a coronation oath upholding Parliament's statutes, and free parliamentary debate was guaranteed. All taxes not sanctioned by Parliament were illegal. No peacetime standing army could exist. The Whigs also tackled the delicate religious question and forced through Parliament the Toleration Act, which amended the spirit, if not the letter, of the discriminatory Test Acts. The new king himself was a Dutch Calvinist. He believed in religious toleration, and the lessons of the past half-century had convinced most Englishmen that enforced religious uniformity could never bring social peace. The Toleration Act kept local civil and political office closed to non-Anglicans, but free and open worship was guaranteed Protestants who believed in the Holy Trinity. Though Catholics, Unitarians, Quakers, and non-Christians were left outside the provisions of this part of the Toleration Act, restrictions against these groups were not enforced. Roman Catholics were excluded from the throne, and the new coronation oath promised to uphold the "Protestant Reformed Religion;" but it now was universally recognized that England's political and social fabric could withstand confessional diversity.

After some wrangling with William, the Whigs won the guarantee of frequent parliamentary elections that became essential to the eighteenth-century constitution. The Whigs wanted no repetition of the Cavalier Parliament or, what was worse, a king ruling without Parliament at all. In 1694, the Triennial Act called for elections at least every three years; in 1716, the act was amended to call for elections at least every seven years. From 1689 to 1713, the needs of war and preparation for the war brought Parliament together annually. The increased length, frequency, and regularity of its sittings assured Parliament a central place in the day-to-day functions of government. Though the king's ministers in the future might cajole, browbeat, and bribe M.P.s into sanctioning royal policies, the Glorious Revolution greatly enhanced Parliament's role in government. Parliament had settled the succession and religious questions, it had regulated the royal prerogative, it provided William with the funds for his war, and it might even impeach his ministers. Surely the king might fill Parliament with his choices, but frequent elections could undo his packing. After 1689, king and Parliament were undeniably interdependent features of the English constitution.

Mary died in 1694, William, in 1702. The couple had no children, so the crown passed on to Anne, Mary's younger sister. Since Anne's numerous offspring had stubbornly resisted survival, the genuine possibility existed that the line descending from James's daughters would end with Anne's death. Therefore, in 1701, Parliament passed the Act of Settlement, fixing the succession in the German House of Hanover, which was directly descended from James I. Suspicious of the new continental attachment, the act added that on his own no English sovereign could send troops to war over lands not linked to his crown. Nor could a ruler leave English soil without Parliament's consent.

Though the so-called Whig program dictated the spirit of the revolutionary settlement, Tory support carried it through. Party loyalties and distinctions still were blurred. William III was the king the Whigs had put on the throne, but his inclination towards royal activism veered more closely toward a Tory than a Whig position. Still, William could count on the Whigs because they were the fountainhead of his support in the war against Louis XIV. London merchants and financiers, as well as the greatest country landlords, had loaned the government sums to fight the war. Customarily, these individuals thought of themselves as Whigs. Others without a direct stake in the war or in conquering Spain's overseas markets identified with the Tories. The "political nation" itself was highly circumscribed. About a quarter million males, one of every ten adults, held sufficient property to vote. Moreover, two-thirds of the electoral districts called boroughs contained fewer than five hundred voters; one-third of them had fewer than a hundred voters. It was not difficult for the crown or an important peer to control election districts. The limited franchise and unreformed districting placed a high price upon votes. By and large, the Tories called for a wider franchise, but both parties represented interests of country proprietors, urban merchants, the armed forces, and civil service rather than individual constituents.

The revolutionary settlement was respectful of Scotland. William rewarded Scottish loyalty by guaranteeing the country's laws, religion, and independent parliament. In 1702, the Scots took Anne as their queen. However, both English and Scottish politicians worried about the loyalty of the wild highlanders to the Hanoverians. Therefore, in 1707, parliaments of both countries agreed to cement ties through political union. The Scottish Parliament was dissolved and forty-five seats in the English House of Commons went to Scots. Scotland kept its legal institutions and established Presbyterian Church. Membership in England's privileged trading companies and the benefits of the Navigation Acts were extended to Scottish merchants. The United Kingdom of Great Britain was born.

Ireland was an entirely different matter. The later Stuarts had done nothing to ameliorate the brutality of Cromwell's conquest. Native Catholics wallowed in virtual serfdom. Presbyterians descended from Scottish immigrants in the northern part of Ireland fared somewhat better. English landlords, usually Anglican and often absentee, owned the greatest properties and controlled the Irish Parliament. But the English Parliament considered all Irishmen of whatever religious persuasion with contempt, and in 1690 the Catholic Irish made a fatal error by supporting James II's abortive effort to reclaim his kingdom. William himself defeated James's Franco-Irish contingent at the Battle of the Boyne, and English fears of future rebellion created a rule of terror and repression that knew no parallel in western Europe. The Catholic population bore the brunt of mistreatment. The so-called Penal Code kept Catholic priests from preaching and Catholic teachers from teaching. Catholic parents were forbidden to send their children abroad to be educated, nor could Catholics sit in the Irish Parliament. Catholics were forbidden from purchasing land, and a child needed only to turn Protestant to dispossess his Catholic father. Professions and most trades were closed to Catholics. To forestall the development of a native

Catholic elite, the English determined to keep Ireland's religious majority economically and socially suppressed.

The Protestant Irish had reason for complaint, too. After 1690 the Navigation Acts continued to treat Ireland as a foreign country. Its merchants could not sell to England's colonies. The Irish were prohibited from manufacturing woollens; their raw wool was to be exported exclusively to England. Thus Ireland was to live off the sale of raw wool and beef, with its absent landlords pocketing the profits. Even the resident Anglicans, however, felt like a conquered people, subject to the economic discrimination and political authority of London.

Queen Anne's reign virtually coincided with the War of the Spanish Succession, the struggle William III had inspired against France. An Englishman, the duke of Marlborough, brilliantly succeeded William as the driving force that brought the anti-French coalition to the threshold of victory. By 1710, however, both Queen Anne and public opinion had grown weary of the war, and the election of 1711 gave the Tories a majority in Commons. Their platform was peace. Anne dismissed Marlborough and packed the House of Lords with Tory peers. In 1712, Parliament and the queen took England out of the war. Two years later, Anne became gravely ill and died at fifty. None of her seventeen children survived her. On her deathbed, she regretted that her young Stuart half-brother in French exile had not become an Anglican and return home to claim his crown. But no Whigs and few Tories wanted the Pretender. As foreseen by the Act of Settlement, the Elector of Hanover became the next English ruler, assuming the throne as George I. After a century of unprecedented shock and dislocation, the England of 1714 was confident of itself and welcomed the future. Nobles, gentry, and the propertied middle classes had welded their separate interests into a common program built around the political settlement of the Glorious Revolution, a social settlement determined by landed, investable wealth, and an economic settlement stressing estate building and international trade. An oligarchy ruled the land.

THE DUTCH NETHERLANDS

In 1650 and 1672, crises occurred in the Dutch Netherlands. Both sets of events were important politically, but they were not revolutions. The structure of Dutch society was barely affected. Battles and large-scale executions were averted. The crises were consistent with the pattern of Dutch history, a pendulum swinging between the absolutist pretensions of the House of Orange and the oligarchic ambitions of the great merchants and shippers.

The social and political structure of the seven United Provinces was unique in Europe. An urban patriciate numbering around two thousand and settled largely in the provinces of Holland and Utrecht had provided the citizenry with a material standard of life that was the envy of the continent. These oligarchs invested in lifetime annuities and offices, bought shares in the East and West India Companies, and built country estates. Because they overwhelmingly financed the Dutch Confederation, the regents of the province of Holland tried to bully or persuade the Estates of other provinces to instruct their representatives in the States General to vote Holland's way. This meant religious toleration, a small army, neutral foreign policy, low taxes, and maintenance of Dutch mastery over international commerce.

The leader of Holland's delegation to the States General was a provincial official called the grand pensionary. It was he who was entrusted to correspond, in the name of the republic, with ambassadors abroad. A respected and feared grand pensionary could be an extremely imposing force in Dutch politics. Offsetting his influence, however, was the stadholder. The stadholderate was a hallowed medieval office, and in the war of liberation against Spain, the personal heroism and martyrdom of the stadholder of Holland, William the Silent, assured the post for the eldest male member of his family, the House of Orange. Four or five other provinces customarily chose this same individual as their stadholder, and the remainder selected a close relative. The States General usually granted command of the armed forces to the stadholder, and he controlled most of the offices put up for sale. The House of Orange held large properties in the Netherlands and Germany and was related to many of Europe's ruling families. The infant who became Stadholder William III was the great-grandson of France's Henry IV and the grandson of England's Charles I.

The wealth and the prestige of the stadholder's family made him very popular among members of the Calvinist clergy, smaller merchants, petty shopkeepers, artisans, and free peasants—all of whom harbored resentments of one form or other against the regent oligarchs. The grand policy of the House of Orange was to weld together the provinces under stadholder leadership. The stadholder of six provinces, Frederick Henry, had wished to continue fighting the Thirty Years' War and to intervene in England to rescue Charles I. But he died in 1647 before effecting his plans, and the regent-dominated States General quickly made peace with Spain.

The succession of William II to his father's offices led to political turmoil in 1650. The regents had good reason to fear William II. Twenty-one years old, impetuous, detesting the peace with Spain, he was eager to take his 55,000-man army to England to throw out Cromwell. Under Holland's instigation, the States General lost no time in depriving the stadholder of funds for his troops, and in July 1650, William responded with a show of force. He surrounded Amsterdam with his army and arrested six of Holland's regents. Though he released them, the city government began arming against the stadholder. Civil war seemed near. At this point, however, an act of nature changed the picture. William suddenly contracted smallpox and died, leaving a widow eight months pregnant.

A week after his father's death, the future William III was born. The regents of Holland seized the opportunity of a vacant stadholderate to tip the constitutional balance in their favor, and allies in the other provinces followed suit. The prince of Orange was specifically denied the stadholderate and command over the army. In his place, the grand pensionary of Holland, Jan De Witt, took command of the republic's destinies. Cromwell gave De Witt a war he did not want, but the Dutchman masterfully maneuvered through the web of provincial politics and raised a fleet. The Netherlands commanded the carrying trade through the Baltic and between Europe, America, and Asia, and it held on through the second trade war with England, from 1665 to 1667. Domestically, however, De Witt was sitting on a powder keg. Again and again, the inland agricultural provinces chafed at Holland's domination of the confederation. Middling burghers and artisans complained that the regents of Amsterdam were soaking up the republic's wealth at their expense. Calvinist preachers denounced De Witt's religious policies, by far the most tolerant in Europe. As the prince of Orange was approaching manhood, all who were naturally suspicious of regent rule threw their hopes round his person. The example of the Stuart restoration gave heart to the Orangists that William could not be excluded indefinitely from public life.

As it turned out, the crisis of foreign invasion overturned De Witt's "Regime of True Liberty." As the third trade war erupted with England in 1672, Louis XIV invaded the Netherlands. Unprepared for war, the republic was traumatized. De Witt was blamed for having sacrificed vigilance for profits. His enemies gained control of the Estates in Holland and Zeeland. The States General recalled how once before the House of Orange had saved the nation, and it asked the frail, shy, twenty-one-year-old William to assume his responsibilities to family and country. William was invested with the essential offices previously denied him—the stadholderates of Holland and Zeeland. He was named Captain General of the army and Admiral General of the navy. Orangists took over important provincial posts and sent more Orangists to the States General. De Witt resigned as grand pensionary of Holland. His brother Cornelius was imprisoned, and when Jan went to The Hague to visit him, an ugly mob greeted the brothers. Both De Witts were dragged to the town square, blamed for the Netherlands's misfortune, hanged upside down, filled with musket shot, and torn apart.

On this inglorious note, the Regime of True Liberty fell. French troops occupied three provinces and a young, inexperienced prince was asked to save the state. That William III managed to do so, while at the same time reestablishing his family's authority over the United Provinces, has made the regime of the De Witts appear shameful by comparison. With some justice, Dutch patriotic historians call the oligarchic experiment of 1650 to 1672 a blot on their country's history—narrow-visioned and materialistic, inviting disaster.

Nevertheless, under these peace-obsessed investors and speculators, a civilization took root that perplexed and amazed all Europe. For the mid-seventeenth century, it was as unique as the Dutch republic itself. Tolerant not only of all Protestant sects but also of Roman Catholics, Jews, and even free thinkers and financing a theater, book trade, and the five most innovative universities in Europe, the regents helped inspire a generation of unparalleled genius in painting, literature, philosophy, and science. It drew directly upon the spirit of cultural openness. Within it flourished the painters Rembrandt, Vermeer, and Jan Steen, the poet Vondel, the philosopher Spinoza, and the scientists Huygens and Leeuwenhoek. Rich and multihued, this civilization contrasted vividly with the stylized classicism taking root in France. It was the genuine legacy of the De Witts.

As stadholder, William III placed his followers into town and provincial administrations; however, he stopped short of converting the republic's unwieldy constitution into a streamlined absolutism. William's preoccupation was to mold the Grand Alliance against Louis XIV and persuade the Dutch magnates of banking and trade that it was in their interest to finance the armies of impecunious allies, such as Austria, Spain, and Sweden. William offered asylum to Protestant refugees fleeing France. He held up the specter of French mercantilism. He persuaded the oligarchs of Amsterdam to pay for the 1688 expedition to England. Thus the events of 1672 produced no revolution, only another swing in the pendulum of Dutch history.

From 1689 until his death in 1702, William shuttled between London and The Hague. Increasingly, Dutch affairs fell into the hands of the grand pensionary of Holland, Anthony Heinsius. Heinsius was no Jan De Witt. First of all, he was devoted to the stadholder and as long as William lived was able to prevent the traditional regent-stadholder political rivalries from erupting into civil strife. Secondly, Heinsius was as convinced as William of the moral necessity of the struggle against France, and due to his prodding, the Dutch expended their material resources to virtual exhaustion in the wars with Louis XIV. However, Heinsius was enough of a regent to reconstruct Amsterdam's leadership in the confederation, and upon William's death without direct heirs, plans for the Estates to elect a successor simply were shelved. The pendulum had tipped once more, and for the next forty-five years, the republic lived without a stadholder. The regents of Holland were back in control. But the Netherlands was becoming a third-class power. The War of the Spanish Succession (1702–13) proved to be a watershed in the republic's history. States with greater depth in manpower and natural resources outstripped the confederation in agricultural and industrial development and were catching up in shipping and shipbuilding. Dutch funds for investment left the country, and the citizenry withdrew into an existence conforming to the size of the republic's population and limited by its natural resources and archaic political structure.

FRANCE: THE FRONDES AND RISE OF LOUIS XIV

A revolt in France erupted in 1648 which threatened to undo the constitution of the state. Its original purpose was to forestall the movement toward centralization and absolutism that had started in the reign of Henry IV. The revolt began with promise, but conflicting interests among the rebels added to the calamities of civil and foreign war, famine, and plague. The great constitutional crisis thus degenerated into a series of miserable and uncoordinated thrusts at the regime and dragged on for more than five years. Recent research has dispelled the old comic opera version of the struggles called the Frondes.[1] Directly or indirectly, perhaps two million people perished. In the end, faced with a choice of anarchy or absolutism, the French nation opted for the *système louis-quatorzième*—the state of Louis XIV—and the Frondes went into history as a tragedy of missed opportunity.

In 1648, the king was child of ten, and the government was theoretically in the hands of a regency of his closest relatives. In practice, however, the queen mother, Anne of Austria, and her companion, Cardinal Jules Mazarin, ran affairs. Italian born, naturalized in 1639, Mazarin had been Richelieu's handpicked successor. He tried to use the skeletal bureaucracy of loyal *intendants* and commissioners to challenge the pretensions of nobles and officers with inheritable posts (see pp. 20 21), but Mazarin's style was better suited to bribe, divide, and undercut than to create an institutionalized base of authority. He controlled the princes' Council of State, but from 1645 on, the officeholders, led by the magistrates in the Parlement of Paris, resisted him. Three years later an open revolt erupted.

The indignation of the officeholders was based on self-interest. In the late stages of the Thirty Years' War, French expenses were extremely high, and the state was chronically short of revenues. As expedients, Mazarin created great blocs of posts in the law courts, tax administration, and local governments. He then sold them to the highest bidder. Many offices were duplicated, augmenting rivalry and bitterness among their holders and angering clients who had to pay the officeholders for their services. Mazarin increased taxes on food and drink. He attempted forced loans and hearth taxes. Still, the state could not pay its bills. Finally, early in 1648, he directed the Council of State to impose a new set of taxes on Paris and suppress payment of most officers' salaries. Officeholders feared a wholesale recall of their positions so that the state could sell them again.

At this point, the chief law court of the realm, the Parlement of Paris, stepped in as spokesman for the officers' interests. The war, an irregular government hungering for revenue, and a countryside suffering from the

---

[1]A *fronde* was a slingshot used by the street children of Paris to hurl rocks and mudballs at each other and passersby.

worst harvest of the century created an atmosphere of national discontent that the *parlementaires*, themselves the most prestigious officers in the kingdom, could exploit advantageously. Already, provincial revolts, endemic under Richelieu, were spreading towards the capital. The Paris Parlement refused to register Mazarin's edicts as law. Its leaders then went further, attempting to reverse the absolutist trend in government that had developed in the past half-century. They demanded a larger share in making the laws and the right to interrogate councillors of state and ministers on policy. They expressed the wishes of the officeholders by demanding the abolition of the *intendants*, an end to office duplication, and state recognition of the inviolability of those offices legitimately held. Finally, the *parlementaires* made a bid at widening their constituency by calling for a lowering of the most important tax in the kingdom, the *taille* (which they and the other officers did not pay) and the freedom of all Frenchmen, irrespective of social rank, from arbitrary arrest. In Paris, shopkeepers, artisans, and the unemployed prepared barricades. Humble peasants and townsmen, who had built the roads, dug the trenches, and filled the ranks during the cardinal's war with the Hapsburgs, now joined officers and judges of quality in order to change the course of events. All looked to the Paris Parlement as the focal point of opposition to Mazarin and his creatures.

In August 1648, Mazarin bungled an attempt to arrest several leaders of the Parlement of Paris, and mobs attacked the royal troops. The great princes at court, traditional malcontents, turned upon the cardinal and Anne. Headed by Conti, Longueville, and Beaufort, they tried at the same time to establish a common front with the judges and lead the mobs. Their very lives in danger, Mazarin, the queen mother, and young Louis XIV fled Paris for estates in the country. In October, a royal declaration yielded nearly every point the *parlementaires* had demanded the previous summer, and France appeared on the verge of becoming a limited monarchy. But Mazarin was simply buying time. He correctly suspected that an alliance of princes, judges, and the people could not last. Unlike the situation in England, where deep-seated religious, constitutional, and political concerns had led to popular support of revolutionaries, in France a handful of judicial officers holding lifetime sinecures had for the moment extended the range of corporate self-interest to a confrontation with the government over the constitution and civil liberties. As he pretended to give way, Mazarin prepared countermoves. Making peace with the emperor, he moved troops released from German service toward Paris. The prince of Condé remained loyal and was placed at the head of the army. In January 1649, Condé besieged Paris, and civil war erupted in earnest.

At this stage, the restive princes turned to arms, and the parlementary front disintegrated. Some judges joined the princes, while others accepted Mazarin's promises of order rather than risk the spectacle of anarchy. A few damned both sides while remaining true to the principles of the previous summer. Aside from a common hatred of Mazarin and a desire to dismember the state among themselves, however, the princes lacked a coordinated program. Unquenchable ambition was what drove them on, and their complex hostilities ravaged France until 1653. Though Mazarin had pulled the army out of Germany, France remained at war with Spain. Spanish armies, royal and noble armies, and irregular guerrilla bands cut wide swaths of destruction through the land. Dismissed veterans and peasants driven from ruined estates joined whatever ragtag group that promised the most booty. The war spared few regions. In many places, food production halted altogether. Crop failure and famine led to property sales at giveaway prices. For the peasants, the civil war was an unmitigated disaster. Twenty-five years later, a spectacular drop in marriages and births was attributed to the demographic catastrophe accompanying the Frondes—the misleading title given the conflict of 1648–53.

In the end, Mazarin returned as savior of the state. He skillfully divided enemies and bribed potential friends. Most *parlementaires* returned to the royal fold, and by 1652 the country was crying for peace. The promise of pardon gave the princes an honorable excuse to lay down their arms, and late in 1652 Paris, the one-time center of resistance, submitted weakly. It took nearly a year to subdue all the provinces, but with the fall of the "people's republic" of Bordeaux in August 1653, the Frondes officially were over.

The failure of the Frondes prepared the way for the absolutism of Louis XIV. Any other alternative had been discredited. Mazarin sought neither revenge nor reprisals. He accepted a surface reconciliation with the erstwhile rebels and a slow, steady reconstruction of royal power. From 1653 to 1661, the cardinal chose his associates well. Disregarding the princes, he turned to the lesser nobility and even bourgeoisie for his most trusted servants. He persuaded officeholders and junior parlementary officials of proven ability to enter the royal service as commissioners. He rewarded his followers with estates and money. As Louis XIV approached the age of majority, Mazarin developed the cult of majesty for the young king. In 1654, Louis enjoyed a magnificent coronation at Reims. The following year, he showed what might be expected when, in full hunting regalia, he burst into a session of the Paris Parlement and prohibited the magistrates from giving their legal objections to a new tax edict. In 1659, Mazarin brought the lingering war with Spain to a triumphant end and scored an even more telling diplomatic victory by marrying off Louis to the eldest child of the Spanish king, Philip IV. This personal union made France an arbiter of the fortunes of the Spanish empire.

The exhaustion that followed the Frondes only covered up the real dysfunctions in French society. Taxation was abusive, and offices still were duplicated and sold. The government borrowed money from private combines and the tax farmers and then turned its "benefactors" loose upon the peasantry to recoup loans and interest. From the Frondes, Mazarin learned that royal power might seize upon the divisions of society, and young Louis XIV sensed the need to emerge as supreme arbiter of them. And, of course, as the most populous state in western Europe, a source of agricultural and commercial riches that ought to have no parallel on the continent, France offered a wealth of opportunity. The king's person provided the unifying structure that society lacked, and alone the king restored a mood of aggressive self-confidence to his people. On March 6, 1661, Mazarin died, willing his superb library to the state that had paid for it. On the following day, the twenty-three-year-old king announced that henceforth he would serve as his own first minister.

LOUIS XIV AND FRANCE

Louis understood the obstacles confronting him. Above all, he needed to raise his throne above the structure of corporate, regional, and individual privilege. The central administrative problem of government was less to make the mass of his subjects obey than to submit the officers of state to the royal will. In this, Louis depended upon his royal agents, the *intendants*. The *intendants'* essential responsibility was investigative—to watch over the courts, militia, police, and tax-collecting officers. With links to the central government assured, the *intendants* soon blended administrative responsibilities with their investigative ones and, in so doing, nibbled away at the functions of all the officers. They oversaw the payment of town debts, helped raise the *taille*, and had the last word in the distribution and collection of all new taxes. They heard complaints of officer malfeasance and seigneurial injustice. They were responsible for public order and maintenance of the militia, as well as for keeping roads and bridges in repair. When troops had to pacify a region, the *intendant* took charge of them and supervised the martial law when necessary. The regularization of the *intendants* as his ex officio agents for justice, finance, and police was the most lasting feature of Louis's administrative reforms. The *intendants* absorbed the fragmented responsibilities of the officers of state, whose functions became increasingly honorific. Colbert dreamed of a France served exclusively by *intendants* and their subordinates, with the officers disposed of altogether.

The *intendants* carried out the edicts and orders prepared in the Royal Council, the heart of the new bureaucratic apparatus. On the major committees of the council sat approximately 150 department chiefs and their assistants. Beneath them were a few hundred junior commissioners and their clerks. Only the chancellor of the Royal Council held an irremovable post, which in time became an empty honor. At the apex of the bureaucratic pyramid was a closed circle of ministers of state, who advised the king during three or four meetings per week, and four secretaries of state, who headed the major departments: the marine, war office, foreign office, and Royal Council. Ministers often doubled as secretaries, and each secretary was also responsible for the internal administration of a demarcated region of France. A secretary therefore corresponded regularly with an *intendant* on mission. As controller-general of finances, Colbert, who was secretary of state for the marine, directed the course of France's economy. But he also had to supervise state manufactures, building construction, and public works. After Colbert's death in 1683 the marquis of Louvois, minister and secretary of state for war, took over the superintendancy of building. The real workhorses of the bureaucracy were the councillors of state and masters of requests who prepared the royal orders and edicts. The most promising among them became ambassadors, secretaries, and ministers.

From minister of state to departmental clerk, all members of the bureaucracy served at the royal pleasure, with the knowledge that disgrace and dismissal might come without notice. Actually, the risks were fewer than one might imagine. Louis XIV had a passion for continuity and order in government. During his fifty-four-year reign there were only sixteen ministers of state, even with three to five sitting at any one time. Louis's controllers-general of finance, war secretaries, and secretaries of state for foreign affairs averaged nearly eleven years apiece in office. The king maintained Mazarin's policy of drawing officials from relatively modest social backgrounds, usually the lesser judicial nobility or bourgeoisie.

Two families, the Le Telliers and Colberts, dominated the ranks of Louis's government, eventually creating ministerial dynasties that worked against the king's express intention of keeping passive, subservient subordinates. The king inherited the lawyer Michel Le Tellier from Mazarin's circle. From the age of fourteen, Michel's son, later made marquis of Louvois, attended high council meetings. Father and son built Louis's army. Surrounded by technicians and strategists drawn from outside the ranks of the *grands*, Le Tellier and Louvois recovered the army from the aristocratic colonel-generals who had purchased regiments and whose loyalty to the crown never was assured. From 1661 on, special *intendants* and inspectors clothed, fed, and formulated strategy for an army that in peacetime grew to 250,000 strong and in wartime doubled that number. The high nobility still led the battlefield charges, but they were subject to the control of the two great war secretaries and their disciplinarians—Martinet, inventor of cadence; Fourilles, reformer of the cavalry; and Vauban, commissioner-general of fortifications. The state assumed complete responsibility over military justice, police, finance, dress, and maintenance. Each parish in France had to supply a stipulated share of troops. As the new infantry regiments became the foundation stone of the French army, the cavalry as preserve of the aristocracy lost prestige. The artillery, heretofore contracted to civilians, was integrated into the newly created engineer corps.

Until his death in 1691, the marquis of Louvois dominated France's military revolution. He fed Louis's belief in the army as the chief instrument of royal glory and power, and the war secretary rose to the central place in the king's government. Finances of state came to be used in accordance with Louvois's recommendations, and his triumph was achieved at the expense of controller-general Colbert, architect of French mercantilism. Pushing the king into war with the Dutch in 1672, Colbert was no pacifist. However, his major achievement was as developer of royal revenues. Following upon Mazarin, this draper's son successfully led the government to abandon its dependence upon loans from corrupt financiers and tax farmers. He took advantage of public hostility towards these money lenders by repudiating payment at the slightest provocation. Colbert advised Louis not to renew the most useless offices of state and also persuaded him to reduce wages to officeholders whenever possible and to find loopholes in sales contracts that permitted restoration to the state of recently alienated properties. By tightening up on abusive practices, filling loopholes, and making certain that most tax revenue actually got to the treasury, Colbert was responsible for doubling royal income, thus complementing his policies of commercial and industrial protectionism. In an age of recession, his program of restraint made the French monarchy financially sound.

The Dutch war (1672–78) changed everything, however. Promising victory daily, Louvois became an appendage to Louis's vanity, and Colbert was reduced to digging for quick expedients. The controller-general had to revert to petty, irritating schemes, like taxing household pewter or raising the excise on salt and tobacco. Serious fiscal revolts erupted in the regions of Bordeaux, Guyenne, and Brittany. In 1675, contemporaries spoke of a new Fronde in the western half of the kingdom. Two armies had to be dispatched to quell the uprising. As under Mazarin, the state borrowed on anticipated revenues. Royal subsidies for new industry dried up, Colbert had to scrap his plan for building the fleet, and the West Indian and northern commercial companies collapsed. In 1680, Colbert pleaded for one-tenth of 1 percent of the state's budget for subsidies to stimulate commerce; he was turned down and in 1683 died out of favor.

The policy of the Dutch war set the pattern for the remainder of Louis's long reign. Military needs subordinated all else. The famine and plague of 1683–84 introduced an age of trials: declining landed income, scarce food, greater fiscal burdens placed on the shoulders of a contracting population. In their search for income, Colbert's successors resorted to the old techniques of currency manipulation and office sales. Tax collectors and garbage collectors, law clerks and funeral criers, judges and wigmakers—all had to buy their posts from the state and pass on their expenses to the populace by way of fees or gratuities. In 1693, a new famine hit, and now not even office purchasers could be found. *Intendant* after *intendant* pleaded for the privileged to pay their share of tax burdens.

In 1695, the *capitation* was introduced, exempting only the indigent and the clergy—though the Church was expected to apportion out a lump sum. Abandoned in 1699, the *capitation* was revived during the War of the Spanish Succession (1702–13). The *dixième*, the first French tax to be based upon voluntary declarations of income, was attempted. Had these two experiments been pursued to their logical conclusion, they might have combined fiscal sanity with social justice. But exemptions destroyed the utility of the new taxes, and they simply added to the burden of the *taille*-paying poor. By the time Louis XIV died in 1715, the state was more in the debt of tax farmers and financiers than at any moment since the advent of Colbert. The deficit was an astronomical two billion *livres*.

Louis's ambition to raise up the throne as arbiter of the life of his subjects was illustrated in two areas of administrative policy: law and religion. Flattering the king with the title "the new Justinian," Colbert wanted codification of the laws to represent the major achievement of the reign. The task was immense. Roman and Germanic legal traditions divided the country from north and south. The clerical courts ruled for the laity on matters such as marriage contracts. Regions and corporations had their own law. More than eighty different civil codes existed, and procedure varied from place to place. Nevertheless, Colbert, along with a commission of experts, took on the job of codification. In civil and criminal law, he never got beyond establishing uniform codes of procedure. Arbitrary and brutal punishments were left untouched. A code was devised to protect forest lands for eventual use in primary industries, such as shipbuilding. A commercial code was drawn up, but because of religious objections, it refrained from establishing legal rates of interest. A code for the marine appeared in 1680 and one for colonies and slaves in 1685. This last, the *Code noir*, did not reprove slave hunting or slave owning, but at least it insisted on the masters' obligation to provide slaves with food, shelter, and the rudiments of religion.

The royal motto was "un roi, une foi, une loi." If the idea of legal uniformity was dear to Colbert, that of religious uniformity particularly appealed to his king. Claiming political power from God alone, Louis took responsibilities for the salvation of his subjects very seriously. He liked to consider himself a kind of super bishop, taking both forms of communion and mediating religious disputes. Louis was convinced of a mission to establish a unity of belief in France, and this led him to quarrel with the pope, some of his Catholic subjects, and all of his Calvinist ones.

Early in life, Louis offered to the Jesuits his confidence in religious matters. In this, as with so much else, he was loyal to the end. In one respect, however, Louis disagreed with his spiritual guides. The Jesuits were uncompromisingly devoted to the pope. They accepted the ultramontane view that all Catholic kings must submit to papal pronouncements on matters of faith and, if necessary, respect the pope's opinions on political questions. On the other hand, Louis's Gallican view stated that where Rome's governance over religious matters clashed with royal policies, national church councils might overrule papal authority. Since the line separating papal from royal responsibilities in ecclesiastical affairs had always been indistinct, Church-state relations were essentially a matter of mutual good will.

Until the end of the Dutch war, the Jesuits had kept squabbles between Louis and the papacy from degenerating into anything grave. Then Louis claimed the power to collect and retain income for sees left temporarily vacant because of the death of a bishop. Innocent XI denied this power, called the *régale*, to Louis. The king convoked an emergency meeting of France's bishops, and the quarrel with Innocent deepened into a full-scale discussion of the entire range of Church-state relations. The bishops affirmed the king's superiority over the pope in all temporal matters and asserted the pope's limited authority in religious ones. They added that decisions of councils of bishops might overturn papal decrees. Undoubtedly, many bishops in the Assembly of 1682 voted more from fear than conviction, and Innocent refused to accept their conclusions. He rejected each of Louis's nominees to vacant sees, and by 1688, thirty-five sees had no bishop. National sentiment rallied around the king, but Louis was at the point of excommunication, and France was on the road to schism; the king had no desire to effect a Reformation. He was devoted to Catholic theology and his Jesuits. Moreover, he was worrying about his own soul. He therefore decided to wait for the intractable Innocent to die so he could work out a compromise with his successor. This he accomplished in 1693. He won his point on the *régale* but withdrew official support for the so-called Gallican Articles of 1682. He promised to cooperate with the papacy and kept his word. The French sees were filled, and the Jesuits breathed more easily.

For most of the reign, Louis was obsessed by a body of his Catholic subjects who called themselves Jansenists. Certain theological views and habits distinguished Jansenists from other Catholics. They rejected frequent communion and the efficacy of good works, and their moral asceticism made them hostile to the humanist, worldly-wise Jesuits. The Jansenists gave French Catholicism a harshness of tone and appreciation for the tragedy of human existence that appealed to many of the century's most sensitive minds. Certain Jansenists were identified with the opposition to Mazarin during the Fronde, and largely for political reasons, Louis developed a special aversion toward them. He translated religious individualism into suspect loyalty to his crown. On several occasions, popes had condemned the movement's chief source book, Cornelius Jansen's *Augustinus* (1640), and in 1653, a papal bull formally declared as heretical five propositions supposedly derived from this work.

Because they usually adopted a Gallican position toward papal authority, the Jansenists might have proven useful allies of the king. However, their leadership was derived from anti-Jesuit intellectuals, parlementary families, and great nobles—groups whom Louis identified as opposing his conception of absolutism. For Louis, Jansenism became a kind of underground church that harbored political and social malcontents, and in the last twenty-five years of his rule, the old king tried to wipe out all vestiges of Jansenist thought. His campaign culminated in 1713 when he goaded the pope into promulgating the Bull Unigenitus, condemning 101 so-called Jansenist principles of faith. Louis's attack backfired badly, inviting a revival of political Jansenism in the eighteenth century. On the eve of the king's death parlementary jurists, peeved officeholders, humiliated great nobles, and discontented merchant-shippers discovered in Jansenism a rallying point against the bureaucratic absolutism that for a half-century had constrained and repressed their corporate interests. Simple priests in poverty-stricken parishes—harboring an understandable hostility towards the great bishops, abbots, and priors designated by the crown to defend its pretensions—considered themselves heirs to the Jansenist spiritual tradition. Their resentments were carried to their flocks. In Paris and other cities during the eighteenth century, an underground Jansenist newspaper circulated widely. It is an oversimplification to trace a straight line between the *Augustinus* and the revolution that exploded a century and a half later. However, in the generation after 1715, Jansenism found renewed strength —indeed, Louis XIV's persecution of it had kept it alive—and was identified with a certain opposition, both corporate and popular, to the authoritarian structures perfected by the king and his servants.

In 1661 the future of French Calvinism did not appear grim. Though amended by Richelieu, the Edict of Nantes (1598) had held for more than a half-century, guaranteeing Protestants religious toleration and civil equality with Catholics. There were nearly a million and a half Huguenots in France. No longer fighters led by potentially rebellious nobles, they were an economically self-sufficient group of professionals, merchants, craftsmen, and peasants. They were concentrated in the western and southern parts of the country but could be found in smaller numbers nearly everywhere. They were especially important in banking and the law. Loyal during the Fronde, the Huguenot community had integrated itself into the life of the nation as well as could any seventeenth-century minority of 10 percent. Colbert saw the Huguenots as providing France with the lifeblood of the country's commerce and industry.

Mazarin treated the Huguenots with benign neglect. Early in his personal reign, however, Louis XIV considered them to be an affront to his authority. At first he decided to use persuasion, pious example, and bribery to win converts. Then he turned to sporadic harassment. He maintained the Edict of Nantes but interpreted its terms with a rigor that invited persecution, prohibiting everything that was not expressly authorized. Nothing in the charter explicitly stated that the Huguenots might bury their dead by day, so they were compelled to bury them at night. Nothing in the edict expressly opened up crafts and professions to them, so they were excluded from serving as judges, notaries, doctors, booksellers, and printers. Discriminatory tax burdens were placed upon them. Endowments for their poor were seized and given to Catholics. Huguenot parents were forced to give their children a Catholic education. Their schools and hospitals were shut down, and churches constructed since 1598 were closed.

After 1680 the Huguenots were assured a scapegoat role. Catholic assemblies of the clergy and Louvois urged Louis to step up persecutions. In 1681, zealous *intendants* began to force Huguenot families to lodge troops, who were permitted a free hand with their "hosts." This latter act stimulated large-scale conversions, which were announced to the king, and a large-scale flight of Huguenots from France, which was not. Louis himself was convinced that his policy of persuasion-coercion had worked. In 1685, he estimated that an insufficient number of Huguenots remained in the country to necessitate a charter protecting them. Therefore, the Edict of Nantes was revoked. The rights of Protestants in Alsace were affirmed, but elsewhere in France, orders went out to destroy Protestant churches and proscribe worship. At the same time that adult laymen were prohibited from emigrating, pastors were given two weeks to leave the country.

Then the dike broke. Perhaps 300,000 Huguenots took flight. Families left by sea and through mountain passes, forests, and fields—heading for places where they could worship in peace. The Netherlands, England, and Brandenburg took most of the refugees; some did not stop until they reached the shores of North America or South Africa. A disproportionate number of those who left were small merchants and industrialists, sailors, teachers, and craftsmen. They brought the linen industry to northern Ireland and helped develop Holland's eighteenth-century printing trade. Back in France, Louis basked in the light of self-delusion. He struck six medals celebrating the extirpation of heresy. Public opinion congratulated him. Poets and painters were inspired to immortalize the deed.

The revocation of the Edict of Nantes proved to be the most glaring domestic error of the reign. Historians still debate the economic effects of the Huguenot flight upon France. Very likely the drop in French agricultural and industrial activity from 1685 to 1715 stemmed more from wartime dislocations and overregulation than from the loss of enterprising subjects. It was in spiritual terms that France suffered its most stunning blow. A Europe weary of religious strife was digesting the creedless messages of Leibniz, Locke, Spinoza, and Newton; in the revocation it saw a reversion to the primitive intolerance of the sixteenth century. Pope Innocent himself doubted its wisdom. In England, the Netherlands, and the Protestant states of Germany, the influx of refugees hardened hatred against Louis and France. In France, Protestantism went underground, and in the mountainous Cevennes in the south it caused a guerrilla war from 1702 to 1705 that took two royal armies to put down. In 1715, at the very moment Louis lay on his deathbed, the pastor Antoine Court held a Calvinist synod of ministers in an abandoned rock quarry outside the city of Nîmes, the first such meeting since 1685.

Practically speaking, Louis built his absolutism upon the foundations of a bureaucratic administration and a magnificent court of nobles performing household functions for him. In theory, the bases were sometimes allegorical—the sun surrounded by revolving, dependent satellites; sometimes they were mythological—the king as Ares, Apollo, or Zeus; most often they were religious. From childhood, the idea had been implanted that Louis was the viceroy of God. As chief theoretician of Louis's absolutism, Bishop Jacques Bénigne Bossuet specialized in justifying the reign by divine premises. Louis was priest-king, the anointed of God, successor to Solomon and David. Bossuet wrote of royal power: "It holds the entire kingdom in position just as God holds the whole world."

A passion for setting things in order, the so-called classical ideal, complemented Bossuet's divine-right theorizing. The idea that monarchical power best serves the well-ordered state is as old as the Egyptians, and Colbert subsidized culture to stress the point. Nearly all forms of artistic, literary, and scientific expression depended upon patronage, and the regime made certain that the king's patronage overwhelmed all other varieties. The state founded academies of inscriptions and *belles-lettres*, painting and sculpture, science, architecture, music, and dance. It nationalized the Académie Française, granting its forty members pensions and comfortable quarters at the Louvre in Paris. One consequence of this control over culture might be expected: a nauseating monotony of obsequities spewed forth from the pen and brush of talentless hacks who knew how to fawn and scrape according to classical rules. Nevertheless, a handful of poets and playwrights did manage to compress a universe of passion, emotion, and human frailty into a framework of disciplined language, strictly defined form, and censored taste.

The classical style was the court style, and the court was Louis's personal work of art. Even before the death of Mazarin, the young king dreamed of settling down in a sumptuous residence of his own. He hated Paris, with its memories of the Fronde, and shortly after his accession decided to convert a modest hunting lodge in a village fifteen miles southwest of the capital into a single, overwhelming building that would serve both as a seat of government and his home. Versailles would not be just another palace. It was meant to epitomize Louis's domination over society, the state, nature itself. Imitated by many other princes in Europe, as a colossus of marble and stone, it never could be duplicated. The planning got underway in 1668, but it was not until 1682 that the king and court could move in. Louis himself prepared the visitors' guide, and throughout the rest of the reign, the work went on. The infant mirror industry, Gobelins tapestry works, and academies of painting and sculpture labored for Versailles without rest. Though

Louis tired of the palace, Europe's image of Louis XIV was inseparable from Versailles.

Within the palace walls, the king was a demigod. Drawn from the security of their provincial redoubts, the great aristocrats of France were tamed, kept at court, and made financially dependent upon Louis. They became an army of retainers jostling for the privilege to attend the royal awakening each morning or the royal retirement each night, to escort Louis on his strolls, or to be asked to accompany him for a weekend at his private residence at Marly. Ministers, secretaries, and their staffs worked in the government wing of the great palace; the nobility housed there endured an unending round of intrigue, parties, and gambling sessions. The discomforts at Versailles were legion. One froze in the winter and roasted in the summer. In the palace corridors, residents mingled with lackeys, peddlers, and prostitutes. Men and women set up camp in antechambers and hallways. A daily coarseness, even criminality, beclouded the superficial pomp and dignity. This was the logical consequence of a situation where several thousand idle individuals milled about, their chief activity to undercut one another and obtain a pension or favor from the king, upon whom all were dependent.

The atmosphere at court evolved with Louis's personality. Prior to the move to Versailles, the spirit was licentious and carefree. In the first twenty years of his reign, Louis had many loves who effaced his shy, devout Spanish consort. Louis was a patriarch, running the lives of his family, dictating and prohibiting affairs and marriages, legitimizing his bastards. He turned the latter over to the care of a woman whose moral influence redirected the spirit of both king and court. This was Madame de Maintenon, a converted Huguenot and widow of the poet Scarron. In 1673, she was admitted to court and obtained 200,000 *livres* to purchase an estate. Ingratiating herself with the king, she became his last mistress. Shortly after the death of Queen Maria Theresa in 1683, she secretly married Louis. Under her influence, the last twenty-five years of the reign exuded an exceptionally rigid, formal religiosity. Personal misfortune—a dozen close family deaths, including those of four heirs to the throne—merged with national misfortune to give Versailles its lugubrious tone. Moreover, the court culture no longer set the pattern for the rest of the country, and the criticism of anonymous pens began to rival the empty praise of court hacks. A few challenges penetrated even Louis's gilded cage. In 1693, the abbé de Fénelon, archbishop of Cambrai and member of the Académie Française, wrote a devastating (and anonymous) "Letter to Louis XIV" in which he called France "one great hospital, desolate, and uncared for." Fénelon laid the blame square at the royal doorstep. Fénelon was no isolated malcontent but rather tutor to the king's own grandson, the duke of Burgundy. In 1711, when his pupil was heir to the throne, Fénelon composed the duke's political program, which advocated voluntary taxation voted by the three Estates of each province, a sum that obviously would render foreign wars impossible to fight; a triennial Estates General of bishops, nobles, and urban patricians who would participate actively in formulating government policies; and an end to state regulation of commerce and industry. Fénelon wished to reverse the trend of bureaucratic centralization. His economic liberalism looked to the future; his feudal politics, to an idealized past. The untimely death of the duke of Burgundy prevented the implementation of the abbé's program; but along with the antimercantilist fiscal schemes of Boisguilbert and Vauban, the program offered institutional alternatives to what Louis and his secretaries had given France over the past half-century. Far more worrisome for the government was the resurgence of civil violence. In 1703 and 1707, there were serious revolts in the countryside.

In the final years of the reign, internal discontent and a desperate shortage of revenue forced the government to revise certain of the political and economic principles upon which its rule had rested. Old corporate groups like the Parlement of Paris joined the chorus of critics, and even at Versailles, the dukes and peers of the realm anticipated the passing of the old king. The system created by Louis XIV as the alternative to the anarchy of the Frondes was losing its grip over a society weary of military defeat, religious wrangling, and state bankruptcy. When the king died in apparent remorse on November 1, 1715, it remained an open question whether his successors possessed sufficient initiative and vision to recoordinate the activities of the government with the aspirations of its subjects.

THE FOREIGN POLICIES OF LOUIS XIV

Certainly the malaise in France in 1715 was a direct consequence of the human and financial costs of a half-century's ambitious foreign policy. To Louis XIV, it was a matter of faith that a grand king should possess a grand plan for Europe. Louis's plan was an empire of client states tied to France through blood and marriage. This was the culmination of a seventeenth-century view holding that relations among states were legitimate extensions of personal relations among princes. Friendships or animosities determined peace or war. Louis was constantly preoccupied with his international reputation and thus meddled in the affairs of other states as though they were affairs of his own family. They often were. Louis, his first wife, and his inveterate enemy, William III of the Netherlands and England, shared a common grandfather—France's Henry IV. The wife of the Hapsburg emperor Leopold I was the stepsister of Louis's queen; the emperor himself was a close relative. To Louis, wars were matters of family pride.

Because dynastic honor meant so much to Louis, ruling houses that disagreed with the French interpretations of honor were subject to abuse and aggression. The last twenty-five years of the reign were dominated by open warfare or alliances that led to warfare. Eventually the mundane idea of a balance of power in international affairs challenged and overwhelmed the French king's grandiose scheme of dependencies and satellites. Though the balance of power concept had failed to keep the peace in the ancient

Greek world or in Renaissance Italy, during the century that had witnessed the great Hapsburg and Bourbon attempts at hegemony, it seemed the only viable alternative to the dynastic imperialism of a single power. Thus it became the cornerstone of diplomacy for the next two hundred years.

In 1648 the Peace of Westphalia guaranteed the religious and political fragmentation of central Europe. The German princes were declared sovereign in rights and powers. No longer did France have to feel the pressures of Hapsburg encirclement from bases in Spain, Belgium, and Germany. On the contrary, as "guarantor of the peace of the Empire," France could intervene in German affairs if she considered the Westphalia settlement endangered. Mazarin's emissaries won recognition of French sovereignty over three fortresses jutting into the empire—Metz, Toul, and Verdun—as well as occupation rights over much of Alsace. Mazarin continued the war with Spain for additional footholds along the Pyrenees and Belgian frontiers, and the end to the Frondes provided France with the opportunity to wear down the decrepit Spanish armies. At the Peace of the Pyrenees in 1659, France obtained Roussillon, Artois, and a cluster of fortresses leading into the Spanish Netherlands. This represented Louis XIV's first gain at Spanish expense. His marriage to Maria Theresa, eldest child of Spain's King Philip IV, opened the door to more.

When Maria Theresa accompanied her debonair groom to her new land, she gave up her claims to her father's throne. However, Louis desired to keep the Spanish succession question open. Flushed with dreams and projects, the young French king proposed to Emperor Leopold I a division of the Spanish inheritance. Leopold was married to a second daughter of Philip, who had not renounced her claims, and thus the emperor rejected the offer. In 1661, Philip produced a son and heir; four years later, the Spanish king died. The infant Carlos was a miserable, sickly prince, but his survival temporarily dashed Louis's plans. Undaunted nonetheless, the French king had his lawyers cook up a claim for Maria Theresa's rights to the Spanish Netherlands and in 1667 sent his troops across the defenseless border. It was a military promenade. Louis occupied a dozen fortresses and prepared to take the entire country. In Holland, Jan De Witt negotiated a defensive alliance with Sweden and England. For the moment, Louis knew when to stop. He turned his troops away from the Dutch frontier and opened peace negotiations with Spain. The Treaty of Aix-la-Chapelle (1668) awarded him not a contiguous piece of Belgium but rather a dozen unconnected towns and dependencies—chiefly Lille, Cambrai, Oudenarde, and Charleroi—stepping-stones for any subsequent movement northward. Vauban began fortifying the advanced posts. The War of Devolution against Spain confirmed the overwhelming superiority of Louis's new 70,000-man army when matched against any one of France's neighbors.

Louis blamed the Dutch for having foiled his plans for dynastic conquest at Spain's expense. Just as Louis despised their politics and religion, Colbert envied their commerce. King and minister agreed upon a new adventure, and Le Tellier increased the army to 100,000. French diplomacy bought off Holland's allies. The Secret Treaty of Dover was concluded with England's Charles II. In the spring of 1672, England and France declared war upon the Dutch Netherlands. Louis himself rode at the head of his army. On June 20, Utrecht fell, and on the same day, the Dutch opened the Minden dikes holding back the Zuiderzee. The work of three generations was ruined, but the French advance was halted. Louis arrogantly spurned the States General's offer of a truce and demanded everything between the Rhine and Meuse. At this juncture, a wave of popular indignation destroyed the De Witts, and William III obtained the offices previously denied him. In tenacity and diplomatic skill this untested, frail young prince was to prove more than a match for the Sun King. He played on European fears of French ambitions, and Spain and Austria joined him in his struggle. The short war Louis had envisioned in 1672 dragged on until 1678, costing France a fortune and discouraging Colbert. At the Treaty of Nimegen, signed in 1679, France added Franche-Comté and more of Spanish Flanders to its gains of the previous decade. But William III had managed to challenge the myth of French invincibility. Victory by military parade was a thing of the past.

His northern frontier fixed and his splendor confirmed, Louis might well have learned a lesson from the Dutch war. But in foreign as well as domestic policy, the 1680s were his most arrogant years. He kept his army, now 200,000 strong, on a war footing and moved his ambitions towards the east. The Rhineland was a mere patchwork of weak principalities, towns, and villages; Louis's policy was to annex all territories possessing a dynastic or historical link to France or its recently acquired possessions. The king established the Chambers of Reunion to decide upon the legality of his claims, and somehow they always ruled in his favor. Then, before the inhabitants of the contested territories could lodge a protest, the troops would move in. The high point of these offensives was the seizure of the great city of Strasbourg, taken in 1681 without even a juridical protest. All of Alsace became French. Force resolved previous ambiguities. The French king gave no hint of when he would be satisfied.

The Chambers of Reunion extended France's eastern frontier and turned nearly all of Europe against Louis. William was able to strike up new defensive treaties with Sweden, Spain, Austria, and several German states, but it took the revival of the Spanish succession issue, coming on the heels of Louis's latest aggressions, to forge these individual treaties into the Grand Alliance. King Carlos II of Spain, the impotent son of Philip IV, proved to be a living corpse. It took a supreme effort for him to move, chew, or mutter. He conserved what energy he possessed for daily meetings with his soothsayers and priests. He would never father an heir. All believed that the Spanish throne would become vacant soon. Leopold I of Austria already claimed it for his second son Charles; Louis eyed it for his grandson, Philip of Anjou.

Meanwhile, the French king continued his thrust into Germany. Not even recognition of his seizures by Spain and the Holy Roman Empire could satisfy him. He invaded the Palatinate and occupied Cologne and Liège. At last, Leopold moved his army towards the Rhine, and the threatened princes took heart. Louis saw the war clouds and decided to seize the initiative. He opened hostilities with the Dutch. William III was now in England, where he had successfully deposed Louis's last major ally, James II. The Grand Alliance was a reality at last. Leopold I led Hapsburg Europe; William III united in his person the two great maritime states. At last it appeared that allied pressures were going to reduce the French king to human dimensions.

With the exception of a single, brief interlude (1697–1702), it took twenty-five years of total war to accomplish this. For Louis XIV, the age of arrogant annexations, like that of military parades, was over. Two successive allied coalitions (1689–97, 1702–13) tested France to the breaking point, and it wound up fighting for its life. The aging grand monarch endured it all stoically. He felt the shortage of men and money; for the first time, he faced military leadership superior to that of his own marshals; the old quick triumphs gave way to wearisome sieges, scorched-earth tactics, and slow occupations. In the so-called War of the Grand Alliance (1689–97) Louis failed to restore James II to the English throne, and at the Treaty of Ryswick, Louis had to concede territorial losses for the first time—certain advanced posts taken during the period of the Chambers of Reunion. He recognized William III as king of England and promised to be moderate. He learned that English and Hapsburg forces, paid with Dutch money, had set limits upon his ambitions.

For three years after the Treaty of Ryswick, diplomats tried to ward off the crisis that the anticipated death of Carlos II posed. Various schemes were proposed to partition the Spanish empire, and Louis seemed to be keeping his word about moderation. The chief opposition to partition came from Leopold I, who considered his son Charles the legal and rightful heir to *all* of Spain's territories, and from the Spanish court, which possessed sufficient dignity to resent the distribution by others of Spain's lands and people. Louis XIV resigned himself to the prospect of an Austrian on the Spanish throne, provided that the two parts of the Hapsburg inheritance should never fall to the same individual and that a certain share of Spain's possessions should compensate a Bourbon prince. William III leaned towards the French compromise rather than the Austrian position.

Nevertheless, the crisis broke on the death of Carlos in November 1700. A month earlier, he had secretly remade his will, and his court approved it as policy. All of Europe knew that the Spanish position was to keep its empire intact. The shock was Carlos's designation of Philip of Anjou,

Louis's grandson, rather than the Austrian archduke, as his heir. A patriotic faction, resentful that Spain had become a satellite of Austrian politics, had been the last to win the ear and guide the hand of the moribund Carlos. The designation of Philip added that the prince must renounce his place in the line of succession to the French throne.

Carlos II died on November 1. News of his will reached Versailles on November 9. For a full week, Louis, his secretaries, and family tried to weigh the options. The English and Dutch supported partition. Would they risk war if France accepted Carlos's testament? Whatever the French did, war with Austria seemed likely, for Leopold was intransigent over the archduke's rights. All sorts of arguments and alternatives were proposed in the Royal Council. At last, Louis called for silence. He had made his characteristic decision. On November 16, he ordered the doors flung open to the palace reception hall and introduced his grandson to the court and ambassadorial corps as Spain's next king. To quell the fears of the English and Dutch, Louis renounced any intention of meddling in Spanish affairs. Anjou was crowned Philip V. Public opinion in England and the Netherlands was against war. The emperor was isolated. It appeared just possible that a feared European conflict over the Spanish succession might be averted.

That it was not must be Louis's responsibility. The calm with which his old adversaries had accepted the will of Carlos II deceived him into believing that he might once more dictate affairs to Europe. He boldly invalidated Philip V's renunciation of the French inheritance. "The Pyrenees exist no longer," he claimed, foreseeing the birth of a great new Bourbon empire. Despite earlier assurances to the contrary, he took over the government of the Spanish Netherlands. He had his grandson award France important trading privileges in the Spanish New World, including the monopoly over African slave imports. Overnight, Dutch slave merchants and English traders who had controlled the contraband to South America turned from peace to war. William III and Heinsius did not need much prodding, for they saw it was the same old Louis. In September 1701, the Maritime Powers renewed the Grand Alliance with Leopold I. Louis rejected all attempts at negotiation. Instead, he called William a usurper and recognized the son of the late James II as England's rightful king. No act could have better solidified English opinion against France. The accidental death of William in March 1702 made no difference. On May 15, England, the Dutch Netherlands, Austria, Denmark, Brandenburg, and most of the principalities in the Holy Roman Empire declared war upon France and Spain.

The War of the Spanish Succession lasted nearly eleven years and so exhausted Europe that no major conflict succeeded it for an entire generation. Battles raged from the Danube to Portugal, into the Caribbean, and on the North American mainland. The victories of the allies at Blenheim-Hochstadt in Bavaria (1704) and Ramillies in Belgium (1706) showed that

Louis could find no commanders comparable to the emperor's Prince Eugene and England's duke of Marlborough. The French were thrown out of the Spanish Netherlands and were forced to defend their own fortresses. The catastrophic famine of 1708–9 was accompanied by threat of an allied occupation of France. Louis asked his adversaries for terms, but a half-century of dynastic arrogance now produced its backlash. The allies ordered him to recognize the archduke Charles as Spain's king and send a French army to Madrid to depose Philip V. However, Louis remained too much the dynastic patriarch to turn on his own grandson. For the first time in his life, he explained a course of action to his subjects. In a circular letter to be read from all pulpits, he wrote that "justice and French honor" compelled him to continue fighting. He asked for prayers and arms.

From 1710 to 1713 matters improved for Louis. His countrymen rallied round their king, and it became the allies' turn to feel war-weary. A platform of peace brought the Tories to Power in England. Leopold I had died in 1705; his successor Joseph, six years later. The archduke Charles became Hapsburg emperor, and neither the Dutch nor English wished to see him add the Spanish crown to his laurels. This would upset the balance of power principle as grievously as would a single Bourbon on the thrones of Spain and France. In 1712, England withdrew from the war. Prince Eugene's effort to crush the French in one final battle, at Denain, fell short. The time was ripe for Louis to bargain for more honorable peace terms than those of 1709.

The Treaties of Utrecht and Rastatt (1713–14) confirmed William III's policy that no single power should be strong enough to exercise hegemony over the continent, and international recognition of the balance of power concept made the peace more durable than had been the case back in 1648. France was weakened but not humiliated. England and Austria were strengthened but not overwhelmingly. Exhausted from having financed the coalition, the Dutch welcomed the lightened responsibilities of a third-class power. To underscore the spirit of balance and compromise, the European parts of the Spanish empire were partitioned among the victors. Philip V kept Spain and its overseas possessions but had to renounce his claims to any French inheritance. Sicily went to the duke of Savoy, and the archduke —now Charles VI of Austria—obtained the old Spanish Netherlands, Naples, Sardinia, and Tuscany. Spain ceded Gibralter and Minorca to England. Brandenburg-Prussia won the Spanish Guelderland. In North America, France abandoned Hudson's Bay, Acadia, and Newfoundland (though retaining some fishing rights) to the English. In the Caribbean, France yielded St. Christophe to England. The French gave some advanced posts in Belgium to the Austrians and permitted Dutch garrisons to reoccupy the "barrier forts" from which they had been expelled in 1702. Louis XIV kept the vast bulk of what had been recognized as his at the Treaty of Ryswick in 1697, including most of his acquisitions in Flanders, Alsace, and Franche-

Comté. The English gained the best commercial advantages. They replaced France as Spain's most favored trading partner and gained special privileges in Cadiz, the *entrepôt* from America. They won a thirty-year right to send an annual 500-ton slave ship to the Spanish New World.

The Grand Alliance had served its purpose. Its membership differed in religion, domestic social practices, and political ideologies. The partnership had creaked and sputtered. In 1713, when England and Holland left Charles VI alone to fight Louis, it fell apart. In the end, however, the balance of nations became deeply entrenched in European diplomacy. Tradeoffs and partitions became the accepted means of resolving disputes, and until the 1790s, no European power again tried to dominate Europe to the extent the Hapsburgs and Bourbons had done in the century preceding the Utrecht settlement.

SPAIN AND PORTUGAL

Virtually no major European state was spared crisis in the midseventeenth century, but some emerged better equipped than others to cope with the challenges of the future. As a political experiment, Cromwellian England proved a failure. However, the Navigation Acts, accompanied by the destruction of guild and corporate interests, opened the gates to economic expansion at home and abroad. The Regime of True Liberty coincided with a blossoming of Dutch art and thought, and the peace cultivated by the regents permitted an accumulation of resources that financed the great struggle of 1689–1713. The chaos of the Frondes cleared the decks for Louis XIV and his secretaries, leading to the construction of the classic absolutist regime.

In 1648, Spain certainly had its share of woes. Both its Dutch and Portuguese dependencies were lost. The Catalan revolt was seven years old. Sicily and Naples were scenes of uprisings among the urban and rural poor, and a plot had been uncovered to foment revolution in all of Aragon. Meanwhile, the war with France dragged on. By 1660, when a humiliating peace was signed with Mazarin, the south Italian revolts had been put down, and Catalonia returned to the empire. Spain was not going to explode from within. Rather, between time of the birth of Carlos II and the Peace of Utrecht, it was the powers of Europe, with their schemes of succession and partition, that reminded Spaniards of their national humiliation.

Theoretically, Spain, like France, was an absolutist state. The government rested upon a bureaucratic mechanism radiating from the king. In practice, however, there were very great differences. In Spain, a privileged minority of great courtiers and churchmen occupied the top rungs of administration. These individuals were secure in their inherited titles, rents, and pensions. There was little distinction between the king's household and the apex of his government. Barely a chance existed for a Le Tellier or Colbert to emerge from relatively obscure origins to high position as servant of the sovereign. The middle and lesser levels of the Spanish bureaucracy were occupied by the *letrados*, individuals with some canonical or legal training who owned their offices and, as notaries, lawyers, and judges, created tiny universes of influence. The *letrado* class reinforced bureaucratic parasitism.

The central government was composed of councils with regional competence (councils for Castile, Aragon, and the Indies), and others with functional competence (councils for war, finance, and the Inquisition). Councillors jealously guarded their posts as property and considered colleagues as rivals. There was no superior council of general competence akin to the French Council of State that might make rapid decisions discreetly and break through the rivalries of jurisdiction and responsibility inherent in semiautonomous government units. Following the disgrace of Olivares in 1643, the first minister, three secretaries, and the royal confessor reverted to the collective role of a central mail bureau, shuffling dossiers and orders back and forth from council to council, transmitting the advice of councils to king, expediting letters and edicts. The country needed an arch-bureaucrat, a Philip II, who could keep the ponderous machinery rolling. But from 1665 to 1700, it was stuck with Carlos II, a human wreck incapable of leadership. One cannot dissociate Spain's misfortunes from the personal woes of its sickly king. The Spanish Church practiced crusading Catholicism; the aristocracy preached Castilian grandeur. The realities of life, however, were a ruined economy, paralyzed administration, disaster on the battlefield, and misery on the throne.

Regional identity and privilege were more important in Spain than in France. Even after Catalonia returned to the fold, Aragon, the great eastern region of which it was part, was a separate world from Castile. The same could be said for the regions of Navarre and the Basque provinces. There were royal commissioners and royal law courts in the provinces, but the wall of thousands of petty officers who held sway over municipalities and collected the king's taxes separated the average Spaniard from the king's servants. The officeholding malaise was worse in Spain than in France. An office brought prestige, a certain amount of tax relief, and service fees. The revenue officers were the most dominant and most despised. They administered nearly thirty different kinds of taxes. Virtually everyone in Spain, including nobles and clerics, paid *some* kind of taxes. But the variety of forms and rates, differing from region to region and social group to social group, dictated local means of collection. This aggravated corruption, and the state remained poor.

Castile's inability to reshape Europe according to the Hapsburg mission left Spain weakened and bitter in 1660. Recognizing the failure of its European policies, the country tried to withdraw into itself, but the succession question and Louis XIV's aggressions kept dragging Spain toward center stage. The government was chronically short of funds. To obtain loans from

English and Dutch creditors, it had to promise shares in the anticipated returns of the American treasure fleet. In 1667 and 1679, Spain lost its Flemish border towns and Franche-Comté to Louis XIV. In the 1680s, it reached the nadir of its fortunes. Its sole export was raw wool. Two-thirds of the American silver was pledged to foreigners. A dizzying spiral of inflation and deflation destroyed the remnants of Castile's industrial and commercial life. The government was paralyzed. The Church offered the populace the consolation of a hundred feast days per year. But there was nothing upon which to feast.

Paradoxically enough, the deepening crisis over the succession contained the seeds of national revival. Spaniards became aware of the fact that they had lost control over their country's destiny, and the testament of the pitiful king, intended to preserve the integrity of his empire, inspired a patriotic fervor that solidified the position of Carlos's successor. At Utrecht, of course, the Anglo-Dutch solution of partitioning prevailed. Gibraltar, Minorca, the southern Netherlands, and Italy were lost, and in the first half of the eighteenth century Spain was the most dissatisfied member of the European family. At home, however, Spanish institutions gave way just enough to permit Philip V to convert the notoriously autonomous councils of government into interdependent ministerial departments on the French model. For the most part, the administrative changes were largely on paper, for the grandees and *letrados* still dominated the personnel. But the new structures were put to good use later in the century.

More important was Philip's handling of the problem of regional autonomy. Around 1690, Catalonia began to experience an economic revival. Compared with Castile, its tax burden was light. A modest immigration from France revived its stagnant textile industry, but the Spanish Succession war halted its advance. Hoping for greater freedoms, Catalonia's nobility and municipal oligarchs had thrown their lot in with the archduke Charles, and Philip considered his richest province in revolt again. Catalonia held out even past the Utrecht settlement, but in 1714, Barcelona fell to royal troops. The institutions of the entire eastern region of Aragon were modified. A captain-general from Madrid assumed wide executive powers, and the area was divided into administrative districts that cut across traditional interior frontiers. The universities, breeding grounds for Catalan patriotism, were suppressed and the council for Aragon was dissolved. By 1716, the autonomy of Catalonia was foredoomed. The difficulty was that the most economically backward region, Castile, was imposing French administrative practices upon the vital periphery. The Catalans called Madrid their leech. Spain was not yet a nation, but a beginning had been made.

On the other hand, Portugal's successful revolt against Spain in 1640 and the Portuguese reconquest of Brazil from the Dutch in 1654 assured its future. Portugal had virtually no industry, but Brazil's coffee, sugar, and gold brought prosperity to the motherland. In 1703, the Methuen commercial treaty put Portugal squarely in Britain's economic orbit. The Portuguese won a near duty-free market for their sweet wines; in turn they accepted British woollens and gave English merchants rights of participation in the Brazilian trade. A landholding alliance of nobles and churchmen ruled the country. The Church owned two-thirds of the rural property and supported half of the population of three million. Compared to Castile, taxes were low. With the ascension of the Braganza kings in 1640, Portugal became a stagnant, feeble, and complacent country, stuffed with piety and the wealth of Brazil.

Chapter Four

Crisis and Resolution: The Center, North, and East

THE COMPROMISE OF POWER: DENMARK AND BRANDENBURG-PRUSSIA

During the 1640s and 1650s, rival political aims of governments and social or regional elites brought England, the Netherlands, France, and Spain to the brink of, or into, civil war. In central and northern Europe tensions existed between sovereigns and Estates, and in some places, it took a good half-century to resolve them satisfactorily. In the German principalities east of the Elbe, the Hapsburg empire, Denmark, and even in distant Muscovy, a social compromise worked out between rulers and landowners settled political crises. During the first half of the seventeenth century, landowning nobles, sitting in government councils and in provincial or national assemblies, had been the chief obstacles to the emergence of bureaucratic absolutism. These aristocrats cast a wary eye upon the extension of political power by elector, king, or emperor, but they had their other eye set upon the maintenance of a subjugated labor force needed to plant and harvest grain for an international market.

After 1648, however, sovereigns tried to assert more of their political authority. If necessary, and if able to, they offered estate owners a compromise of power. In return for extended controls over the fiscal, administrative, and military aspects of the state, the sovereigns guaranteed their nobilities vast seigneurial controls over peasant labor. Tightly or loosely leashed by their sovereign, landlords could run local government. Rural workers fell into neoserfdom, without civil rights, used or sold like beasts.

Denmark offers a classic example of the "compromise of power." In 1648, the Danish monarchy was Europe's oldest and most aristocratized Kingdom. About 150 families owned half the land and controlled all local administration, including civil and criminal justice. A Diet of three Estates, dominated by the nobility, chose the king. Only the province of Norway was free of domination. There a peasant society created its own structures in which rich farmers, not titled aristocrats, controlled poor ones.

In 1648, Frederick III was elected king of Denmark. From 1655 to 1660, a disastrous war with Sweden cost the country all its lands across the "Sound" and control over the tolls merchant ships paid for transport through it. When the national Diet met in Copenhagen in 1660, the treasury was empty, the nobility refused to give up its tax exemptions in the moment of crisis, and the lower Estates were in an ugly mood. Clergy and burghers urged Frederick to impose a consumer tax on everyone, and some advisors of the king urged him to set up an absolute monarchy. Frederick took his chance. Slamming shut the gates of Copenhagen, he summoned the burgher militia and declared the Danish crown hereditary.

Within the next five years, the king's party consolidated the daring coup d'état. A glorious coronation took place and an absolutist constitution was offered the Estates. The Diet disappeared, the aristocratic Royal Council was reduced to a royal household, and a bureaucracy of *intendants*, and commissioners was established to run the state's fiscal, judicial, and administrative agencies. The king reserved the right to name town officials, and a new royal tax was placed on all towns and all lands. Aware that they had been outfaced, the landlords swallowed the pill rather than risk revolt. The constitution made no effort to tamper with their seigneurial rights over the peasantry. It was enough to shear the aristocracy of its political importance. Old nobles eventually merged with ambitious parvenus into the king's bureaucracy, and their tenants now had to pay taxes both to king and seigneur. The abolutist solution to Denmark's political and social problem endured for the remainder of the ancien régime.

The political and social example of Denmark was repeated, though less brutally, in many of the German principalities that tried to rebuild from the wreckage of the Thirty Years' War. In those parts of Germany that had lost from half to two-thirds of their prewar population, the manpower shortage was critical. Nobles managing their own estates needed labor, and princes needed taxpayers. Both wished to keep peasants from fleeing to the blessed anonymity of towns by fixing them to the soil. Indebtedness and service obligations tied peasants to their lords. In return for concessions that ensured their absolutism, several German princes during the 1650s guaranteed their aristocrats the labor of a servile peasantry and thereby sealed the fate of thousands who might otherwise have taken advantage of the general impoverishment of society to bargain for their liberty.

Frederick William, elector of Brandenburg (1640–88), was intent on establishing strong political authority over the disparate mosaic of rural regions and corporate towns that recognized him as sovereign. Apart from Frederick William, no unifying principle tied these lands together. They were scattered from the Rhine to the Niemen rivers, separated from one another by states over which Frederick William had no authority whatsoever. Even in the heartland, the electorate of Brandenburg, territorial Estates and town councils jealously withheld from Frederick William the right to grant and spend tax money, make clerical appointments, and recruit for local bureaucracies and defense. Frederick William wanted both control over the tax-collecting apparatus and an army devoted to his person alone. As a tool and agency of government, a loyal army could coerce the Estates into making further concessions. In 1650, Frederick William wished to go to war against Sweden, but the Estates of Brandenburg refused him subsidies. Wrangling continued until 1653, when a compromise was reached. In return for six years of guaranteed funds, Frederick William agreed to recognize tax exemptions for all estate owners. Only townsmen and peasants were to foot the bill. Furthermore, the elector agreed to respect the landlords' civil and criminal authority over the peasantry, and he acknowledged serf status for all peasants unable to produce contractual evidence to the contrary. Whenever a "Junker," a noble landowner in Brandenburg, dispossessed a peasant, the elector agreed to look the other way. Landlords might demand unlimited services from their peasants, and they were permitted to export grain and wool and import wine, salt, and cloth—all duty-free.

It may appear that the landlords of Brandenburg got the better part of their bargain with the elector. However, he used his small army well in the Swedish war, and instead of disbanding it after the conflict, he maintained it as a lever for further subsidies. After 1660, he informed the Estates of Brandenburg and East Prussia that his request for subsidies no longer was negotiable. He hired loyal Junkers as his commissioners and had them ride out into country districts, an armed company behind, to make certain his decrees were obeyed. Eventually, Frederick William transformed the Estates of Brandenburg into regional assemblies beholden to him. Military force tamed the Estates of East Prussia. Though Frederick William had difficulty cowing his more distant domains, he set the tone for the eighteenth-century Prussian monarchy. Every element in society had a distinctive function. The peasantry bore the major fiscal and labor burden. All townsmen were to pay purchase taxes on the articles they used. Landed aristocrats and a few ennobled commoners led the troops, controlled the peasantry, and served the state as its fiscal and judicial agents.

Up from 2,000 in 1656 to 45,000 in 1678, the army formed the institution that welded together the domains. The War Commissariat, a governmental agency that supervised lodging, supply, and food for the troops, as well as collection and expenditure of taxes, became the regime's most important administrative agency. Early in the eighteenth century, the *Amtskammer*, the treasury accounting for income and expense, merged with the War Commissariat in Berlin, thereby guaranteeing indissolubility of the military, fiscal, and financial offices of the Prussian state. Half the state's revenue was funneled back into the army. Its officer corps was the special preserve of the aristocracy, but the emphasis was placed on ability and not social rank.

A particularly capable noncommissioned officer might advance toward nobility through the army.

The army's devotion to the ruling house of Brandenburg, the Hohenzollerns, set the tone for the development of a loyal civil service. It was not so incorruptible as nationalist Prussian historians would like us to believe, for even in Brandenburg, public office might help build private fortunes. However, Frederick William's budding bureaucracy was the envy of most neighboring states. Its members were expected to be dutiful governors, revenue collectors, and judicial and customs officials. By and large, Frederick William was popular enough to command their loyalty, if not affection.

The elector worked hard to rebuild Brandenburg from the damage of the Thirty Years' War. He was sincerely interested in economic improvements and tempted rural immigrants with tax exemptions. He built the Oder-Elbe canal to divert downriver traffic away from the Swedish port of Stettin and encouraged both tobacco raising and truck gardening. By prohibiting imports of woollens and dressing his army in the celebrated home-produced dark blue, he ensured the growth of a blossoming industry. State-protected glass, iron, and copper industries emerged. The elector's religious policies marked him as the most tolerant sovereign of his age. His tolerance was built not upon religious indifference but upon principle and social pragmatism. Lutherans and Calvinists comprised the religious majority in his domains, but pockets of Catholics, Mennonites, and Protestant sectarians who were little welcome elsewhere found refuge with the elector. A devout Calvinist who had spent his formative years in Holland, Frederick William conceived of a new university with a faculty drawn exclusively from victims of religious or political oppression. He opened Brandenburg to French Huguenots, Austrian Lutherans, Polish Unitarians, and even Jews. He endowed Catholic churches and schools.

The fundamental achievement of the Great Elector was to mold the patchwork of towns and provinces he had inherited into a collection of regions overseen by his personal army and bureaucracy. State service was supposed to melt away the local loyalties of all the provincial aristocracies. When he died in 1688, Frederick William had achieved his goals more effectively than any other contemporary ruler. His son Frederick III (1688–1713), who reigned between a constructive, diligent father and a brutally strong son, was stamped in a different mold. Under him, Brandenburg was added to the list of small German states dazzled by the splendor of a royal title and royal trappings. For recognition as king in his East Prussian domains, Frederick loaned Emperor Leopold I several thousand crack troops. In 1701, at enormous cost, Frederick dragged his court from Berlin to Königsberg for the lavish coronation. He embellished Berlin with gardens, buildings, and statuary and invited the eminent scientist-philosopher Leibniz to become charter president of the state's new Academy of Science. With its unique programs in comparative religion and jurisprudence, secular history, and experimental science, the University of Halle was founded under Frederick's patronage.

Though Frederick was largely frill, in one respect his vanity bore fruit for his state. He was the first Hohenzollern to view his collected domains as an indissoluble entity. Not even the Great Elector, who tried to divide his lands among the children of his two marriages, had possessed this vision. Frederick's first political act, to throw out his father's will, proved to be his most important one. His own son's first act was to get rid of his father's court. By 1713, the state of Brandenburg-Prussia was well-established in Europe. The army had fought courageously under Marlborough and Prince Eugene. Succeeding his vain and spendthrift father, Frederick William I decided to restore the country to its proper financial moorings.

FROM HAPSBURG DOMAINS TO DANUBIAN MONARCHY

Until 1806, the Holy Roman Empire persisted as the great fiction of European politics. Though an imperial constitution, Diet, and law courts existed, the Peace of Westphalia had destroyed the empire as a confederation. The emperor and his princes distrusted each other, as did the princes and free towns. Catholic and Protestant princes, as well as ecclesiastical and secular ones, were mutually suspicious. It was nearly impossible to raise taxes, get laws passed, or raise an army for the empire. No imperial foreign policy existed. Genuine sovereignty in Germany resided in the governments of the three hundred–plus states and cities that filled the empire, and the political trend of these states was toward the construction of individual princely absolutisms. The princes wanted to keep the empire weakened. So did Louis XIV, who consistently involved himself in imperial affairs, buying off princely clients. Princes opposing the Diet's declarations of war against France remained neutral or even joined Louis against the emperor.

Though the empire was impotent, it retained a role in European politics because of the Austrian Hapsburgs. Except for a brief interlude in the eighteenth century, the senior male Hapsburg was regularly elected Holy Roman Emperor. Whenever possible, he stimulated discord among the princes, particularly the powerful ones, if this could strengthen his own hand as mediator and conciliator in Germany. But the most important method of improving his constitutional position was by increasing his control over the variegated dynastic lands of his family, both within and outside the empire. Whenever confronted with revolts of Estates and regions, the Hapsburgs instituted the compromise of power that we have noted in previous pages, but their eventual triumph was less complete than that of the king of Denmark or the elector of Brandenburg. The Hapsburgs scarcely envisioned the many distant regions attached to their dynasty as parts of a unitary state. What they hoped to do was dominate each region singly and have each region pay its tax share for the maintenance of the whole. The Hapsburg lands contained dozens of different ethnic groups and nationalities, chief of which were the Germans, Czechs, Slovaks, Magyars, Croats, and Serbs. Language and religion created barriers among the peoples. The reigning Hapsburg prince had different constitutional agreements with elites of the various regions, but an ability to manipulate opportunity laid the foundations for the Danubian monarchy.

After the death of Emperor Ferdinand III in 1657, it took Leopold I a year to accumulate all his titles, including securing election as Holy Roman Emperor. But the Hapsburg domains had been relatively free of crisis since the end of the Thirty Years' War, and Leopold concentrated upon establishing a front line of defense against the Turks who occupied one-third of Hungary. The great Hungarian magnates and lesser gentry urged the emperor to mount an offensive to free the entire country from the Turks. However, Leopold preferred a truce that would recognize the current frontier. A victory at St. Gotthard in 1664 won Leopold the truce he sought and infuriated the Magyars. Relishing a wealth of "liberties" dating back to the thirteenth century, including the right to resist their Hapsburg sovereign when they considered themselves betrayed, the Hungarian nobles staged an ill-conceived revolt against Leopold. The emperor suppressed it easily, tried the perpetrators in an Austrian court, and executed four of them. The unsuccessful rebellion then gave Leopold the opportunity to occupy the non-Turkish part of Hungary with German troops and teach a lesson to his recalcitrant subjects, who controlled and collected taxes, ran their own armed forces, directed their own local affairs, and mercilessly exploited their peasants. A military governor took over, and suspected sympathizers in the abortive revolt of 1665 found their lands confiscated. From 1671 to 1678, the Hapsburgs demolished Hungarian institutions and ruled through terror.

The reconquest of Hungary, however, failed to hold. In 1678, guerrilla warfare erupted, and Leopold slowly moved towards a policy of compromise. The Turks were preparing a new offensive against the Danube basin. In 1683, they had to be repulsed from Vienna itself. Four years later, the Hapsburgs reached an agreement with the Magyars. Property confiscations would cease, and the Austrians promised to liberate the entire country from the Turks. They agreed to guarantee Magyar landlords the state's backing in the economic and social subjugation of the peasantry. Serfdom was acknowledged officially. In return, the Hungarians had to recognize that their crown was hereditary in the Hapsburg house, and they had to give up their long-coveted "right to resistance." The Hungarian Diet was restored but made to understand that Hapsburg requests for subsidies were to be taken seriously. German troops would remain in Hungary, and in 1699, the Hapsburgs at last won the southern part of the country from the Turks. It was incorporated into the new constitutional statute.

For many Magyars, compromise was equivalent to defeat, and in 1703, still another rebellion broke out in Hungary. Led by the magnate Francis II Rokoczi, it began as a patriotic revolution, uniting all social groups and religious faiths against "Germanization." However, Leopold and his successor Joseph divided and conquered, and the Peace of Szatmar (1711) confirmed the agreement of 1687. The Austrians cajoled and flattered the greatest magnates by offering them administrative posts in the Hungarian "department" in Vienna. The magnates' preponderant role in the Hungarian Diet was confirmed, while Hapsburg law protected both their seigneurial powers and native offices. The price they paid was loyalty to the regime. In the rural areas, the gentry grumbled that the natural leadership had sold out the country. From their vantage point, there was some truth in this. For the Hapsburgs and the great Hungarian nobility, however, the theme after 1711 was reconciliation. Until the nationalist revival at the end of the century, Hungary was tamed.

Without the revival of Austria's international posture, Leopold and Joseph could not have pacified Hungary as well as they did. The emperors gained from the Grand Alliance against Louis XIV, but even more remarkable was their liberation of the northern Balkans from the Turks, particularly from 1683 to 1699. The Turks broke the truce they had signed with Leopold in 1664, and renewed their drive northward. By July 1683 their motley force of 200,000 soldiers, artisans, merchants, and camp followers reached the gates of Vienna. Leaving the capital in the hands of the town garrison, Leopold called upon the Christian princes of Europe to relieve the defenders. The city was about to fall in September, when an army led by Duke Charles of Lorraine and King John Sobieski of Poland swept down from the Kahlenberg heights and routed the Ottomans. The Hapsburgs rallied, offered their compromise to the Hungarians, helped the pope organize a holy league against the Turks, and forced the Peace of Carlowitz (1699) upon their foes. Hapsburg control over Transylvania and nearly all of Hungary was assured, and subsequent victories over the Turks in 1717–18 added the most fertile regions of Serbia, the rest of Hungary, and parts of Wallachia and Moldavia to the spoils gained at Carlowitz. Within a generation, the Hapsburgs had replaced the Turks as the predominant Balkan power, and their thoughts of carrying a crusade to Istanbul itself seemed realistic.

The heartland of the eighteenth-century Hapsburg domains lay in the Danube valley, but the Peace of Utrecht added most of Spain's Italian territories and the southern Netherlands as Charles VI's consolation prize. The peoples of Charles's empire were more heterogeneous than ever, but his house showed little skill in channeling the wealth of its possessions for the betterment of the state. Chronically short of funds, the emperor failed to create a bureaucracy of commissioners whom he might impose upon regional aristocracies. Nor could he convert regional aristocracies into a service class for the state. With absentee landlords drawn from the other nationalities of the empire, the Hungarian magnates who came to Vienna supported territorial accumulation, but they shrank back with horror at any thought of consolidating the accumulations into a functioning unit.

Outside Vienna, in lands whose social structure rested upon rural bases, aristocracies continued to stand as barriers between the government and peasants. In Austria proper, in Italy and the Alpine valleys, in Belgium and Silesia, local nobles and clergy collected from tenants both rents and tithes, in addition to the state's taxes. In Bohemia, Moravia, the Balkans, and Hungary, noble landowners held the power of life and death over their serfs. Peasants had to devote three to five days of free labor to seigneurs who administered the state's revenue, exercised imperial and private justice, and monopolized mills, taverns, stores, and seed supplies. The nobility paid no taxes, and they made certain that the peasant's contribution stayed in the region.

Subsidies from regional Estates and diets could not meet the costs of the conquering Hapsburg army, so the emperor begged from the English and Dutch or borrowed at exorbitant interest rates from his own aristocracy. The reconquest of Hungary provides a good example of the compromise of power in central Europe. Lacking institutional reform, however, the Hapsburgs were unable to exploit their dazzling outward successes for the profit of their house or the state.

"ECLIPSIS POLONIAE"

From his vantage point, however, the king of Poland envied the Hapsburg emperor. In the second half of the seventeenth century, the course of Polish history was fraught with political crises. Though Polish kings would have welcomed a compromise of power resembling the Hungarian solution, nothing of the sort ever emerged. The aristocracy dominated regional governments and paralyzed central government. Its members viewed this use of power as a supreme virtue and therefore saw no necessity for compromise, regardless of the king's desires. Without the aristocracy's consent, the king had no army, no income, and no bureaucracy.

After Russia, Poland-Lithuania was Europe's largest country. In 1648, its population was ten million, but fewer than half were ethnic Poles. In the north, east, and southeast, respectively, lived large groups of Lithuanians, White Russians, and Ukrainians—self-contained minorities understandably hostile to the emergence of whatever national consciousness a strong ruler might inspire. Throughout Poland, ethnic Germans lived in hundreds of their own enclaves. Religious diversity added to ethnic diversity. A half-million Jews possessed their separate culture in towns and villages that dotted the eastern part of the country. Poles and Lithuanians usually were

Catholic, White Russians were Orthodox or Uniate, and Germans were customarily Lutheran.

Great magnates so dominated their regions that the government of Poland was nearly as decentralized as that of the Holy Roman Empire. Furthermore, nearly all the magnates had their retinues and private armies. The gentry of their region were their men, not the king's. The great nobles controlled local diets and could form legally recognized confederations to resist the king or one another. The magnates endowed churches, constructed fortresses, and founded towns. Along with the hierarchy of the Catholic Church in Poland, they comprised the upper house of the national Diet. The king was obliged to select his high officials from among them. They supplied him with subsidies and an army, both infinitesimal in size. Representatives of the lesser nobility, the gentry, sat in the lower house of the national Diet. Both houses elected the king and wrung from him a pledge to do nothing that would upset the constitutional status quo. In 1652, to insure a power vacuum at the center, the national Diet adopted the *liberum veto*. Hereafter, not only was unanimity of both houses necessary to pass any major piece of legislation but a single adverse vote was sufficient to nullify all previous legislation passed at the session and dissolve the Diet. Thus government was effectively paralyzed. From 1655 to 1717, forty-eight of the fifty national Diets convoked produced no legislation. Foreign powers bribed Diet members and manipulated confederations. No other European state was subjected to more outside interference in its affairs than Poland.

The inability of the Polish king to raise an army forced him to depend upon large bands of seminomadic warriors to defend the southern frontier against the Turks. The Cossacks—horsemen, lumberjacks, herdsmen, hunters, and petty traders—lived, or rather roamed, along the Dnieper, Don, and Volga rivers in Poland and Russia. All who wearied of the constraints of sedentary existence, including runaway serfs, freebooters, and criminals, joined the Cossacks. Technically, they owned no land and paid no dues or taxes. By 1648, however, the westernmost ones showed signs of settling down, and "registered Cossacks" found winter shelter in Polish towns. As they took up farming on frontier lands, they came into conflict with the great Polish magnates of the Ukraine. The latter, large-scale grain producers for the western market, wished to exploit these virgin lands themselves and press agricultural Cossacks into serfdom.

In 1648, clashes between Cossacks and magnates erupted into social warfare. The Cossack leader Bogdan Chmielnicki invited peasants to join the revolt, which became an enormous rural uprising. Chmielnicki's motley army turned upon magnates, their rent collectors, the Catholic clergy, and Jews. The Cossack leader wished to carve an independent Ukrainian republic from the southeastern part of Poland, but he also knew it was only a matter of time before his support would melt away. Therefore, in 1653 he revised his earlier plans and offered Czar Alexei of Russia tax collection rights over Ukrainian towns and the lion's share of lands taken from the

Polish magnates in return for Russian protection of the Cossacks and recognition of their liberties.

To the Poles, this robbery meant war with Russia. For the next fifteen years, Polish history was a litany of misfortunes. The magnates withheld an army from King John II Casimir. Cossacks and Russians plundered the Dnieper. A second front opened in Lithuania, and in 1655 Sweden entered the war to beat the Russians to Warsaw. Swedes occupied Warsaw and Cracow; John Casimir fled the country; the magnates offered homage to the Swedish king. Brandenburg, the Hapsburgs, and even the Dutch intervened. The west European powers feared a partition of Poland that would make the Baltic a Swedish lake and place the Russians on the frontier of Germany. A native resistance movement erupted in Poland, but the war dragged on until 1667. When the Treaty of Andrusovo finally terminated the conflict, Poland was saved from complete dismemberment. The price, however, was the loss of one-fifth of its territory to Russia.

Diplomatically, Poland became the prize pawn on the European chessboard. Socially, the regime of rural servitude hardened. Twenty years of warfare cost Poland almost 30 percent of its population. Driven from their ruined villages, tens of thousands of peasants and hundreds of gentry became a rural proletariat floating through the countryside in search of food. The winners were the great landlords who occupied deserted properties and offered a hovel to poor creatures ready to sell away a lifetime in service dues. The patriotism of the late 1650s expressed itself not in constitutional reform but in widespread persecution of Protestants, Germans, and Jews. The regional diets remained in force. John Casimir's attempt to abolish the *liberum veto* and select his own successor resulted in a magnate uprising and the king's abdication in 1668.

John III Sobieski's (1674–96) international reputation as a warrior-king redounded upon the Polish aristocracy and helped him relieve the Turkish siege of Vienna in 1683. At home, however, Sobieski could get nowhere. On his death, the Diet failed to agree upon a successor, and two magnatial cliques brought the country to the brink of a new civil war. As candidate of one of the groups, the elector of Saxony rushed to the capital and was crowned. Assuming the throne as Augustus II, he offered his new subjects a tempting economic union between Saxon industry and Polish agriculture. Moreover, Polish ports gave Saxony an outlet to the sea. Dazzled with his new crown and blind to Poland's traditional weaknesses, Augustus extended his vision northward.

During the 1696–97 period, Peter I of Russia and Charles XII of Sweden assumed command over their states. Twenty-four years old, overshadowed since childhood by his aunt and mother, Peter was anxious to prove himself. Charles was an untried adolescent of fourteen. Sweden's territories were scattered from the eastern reaches of Finland to Bremen near the Dutch frontier, and the underpopulated Scandinavian state seemed hardly prepared to defend them. Augustus therefore tempted both Peter and the Danes with a share of Charles XII's inheritance, but the Polish king underestimated Charles's extraordinary capabilities and overestimated Russia's strengths. In 1700, the Swedes annihilated the Russian army at the Battle of Narva. Charles smashed his way into Poland, deposed Augustus, occupied most of the country, and set up his own puppet-king, Stanislas Leczcynski.

As in the 1650s, remorse, followed by an indignant wave of patriotism, settled over the Polish gentry. Peter recovered, and the magnates urged him to rid the land of the Swedes. The country became a battlefield again. Charles met disaster in Russia, Leczcynski was deposed, and Augustus restored. Had Peter desired it, the old constitution might well have been scrapped and Augustus placed upon the throne in fact as in name. Coming as a liberator, however, Peter forced war contributions on Poland to pay for his struggles against the Swedes and Turks. He encouraged magnatial rivalries and refused to take Russian troops out of the country. Augustus was forced to abandon ideas about abolishing the *liberum veto* and make the monarchy hereditary. He became another in the long line of frustrated and embittered kings of Poland, and his country sank back into its habitually enfeebled role until the late eighteenth century, when Poland's neighbors, then too civilized to fight over it, secured their aims by dividing it peaceably among themselves.

THE SWEDISH METEOR

In Poland, the compromise of power remained incomplete because the aristocracy shackled both sovereign and peasantry. In Sweden, Charles XI outmaneuvered his magnates without sacrificing his peasants. Charles manipulated the political and social forces of his realm so skillfully that not even military disaster in the following reign could undo his work. During most of the eighteenth century, the royal personality was effaced, the royal administration still ran the country, and society rested upon the freest peasantry in Europe.

In 1648, Finland and Estonia were attached to Sweden's large Baltic empire, and a series of peace treaties during the previous thirty years had won prizes from Karelia, Livonia, and Ingria in the east; Bremen and Verden in the west; a pair of Norwegian provinces; the German regions of western Pomerania; and the ports of Wismar and Stettin. This scattered empire was constructed upon a kingdom of a million people, whose forests and iron mines needed Dutch capital and whose power the Dutch and English tolerated as long as ports and seas remained open to their commerce. Swedish society was rural, resembling western Europe's more than that of neighboring Brandenburg or Poland. The peasants were not serfs. A large number of them held full ownership of land, while others leased land from the aristocracy or the crown. The crown peasants even sent representatives to the national Diet, meeting in Stockholm. The nobles' estates were modest in size, and the greatest Swedish aristocrats did not control regions and clients. Rather, they served in the army and Royal Council. Of course, they had representation in the national Diet, but so too did the Lutheran clergy and small group of burghers.

From 1650 to 1680, however, the delicate balance of traditional Swedish society was nearly upset. During the Thirty Years' War, Queen Christina desperately needed cash, and she therefore sold crown lands to nobles at cut-rate prices. She also rewarded faithful officers in the war with large tracts in Finland. Peasants who had enjoyed relative prosperity leasing the state's properties found they had new landlords, veteran officers of the war who had seen serfdom in Germany and western Poland and were eager to apply it to their Swedish lands. The new landlords charged their tenants with unheard-of dues and services, and Christina did nothing to reverse the trend. If anything, the idea of a splendid magnatial aristocracy appealed to her own inclination to transform backwoods Sweden into a dazzling kingdom whose palaces, theaters, and libraries would be the envy of the north.

When the Diet gathered in Stockholm in 1650, the peasants, clergy, and burghers pleaded with the queen to take back the lands she had awarded. Because she was contemplating abdication and wished to name her own successor, her nephew Charles Gustav, Christina pretended to heed the aggrieved Estates. Once Charles was nominated, however, she did nothing. The alienation continued. After his accession, Charles X tried to slow down the process, but war in Poland and against Denmark from 1655 to 1660 further strained the state's resources. In 1660, Charles X died prematurely, leaving a child as successor. The newly enshrined magnatial aristocrats now found themselves in control of the state and were prepared to turn Sweden into a monarchical republic on the Polish model.

They nearly did so. From 1660 to 1680, peasants sank more deeply than ever into debt and resignation. They were subject to the landlord's civil and criminal jurisdiction and could be evicted without notice. As the magnates grew richer, the state grew poorer. In 1674, however, the aristocratized Royal Council committed a fatal blunder. It involved Sweden in a new war with Denmark and Brandenburg that it could not afford. When peace arrived five years later, Sweden managed to keep its empire intact, but the state was near bankruptcy.

No longer a child, Charles XI had proven himself on the battlefield and was determined to take command of his country. In 1680, he called together the Diet, ostensibly to find a way to pay the outstanding war bills. The lower Estates surprised even the king by their boldness, suggesting a wholesale reacquisition of alienated state lands and establishment of an absolute monarchy. Even the gentry who served in the army and civil service and whose wages were in arrears joined the cry. The great magnates had had their day. A royal survey disclosed that 72 percent of the land was owned by the nobility. The king repossessed great estates that the crown had alienated within the past half-century, and he promised the peasants that he would not abandon them to serfdom as long as they paid their taxes, rents, and dues to the state. They willingly exchanged masters. The nobility was told to be satisfied with careers in the army and royal administration, and the state entered a period of rigid austerity. Charles avoided foreign loans but encouraged foreign investments. During his reign, Sweden's iron exports doubled. The army was rebuilt, but costs for maintaining it were cut. Charles XI's bloodless royal revolution, which had tamed the aristocracy and achieved financial balance while rescuing the peasantry from impoverishment and exploitation, was the envy of contemporary sovereigns. In 1693, a grateful Diet declared Charles "by God, Nature, and the Crown's high hereditary right . . . an absolute sovereign king, whose commands are binding on all, and who is responsible to no one on earth for his actions. . . ."

When the king died in 1697, he left an heir of fourteen and a state well-prepared to defend itself. Augustus of Poland and Peter of Russia counted upon an aristocratic revival that would overturn Charles XI's reforms, weaken the state, and invite foreign intervention. But they underestimated the new king. Descended from a line of warriors, reared in the Lutheran piety of a court that ignored learning and the arts, Charles XII assumed the role of an impetuous military commander. The aristocracy supported him and the rest of the country followed. A brilliant battlefield strategist, for sport Charles rode horses to death. At the age of seventeen, he landed his army at Copenhagen and forced Denmark out of the coalition with Russia and Poland that intended to dismember his state. Several months later, at Narva in Estonia, he surprised a Russian army five times the size of the Swedish force of 8,000. Aided by a snowstorm that blew into the faces of the Russians, he scored such a decisive victory that Peter abandoned the battlefield, his army in ruins. Within half an hour, 15,000 were dead and 20,000 were taken prisoner.

All of Europe was stunned. William III and Louis XIV both courted the teen-aged warrior, but Charles had little interest in the Spanish Succession question. He still had a score to settle with Augustus II. The Swedes poured into Poland, deposed Augustus, and forced a rump Diet to elect Stanislas Leczcynski as king. Charles left Stanislas a Swedish occupation force. Then he turned his attention upon the Hapsburgs, scolding Joseph I for mistreating his Protestant subjects. For all his military daring, Charles bore a religious strain in his politics that was reminiscent of another age. His hatred of Augustus II was inflamed by the fact that the Saxon was a renegade Lutheran turned Catholic for the Polish throne. Emperor Joseph promised that he would treat non-Catholics in a more kindly way. Once more Charles moved eastward.

Peter's recovery after Narva forced Charles to confront the Russians. The czar had learned that without a complete overhaul, his army never could stand up to a disciplined, well-trained force. From scratch, Peter built a volunteer infantry, then a commissariat, and even an artillery. He systematized the peasant levy and established a school of tactics for young officers. In 1703, he scored a couple of small successes against the Swedes in Ingria and defied Charles by building his anticipated new capital on Swedish-claimed soil. In September 1707, Charles moved across Poland with 43,000 troops. His goal was nothing less than Moscow. However, in the face of disease, bad weather, and Polish guerrilla resistance, his advance bogged down. It took ten months to reach the Dnieper, still in Poland. In July 1708, as his supplies dwindled, Charles received an offer of help from the Cossacks, who accused Peter of interference in their affairs. The Swedish king decided to cut a wide detour through the Ukraine, where he might find food, and link up his forces with both the Cossacks and a second Swedish army moving down from the Baltic.

At this juncture, however, more misfortunes and miscalculations occurred. The Russians burned the countryside as they retreated. Guerrilla forces wiped out nearly half the Swedish army sent to relieve Charles, and the Cossacks did not help. The terrible winter of 1708–9 struck the Ukraine early. After eight years in the field, Charles's surviving troops longed to go home. Still, the king would not deflect from his goal. Though the Swedes already had lost over half their army and the king himself was badly wounded, Charles challenged Peter to fight. While Charles besieged the town of Poltava, the Russians finally attacked. Outnumbered two to one, their king incapacitated, hungry, tired, and without supplies, the Swedes came close to pulling off another miracle. Carried from place to place on a litter, Charles defied death itself. At length, the Russians wore down their old tormenters, and with a thousand survivors, the Swedish king fled into Turkish territory.

Poltava heralded the end of the Swedish empire and the beginning of the Russian one. Russia, Denmark, and Brandenburg seized Sweden's Baltic lands. Peter cleared Poland of Swedish troops, deposed Stanislas Leczcynski, and reestablished Augustus II as a Russian puppet. In September 1714, after a series of fantastic adventures among the Turks, Charles arrived home. Undaunted as ever, he was filled with plans and projects. Stralsund, his last German port, fell to the Prussians, but he believed that a new victory would revive his countrymen. The Danes had always been his easiest victims, so the king pulled together his last army and marched across the frontier into Danish-held Norway. In December 1718, while besieging the obscure fortress of Fredriksten, a stray bullet finally caught up with the Terror of the North. Upon Charles's death, his generals called off the campaign and the army went home. Two years of negotiations confirmed most of Sweden's wartime losses: Hanover took Bremen and Verden;

Prussia got Stettin and half of Swedish Pomerania. By terms of the Treaty of Nystad (1721), Peter saw his hold on Ingria, southeastern Finland, Estonia, and Livonia confirmed. Like Denmark, Sweden was finished as a great power.

Charles XII left a disputed succession. The Diet elected the king's youngest sister as queen but hedged her powers and threw out the absolutist blank check presented to Charles XI back in 1693. However, Sweden did not revert to the chaos of Poland. For more than fifteen of his twenty-one years as king, Charles XII had been out of the country, and the bureaucracy had run the government. From 1718 to 1772, the four-Estate Diet and civil service shared the responsibility of governing while the monarchy was eclipsed. Sweden's eighteenth-century foreign policies were tailored down to its size and strengths, and despite Charles XII's military adventures, the social-administrative revolution effected by Charles XI proved to be the most enduring legacy.

FROM MUSCOVY TO THE RUSSIAN EMPIRE

In 1648 Moscow was worlds apart from Paris, London, or even Warsaw. Nevertheless, it shared with these capitals severe social tensions. Untempered by Estates or a legal tradition, Russia was unlike any state in Europe. In the sixteenth century, the czars had developed the concept of a pure service state in which clearly defined social groups owed to their imperial majesty a set of obligations peculiar to their station. The czar owned the state. Aristocrats led his army and administered his central and provincial governments. Peasants were to render labor services to noble landowners and pay taxes. Townsmen provided the state with a percentage of the revenue they derived from commerce. The czar identified the privileged elements of Russian society. To the nobility and Church he donated lands and peasants, and the regime bound the peasantry to lord and land. The czar could grant monopolies, lands, and titles to foreigners who established foundries and iron works or who directed the export-import trade. Towns had no municipal liberties. The state channeled and directed internal commerce. In 1654, an imperial decree accomplished what Colbert could never do in France. It abolished all internal tolls.

Theoretically a despotism, the state possessed internal checks that kept it from becoming a model of ruthlessness. The czar's government was poorly organized and, except at the very top, devoid of hierarchy. Departments were created to respond to the needs of the moment and then retained. In the 1680s, eighteen separate bureaus managed army affairs. Coordinating departmental duties was foreign to Russian tradition, and sheer distance permitted the provinces to maintain their own rhythm of existence. Country officials were summoned to Moscow irregularly to dispute with the czar's agents over regional tax responsibilities or land grants, and then they returned home.

The Orthodox Church also counterbalanced the theory of despotism. The model of church-state relations was Byzantine. The ruler controlled and protected the church. Split off from its Greek foundations, however, Russian Orthodoxy lacked a systematic theology and inspired neither moral conduct nor scholarship. Essentially, it was a folk religion, thriving upon superstition and ritual. Czar and hierarchy might agree that the Russian Church must change if it were to compete successfully with Catholicism or Protestantism, but they were equally aware that to tamper with icon worship or liturgy might have explosive social results. In the sixteenth century, the Church had grown wealthy. Tax-exempt monasteries and priories had been willed vast estates complete with serfs. The pervasiveness of popular religion and the economic power of the Church mitigated against tight state control.

The Moscow riots of 1648 began as protests of townsmen against increased use taxes on salt. The government could cope with petty tradesmen, but when the palace guard joined the discontented Muscovites, matters became critical. Violence erupted in several provincial towns, though the countryside remained quiet. The government negotiated with the guards, who abandoned the burghers, and the uprising petered out. The revolt convinced Czar Alexei and his advisers that a legal charter should be drawn up, clearly enunciating the autocratic constitution of the Russian state and the responsibilities and obligations of the social groups serving it. A commission set to work immediately. Completed in five months, the Code of 1649 froze society. All elements were beholden to the state. Only the service nobility and the Church could own land and peasants. Townsmen were tied to their place of residence, but foreigners and country people were prohibited from competing in town commerce. The Church could no longer acquire tax-exempt properties, and a new government department was established to oversee Church administration. Serfdom was enshrined as an immutable institution, the peasant and his entire family tied to a landlord's estate. Should the peasant run away, the landlord's claim to possess him would never lapse.

The tightening of state control over the Church led to the rise in influence of the czar's good friend, the Orthodox priest Nikon. The priest was absolutely convinced that the state must remove Russian Orthodoxy from its dependence upon ritual and magic and bring it closer to its Greek roots. In 1651, Alexei named Nikon patriarch of Moscow, and the priest drew up a new service book deemphasizing and eliminating what appeared to be superstitious forms of worship. Imposed upon the country clergy, it immediately provoked a widespread hostility among those who viewed the reduction of the number of hallelujahs and genuflections in the service as tampering with God's law. Tens of thousands refused to part with the "Old

Belief" and defied the Code of 1649 by running away from their villages to the Cossacks in the south or the wilderness in the east. Nikonites were accused of having been seduced by the devilish triad of Catholicism, science, and geometry. Increasing in number and vigor, "Old Believers" became the caretakers of an indigenous antiwestern tradition that considered itself more authentically Russian than the czarist regime itself. Developing characteristic habits of rigid moral puritanism, the Old Believers became the great frontiersmen of Russia, colonizing Siberia and the southeast, moving on whenever the arm of the state came too close.

Though Nikon's political ambitions led to his disgrace in the 1660s, the social tensions of the previous twenty years erupted in widespread violence. Old Believers and escaped peasants moved into the valleys of the Don and Volga, where they came into contact with unruly Cossack bands. Only a charismatic leader was needed to turn the mob into an army. A Cossack chief named Stenka Razin provided this leadership. In 1668–69, the western bank of the Caspian fell to Razin's forces. He then turned them abruptly towards Moscow. Soldiers, country priests, townsmen, and peasants supported the crusade. To many, Razin was a saint, a deliverer promising an end to war, taxation, serfdom, and the replacement of despotism with assemblies of the people.

At its height, Stenka Razin's uprising involved several hundred thousands and was the most spectacular popular rebellion in seventeenth-century Europe. As the human wave pushed towards the northwest, estates went up in flame and towns fell. In 1670, however, Razin lost control of his following. Tensions erupted between Cossacks and newcomers. Razin was betrayed, carted off to Moscow, tortured, and publicly executed. His splintered forces still terrorized the countryside but no longer posed a threat to the regime. The landholding service nobility was amply rewarded for remaining loyal to Alexei. The Code of 1649 stood, and the landlord enjoyed total property rights over those who worked his estate. By 1680, Russia's social crisis had been settled theoretically in terms of a compromise of power that was consistent with trends in central and eastern Europe. However, it remained for the state to create the instruments of power that converted absolutist claims into force across millions of square miles of desert, forest, and ice.

Alexei died in 1676. From his first marriage, there had survived a girl, Sophia, and two boys, Feodor and Ivan. From his second marriage, a son, Peter, was born in 1672. Though Feodor succeeded his father, he died in 1682. Ivan was mentally incompetent. Since the Russian state possessed no law of succession, such matters usually degenerated into palace intrigue. Peter's mother and her family, the Naryshkins, proposed the ten-year-old boy as the new czar. The patriarch of Moscow gave his blessing, and a mob of Naryshkin followers, hurriedly labeled the "Assembly of the People," acclaimed Peter. However, Sophia did not relish being thrust aside so easily.

Controlling the palace guard, she and her lover, Vasili Golytsin, murdered all the Naryshkins they could find. Miraculously, Peter and his mother were spared. Sensing the need to avert a backlash, Sophia proposed an imaginative compromise. Peter and his dimwitted half-brother would be recognized as co-czars and Sophia would serve as regent. This was appropriate enough for state occasions, but Sophia's real aim was to keep Peter out of the picture as much as possible.

From 1682 to 1689, the boy and his mother were forced to live in a village outside Moscow. Left to his own devices, he roamed the countryside and caroused in the "Foreign Suburb," located midway between his village and Moscow. For two centuries, several dozen western merchants, technicians, and army officers had resided there, insulated from Russians whom they despised and who feared them. Learning to share their prejudices towards his countrymen, Peter struck up friendships with several soldiers of fortune. From them, he learned the rudiments of military geometry and developed a passionate interest in naval matters. Peter learned a little German and Dutch, but his education was hardly regular. His mother could not control him, and Sophia kept her distance. An artisan and bully, Peter drilled his companions, terrorized the peasant girls, and built sailboats.

Paradoxically enough, the regime of Sophia and Golytsin prepared Russia for Peter in several ways. Golytsin envisioned an aggressive foreign policy. He wanted to draw the Muscovite state closer to Europe and develop contacts with the Orient. He wished to introduce western technology to his backward state and considered the great boyar landowners, Orthodox Church, and palace guard as the chief obstacles to progress. Time, however, was not with Golytsin. In 1689, his enemies staged a countercoup and deposed Sophia. The regent was placed in a convent and her western-looking adviser was exiled. Peter's mother offered the front of respectability for the corrupt gang of nobles who seized the government, while young Peter bided his time. In 1694, his mother died, followed two years later by his half-brother Ivan. Peter was sole ruler at last, and his pent up energies exploded in every direction.

Peter was the first European ruler to commit mind and heart almost exclusively to the technological improvement of his state. His motives were clear-cut. The modernization of Russia was the surest way to tighten his hold upon the country and impress the country upon the world. That Russian society and civilization might resist his vision was irrelevant. He would bend the nation to his purpose. He never swerved from his faith in example from above. Near the close of his life he wrote: "Our people are like children who would never set about their ABC's unless their master compelled them."

Force of arms offered a shortcut to national goals, one of which was to turn Muscovy into a sea power. The country did not even possess an ice-free port. Swedish Finland, Ingria, Estonia, and Livonia closed off the Baltic.

Tartar Crimea, a tributary state of the Turks, controlled the entrance to the Black Sea, and the Ottomans blocked the passage to the Mediterranean. The Crimean bases seemed the most vulnerable point to the czar. In 1698, he captured Azov and began to build a fleet. He planned harbors for the Don and a canal link between the Don and Volga. However, the Mediterranean was still in hostile hands. In 1697, however, a potentially more realizable opportunity beckoned. Charles XI of Sweden died, and Augustus of Poland offered Peter a slice of the Swedish Baltic empire. The czar shifted focus. The Baltic would be his window on the west. It took thirteen years to dispossess the Swedes, but Peter nevertheless lived long enough to see the Peace of Nystad consolidate his great triumph.

Russia replaced Sweden as the chief Baltic power and turned Poland into a satellite. Hoping to emulate the Austrian example in liberating the Balkans from the Turks, in 1711 Peter moved his army into Moldavia. He expected the Christian populations to rise up against the infidel and welcome the Russian armies as their saviors. In his enthusiasm, however, Peter overextended his forces, and the entire Russian army was surrounded on the River Pruth. Peter had to surrender or face annihilation. He returned Azov, thereby closing the Balkans and Black Sea to Russian expansion for another half-century.

Peter understood that conquest might make Europe fear Russia but not welcome it. He longed to divest the West of its suspicions of Russian power and scorn for its institutions. By borrowing experts and techniques from Europe, he believed he could strengthen the state as well as integrate it into the community of nations he so envied. Peter was convinced that he could accomplish his aims through personal example and thus embarked upon two "Great Emissaries" to the West, the first in 1697 and the second in 1716. During the first voyage, he traveled as a private person, working with his hands at the dockyard of the Dutch East India Company, spending fifteen weeks at an English shipbuilding town, and observing Parliament. On the return journey home, via the Netherlands, Leipzig, Prague, and Vienna, he contracted expert seamen, gunners, shipwrights, mathematicians, surgeons, and engineers, who followed him shortly along with their books and instruments.

In Vienna, Peter learned that the officers of the palace guard were meddling in dynastic politics again. Goaded by boyars worried about the czar's apparent impiety, devotion to foreigners, and mistreatment of his wife, four regiments revolted. Peter rushed back to Moscow, only to find that the uprising had been suppressed. Suspecting a conspiracy to place Sophia on the throne, Peter decided to settle the matter. Fourteen torture chambers were erected outside Moscow. Dismissing the entire Moscow guard, whom he considered poor soldiers and worse plotters, the czar wiped out its leadership. Charges were filed, courts-martial were held, and hundreds were whipped, garroted, beheaded, hanged, or buried alive. Peter had an execution block set up directly outside Sophia's convent window. At this moment, the first contingent of western experts arrived.

Any summary of Peter's internal reforms runs the risk of suggesting that they were conceived in a reasonably systematic fashion. Nothing could be further from the truth. One order might contradict another, and none ever considered the psychological unpreparedness of the Russian people for change. Though it was characteristic of Peter to emphasize the outer, superficial, or symbolic aspects of modernization, such as trimming robes or clipping beards, other changes were shattering and created the matrix into which modern Russia was molded. Peter consulted neither intermediate bodies nor entrenched groups. With the stroke of his pen, the czar dismissed overlapping boyar councils and erased provincial governments. In 1700, he divided the country into eight regional districts with a governor and staff for each. After Poltava, these eight districts were further divided into smaller units, and local landlords were fixed to them. Officials responsible to the czar alone were to collect taxes, grain, and soldiers. Those accustomed to pocketing the lion's share of revenue grumbled, but they did not resist.

Peter also tackled the central administration. He appointed a Senate of nine trusted men to handle day-to-day affairs and to execute the czar's orders. Peter had no patience for the interminable deliberations of the old boyar councils. The Senate better suited the needs of crisis government, and the councils were thus doomed. Provincial officials sent reports to Senate members, who dispatched agents and spies to the provinces. Even the senators were subjected to scrutiny by Peter's procurator-general. The czar also established departments with specific functional authority over foreign affairs, the army, navy, mining installations, and manufactures. Each department also made long-term recommendations and established systems of procedure, including majority rule. Thus Peter offered Russia the framework of a coordinated governmental apparatus, though the country lacked trained personnel to fill it. Peter imported technicians and army officers, but an instant civil service was another matter. The czar's cronies rubbed against haughty boyars ill-fitted for their new roles. Social tensions and mutual jealousies abounded. Neither corruption nor human inefficiency could be erased overnight.

Old Muscovite society had not only distinguished among peasant, townsman, and noble but it also had recognized various categories of peasants: slaves, serfs, freeholders, and colonists. Each group accordingly paid specified types of household taxes to the government. The Code of 1649 had gone far toward creating a uniform serf-peasantry, and Peter completed the job by substituting for the old impositions a single poll tax on five million male family heads. With the peasant village now in bondage to landlord and state, Peter went after the privileged members of Russian society. By prohibiting the division of private estates, the czar channeled the younger sons of landlords into the army, navy, and civil service. Peter institutionalized a system of ranks for state service that corresponded to the military's, and the two hierarchies became the official mark of status for those outside peasant society. Of the fourteen grades in the civil service, the highest eight conferred nobility. Aristocrats were urged to compete for the top grades, and nonnobles understood that state service was the only avenue to social distinction.

Peter's ruthless fiscal policies were effective. From 1710 to 1724, revenues tripled, and despite war the budget was balanced. Nor did the industrial primitiveness of Russia daunt the energetic czar. He had inherited a substantial mining enterprise in the Urals, but the sheer size of the country and its lack of a communications network dictated the existence of hundreds of self-supporting economic units, dependent upon handicraft production. However, peasant villagers could not clothe Peter's army or make sails for his navy. He ordered the construction of specialized factories, encouraged foreign investment, and took state-owned serfs to be trained as iron workers, cannon founders, and textile laborers. Vagrants, poor women, and orphans were put to work. The best-developed industry, iron production, spread from Perm in the Urals to the region around Lake Onega and St. Petersburg. A former peasant, Nikita Demidov, was the industrial genius behind the growth of Russia's heavy metals. By the mid-eighteenth century the country produced as much pig iron as the rest of Continental Europe combined.

The czar was almost wholly responsible for the birth of his country as a commercial power. In pre-Petrine Russia, Archangel, the only important port, was controlled by Dutch and English tradesmen, who handed the czar's government a pittance in the form of customs revenue. The acquisition of Sweden's east Baltic empire altered the picture completely. Suddenly the great *entrepôts* for Polish grains, the towns of Riga, Reval, and Viborg, were in Russian hands. Peter envisioned the Baltic as the nerve center of his country. Out of the region's ice and mud would arise its living monuments, the capital of St. Petersburg and naval base of Kronstadt. No insulated Versailles, St. Petersburg was to be Russia's hub of world commerce, as well as a royal residence and administrative capital. Peter cajoled, bribed, and bludgeoned businesses to establish themselves in St. Petersburg. He began building a network of canals from the Caspian to his capital. In his own lifetime, Peter saw the city emerge from nothing to a busy port. In 1713, a single ship laid anchor there, but in 1725 the number rose to nearly five per week. An Amsterdam or London was not created overnight. However, St. Petersburg's merchant community was comprised mostly of Russians who developed connections with Turkey, Persia, central Asia, and China, who gained control of the iron, pitch, and tar of the hinterland, who persuaded Peter to finance the Bering expeditions to charter the straits between Siberia and Alaska, and who even planned an East India Company. Russians were learning the techniques of western commerce, and this brought Peter immense satisfaction.

In other respects, however, the breakthrough was less promising. The ships that left St. Petersburg, Riga, and Revel laden with iron, naval stores, wheat, and silks were seldom Russian. Russians were still too unskilled to undertake banking and insurance. Nevertheless, none of Peter's contemporaries understood bootstrap economics as well as he, and St. Petersburg offered the enterprising individual an unparalleled opportunity at pioneering. The state provided incentive, monopolies, and privileges. Within a generation, St. Petersburg became Russia's most cultivated and beautiful city.

Peter encountered opposition to his projects from the Church. It was the most privileged institution in Russian society, with an income untouched by taxation and lands tilled by hundreds of thousands of serfs. Its hold on the people was unrivaled by any secular ideology the czar could hope to conjure. Peter himself was a believer. His letters are filled with Biblical illusions, and he was genuinely interested in missionary activity among the non-Christian peoples of his empire. He also feared and hated the institutionalized Orthodox Church. To him, the patriarchate of Moscow, seat of Church government, was obscurantist, corrupt, and an obstacle to his vision of a new Russia. The patriarch, Adrian, despised foreigners, repudiated any change in Russian life, opposed the "Great Emissary," and scolded the czar for his private life. When Adrian died in 1700, however, Peter decided to bring the Church into his net of activity. He delayed nominating a new patriarch and instead picked a layman as temporary administrator. Citing the financial crisis after Narva as his reason, he commanded Church revenues to be diverted for the government's use. No other European sovereign would have succeeded at this, but Peter maintained the "emergency" until 1721. Then he dissolved the patriarchate altogether and replaced it with a holy synod, a committee of eight priests of unquestioned loyalty with a layman presiding. This was nothing more than a faceless body subservient to the regime. The synod took command of the essentials of Church organization and government and controlled income, appointments, and building construction. It oversaw the education of priests and ordered the clergy to stress morals and patriotism instead of ritual and prayer. Peter allowed the number of monks and nuns to dwindle through natural attrition and appointed army veterans to monastic vacancies. By passively accepting Peter's humiliating blows, official Orthodoxy showed the czar that he had nothing more to fear from it. Old Belief persisted. Many fled the regime of the "crowned Satan" for the reaches of the Arctic and Siberia. Those who returned to society paid discriminatory taxes and kept wide the gulf between the czar's upper-class society of courtiers, bureaucrats, and industrialists and the rest of Russia.

Additional resistance and personal misfortune marred Peter's last years. From 1719 to 1726, an estimated quarter-million serfs fled to the east. The Cossacks were always restless. Finally, there was the problem of the great Muscovite aristocracy, the only element of the old privileged society that Peter had neither destroyed nor mastered. Their government councils dissolved, the boyars grumbled over their place in the Table of Ranks beside the foreigners and self-made men of the new bureaucracy. The Muscovites resisted passively, resigned to riding out the Petrine storm. Time, they believed, was on their side. Alexei, Peter's son by his first marriage, passionately hated his father. When Peter married a Latvian camp follower, it became clear that given the chance, Alexei would undo all his father's work. This meant the abandonment of St. Petersburg and the Baltic and returning the government to boyar councils.

Though the aristocracy chose to await Peter's death, Alexei could not. Intimidated by Peter's rages and threats of disinheritance, Alexei ran away in 1716. First he sought refuge in Vienna, at the court of his brother-in-law, Emperor Charles VI. The czar sent emissaries after him, and they finally chased him down in Naples. He returned to Russia where father and son staged a tearful reconciliation. However, haunted by prospects of Alexei's accession, Peter succumbed to a morosity that nearly broke him. Finally, he had Alexei arrested and ordered the application of tortures so as to learn the czarevitch's genuine motives. The questioners proved too conscientious, and in 1718, Alexei died under the strain. It was political murder, and Peter's responsibility was total. Peter died eight years later without naming his heir, and once again a succession crisis loomed. The senate quickly set up the tsar's widow Catherine as empress, but she died in 1727. For the next fourteen years, faction and clique fought bitterly over the Petrine inheritance, and the country never was in greater danger than during this time.

Most of the revolution held, however. The Muscovite boyars misjudged the intentions of the bulk of the country nobility. That the gentry had been bludgeoned into service by the czar there is no doubt. That its members considered many aspects of this service oppressive, particularly the years in the army and the drudgery of tax collecting, there is no doubt. That they feared the regime at St. Petersburg also cannot be denied. However, the Table of Ranks provided certainty that the highest offices of state were open to the most able and most ambitious and were no longer the exclusive preserve of the great boyars. In a well-ordered service state, an obscure squire might realistically contemplate becoming a general, senator, or department head. During the eighteenth century, provincial landlords and even one-time serfs illustrated this paradoxical society frozen in the law but mobile because of circumstance. Peter the Great's obsession to catch up with the West became the key element in Russia's increasingly complex heritage. The complacency of isolation had to yield room to a spirit of competitiveness in which individual ambition, channeled through service to the state, might produce vast rewards. The Russian compromise of power worked to the mutual advantage of the regime and landholding gentry. Its victims were great boyars, churchmen, a czarevitch, and several million peasants.

Chapter Five

Europe and the World

In the second half of the seventeenth century, relations between the European states and their advanced posts in America, Africa, and Asia assumed wider dimensions, as determined by commerce and warfare and influenced by religion. Mother countries demanded agricultural products and raw materials from their colonies either for sale at home or reexport abroad, and these goods were to be transported on the motherland's ships, which were to be manned by her crews and financed by her investors. Moreover, the colonists were supposed to purchase manufactured and industrial products from the motherland. Around the 1670s, calicoes and cottons from Asia and coffee and sugar from America began finding a European market, thus necessitating more efficient exploitation of native labor in the Far East and slave labor in the West. European rivalries, particularly between France and its enemies, extended to the colonial world. Now European armies fought pitched battles on overseas soil, and warfare strengthened the bonds between motherlands and their colonies. Finally, the age witnessed an extension of Catholic Europe's religious mission to the world, particularly in the direction of Asia. The effort dramatically brought home lessons in the perils of evangelization and affected Europeans themselves in ways that missionary priests could never have foreseen.

NORTH AMERICA

Cromwell and the later Stuarts considered the English mainland colonies of North America the centerpiece of a coherent imperial network that was subordinate to England and subject to its laws. The colonies had been founded as discrete units, protected by individual charters that determined their governance, but they deeply resented potential threats to religious traditions or economic concerns. Massachusetts Bay, in particular, wished to develop native manufacturing in defiance of the Navigation Acts and of the idea of subordinating colonial interests to imperial ones.

The Lords of Trade in London comprised the chief policy-making board for America. In 1684, upon the insistence of James, duke of York, the Lords agreed to establish a Dominion of New England that would revise, and ultimately dispense with, the individual charters held by Massachusetts Bay, New Hampshire–Maine, Connecticut, and Rhode Island. When James became king a year later, he intended to investigate all the North American colonial governments with an eye toward dissolving the twelve provincial assemblies and awarding their authority to tax, legislate, and select judges to royally appointed governors and councils. James also promised the colonies religious toleration, which colonists feared was a convenient screen for Catholicizing.

Certain that a new colonial union under royal leadership was necessary, James annulled the charters of Massachusetts Bay, Connecticut, Rhode Island, and New Hampshire–Maine. In 1687 the royal colony of New York joined the enlarged Dominion of New England. Sir Edmund Andros, a devoted courtier, was named dominion governor. Massachusetts Bay became a sullen, embittered colony. Its tenant farmers, frontiersmen, fishermen, and urban craftsmen joined the Puritan oligarchs recently dismissed from the old colonial assembly in unified resistance. When Boston learned of James's "abdication" early in 1689, the city exploded with joy. New England proclaimed its solidarity with the Glorious Revolution, and Governor Andros was thrown into prison. William and Mary restored the original charters to Connecticut and Rhode Island. By agreeing to have property rights rather than religion form the chief basis for suffrage, Massachusetts won back its charter. New Hampshire–Maine became part of an enlarged Massachusetts Bay.

To the north, French Canada was a completely different world. Louis XIV had little interest in his unexplored trans-Atlantic possessions that in 1660 possessed only 2,000 non-Indians, mostly missionaries and trappers. However, Colbert saw a place for them within his mercantilist system. Canada could supply fish and leather for France's West Indian sugar plantations, and both colonies could serve as dumping grounds for French manufactures. First, Canada would have to be settled. Despite Louis's avowed reluctance to encourage emigration, adventurous noblemen were attracted by the prospect of extending the seigneurial system to the New World. By 1670, Canada's French population grew to 7,000. Though England's acquisition of New York in 1667 barred French advance southward along the St. Lawrence, the expansionist vision of the governor of New France, Louis de Frontenac, and the king's *intendant*, Jean Talon, led to the exploration of and claims to tracts bordering the Great Lakes and the Mississippi. The English thus became hemmed in between the Atlantic and the Alleghenies. In 1682, the French explorer Cavelier de la Salle reached the mouth of the Mississippi and claimed the lands on both banks in the name of his unappreciative king. In contrast to New England's compact network of farms, towns, and fishing villages, New France remained a long thin string of isolated settlements running over 300 miles through the wilderness, from Trois Rivières and Montreal through Quebec and Hudson's Bay. The enormous Louisiana territory contained only a few fortified places. Wherever the French settled the land, a seigneurial class oversaw a peasant society, and the peasants in turn longed for the woods.

The War of the League of Augsburg (1689–97) brought the English and French colonists into open conflict. New Englanders hoped to conquer Canada, and Frontenac dreamed of a descent upon Boston and New York; but neither side possessed sufficient troops and arms. At the Treaty of Ryswick, the old boundaries remained intact, and the French still blocked the westward expansion of the English coastal colonies. Meanwhile, William III and the Whigs looked upon colonial autonomy as skeptically as James II and the Lords of Trade had. Pressures once more mounted to abrogate the colonial charters. Before any policy decisions could be made, a new war in Europe extended to America. In 1711, an Anglo-American army left Boston to conquer New France but was shipwrecked in the St. Lawrence estuary. Campaigns took the form of murderous frontier raids and reprisals. Both sides made alliances with native Americans and exploited tribal rivalries. At the Peace of Utrecht in 1713, the French gave up Acadia and Newfoundland. However, Canada was still theirs, and their claims to the Mississippi Valley remained in full force.

In 1713, New France contained 19,000 Europeans, but the demographic preponderance of the English colonies was overwhelming. Along the Atlantic seaboard were 400,000 English-speaking settlers. They had always been uncompromisingly particularistic about their habits and institutions. New Englanders reveled in their universal literacy, dissenting Protestantism, urban civilization, and local self-government. Unlike the aristocratic slave-holding planters of Virginia and the Carolinas, they had no desire to submit to London. New York and New Jersey were too royalist for them, Maryland too Catholic, and Pennsylvania too Quaker. At the same time, tensions were rising between the wealthy who controlled all the colonial assemblies and the unrepresented pioneers pushing out towards the wilderness. For the moment, the new dynasty in England promised to let matters rest, though the terrain was prepared for political and commercial disagreements between the colonists and the homeland, for social disagreements among the colonists themselves, and for renewed conflicts between French and English Americans.

LATIN AMERICA AND THE CARIBBEAN

By 1648, European civilization in Florida, Mexico, and South America was nearly 150 years old. The lands claimed by Spain contained more than ten million people, two million more than in Spain itself. Eight million were indigenous, while the remainder were whites, blacks, and people of mixed racial stock, representing the most important transplantation of European culture anywhere in the world. However, Spain's misfortunes meant a loosened grip on its colonies. Interlopers successfully challenged the homeland's trading monopoly, and the Spanish colonial administration governed by the Council of the Indies in Seville could no longer control Latin America's plantations and autonomous towns. Already the colonists were learning to fend for themselves. When revolution struck Latin America in 1811, the political fragments had been long settled. The republics that ultimately formed were the consequence of the weakness of the homeland.

A colonial aristocracy, the Creoles, filled the vacuum left by Spain. Though the viceroys, governors, treasury agents, and judges of New Spain (Mexico) and Peru were drawn from Europe, town councils and municipal magistracies were packed with American-born officeholders. Supported by a wealthy and influential clergy, the Creoles established the pattern of life in colonial society. Economically, it was built on a system of estate-labor enserfment (the *encomienda*); socially, it was built on racism (the exclusion of persons of mixed blood from the universities and professions); and politically, it was built on officeholding. All government posts, except the top one of viceroy, were sold, and the officeholders were businessmen out to maximize profit from their posts. The traffic in offices was notorious. Court favorites obtained them from the king and sold them to speculators who then found Creole purchasers. The holders of offices associated with legal or political duties charged for whatever services they dreamed up, and thus large sums of money went into uncreative favor-hunting enterprises that aggravated the stagnant, exploitative character of life in the colonial world.

Two major factors turned Spain's American empire into a liability in the second half of the seventeenth century. The homeland's commercial monopoly over the colonies broke down, and the silver yield of Mexico and Bolivia decreased catastrophically. While Dutch, English, and North American smugglers took care of New Spain's consumer needs, the Spanish treasure fleet stopped making its annual voyage to Cadiz. Spain grew unable to supply the cheap labor that the agrarian habits of Latin America demanded. Because the Spaniards had failed to develop West African slave stations, the government leased out short-term monopolies to the highest bidders. Merchant companies from Portugal, England, Genoa, and Holland held the supply contract, called the *asiento*, but smugglers from everywhere responded to the demand for slaves.

From 1648 to 1713, Spain knew nearly forty years of warfare. Privateering off the Latin American coasts became more organized and periodically interrupted commerce. At the Peace of Utrecht, the allies left Spanish America intact, both the English and Dutch preferring to break through the paper monopoly of Spanish trade rather than assume the responsibilities of governing lands whose natural resources appeared to be exhausted. In response to the problems of New Spain King Philip hoped to reform colonial institutions, and he did manage to slow down the sale of offices. He also planned to introduce *intendants* to attack corruption and made genuine efforts to appoint qualified adminstrators to the highest colonial posts. Renewed measures were taken to protect the American coasts against smuggling. However, Creole society resisted any concerted attempt to re-strengthen the bonds between motherland and colony, and eighteenth-century Spain lacked the sustained vigor to try.

In 1630, the Dutch had managed to seize control of Brazil, but in 1654, newly independent Portugal regained possession of its sprawling, barely explored colony. The settlers maintained a coastal civilization built upon a sugar-tobacco economy fed by regular infusions of slave labor from Portugal's African stations, Angola and Mozambique. Though more sparsely settled, Brazilian coastal society resembled that of Spanish America. Both were dominated by a landed aristocracy that was suspicious of the home-land and contemptuous of lower orders. Toward the 1680s, however, Brazil experienced a boom that knew no parallel anywhere else in the colonial world and transformed it into a pioneer land. Not content with settling in the civilized regions, an influx of Portuguese adventurers pushed deeply toward the west and south, where they cleared land for cattle raising and leather production.

However, gold was what wrote the greatest chapter in Brazil's colonial history. As far back as the sixteenth century, handfuls of tough, lawless adventurers searched the Sao Paulo plateau for precious metals. A few made strikes, but the overwhelming majority either perished in the wilderness or returned to the sugar and tobacco plantations, where they became foremen and slave drivers. In the 1680s, as strikes increased in frequency, immigrants and coastal inhabitants caught the fever and plunged westward toward the Minas Geraes and Matto Grosso. Up to 30,000 pioneers, dragging twice that number of black slaves behind them, pushed on toward the foothills of the Andes. Portugal took its percentage from the strikes. From the 1690s until 1715, it received as much gold from Brazil as Spain had received from all of its possessions in the previous 140 years. Gold created the Portuguese wine industry and helped pay for the armies that wore down Louis XIV. In Brazil, it forged a frontier world more individualistic and unruly than the stagnant, settled coast, possessing a vitality that was unique in Latin America.

The deterioration of the Spanish navy opened the Caribbean to adventurers from all over Europe, and governments as well moved in for the spoils. At St. Christophe, Martinique, and Guadeloupe, the French already had constructed a flourishing society and economy based upon slavery and sugar. To prospective settlers, the isles were far more attractive than Canada, and by 1650, 15,000 Frenchmen and 12,000 black slaves lived and worked there. In 1664, Colbert decided to regulate both immigration and the economy of the Antilles. He established the French West India Company to monopolize trade, but investment proved inferior to expectations, and in 1674, the islands were opened to all French vessels. Martinique and Guadeloupe were large and fertile. Sugar could be grown cheaply. Moreover, their location northeast of Caracas made them ideal way stations for smuggling goods into Spanish America. As the French Antilles became the focal point for privateering in the Caribbean, European merchants and shippers urged their governments to exploit the region at Spain's expense. From 1655 to 1670, England seized Jamaica, eastern Honduras, and the Bahamas. The Dutch held Caracas, and the French captured Haiti.

The late seventeenth century witnessed the perfection of the legal and illegal forms of the so-called Triangular Trade. The Caribbean was the nerve center of this commerce. The Dutch poured Africans into the West Indies. The slaves worked the plantations, which sent raw sugar and molasses to Europe's Atlantic ports, where the cargo was refined or converted into rum. The ships then headed to West Africa for more slaves. Newfoundland cod fed the black, and cheap European cloth dressed them. The French isles had the best-developed commerce in sugar and slaves, though Dutch shippers derived the greatest profits from this commerce. New England merchants defied the Navigation Acts by heading straight to Martinique for sugar and molasses. They willingly supplied the French planters there with fish, wheat, meat, tools, and timber. Skillful at cutting production costs, the French planters passed on the savings to whoever wanted their sugar. English merchants from Jamaica and Bermuda purchased raw sugar from the French and sold it illegally in London for less than the price asked by their own planters. Caught between high production costs and the loss of all their markets, English planters on Jamaica and Bermuda pleaded with Parliament to enforce commercial prohibitions between New England and the French Antilles. In the years following the Peace of Utrecht, they were instrumental in fomenting international tensions wholly out of proportion with their government's interests. Conflicts were provoked between Britain and Spain over their smuggling, then between Britain and France over their rivalries with French planters, and finally between Britain and the North American colonists over the latter's insistence upon trading for the best price irrespective of the nationality of the partner.

AFRICA

To seventeenth-century Europeans there were three Africas. North of the Sahara lay the Africa of Islam. Its eastern fringe was Egypt, a province of the Ottoman empire but in reality divided among semi-independent prefects whose civil wars kept Egypt in perpetual chaos and out of touch with the

Mediterranean world. West of Egypt lay Tripoli, Tunis, and Algeria, technically Ottoman regions as well but in reality autonomous provinces under
native deys and beys. Despising and fearing its coastal inhabitants, Europe
called this entire region Barbary. Under Barbary's flags, Moslems and renegade Christians alike participated in freebooting as an industry. West of
Algeria lay the cherifate of Morocco. From 1672 to 1727, the cherif Moulai
Ishmael pacified an empire that drove southeast to the Sudan. He ordered
and hierarchized Moroccan society and built a capital, Meknes, which
he ringed with fortresses. Blacks from the Sudan formed the bulk of his
150,000-man army. Moulai Ishmael conceded a trading station each to the
English and Portuguese, and the Spaniards held two of them. Periodically,
he would skirmish with the Europeans in their enclaves, but above all, he
desired civilized relations with their governments. Therefore, he exchanged
African cloths, indigo, ivory, and dates for European arms and munitions.
He suppressed piracy and fought Barbary's freebooters. He prided himself
on running the only indigenous African state with regular diplomatic contacts with Europe.

South of the Sudan lay black Africa. For centuries, nomadic Arab slave
hunters had eaten deeply into the vitality of the central part of the continent. However, the gravest menace of all proved to be the European slavers.
The Portuguese dream of a Catholicized black civilization stretching from
the Cape Verde Islands to Angola sadly yielded to the incentive of profits
in human flesh, and the Portuguese won the dubious distinction of being the
first Europeans to transform black Africa into a reservoir for America's
servile labor. In the seventeenth century, the Dutch took over the slave
trade along the Guinea coast in western Africa, and after 1715, the French
and English became the great European traffickers there. Promising rewards in rum and guns, the traders incited native chiefs against one another
and bought prisoners of war. Europeans rarely penetrated beyond the coastal stations. In eastern Africa, Arab merchants displaced the Portuguese as
the leading slave traders.

It is impossible to calculate the toll Africa had to pay for a forced emigration that reached 100,000 per year and in the eighteenth century averaged
75,000 annually. The victims were the most physically robust of its people—
young men from defeated armies and young women with the best chances
of procreating. Throughout the eighteenth century, the central section of
the continent knew incessant tribal warfare and demographic regression.
Native confederations to resist the Europeans and Arabs failed to hold
together. On the other hand, the native Ashanti, Benin, and Dahomeyan
kingdoms along the gulf of Guinea themselves profited from slave sales until
nineteenth-century forms of European exploitation based upon partition
and occupation eradicated them as political units.

On the entire continent, the southern tip alone served as a base for
European settlement in the seventeenth and eighteenth centuries. Since the

days of da Gama, the Portuguese had stopped periodically along the Cape of Good Hope. In 1652, the Dutch built a supply station for ships. Subsequently, the surgeon Jan van Riebeck led fifty Dutchmen to found the Cape Colony, and by 1680, more than 600 settlers had arrived, land-hungry and searching for a spiritual climate more receptive to their fundamentalist Calvinism than the tolerant, Arminian Netherlands. Five years later, the first boatload of Huguenot refugees from France joined them. Pushing into the interior, the pioneers broke with their European origins to a greater degree than did the English, French, and Latins in seventeenth-century America. Sustained by courage and religion, these Afrikaaners considered themselves a new chosen people. Their initial tolerance of the natives gave way to powerful sentiments of racial superiority. They took slaves. By 1715, the Afrikaaners had pushed through the mountain passes, overwhelming Bushmen and Hottentots to find good country beyond the reach of the East India Company that administered the coastal station. The European population of South Africa had reached 5,000. By the close of the eighteenth century, it increased fourfold.

ASIA INSIDE EUROPE: THE OTTOMAN TURKS

In the seventeenth century, the Ottoman Turks were the only Asians to dominate significant numbers of Europeans. From its vaguely defined limits along the Persian Gulf and south of the Caspian Sea, the Ottoman empire exerted hegemony over the Middle East and Anatolia, laid claim to Egypt, and called the Barbary States vassals. The Turks considered the eastern Mediterranean, Black Sea, Red Sea, and west Caspian as their waters. The heartland of the empire was in the Balkans, where Ottoman rule extended over Christian Greeks, South Slavs, Croats, Slovenes, and Magyars. At the empire's peak in the early 1680s, its northwest frontier was a bare eighty miles from Vienna, and in 1683, the Turks besieged the Hapsburg capital itself. The peoples subject to the Ottomans numbered from twenty-five to thirty million, belonging to assorted cultures and nations that grudgingly submitted to a tribute-collecting army of occupation, grasping governors, and province chiefs. The Turks could offer their subjects neither a moral nor legal justification for empire. The only reason for conquest was the extension of Islam, and even here the Turks no longer forced the issue.

Lacking a priesthood, the Ottoman empire could not be called a theocracy in the western sense. Nevertheless, Islam permeated all Turkish institutions. The fundamental reference for settling legal and adminstrative questions was the Koran, and the sultan's decrees were based upon his reading of Islam's holy book. Because they were also descended from Abraham, Christians and Jews were tolerated, though they had fewer rights and responsibilities than Moslems. They might participate in government, largely because the Turks had little aptitude for administration. Expelled Spanish Jews and Moriscos proved a boon to the Ottomans, providing them with artisans, businessmen, administrators, physicians, and sailors. The appeal of the warrior state for European talent is a thread running through Turkish history.

The empire was built upon the tribute of subject peoples, and it thrived on conquest. Peace glutted Istanbul with bored troops and provided opportunities for intrigue and revolt. The chief army officers, the *sipahis*, controlled hundreds of clients and their men. The Balkans replenished the army every generation. During five-year intervals, up to 15,000 able-bodied boys were taken from their parents, reared in special camps as Moslems, granted legal and social privileges, and taught an esprit de corps. They formed the sultan's elite guard, the Janissaries. In the seventeenth century, however, far from being the bedrock of the sultan's power, the Janissaries were the most dangerous element in the state. If the sultan was unable to pay their wages regularly, their discipline grew lax, and they became a restless force for sale to the highest bidder.

The lack of binding constitutional principles and legal understandings between ruler and subject, combined with the liberty of each sultan to interpret the Koran according to his particular political ends, made the Ottoman state seem like a hopeless tyranny to Europeans. Moreover, in the seventeenth century, political factionalism became particularly virulent. Since there was no rule of succession, relatives of the reigning sultan built their constituencies at court and in the harem and outbid one another for Janissary support. Government degenerated into a welter of intrigue and instability, which had serious consequences for the empire. Transylvania and Moldavia in the Balkans edged toward autonomy under native chiefs, and the Persians advanced upon the eastern frontier. In the 1630s, an energetic sultan, Murad IV, regained command of the state and forced the Persians to make peace. On his death, however, the old anarchy renewed itself, and in 1648, unpaid Janissaries deposed and murdered Murad's successor.

A seven-year-old child, Mehmed IV, was placed upon the throne and for his safety locked in his late father's harem. For the next eight years, the empire reached the nadir of its fortunes. Thirteen grand vizers, roughly prime ministers and chiefs of the army, rose and fell. Bread riots were endemic in Istanbul, revolts broke out in Anatolia and the Balkans, a war with Venice went very badly, *sipahis* in the provinces took over as petty tyrants, and sectarian dervishes stirred up religious passions and social unrest. Finally, early in 1656, a seventy-one-year-old former governor from Albania, Mehmed Köprülü, demanded total power. Janissary officers stood behind him, and he became grand vizer. Köprülü pitilessly purged government councils and eliminated all potential opposition. He pacified Anatolia and chased the Venetians from the Dardanelles. Köprülü's methods were ruthless, but they saved the state. In 1661, the old man died, and his twenty-six-year-old son succeeded him as grand vizer.

Ahmed Köprülü was an urbane, cultivated statesman and gifted military commander. He put the army to use again in the Balkans. Pacifying rebellious Transylvania, Ahmed set his sights upon the habitual and elusive goal of the Ottomans, the capture of Vienna. Its possession, Ahmed judged, would shatter the Hapsburgs and ensure Turkish control of the Balkans and Hungary for at least another generation. Therefore, an Ottoman army of 100,000 pushed northward but, in August 1664, was stopped at St. Gotthard (see p. 82). Emperor Leopold I hurriedly signed the Treaty of Vasvar with the Turks, recognizing their control of most of Hungary and their suzerainty over Transylvania.

In 1676, Ahmed Köprülü died, and his brother-in-law Kara Mustapha replaced him as grand vizer. Kara Mustapha cherished the idea of a renewed offensive toward Vienna, and the Magyar rebellion against the Hapsburgs provided him with the opportunity. Conspiring with Magyar chiefs who consented to Ottoman suzerainty, Kara Mustapha gathered together a magnificent cavalcade of 200,000 and reached the walls of Vienna in July 1683. Instead of immediately storming the city, the grand vizer adopted the strategy of a deliberate siege. The Hapsburgs thereby gained a respite, and Leopold pleaded with the princes of Christendom to save his capital. A relief force of Bavarians, Saxons, and Poles reached the Danube early in September. On September 12, the Christian army swept into Kara Mustapha's camp and crushed the besiegers, softened by two months of inactivity. The Turks suffered the most inglorious defeat in their history. Abandoning tents of silk, treasures, and slaves, they fled in panic. For the disgrace, Kara Mustapha was strangled and Mehmed IV was deposed.

This time, however, no change in leadership renewed the empire. Moving to the offensive, the Austrians captured Buda and smashed the Ottomans at Mohacs, where Hungary had lost its independence a century and a half earlier. Prince Eugene of Savoy destroyed the Turkish army at Zenta in 1697, and Peter the Great took Azov a year later. In 1698, for the first time in their history, the Turks sued for peace. At the Peace of Carlowitz (1699), they acknowledged the loss of Transylvania, nearly all of Hungary, and parts of Slavonia and Croatia to the Hapsburgs. The Venetians took Dalmatia, the Morea, and the Aegina. Poland obtained Podolia. In 1702, the Ottomans signed away Azov to the Russians. No longer were the Turks a menace to Europe. In 1718, at the Treaty of Passarowitz, they surrendered to the Hapsburgs lands south of the Danube, including their Balkan capital of Belgrade, the remainder of Hungary, and part of Wallachia.

Battlefield defeat not only shrank the empire but also changed its character. The Janissaries turned to petty trades in Istanbul, and the military vitality of the state was sapped. Incapable of adjusting institutions to peace, government reverted to rounds of conspiracies. In the provinces, wealthy

Greek Christians and *sipahis* rivaled one another for tribute-collecting rights over sullen populations. In place of leading armies into the Balkans, the sultan and his officials retired to Istanbul and Adrianople, where they indulged themselves in extravagant dances, concerts, and Chinese shadow-plays or took their martial glory vicariously by cheering on favorite participants in mock sea battles fought in the Dardanelles. Late in the century, again at war with European powers, the Ottomans found themselves on the defensive. Austria and Russia moved to clear the Turks entirely from the Balkans. Greeks and South Slavs stirred to throw off three centuries of humiliations. Europe's ancient terror was a generation or two away from becoming its sick man.

EUROPE AND THE ORIENT

Fortresses in the Canadian wilderness, sprawling sugar plantations in the Haitian countryside, tidy farms in the Transvaal, and gold mines in the valley of the Paraná characterized the triumph of European arms over nature and non-Europeans. The pace of conquest varied, yet it was an inexorable process that assumed full force in the eighteenth and nineteenth centuries. The indigenous peoples of America and black Africa were the earliest and most important victims of the tide, for even though Europeans gained commercial preeminence in the Orient, civilizations there discouraged colonization and resisted evangelization.

Initially, however, it appeared that India would offer an opening. During the second half of the seventeenth century, the Mogul empire of north India was cracking. Shah Aurengzeb (1659–1707) was a fanatical Sunnite Moslem, whose contempt for non-Moslem vassals resulted in enormous revolts among the Sikhs, Radjputs, and Marathas. From the 1680s on, civil war racked the subcontinent, and at Aurengzeb's death, disintegration of the Mogul state seemed complete. The Sikhs and Radjputs established their confederations in the northwest, but the Marathas could neither maintain permanent control over the center nor conquer the old satellite states of the Mogul empire in the south. The bloody struggles in India worked to the advantage of those prepared to exploit the divisions, and there was no shortage of Europeans willing to attempt just that.

The Portuguese had been the first Europeans to obtain commercial concessions and the right to establish trading stations along the coast of the subcontinent. By 1670, however, all that remained of da Gama's heritage were the outposts of Goa and Diu on the Indian Ocean. Though the Dutch had taken Colombo on the island of Ceylon and Cochin near the southwestern tip of the subcontinent, they were mainly interested in controlling the spice trade of the Moluccan archipelago and Indonesia, while the French at Surat and the English at Bombay and Madras wished to control India's coastal commerce. Chartered companies were the essential agencies of control. The English East India Company administered itself while the French company was an arm of the French government. Each firm had a resident governor general, and each was expansionist. From the 1670s on, a west European craze for light textiles, particularly brightly dyed cottons and calicoes, gave vent to a new flurry of commercial activity. The French added their trading stations at Pondichery, just below Madras, and at Chandernagor in the Bengal. In 1690, the English founded Calcutta.

Subsequently the disintegration of the Mogul empire drew the French and English into the chaos of Indian politics. To protect trade lanes the French governor François Marin sided with local chiefs, and both the French and English constructed fortresses and armed ships against pirates. Defending Bombay, the English fought pitched battles against the Marathas. They coined money, raised native troops, and made treaties with neighboring princes. The spread of Europe's wars overseas from 1689 to 1713 forced the rival East India companies to seek out native allies, and peace in Europe did not necessarily extend to India. Either as employees or soldiers of their respective companies, hundreds of adventurers set sail from Europe seeking their fortunes in Asia. Individual greed fed commercial and national rivalries. By 1740, the governor of the French company, Benoît Dumas, controlled a host of alliances with native princes, created battalions of Hindu troops, enjoyed the title of nabob, and extended French influence from Bengal to the gates of Bombay. This was no longer mere commercial exploitation. It was a bid for empire that the English had to challenge.

Nothing comparable to the Mogul empire encountered the first Dutch merchants to Indonesia early in the seventeenth century. The small Moslem sultanates that had thrived upon the localized spice trade simply traded with the Dutch. With the establishment of the East India Company in 1621, the Dutch began purchasing plantations. They exchanged Indonesian silks, spices, and pepper for Persian coffee, Indian cottons, and Chinese porcelains. Then they sent all these products to Europe. By the 1680s, most of Indonesia's sultans were Dutch vassals, retaining internal sovereignty, and enjoying the Europeans' "protection" in return for yielding a monopoly over stipulated exports. The Hollanders made no secret of their aim of pure economic exploitation. After a generation of contact and even intermarriage with the natives, the company's planters and merchants sealed themselves off from Indonesian society. Lacking the manpower to exercise total control over the sources of production, the Dutch eventually concentrated on carrying and selling goods. Until the mideighteenth century, their East India Company dominated Asia's carrying trade from Ceylon to Japan and controlled shipments to Europe of Indonesian pepper, nutmeg, and cinnamon. As in the Baltic and Atlantic, their specific role in the Far East was to ship products, particularly the products of others.

While the Europeans in late seventeenth-century India faced a decaying empire, those who penetrated China found one on the ascendancy. In 1664, the native Ming dynasty had succumbed to invading northern tribes, the Manchus. The Ming emperor was deposed, and in 1661, the year of Louis XIV's accession as sole ruler in France, a young Manchu warrior, K'ang-Hsi, became emperor of China. His impact upon eastern Asia proved at least as great as the Sun King's upon western Europe. During his sixty-one-year reign, K'ang-Hsi wiped out the vestiges of Ming resistance and crushed the pirates of the South China Sea. Pacifying the tribes of central Asia, he set the stage for the greatest territorial advance in China's history, which by the mideighteenth century reached the borders of India and turned southeast Asia from Burma to Vietnam into tribute-bearing states.

Under K'ang-Hsi, Manchu China entered her golden age. The state was reconstituted along military lines, and the Manchus established a bureaucratic aristocracy that rejected commingling with the natives. Army officers doubled as government officals, and Manchu soldiers took over the best lands. The conquering minority was exempt from taxation. Its members were prohibited from marrying Chinese women and by virtue of physiognomy, dress, and social habit stood apart from the mass. For the Chinese, the Manchu conquest was a rude shock. Thousands of bureaucrats chose suicide, while others joined in a fruitless guerrilla warfare. The Manchus destroyed the landlord system that had bound hundreds of thousands to Ming courtiers and favorites. This won the peasantry. The conquerors also adopted Chinese institutions that might serve the state, such as the examination system for the civil service and the tenets of orthodox Confucianism. K'ang-Hsi himself remained true to his warrior origins and spent several months each year at the head of his troops. His proudest accomplishment remained the taming of Mongolia. He was sincerely interested in both Buddhism and Christianity and took European Jesuits as close advisers. It was the tolerant, cultivated side of the emperor that captured the imagination of eighteenth-century Europe, which envisioned him as the archetypal Oriental sage, a philosopher-king.

Manchu China was open to Europeans, but it also had the power to resist them. The Treaty of Nertchinsk (1689) closed the Amur Valley to Russian settlement but opened the caravan route from Moscow to Peking. After 1702, the English, French, and Dutch began carrying Chinese tea to Europe. Though the Dutch had been transporting porcelain, lacquered ware, silks, and plants about Asia and to Europe, a seemingly insurmountable problem inhibited the establishment of genuinely great trading ventures. Except for gold and silver, the Manchus wanted few things that Europe could offer. Until the English East India Company was able to dump Indian cottons and opium into China, the great tea trade remained in its infancy, emerging only at the end of the eighteenth century.

Just as China slowly opened, Japan rudely closed. The emperor resided in the royal city of Kyoto, and his mayor of the palace, the *shogun*, oversaw the Council of State, ministers, and provincial governors. Until the middle of the sixteenth century, great landowners aided by their military retainers, the *samurai*, ran Japan. Civil war was endemic. The Japanese aristocracy had just finished another cycle in 1603, when Tokugawa Ieyasu became *shogun*. He forced the surviving landlords to assume government posts and spend every second year at the administrative capital, Yedo (Tokyo). All the landholders in Japan, including the powerful Buddhist orders, saw the reins of state service tightened around them. As the Tokugawas froze the social life of the state, defining specific roles for *samurai*, nobles, merchants, and peasants, they moved to save Japan from foreign contamination. In 1638, Japanese were prohibited from leaving the country, except by specific dispensation. European merchants and missionaries were expelled. Only a few Dutch, clustered together on a tiny island in Nagasaki harbor, where they could have no contact with the population, were allowed to remain. Japanese Christianity, which had 300,000 converts at the beginning of the seventeenth century, was suppressed. Martyrdoms reached 40,000, perhaps the most ruthless persecution ever committed against a Christian community. Meanwhile, only a few Dutch ships exchanged Japanese copper for Indian textiles and Indonesian spices. Until Commodore Perry boldly sailed into Nagasaki harbor in 1853, the West showed little interest in a nation that feared and scorned it.

In the Philippines, where sixteenth-century Spaniards discovered a culture much less sophisticated than what they found in India or China, Europeans most effectively implanted themselves. By the 1620s, two generations after their arrival, the Spaniards had converted two million Filipinos to Catholicism. They superimposed a centralized administration upon the island but handed local power over the populace to Europeans or natives assigned huge estates according to the *encomienda* system. The estate owner collected dues, tithes, and taxes, paid wages at his discretion, and controlled local justice. The Spaniards were largely interested in exploiting the Philippines as a vital commercial link between the Orient and Latin America. Each year, a galleon crossed the Pacific laden with Ceylon tea, Indonesian spices, Chinese silks, and Siamese teak. The Dutch tried to transport Chinese goods to Manila, but the Chinese insisted upon Mexican silver in exchange for their textiles. Seville and Cadiz wanted this drain of precious metal stopped or curtailed, but Manila and Mexico wanted it extended. Until the American veins were exhausted, the colonials prevailed over the homeland's interests. The only Asian country where Europe's religion gained more than a tenuous foothold, the Philippines experienced an exploitation of the land that resembled the Latin American plantation and served as a commercial link between the world's oldest civilization and her youngest.

THE MISSIONS

In the sixteenth century, Portuguese missionaries had evangelized success-fully in America and Asia. On the other hand, the zeal to win souls in black Africa soon was overwhelmed by the lust to chain bodies, and the slaver superseded the priest. In the New World, the Portuguese and Jesuit mis-sionaries defended native converts from exploitation by plantation owners, ranchers, and mining bosses. However, the great influx of Africans into Latin America made evangelization both more important and more dif-ficult. To slave masters, lessons on the equality of souls before God smacked of subversion, and the missions worked out a rather dubious compromise with society. Declared incapable of sustaining themselves, Africans were said to need masters who would treat them with firm paternal benevolence, nourishing and clothing them adequately. They were to be baptized and taught the elementary rudiments of faith. Uncomfortable with their accep-tance of black slavery, missionaries in the New World worked hard to prevent the indigenous populations from falling into the same category as the unfortunate Africans. In 1610, Jesuits established a refuge for natives in Paraguay, where colonists could not enter without permission of the priests. Most white immigrants considered the missionaries as meddlers, needlessly complicating social and economic relations that of necessity were based upon separatism and inequality. The episcopal hierarchy in the New World often shared the position of the settlers. Nevertheless, the missions kept the spark of social conscience flickering in a society depend-ant upon servile labor.

In Asia, where the missions often confronted mature societies and highly developed religious codes, the initial successes of the Portuguese and Jesuits were gratifying. By 1600, there were 300,000 Christian converts in Japan, an equal number in India, and a million and a half in the Philippines. China appeared ready for evangelization. Natives often had social or political reasons of their own for converting. In India, Christianity was attractive to low-caste women who wished to marry Portuguese. In Japan the Western-ers' religion won over landowners and *samurai* who wished to illustrate their independence of the *shogun* or Buddhist monks. By the seventeenth century, the Jesuits were responsible for Catholicism's Oriental mission, and Protestantism made virtually no impact. The Jesuits considered the missionary techniques of their predecessors as superficial. They insisted that converts learn the roots of basic doctrine, but they also adapted doc-trine to accommodate native habits, customs, and traditions. Rome praised the attempt to make new Catholics comprehend as well as believe, and initially the papacy showed itself remarkably tolerant of Jesuit respect for native cultures. By 1700, however, philosophies of evangelization that called for the converts' total submission to orthodox doctrine challenged

Jesuit methods. Stemming from Saints Paul and Augustine, they represented a purer approach to winning souls than that employed by the Jesuit fathers. But they also cost the Church Asia.

In India, the basic difficulties concerned the caste system and native beliefs in pantheism. During the first half of the seventeenth century, an Italian Jesuit, Father Robert di Nobili, insisted that Christianity's future in India depended upon its penetration of Hinduism. Therefore, Nobili tolerated the caste structure and began preaching to the highest ones, the Brahmins. An aristocrat from Rome, Nobili easily adopted the dress and habits of a holy man living in prayer and penitence. He resided in a rude hut, ate vegetables and drank water, abstained from beef, and passed his days in contemplation. He learned Indian dialects and read Indian poetry. Brahmins visited Nobili and admitted him to their caste. He translated the Psalms into Tamil. Claiming that he had brought a fifth Veda that complemented the four books of Hindu teaching, Nobili was highly successful in baptizing Brahmins. When he reached a native rite that even he could not accommodate to his syncretic Christianity, he called it political or social custom. Conscious of his rank in Indian society, Nobili kept his distance from native inferiors. He proferred them Communion on the end of a long stick or left the wafer at their door.

Nobili's techniques illustrated all the dilemmas Christianity would have to face in the mature civilizations of the Orient. His mission on the Malabar coast won 100,000 converts, but other priests denounced him as a secret Hindu. Asked for an opinion several times, the papacy approved Nobili's methods but in 1645 and 1649 noted the incompatibility between Christianity and the caste system. Nevertheless, Nobili's disciples followed in his footsteps, and by 1700, nearly a million Indians had accepted Catholicism. Partly based upon Dominican jealousies, in Rome a mood was developing against the Jesuit missions in the Orient. It also opposed the practice of religious syncretism and stressed the need for pure and total conversions. Reporting on the missions in India and China, in 1704 a papal legate, de Tournon, recommended condemnation of the "Malabar rites," calling them contrary to Catholic orthodoxy. With a million souls at stake, Rome fell short of invalidating the conversions already made. In 1745, however, Pope Benedict XIV formally declared the hostility of the Church to caste distinctions and Hindu customs. New conversions ceased, and old converts returned to the ancestral faiths.

The hostility of the Japanese Tokugawas to both Buddhism and Christianity was political. Christianized landlords and Buddhist monks had opposed the growth of the centralized state, and the *shoguns* persecuted their enemies ruthlessly. Officially proscribed and amply supplied with martyrs, Japanese Christianity went underground. By contrast, China opened the gate to evangelization. In their commercial enclave at Maçao, the Portuguese had made a few thousand converts in the sixteenth century. The

Jesuits, however, ingeniously accommodating Catholicism with Chinese customs and beliefs, made the greatest progress. Their skill in medicine, mathematics, and astronomy gave them access to the imperial court, and they became privileged subjects.

As early as 1600, a pair of Italian priests had introduced the Ming aristocracy to a Christianity that gave highest priority to principles of divine justice and divine reason. The Jesuits arrived and quickly displayed outward respect for Chinese civilization. They donned the costume of the scholar aristocracy, kneeled during audiences with officials, spoke humbly of themselves, and addressed their hosts with the accepted forms of exaggerated praise. They tolerated ancestor worship as a practice intended to teach respect for one's heritage, particularly useful in maintaining the social order; they even tried to accommodate nature worship with Christian principles. High Ming officials converted to Christianity. After a brief period of official hostility, the Manchus welcomed the Westerners as well. Father Scholl, superior of the mission to China, was named mandarin of the first class and appointed chief of the imperial department of astronomy, an important post in a country where astrology was a passion.

Ingratiating themselves at the court of K'ang-Hsi, the Jesuits also went out into the country. They built churches and by 1670 had won 300,000 converts. They served the emperor as military engineers, artillery experts, and diplomats. They helped negotiate the Treaty of Nertchinsk with the Russians. In 1692, a French Jesuit cured K'ang-Hsi with quinine, and in recompense, the emperor officially proclaimed the liberty of public Christian worship throughout China. The Jesuits had reason to hope that they were forging an Oriental Constantine.

Not only did the Jesuits bring Christianity to China, but they also brought China to Europe. In doing so, they provided impetus to an intellectual mutation that had been taking root since the Thirty Years' War. To the deeply troubled European civilization of the late seventeenth century, the Jesuit image of a near utopian civilization governed by moral sages uncorrupted by intolerance, passion, or material desire offered a refreshing contrast. K'ang-Hsi was viewed as a philosopher-king whose sense of justice and virtue made Leopold I or Louis XIV seem like moral pygmies. Europe swallowed fact and fancy about China. For the first time, a significant body of Western intellectuals cast doubts upon the ethical superiority of their own civilization, and this occurred at the precise moment when Descartes, Leibniz, and Newton were providing that civilization with rational explanations about the physical universe that Eastern sages could not hope to match. Cognizant of their technological and methodological superiority over all other peoples, Europeans were starting to ask: What was the value of all the new knowledge if one didn't know how to live?

For many, the most disturbing immediate problem posed by the discovery of China was its impact upon the historical veracity of the Bible. According to the calculations of the Jesuit scholar Martini, the Celestial Empire had been founded 660 years before the accepted date of the biblical deluge. However, Chinese annals contained no reference to the Flood. Could it therefore have been merely a local episode, important only to the Jews and their immediate neighbors? Scholars estimated that Oriental civilization preceded even the accepted date of Adam's fall. Was it possible that he was the ancestor of the Jews alone, and not of humanity? China past and present was calling to question the universal necessity of Christianity while suggesting that biblical chronology was incorrect.

The seeds of self-doubt that the Jesuit image of China had planted in Europe coincided with the mood in Rome for investigating Jesuit missionary practices in India and China. Dominicans and Franciscans who had practiced mass conversions in the Philippines insisted that Chinese nature and ancestor worship were polytheistic. The Jesuits responded that in their hearts the Chinese worshipped the true God. Gentle prodding rather than wholesale condemnation of their customs would result in the conversion of millions. The Jesuits pointed to encouraging signs: in 1688, during the funeral procession for one of their number, imperial guards marched behind banners of the Virgin and child Jesus. Four years later, the emperor gave his blessing to free Christian worship. By 1701, more than 100 missionaries served in 244 churches in China.

In Europe, however, the tide had turned against the Oriental missions. In 1700, the Sorbonne condemned ancestor worship and other "Chinese rites." Four years later, the legate de Tournon, fresh from his investigation of Jesuit practices in India, arrived in Peking. By his arrogance, de Tournon so irritated K'ang-Hsi that the emperor expelled him from the country. In 1707, Pope Clement XI declared the Chinese rites idolatrous and ordered the Jesuits to repudiate them. K'ang-Hsi was infuriated that Europeans who could not even read Chinese characters were judging as idolatrous practices that he himself considered to be civil, not religious, customs. The emperor expelled missionaries who abided by Rome's decisions. By now, however, the Chinese themselves were questioning the compatibility of Catholic orthodoxy with their traditions. The dualism of Christian theology was unintelligible to them; the exclusiveness of the Western religion was repugnant; its glorification of poverty presented a danger to society. Even China's earlier receptivity to European technology and the fruits of inductive reasoning waned.

Paradoxically, the Oriental hold upon secular European culture grew progressively stronger. Among the leisured classes in Europe, the outward trappings of Chinese civilization became a rage. Porcelains, lacquer ware, furniture, and the architecture of the pagoda and pavilion captivated tastes. Flora and fauna of the East adorned arboretums and zoos in London and Paris. Great atlases of China, India, and the Pacific were printed. Learned societies published papers on Oriental customs, and novelists gave birth to the Oriental tale. Except for the clergy, the West's reception to the East remained warm. China above all was wise, with much to teach. The philosopher Leibniz planned on importing Chinese scholars for the instruction of Europe's statesmen and thinkers. He dreamed of a new international language of the learned, based upon Chinese ideograms. In the end, Rome's feud with the Jesuits gave eighteenth-century sinophilism a genuine cutting edge. Admitting the value of the East became a way of identifying what was wrong with the West. The early Enlightenment thinkers, pro-Chinese and hostile toward Rome, created in the image of the Orient what they wished their Europe would become.

Chapter Six

The Age of Reason

THE RELIGIOUS CULTURE

For the overwhelming majority, religion remained the most important cultural force in European civilization. The decisions of governments were often based upon religious motives, while scientists and philosophers had to consider the religious climate of their societies before publicizing their discoveries. The epoch opened with the settlement of a religious war and closed with religious crises smoldering in places as far removed as France and Russia. The European penetration of the Orient depended upon missionary activity and foundered upon the shoals of religious controversy. Queen Christina of Sweden abdicated for religious reasons, while King James II of England was deposed for them. Most rulers believed that God had chosen them to govern. The Hapsburgs considered divine intervention to have been responsible for their successes over the Turks, and even the idea of a crusade still flickered. Women and men remained willing to endure persecution and death for their beliefs. Everywhere, devout sectarians challenged the conscience and stimulated the anger of the majority: Puritans and Catholics in England, Huguenots in France, Pietists in Germany, Lutherans in the Hapsburg lands, Old Believers in Russia.

Catholicism retained a remarkable vitality. In Spain, Portugal, and Austria, magnificent baroque abbeys and churches soared in testimony to the triumph of the Counter-Reformation. There the Church owned up to half the land and collected the tithes of an overworked peasantry. France revealed another face of Catholicism. There king challenged pope, saintly men and women challenged king, and the religious controversies of the day filtered down into the parishes. Amid Europe's Catholic peasantry, religion was all-consuming and laden with superstition. Believers sacrificed animals to the Virgin, prayed to the new moon, and venerated the sources of streams. They made curative pilgrimages to sites of miracles. Book peddlers carrying their wares to villagers able to read aloud to others had their sacks filled with saints' lives, collections of psalms, catechisms, and stories linked to Christ's Nativity and Passion. The faithful believed in the necessity of witch hunts and resisted the Church's attempt to stamp them out. Satan was everywhere, and his creatures had to be eradicated. Thus social noncon-formists, the mentally unbalanced, heretics, vagabonds, Jews, and Moors were the scapegoats upon whom people thrust responsibility for their pri-vate sins.

After 1650, the Church made a supreme effort to spiritualize peasant Catholicism and reduce its magical content. A better-educated clergy was sent to rural parishes, placing stress upon scriptural teaching, the sacra-ments, and the catechism. The Church attacked semipagan folk festivals and declared war upon the veneration of bric-a-brac that transformed churches into sacred warehouses. Wherever tolerated, Jesuits reinvigorated Catholicism as royal confessors and teachers in schools and colleges. They were receptive to the new science and led the Catholic reconquest of Bohemia, Poland, and Hungary. They had ambitions for Russia and, as we have seen, the Orient.

In Protestant Europe, the prince was chief administrator of a country's Church, even though he might not share the confession of the majority of his subjects. If one was not ruler, however, deviation from the majority usually spelled civil disabilities, special taxes, and occasionally expulsion. Subservience of the Protestant Churches to the prince possibly led to sterili-ty of faith, indifference, and Catholic advance, particularly in the Lutheran regions of Germany and Scandinavia. By reading decrees from the pulpit, helping recruit for the army, registering births, marriages, and deaths, and preparing tax lists, the German Protestant clergy doubled as political func-tionaries. Each Sunday, pastors preached to the flock the virtues of integri-ty, submission, and obedience.

Yet, it was within this orthodox environment that Pietism, the continent's most important Protestant revival, occurred. Pietism was a grass roots movement of individual believers desirous of restoring zeal, passion, and social concern to both Lutheranism and Calvinism. Most Pietists invigorat-ed the traditional confessions, but others splintered off into new sects. Firebrand preachers and tireless hymn writers inspired the flock. Fellow-ship centers admitted all social elements to their halls, from nobles to vagrants, and thousands learned to read their Bibles in the movement's primary schools. The rays of Pietism extended to Scandinavia and Holland. They inspired Methodism in England and the Great Awakening in Amer-ica. In Germany, Pietism rescued Protestantism from the stranglehold of the state, offered the laity a deep religious experience, and even provided a semblance of cultural unity to a civilization fragmented into hundreds of political pieces.

Eastern Orthodoxy knew nothing comparable to the Jesuits or Pietists. In the Balkans and Russia, revival took the form of movements resisting liturgical or administrative Church reforms. In the lands under Turkish occupation, Slavic Christians resented that their Church, suffering its Babylonian Captivity, was headed by the sultan's Greek puppet in Istanbul. This patriarch and his officials collected the sultan's tribute, recruited for his armies, and sought to "purify" Slavic folk rite and liturgy with Byzantine forms. Thus, the Balkan peoples welcomed Peter the Great as liberating them from the infidel and his Greek servants. However, many Russians who saw Peter firsthand regarded him otherwise, as an Anti-Christ who retained Nikon's liturgical changes, poked fun at services, cut beards, expropriated monasteries, and secularized Russia's Church administration. Deep inside the country, far away from St. Petersburg and its spirit, the reaction set in. Priests simply ignored the reformed rites, stuck to the old Russian forms of prayer, and insisted upon the magical properties of their service. Thus Holy Mother Russia engaged in a conspiracy of unresponsiveness that would pay dividends in subsequent generations. In Russia as well as the Balkans, cultural nationalism had religious roots.

Despite elements of spiritual revival in the late seventeenth century, secular values were rapidly influencing European life. By 1715, it had become unacceptable to go to war in the name of rival Christian creeds, and within states themselves, some princes began to see the political and social impracticality of inconveniencing religious minorities. In their quest for new settlers, German princes in Brandenburg and Saxony deemed religious affiliation to be a private, not public, matter, a position which the Dutch were to accept too. A sense of piety caused Cromwell and Sweden's Charles XII to respect the religious convictions of most other Protestants, and whatever discomfort Catholics and Anglicans suffered during the English Interregnum of 1649 to 1660 was due to their suspect politics. Since credal affiliation could easily be confused with political loyalty, bigoted rulers like Louis XIV or Leopold I failed to see how non-Catholics could ever be loyal subjects; and even Cromwell had ingrained doubts about non-Protestants. Nevertheless, citizenship as a secular idea was taking root.

Religious toleration was assisted by a growing critical spirit regarding matters of faith that ridiculed unproven credulity and weakened traditional belief. Out of the carnage of the Thirty Years' War and Puritan revolution emerged the first generation of European intellectuals to repudiate witch hunts, scorn oracles, and deny the supernatural message of comets. Contempt for superstition evolved into doubts over more hallowed forms of dogma, especially that which appeared to contradict the course of natural phenomena. Europe's most honored scientist, Sir Isaac Newton, considered himself a devout Christian and his incessant labors on biblical chronology revealed him to be a highly pedantic one. Still, Newton's theories of the physical universe rendered it impossible for him to accept the dogma of the Holy Trinity, and his honesty was respected. In such a climate, intolerance had to be on the defensive.

The well-publicized view of René Descartes offered an important theoretical justification for religious toleration. In his *Discourse on Method*, Descartes enunciated rational supports for the existence of God. Insisting, however, that his overriding concern was with matters of knowledge and not belief, he avoided pursuing questions of dogma. Nevertheless, the Catholic Church sensed the potential danger of summoning privileges, doctrines, and institutions before the bar of Reason, and Descartes's *Discourse* was placed on the Index of prohibited books. The gesture was futile. Dutch, French, and Swiss presses poured out editions and translations. By the end of the century, Cartesianism was a respected philosophical school, and in Catholic France, it was even dominant. Moreover, it served toleration's cause. If religion was exempt from rational analysis, a humanly contrived institution, the state, could not determine which religion was correct and which was false. In England, a rival philosophical school, empiricism, offered an even more perplexing hypothesis. Rejecting Descartes's position on innate ideas, empiricism held that our experience determines the sum of our knowledge. Therefore, should not religious truth, like knowledge, derive from universal consent? The immense variety of religions ought to cast a long shadow of doubt upon the absolute validity of any single creed, the will of princes and opinions of their theologians notwithstanding.

The father of modern empiricism, John Locke, remained an Anglican because Anglicanism best responded to his own experience. Locke, however, had no motive for refusing to respect the beliefs of others. Furthermore, Locke conjured up the idea of a widespread "Invisible Church," a voluntary association of individuals united in their desire to worship God. Locke's position was compatible with that of the German philosopher Leibniz, who spent a lifetime seeking common religious ground for Protestants and Catholics. And Jesuits in the Orient, who tried to accommodate Catholicism to religious principles shared by reasonable, civilized pagans, surely were under the influence of a new mood of religious tolerance. Most significantly, a quest for "natural religion" captivated intellectuals of the period. Scientists and philosophers sought out religious precepts that governed the human consciousness as universally as the laws of motion were shown to govern the physical world. The story of fallen humanity, the passive plaything of evil, earthly forces, needing a redeemer outside nature to attain salvation, gave way to a conception of the individual as a divinely created being placed upon the earth as God's pampered child expressly to unlock His secrets in nature. "The heavens declare the glory of God," became the watchword of the fathers of natural religion. Because God must embody Supreme Reason, the Christian cosmology of a universe suffused with corruption no longer made sense. Rather the majesty of God manifested itself in natural laws. Physical scientists became the theologians of the future, authoring bombastically titled texts such as *Physico-Theology, or a Demonstration of the Being and Attributes of God From His Works of Creation.*

Others used mathematical formulas to try to prove particular confessional viewpoints. However ludicrous the approaches appear, religion was being emancipated from terror, fear, and prejudice, and an especially critical eye was being cast upon the teachings of both Protestant and Catholic Christianity.

For good reason, guardians of the Christian tradition were worried. The bitter Jesuit-Jansenist controversy, revocation of the Edict of Nantes, and Rome's mishandling of the controversy over the Chinese rites invited attacks on Christian dogmatism. One of the most effective critics was the journalist-pamphleteer-scholar Pierre Bayle. A Huguenot from southern France, Bayle knew intolerance firsthand. While Bayle fled the persecution of Louis XIV and found refuge in Rotterdam, a less fortunate brother lost his life to the *dragonnades*. William III liked Bayle's sardonic denunciations of the French king and his offensive against superstitions. However, Bayle's submission of bible history to the test of Reason and scholarship proved too much even for enlightened Holland, and his pen cost him a university professorship. Still, he remained active. Bayle argued that atheists might possess moral codes as elevated as the devout. He wondered whether God could be all-knowing and all-benevolent if He had foreseen the Fall and done nothing to avert it. In his *Historical and Critical Dictionary* (1695–97), Bayle spared no sanctimonious tradition, no inconsistent or intolerant doctrine, no barbarity committed in the name of divine revelation. Bayle doubted every unproven hypothesis and submitted all to Reason's test. To his mind, proof by universal consent might simply mean that everyone could be wrong. Treading paths even Descartes called off limits, this independent thinker insisted he was a Christian. His Christianity, however, could never be the repository of unquestioned tradition and fundamentalist belief.

Nor could it be for his Catholic contemporary, the French Oratorian priest Richard Simon. Expert philologist and ancient historian, Simon is one of the founders of modern biblical scholarship. His histories of the Old and New Testaments (1678, 1702) included allegorical and symbolic interpretations of many texts, and he challenged Protestant literalism. Catholic orthodoxy tried unsuccessfully to silence him. Like Bayle, the Oratorian priest protested his good faith. He was certain that in excluding myth from Christianity he was performing a service for belief.

However, biblical scholarship could not remain for long in the hands of critics who wished Christianity well. Bishop Bossuet thundered: "A great battle is being mounted against the Church, under the banner of Cartesian philosophy." Scholarly efforts to apply to religion the reasoned proofs of scientific inquiry seemed to be leading either to skepticism or sophistry. The Churches could bid good riddance to Saint George's dragon, the portable head of Denys the Aeropagite, and much of the myth in folk religion. But could Genesis, biblical chronology, or the Incarnation itself survive the probes that now were entering the body of Christian lore? Was it really necessary for science and mathematics to pinpoint the celestial position of paradise? Orthodox hierarchies agreed with most Pietists, Jansenists, and Old Believers that reasoned criticism might indeed be the devil's curse. For the first time since the fourth century, Christianity was placed on the defensive; and the threat was from within.

THE GOD OF THE PHILOSOPHERS

For philosophers compelled to explain the reciprocal relationships between man and God in terms conforming to Reason, it no longer was a question of God the savior, but rather of God the author of Nature's laws. Such thinkers wished to enter the realm where Descartes had feared to tread and construct entire theologies in accord with the universe of measured facts. The dangers were obvious. For example, once the English philosopher Thomas Hobbes concluded that matter alone conformed to objective reality, he lost God altogether. However, atheism based upon a materialist world view won few converts in the seventeenth century. The search for a rationally explicable God was more appealing. It might generate from the Cartesian construct, the product of the thinker's ability to reason abstractly, or it might emerge from the empiricist mold, born of experience and pragmatic need. Whatever the approach, the minds and eyes of most European intellectuals from 1648 to 1789 were focused upon the author of Nature. Whether or not this deity satisfied emotional or existential needs was parenthetical.

The system of Baruch Spinoza was among the most important of the new creeds. Born in Amsterdam to a family of Portuguese Jews who had fled persecution, Spinoza imbibed both his ancestral religion and the new science. The conflict of his learning became readily apparent, and at twenty-four, Spinoza was expelled from the synagogue for expressing ideas antithetical to Judaism. He spent the remainder of his days at his trade of lens grinding and at working out a metaphysics, ethical system, and political theory. The audience of this humble renegade Jew was impressive. He knew the De Witts and corresponded with princes, the secretary of England's Royal Society, and Leibniz. Fearing that an official academic position might compromise his liberty of thought, he declined a professorship at the University of Heidelberg. His career exemplifies the evolution of the philosophers' Europe, in which customary political, religious, and social barriers had fallen.

Spinoza made his reputation with an impressive critique of Descartes's thought. Mind-body dualism did not convince him at all; nor could he dispense with God as an active force in the physical world. Nevertheless, as a rationalist, Spinoza had little use for unproven scriptural claims and miracles, a personal savior, and established Churches. He envisioned God as primary reality, not necessarily creating the universe and then standing aside, but identical with the universe, immanent in both matter and thought. People were part of Him, indistinct from Him, modes of divinity as it were. Spinoza was a pantheist, with a spiritual home neither in Judaism nor Christianity, and he was anathema to the Cartesians. Above all, Spinoza was a moralist and builder of an ethical system. If God was all, the individual who understood himself as indistinct from God would reject the folly of personal desire and not be tormented by guilt and sin. He would opt for a brotherhood of the spirit with other creatures, recognize the unproven subjectivity of sectarian theologies, and depend completely upon the God of Divine Reason. The lifetime of the perceptive individual would be spent in contemplation, study, and the perfecting of his morals.

Because the concept of God the creator was so deeply ingrained in the Western religious tradition, Spinoza's pantheism was usually misconstrued as atheism. Fellow philosophers asked how morality could be built upon anything except divine commandments. How much safer it would be to use Cartesian principles as proof not only of God's existence but also His workings. This is what a French priest, Nicolas Malebranche, attempted to do. Malebranche concluded that divine intervention was what made the body obey the mind's will. Certainly Nature functioned according to God's laws, but human action necessitated the occurrence of countless little miracles. To some rationalists, this constant intervention smacked too much of mysticism, while the Catholic Church condemned Malebranche for his loyalty to Descartes. Nevertheless, European intellectuals hungering to make Cartesian rationalism compatible with Christian belief chose Malebranche as their high priest. His fame was such that Chinese philosophers asked the Jesuits about him. Above all, he frustrated the spread of Spinoza's theories.

By 1715, newer explanations of the philosophers' God were catching hold. The most important of these was promoted by Leibniz. Scholar, courtier, and diplomat, advocate of religious union and discoverer of infinitesimal calculus with Newton, Leibniz shared the peak of Europe's intellectual life. His correspondence was large and influential. He founded learned academies and contributed more to the free exchange of ideas than anyone else of his time. He could not abide Spinoza's pantheism, and Malebranche's elaborations of Descartes seemed inconsistent with his own conceptions about the workings of the universe. Entranced by the concept of infinitesimals and the discovery of both microscopic cells and spermatazoa, Leibniz theorized a universe filled with tiny self-contained metaphysical organisms called monads. These were the necessary agents of divine creation, independently operating. Yet, it was essential for monads to relate to one another. How, for example, could mind perceive tree? Leibniz held that God synchronized the movement of monads. For every perception within a monad at a given time, there arises a corresponding perception within another monad. Taken as a whole, the activity of monads fulfilled a divine plan of preestablished harmony. God acted freely to foreordain this most systematically logical of worlds, and God is benevolent. Vulgarized, Leibniz's notions brought him enormous popularity in the early eighteenth century and helped create one of the most complacent attitudes of mind in Western intellectual history. Faith in preestablished harmony guaranteed a sufficient reason for why anything should be as it is, since God knows and plans for the best. Leibniz's enthusiastic disciples attributed to him the resolution of the problem of evil. Confidence in the ability of divine intelligence to manipulate monad after monad according to a providential pattern was a tempting means of explaining away the most seemingly incomprehensible horror without reference to bothersome points on the origins of evil and human corruption. Leibniz's *Theodicy* (1710) and commentaries on it went through dozens of editions.

Their criticisms of established religion notwithstanding, the philosophers often looked like old-fashioned sectarians hurling so-called truths at one another. To further complicate matters, some, like Hobbes and Leibniz, paid lip service to traditional Christian formulas while disbelieving them. More than most, John Locke was disturbed by the difficulties of reconciling Reason with Revelation. He accepted the validity of certain extrarational ideas on the basis of what he called their clarity, but he was uncomfortable doing so. Blaise Pascal stands out, however, as having served science and tested some philosophic theologies, only to find them wanting. He returned to Christianity simply because, in his view, it best explained the human condition. Born in 1623 and living only thirty-nine years, Pascal haunted subsequent generations long after Malebranche's occasionalism and Leibniz's monadology had lost their disciples.

As a brilliant young mathematician, Pascal had spent much time among the critics of orthodox Christian doctrine. In 1646, Jansenism attracted him, and his *Provincial Letters* (1657) provided a highly effective polemic against Jesuit theories on grace and salvation. Moreover, Pascal underwent a mystical experience during which a sense of his human weakness overwhelmed him. He offered himself to the God of mercy and spent the remainder of a life wracked with pain and illness composing epigrams that reduced arguments to a few trenchant words or sentences of revelatory insight. After his death, several hundred of these were found. First published in 1670, the *Thoughts* have become one of the masterpieces of French literature. Systematizing them is impossible, but they prove that Pascal never relinquished the reasoning process. Like Descartes, he subjected all knowledge to question and doubt. Applied to Nature and Nature's God, however, Reason taught Pascal nothing. Instead of gaining a sense of security from the celestial harmonies, Pascal found himself "engulfed in the immensity of spaces whereof I know nothing, and which know nothing of me. I am terrified. . . . The eternal silence of those infinite spaces frightens me." When he examined the human condition, Pascal discovered passion, self-interest masquerading as Reason, foolishness, and just plain error as customary guides. Observing that all he knew affirmed the tragedy of human existence, Pascal pleaded with philosopher, skeptic, and unbeliever to take the leap of faith. If the Christian God exists, all is won. If He does not exist, nothing is lost. But to a generation of intellectuals who failed to share Pascal's fears of the infinite spaces, Pascal's wager made little sense. He wanted to address himself to the intellectuals of his day, to point out the folly of their rational cosmologies, and to win them back to a religious position that he considered consistent with humanity's genuine state. But he was both too late and too early. Euphoric over the use they could make of mathematics and empirical science, Pascal's contemporaries were caught up in the spirit of discovery rather than bewilderment, and the secularization of European culture was quickly becoming a fact.

THE SCIENTIFIC CULTURE

That Pascal's plea went unanswered was partly due to a new image of scientific inquiry that had emerged in the first half of the seventeenth century. Systematic analysis and experiment turned previously accepted conclusions about the state of reality into apparent guesses built upon casual observation. The idea of the universe as a living, breathing organism, comprehended according to its qualities or principles of behavior, where miracles and spontaneous generation were accepted, was repudiated in favor of a conception of the celestial machine, understood only through measurement, calculation, and quantitative prediction of its working parts. A new method, commencing with axioms, definitions, postulates, and hypotheses and concluding with experiments, was enshrined as the only way to discover certainty about the workings of the real world. Mathematics would compel Nature to unlock her secrets.

By 1650, devotees of the new method, known as the geometric spirit, represented the most important intellectual community in western Europe. Members visited and corresponded, exchanged theories in books and letters, and acquired a fraternal sense that transcended national boundaries, religions, and political ideologies. They were creating a new culture. At the same time, the gulf between themselves and the overwhelming majority of Europeans had become immense and, by decision of the geometers themselves, unbridgeable. For the first time since the fall of the Roman Empire, an intellectual elite was pursuing approaches to God, man, and the universe that the rest of Europe could hardly comprehend, much less share. Nor did the new elite mask its contempt for the older culture.

The protectors of the older culture were the universities and the Churches.

With few exceptions, European universities in the midseventeenth century were medieval institutions. Nonexperimental science had a revered place in the mathematics quadrivium and Aristotle's natural philosophy in the arts. Scientific education took the form of lectures and commentaries upon Euclid, Ptolemy, and Galen. At the Sorbonne in Paris, Descartes was condemned, and Harvey's theories on blood circulation rejected out of hand. The contempt of university-educated physicians for surgeons empirically trained in modest surgical colleges held back the development of modern medical practice. Professors in the older universities who were receptive to certain new theories did not dream of practical research. They only asked for the right to offer mathematical and empirical methods as possible alternatives to Aristotle and the ancients. The new science made slow inroads. The admission of Isaac Newton to the Cambridge faculty and Edmund Halley to Oxford's linked these hallowed institutions to researches conducted in London by the Royal Society. Guided by a progressive physician, Herman Boerhaave, Leyden University incorporated findings in physiology, chemistry, botany, and physics into its medical program. Nevertheless, Leyden was exceptional. Most older universities were bound by their corporate character and traditions, their faculties filled with pompous beadles entrenched in the security of privilege and thriving upon academic ritual.

It was in Germany that the modern state-sponsored university emerged. At Halle in Brandenburg (1694) and later Göttingen in Hanover (1734), faculty were civil servants, the brainpower of the emerging bureaucracies. Professors were to do research and teach. To the political authorities they submitted regular reports of their work and their students' attendance at lectures. Though the professor as state servant was to have tragic consequences for modern Germany, in the eighteenth century, the faculties of Halle and Göttingen rose to preeminence. Princes paid for libraries and scientific equipment. Professors ranged freely over a panorama of scientific and humanistic learning. The cooperative research seminar was born, the prototype for the community of scholars unencumbered by the past.

Nevertheless, it was outside the universities that the new culture became fashionable. Wishing to bask in the sunlight of their beneficiaries' discoveries, princely patrons subsidized private research. Under government protection, learned societies emerged. The model was the Accademia del Cimento of Florence (1657–67), supported by the Medicis, where for the first time, professionals met for the exclusive purpose of conducting cooperative experiments and publishing their research. The most spectacular new organization, the Paris Academy of Sciences, was underwritten by Louis XIV. For about eight years, a group of Parisian savants had been meeting irregularly. In 1665, Colbert offered them a place on the king's payroll, comfortable living and working quarters, and the promise of an astronomical observatory. Members comprised a privileged elite, but their lives were regimented. They had to live in Paris, meet twice weekly, and agree to government-defined holidays. Academicians understood the price of royal patronage, but only rarely did Louis's bellicosity and intolerance cost him a scholar. From the beginning, the Paris academy stressed the useful aspects of research, and its concern for technology and demonstration opened scientific inquiry to a wider public than had been the case earlier. Because of the academy, the new culture appeared less mysterious, less subversive, and more respectable.

The Royal Society in London was much different from the Paris academy. Private individuals, not the state, subsidized it. Chartered in 1662 and publishing its *Philosophical Transactions* from 1665, the Royal Society remained both underfinanced and free from political influence. Presided over by Isaac Newton from 1703 to 1727, it was particularly revered in the world of early modern science. Of primary importance were experiments in mechanics and optics, but it also promoted smallpox inoculation. Elsewhere in Europe, where absolutist princes hankered after investments in prestige, the French institution rather than the English served as the prototype. In underdeveloped states, the academy could become an important agency of government. Peter the Great's academy, established in 1725, supervised education, book publishing, and technological innovations. In more advanced states, provincial academies blossomed. They specialized in science but also contributed to local history and folklore. By 1760, France alone had forty such institutions.

The most important generation in the history of science had been that of 1620 to 1650, when Galileo, Kepler, Harvey, and Descartes rejected the formulations of Aristotle, Ptolemy, and Galen. Doubt, experiment, observation, and reason overwhelmed the prestige of the past, and demands for precision caused scientists to concentrate upon the concrete and the measurable. Laggard as it was, after 1650 technology, too, betrayed concern for exactitude. Scales, barometers, compound microscopes, and telescopes were perfected. In 1656, Christian Huygens demonstrated how the isochronism of the pendulum could be incorporated into a mechanical clock, thus creating a measuring device that all could use. In 1690, Sir William Petty published his *Political Arithmetick*, the first serious attempt to estimate the number of individuals belonging to occupational groups within society itself. Several years later, the French academician Bernard de Fontenelle underscored the prestige of the scientist when he wrote: "A work on morals, on politics, and on criticism, perhaps even on eloquence, will be better ... if it is written by a geometer."

The central scientific event of the century was the discovery of a mathematically and empirically verifiable law of motion that indisputably confirmed the mechanistic interpretation of the universe. The *Mathematical Principles of Natural Philosophy* (1687) of Sir Isaac Newton became the point of reference for all the exact sciences. Newton synthesized the advances in celestial mechanics that had been developing ever since the problem of a mathematically defined force of attraction in the universe had been touched upon two centuries earlier. Newton proved that bodies in the heavens and on earth were subject to the same laws of motion.

Newton's great synthesis emerged in two bursts of creativity, each lasting approximately a year and a half. The first occurred in 1665–66, when Newton was in his early twenties. He had rejected the Aristotelian theories on planetary movement, and the unverified Cartesian hypothesis of a universe filled with celestial fluid that sustained the sun and planets seemed to him absurd. Nor could he believe Descartes's claim of planets whirling about in vortices. Cartesians, Newton thought, looked at the universe as a whole rather than as particular phenomena. In Newton's view, only a meticulous analysis of the particular could lead to a valid explanation of the whole. Reflecting upon his conclusions drawn in 1665–66, Newton later wrote: "[I] compared the force requisite to keep the Moon in her Orb with the force of gravity at the surface of the earth, and found them to answer pretty nearly." But "pretty nearly" was not mathematical proof of a theory of universal gravitation. Newton could go no further in his calculations and for the next twenty years concentrated mainly upon calculus, optics, and alchemy.

Many others remained profoundly disturbed when mathematical and empirical investigation failed to support Descartes's fluid vortex hypothesis of planetary movement. Newton's contemporaries Robert Hooke and Edmund Halley wrestled with alternatives illustrating the mutual attraction of heavenly bodies, but verifiable proofs eluded them. In 1684, Halley went to Newton with his dilemma. To his surprise, he learned that Newton had been working with the problem of motion twenty years earlier. Halley urged Newton to take up his work again. Because the old notes were lost, Newton began afresh. This time the route proved smooth. In fewer than three years the *Mathematical Principles of Natural Philosophy* became known to the community of science. Aware of the distance of earth to moon, computing the lunar orbit, and checking his computations against observed facts, Newton discovered that, according to his theorem of inverse squares, a single law of motion existed and held as true for the transits of planets as for a falling body. Thus Descartes's general appreciation of Nature was confirmed, even as the details of his hypothetical vision of planetary motion were rejected.

Newton's discovery electrified European intellectuals. If he was correct, the idea of celestial uniqueness had to be discarded. What was true of bodies seen through the telescope applied to bodies seen through the microscope. England honored him with a seat in Parliament, knighthood, directorship over the mint, and presidency of the Royal Society. He became the first "natural philosopher" to be so treated by his country within his lifetime. English, Dutch and many German scientists accepted the theories of the *Mathematical Principles.* For political reasons, however, the Paris academy refused to abandon Descartes; and the French universities stayed with Aristotle.

Though Newton had confirmed that the mathematically deduced and empirically observed were the twin measures of reality, he shunned a purely materialist conception of the universe. He offered an olive branch to the defenders of the older culture by postulating the existence of a divine mystery behind the marvelous mechanism of the physical world. God was not simply a watchmaker who created His masterpiece and then stepped aside. God was living and real, though to be sure, closer to the scientist-philosopher than to the theologian. In his *Optics* (1704), Newton wrote: "The main business of natural philosophy is to argue from phenomena without feigning hypotheses, and to deduce causes from effects, till we come to the very First Cause, which certainly is not mechanical." Newton's legacy was to have uncovered, through the application of mathematics, systematic observation, and experiment, a reasoned harmony lying behind the surface disorder of the physical universe. Treated as a seer by his allies and as an occult magician by his enemies, he admittedly did not work in a scientific void. Throughout the second half of the seventeenth century, a wide range of cumulative advances in mathematics, chemistry, geology, medicine, and biology accompanied work in celestial physics, all of which helped confirm the mechanistic interpretation of the universe.

By virtue of their challenges to Descartes, the "corpuscularean theorists" helped establish the intellectual mood conducive to welcoming Newton's theories. To Cartesians, the assumption of a universe of densely packed, constantly moving, coarse and fine particles, all immersed in a celestial fluid, meant that there were empty spaces, with neither particles nor fluid; this was unthinkable. From 1644 to 1654, in a controlled laboratory environment, experimenters claimed to have discovered a vacuum. This challenged the theoretical certainties of the Cartesians and inspired the most celebrated of the "corpusculareans," the Englishman Robert Boyle, to arrive at his law that the volume of gases varies inversely according to the amount of air pressure upon it. Like Newton, Boyle rejected unverifiable Aristotelian conceptions.

Just as the Cartesians had been wrong in denying the possibility of a vacuum, so the universities erred in reducing matter to the four elements of fire, air, earth, and water. This ancient way of analyzing matter had lain at the heart of the qualitative explanations. Fire was dry and hot, earth dry and cold; air was moist and hot, water moist and cold. Matter reacted in predictable ways not because of physical laws but because, like human beings, it longed for certain states. A stone fell because it yearned for earth; smoke rose because it yearned for air. In *The Sceptical Chymist* (1661), Boyle ridiculed the qualitative explanations of the workings of matter, and he removed chemistry from the domain of the magical and sinister. Boyle's achievement, however, remained incomplete. He never did systematize

according to their physical properties what he called "primitive and simple
... unmingled bodies," and he never quite forsook the kitchen for the
laboratory. Alchemy tempted him, as it did Newton, causing him to work
at cross-purposes. Boyle never tired of emphasizing the possibilities of
science, and he was convinced that the new learning awarded a greater glory
to God. He set aside a sum to pay preachers to lecture on the compatibility
of science and Christianity. His enthusiasm misapplied, it was said that few
doubted the existence of God until the Boyle lecturers set out to prove it.

What we today call the biological sciences were in their infancy. They too
became indebted to a mechanistic outlook and experimental methodology.
When he outlined his theory of blood circulation in 1628, William Harvey
liberated physiology from its ancient Galenic standard. In the second half
of the century, the microscope became inextricably linked to physiology.
Thoroughly entranced by the microscopic, a Dutch draper, Anton van
Leeuwenhoek, perfected a 300-power instrument and delighted in entertaining his acquaintances with the wriggling universe beneath its lens. He
insisted that he had observed the perfect form of a sheep in an embryo
one-eighth the size of a pea. Though an amateur, van Leeuwenhoek nevertheless discovered spermatazoa and protozoa. He even began classifying
bacteria into species, and he corresponded regularly with the Royal Society,
which published his articles. Upon his death, the society received his trea-
sured microscopes.

Despite their innovators, physiology and biology lacked universally accepted and verifiable principles of classification. Physics at least had its
geometrized superstructure built upon a comprehensive body of precise,
ascertained facts. Life scientists, however, groped amidst conflicting systems, names, and descriptions. They were looking for a "natural" system
of classification that would uncover the genuine, unifying relationships of
living things. In botany, matters were particularly critical. The passion for
collecting Europe's flora and fauna and the discovery of exotic plants made
establishing principles of classification imperative. An intuitive genius, the
Englishman John Ray classified nearly 20,000 identifiable plants according
to their community of origin. Ray was the first to use the term *species* in
this way, and his French contemporary, Pitton de Tournefort, a professor
at Paris's Royal Gardens, developed the term *genus* for a definable group
of related species. Finally, in the next generation, the Swede Carl Linné
brought the work of Ray and Tournefort to a triumphal conclusion. Linné's
most lasting innovation was in nomenclature, the dual name. The first was
generic, shared with other species (*Rosa*); the second represented the species itself (*Carolina*).

The belief in the fixity of species confronted the study of vertebrates with
an obstacle that Newton's triumph seemed to make all the greater. It was
not until after 1750 that the possibility of evolution challenged the idea of

an unchanging natural order. Before then, biologists believed that they had to provide an analogy to the regularized, harmonious universe of physical matter uncovered by the Newtonians. Since this universe was based upon the principle of static reality, with change abhorrent to its workings, the celestial physicists saw little need to challenge the view that the earth was 5,700 years old, and that all plant and animal life in existence around A.D. 1700 had been present at the dawn of creation. Geologists, however, were finding in various layers what they thought were skeletal remains of creatures no longer in existence. Such discoveries challenged biblical chronologies and turned the Flood in Genesis into merely the latest of a series of ancient marine catastrophes. How many extinct creatures once roamed the earth and swam in its waters? In 1710, addressing the Paris Academy of Sciences on fossils, Fontenelle underscored their role in natural history: "Here are new species of medals whose dates are more important and more certain than all the Greek and Roman medals combined." The Newtonians had provided momentous answers; but in their wake, others were asking troubling questions.

By 1715, the idea of a universe that works had replaced the idea of a universe that feels. Descartes had insisted upon the substitution of fact for imagination; Newton had taken him at his word, and deduction, observation, and experiment had triumphed. The future branches of modern science still were at different stages of development. Physics and mechanics were the standard for all the rest. The sciences of classification were groping for methodologies, and geology was in a perplexed state. Despite the air pump, microscope, and other instruments of measurement, technology remained too undeveloped to affect the lives of the majority of Europeans. In the 1690s, attempts were made to find new sources of power by applying steam to the piston and cylinder, though it was not until 1712 that the imaginative English blacksmith Thomas Newcomen harnessed steam power sufficiently to make an engine of highly limited use. Around the same time, the passion for improvement reached into agriculture, the area, of course, which touched most closely upon the well-being of society. Borrowing ideas from intensive cultivation in the Netherlands, some Englishmen began abandoning the fallow for systematic methods of crop rotation. The "New Husbandry" operated on a cycle of clover, wheat, turnips, and barley. No one yet understood just why clover and turnips invigorated the soil, but observation and experiment proved that they did. In the 1720s, when the English gentleman farmer Jethro Tull showed that pulverizing the soil produced effects similar to manuring it and invented the horse hoe to effect his ideas, the long-delayed marriage of science and agriculture seemed to be approaching reality. Though technology still lagged behind theory, methodology and newly acquired optimism for the future linked Newton to Newcomen and Tull.

EMPIRICISM: PSYCHOLOGICAL, SOCIAL, AND POLITICAL THOUGHT

The subjugation of the physical universe to mathematical and empirical analysis inspired seventeenth-century thinkers to apply reasoned judgment to ethics, political theory, psychology, and jurisprudence. Spinoza, Malebranche, and Leibniz were confident that they would solve metaphysical problems as comprehensively as the celestial mechanicians had solved physical ones. Only careful definitions, tightly reasoned analyses, geometrical demonstrations, and meticulous observation of God's work through Nature were needed. That scientific and philosophical problems might call for differences in approach was barely conceivable to thinkers flushed with the power of the new methodology. Though some tried to prove via mathematical formulas the existence of good and evil in people's hearts, it became clear that empirical study was more useful than abstract analysis in probing the realities of human existence and one's place in the social and political environment. Of course, observation and experiment enjoyed places of honor, especially as checkpoints, in the findings of the great theorists of matter; and the less developed sciences of biology, chemistry, botany, and geology were almost entirely dependent upon empirical techniques. By 1715, psychological, social, and political theory were awarding precedence to the world of observable fact.

Three Englishmen—Francis Bacon (1561–1626), Thomas Hobbes (1588–1679), and John Locke (1632–1704)—spanned more than four generations of empiricist thought. Bacon set down the guidelines. He assumed that the sum total of phenomena was finite; observation and the collection of facts formed the basis of inductive proof; experiments must be deliberate and rationally conceived; and the ultimate end to knowledge was humanity's mastery of Nature. Bacon's secretary, Hobbes, disregarded the immaterial side of Cartesian dualism, believed that reality consisted exclusively of matter in motion, was persuaded that universal laws had nothing to do with reality, and placed all on the side of the senses. Unlike Bacon, Hobbes was primarily interested in the reactions of people battered about by a universe of fleeting matter. Responding entirely to the needs of the senses, the Hobbesian individual was constantly in competition with other humans. Knowledge was uncertain. Religion and morality were intended either to counteract the most ruthless aspects of competition or else subject some individuals to the rule of others. Profoundly pessimistic about humankind, Hobbes nevertheless insisted that his conclusions were based upon painstaking observation of his fellows and a careful reading of history. His own life affirmed his faith in uncertainty. A defender of Charles I, he fled to France in 1640. However, Cromwell invited him back, and his masterpiece, the *Leviathan*, was published in London in 1651. Though Charles II protected him, Hobbes's materialism earned him the reputation of a dangerous character, and his enemies called the Great Plague and Fire of London divine retribution for his presence. Timid by nature, yet repudiating nothing he had written, Hobbes died in 1679, at ninety-one, certain that experience justified his pessimism.

For nearly a half-century, the life of John Locke overlapped that of Hobbes. The two thinkers lived through the Civil War, Interregnum, and Restoration. Like Hobbes, Locke experienced political exile, and with Hobbes, he shared a belief that the primary way to learn about humanity and the world was empirically. But here all resemblance stopped. Hobbes was convinced of the instability and unpredictability of life, of the individual's unquenchable egoism, and of the inevitability of social conflict. On the other hand, Locke left room for hope. His *Essay Concerning Human Understanding* (1690) was meant to refute Descartes's principle of innate ideas and to show that trustworthy knowledge derived exclusively from human experience. Locke agreed with Hobbes that simple ideas were products of our senses. He added, however, that individuals reflect upon simple ideas and refine them. Locke was vague as to how the mind sorts out and arranges the products of experience, and what he called the principle of innate rationality appears to be human conscience. This rationality transforms our sense-derived ideas into complex ones, and these complex ideas become the guides for our conduct, morality, law, religion, politics, and aesthetics.

Locke developed a related theory of overpowering consequence. Since we are so dependent upon our senses for ideas, our environment molds us. Conversely, our complex ideas, the product of our "reflective experience," may transform and ameliorate our environment. A generation reared upon Cartesian faith in reason, dazzled by the discoveries of the celestial mechanicians, and increasingly skeptical about traditional theologies and original sin took to Locke's sanguine empiricism with an enthusiasm Hobbes could hardly have expected. Locke's *Essay* marked a revolutionary event in the history of ideas. Upon its hypotheses and conclusions arose the fundamental liberal belief in moral and material progress. Though Locke stated that the concept of God was the clearest complex idea one could hold, his psychology was uncompromisingly secular. Humanity alone controlled its destiny.

Just as Descartes, Spinoza, Pascal, Bossuet, and Leibniz were keenly interested in political theory, so too did Hobbes and Locke apply their secular empiricism to politics. No one lived in a vacuum. Rebellion, revolution, and regicide had plagued the first half of the seventeenth century. Though international warfare rather than internal revolts dominated the second half, political thinkers remained obsessed by the fundamental problems of defining the nature of sovereignty, purpose of government, and proper role of the subject.

Theorists of divine right absolutism, such as Bishop Bossuet, court preacher at Versailles, had certain answers. Governments were obviously ordained by God, and subjects were obliged to obey these governments. Nothing could be clearer than the words of St. Paul, whom Bossuet quoted in his *Politics Drawn From the Very Words of Holy Scripture:* "Let every soul be subject to the higher powers. For there is no power but of God and the powers that be are ordained by God. Whosoever therefore resisteth the power resisteth the ordinance of God." Hereditary monarchy was the most appropriate "higher power." It offered a parallel to the divine order and was chosen by God for ancient Israel. Far from resting his argument exclusively upon biblical fundamentalism, however, Bossuet also showed that individuals craved paternal government, that absolutism was the best insurance against division in the state, and that hereditary rule was the "most natural and self-regenerating kind." Distinguishing between absolute and arbitrary government, Bossuet reminded princes that they must respect the fundamental laws of the state and the property of their subjects. Against an unjust ruler, the subject might make nothing more than respectful remonstrances. Antithetical to scripture and a violation of public order, civil disobedience was intolerable. The ultimate weapons of a suffering populace were prayers for the tyrant's conversion.

Like Bossuet, Hobbes was a convinced believer in absolute government, though his method of justification did not endear him to divine right theorists. Hobbes's thought had little room for the Christian God, and his world was suffused with swirling matter and individuals who followed their instincts and responded to their senses. The political theory of Hobbes's *Leviathan* derived from the cosmology of the work. Hobbes began by placing the individual in a hypothetical environment that preceded the establishment of political society. In the Middle Ages, such an environment was linked to Eden, where humans behaved according to natural laws ordained by God. Early in the seventeenth century, the political thinker Hugo Grotius, while not dispensing with the device of a state of Nature, secularized the principle of natural laws by postulating them upon the workings of human reason. Even if God did not exist, Grotius hypothesized, the laws of nature stood, being indistinguishable from moral principles. Devoid of either moral or divine laws, Hobbes's state of Nature was a microscopic version of his universe. Within it, individuals obeyed their private instincts and were restrained only by fears of reprisal and their own violent death. Scoffing at the idea of a social instinct that, according to Grotius, drew people into cooperative activities even before the formation of organized society, Hobbes envisioned within the state of Nature a state of "war of every man against every man." Lacking laws of nature, "the notions of right and wrong, justice and injustice, have no place." Mere existence was conflict, "and the life of man, solitary, poor, nasty, brutish, and short."

Inside the state of Nature, the freedom of one individual threatened the survival of everyone else. Then, for a moment, according to Hobbes the single most important instant in human history, people applied their powers of reason to their need for self-preservation. Among themselves they agreed to surrender their liberty and "confer all their power and strength upon one man, or upon one assembly of men." This act of self-preservation created a "mortal god," the great Leviathan, the omnipotent state. Its sovereignty was absolute and its power unlimited. It defined justice, morality, and religion; it made no reciprocal concessions to subjects. Its purpose was wholly to maintain order and avert dissension. Mass rebellion against it was social suicide, for such activity incited a return to the state of Nature. Only when the sovereign failed to provide necessary security did a rationale exist for subjects to transfer authority. Unpleasant as the *Leviathan* was, as a piece of political philosophy it represented a landmark. Out went the religious, moral, feudal, and constitutional underpinnings of the state. In came a total, self-sustaining view of political authority.

Hobbes broke with the past in another way. For him, political society originated as a voluntary association of individuals, equal in their freedom and misery. Neither religious commandment nor moral vision lay behind the social act. The state and its laws were artificial creations, and Hobbes saw no need for subjects to urge rulers to govern according to higher principles than utilitarian ones. For him, natural laws never existed. Subsequent thinkers, however, revived them and made them indisputably secular, the embodiment of mankind's pristine, inherent rationality. Because natural laws were positive, even benevolent, it was the duty of government to preserve their character. Faith in the reality of natural laws was consistent with faith in the reality of the mechanical workings of the universe. It was consistent with faith in natural religion that philosophers and deists extolled. Almost in reaction to Hobbes's gloomy prospects, the idea of a voluntarily contracted society merged with a revival of natural law theorists to create a political theory that placed unprecedented confidence in the capacities of human beings to work out their destinies.

The natural law theorists themselves were not a homogeneous group. One school argued that strong government provided the most effective instrument for expressing natural law and defending natural rights. The most celebrated spokesman for this position was a Saxon professor and jurist, Samuel von Pufendorf, who served two of the most effective rulers of his day, the Great Elector of Brandenburg and Charles XI of Sweden. For Pufendorf, as for Hobbes, people established political society as a vehicle for restraining themselves. Yet the purpose of government was protective, not repressive. For this reason, the subjects made a second contract, this time with their newly appointed government. The subject affirmed loyalty to his ruler; the ruler agreed to respect the natural rights of the subject. Pufendorf's view appealed to the princes of the Holy Roman Empire, who believed they were protecting their subjects from social anarchy while defending them from the pretensions of the emperor. In the mideighteenth century, the so-called Enlightened Despots of central Europe drew their rationale for absolutism from Pufendorf.

A second body of natural law theorists did not share Pufendorf's elevated view of the powerful state. On the contrary, these critics thought it naive to entrust governments with defining and then defending natural rights. Uninterested in protecting subjects, absolutisms were built upon the principle of a hierarchical society and existed only as long as the few could dominate the many. Therefore, the people, and the people alone, must define the meaning of natural rights and laws. This doctrine originated in England during the 1640s, where revolution had given birth to Europe's boldest political climate; its advocates, called the Levellers, held that since the laws of Nature were founded upon the collective reasoning power of mankind, it made no sense to delegate to a political regime the right to reinterpret the laws. The people must remain sovereign.

If Reason rules the state of Nature and political society represents such a threat to natural rights, why bother to form governments in the first place? In *Oceana* (1656), James Harrington, an old crony of Charles I who refused to choose sides in the Civil War, responded with the view that all regimes—monarchies, aristocracies, or republics—are beholden to the propertied and exist to defend the interests of landowners. In the next generation, more clearly than Harrington had done, John Locke incorporated the protection of property rights into a political theory supporting natural rights. Locke's amalgam appealed to the victors in the Glorious Revolution of 1688–89 and became the commonplace for the English ruling classes through the eighteenth century. Because he hated absolutism and said so, Locke also became a model for continental liberals. His legacy was to show that both security and freedom were compatible features of civil society.

Locke's *First Treatise on Government* and a good deal of the *Second Treatise* were written from 1679 to 1683 to refute Sir John Filmer's advocacy of divine right monarchy. Unfortunately, the last four years of Charles II's reign were bad ones for opponents of absolutism. A physician with a research post at Oxford University, Locke was associated with Shaftesbury and the Whigs. Fearing imprisonment during the Tory reaction of 1683, he fled to Holland. Political exile nurtured his distaste for unregulated governments, and the fall of James II brought him home in 1688. Thereupon, he polished up and published his two treaties. For the remainder of his life, Locke lived quietly near London, in contact with scholars, scientists, and politicians, enjoying fame as the father of empiricist psychology and the leading theoretician of the Glorious Revolution.

Locke's *Second Treatise*, his more important one, opens in the state of Nature, where "everyone has the Executive Power." Freedom there is not the anarchic, obliterating kind outlined by Hobbes but rather a natural freedom defined by natural law. There, human reason interprets natural law.

Any individual who constricts the freedom of another is committing a transgression. However, distinct disadvantages exist in the state of Nature. The laws of Nature are not written, nor is there an impartial judge who can try and punish transgressors. An aggrieved party has no other choice than to fight it out with his attacker in much the same way states do in the "community of nations," where no supranational court of justice exists. Locke insists, however, that in the state of Nature Reason guides individuals and conflict is the exception. As evidence, people remove raw materials from Nature, apply their labor to these materials, and convert them into useful products. This activity gives the individual title to property. "As much land as a man tills, plants, improves, cultivates, and can use the product of, so much is his property.... God gave the world to men in common.... He gave it to the use of the industrious and rational, and Labor was to be [mankind's] title to it." To guarantee themselves a juridical device that will protect their natural and material possessions, individuals create civil society.

A contract among individuals forming civil society marks the first step out of the state of Nature. The second step occurs when society institutionalizes protection by authorizing government. The purpose of government is the establishment of a legislature and magistrates "with Authority to determine all the controversies and redress the injuries" individuals might suffer at each other's hand, in other words, to guarantee natural rights and rightful property. While Pufendorf glossed over the fact that the state itself might present the greatest danger to rights and property, Locke saw it clearly. The relationship between the citizenry and legislature was not indissoluble. Government was a trust: "The Legislative acts against the Trust reposed in them, when they endeavor to invade the Property of the Subject, and make themselves, or any part of the community, Masters or Arbitrary disposers of the Lives, Liberties or Fortunes of the People." But who should determine whether government has overstepped its bounds? "To this I reply," wrote Locke, "the People shall be judge." Breaking with Hobbes and Pufendorf, Locke approved of throwing out the rascals, either through elections or other means. Rid of repressive government, the people do not fall back into a state of Nature. The first contract stands. Civil society must simply establish another government, more worthy of its trust than the preceding one.

Therefore, within society and under government, Locke's individual retains as far as possible the rights he held in the state of Nature. Eighteenth-century Whig aristocrats assumed that Locke's "people" were the "political nation," that is, those who possessed valuable amounts of landed property. These were the individuals with most to gain from a benevolent government and most to lose from a repressive regime. The propertied made certain that the "Legislative" in England represented their interests and voted according to their wishes. But Locke's heritage extended far beyond the country houses of the gentry. Frederick the Great might discover his spiritual ancestry in Pufendorf. American and French revolutionaries found theirs in the timid Oxford don whose major concern remained citizens' rights and not subjects' duties.

BAROQUE, CLASSICISM, AND REALISM

The years 1648 to 1715 were filled with contradiction and paradox. Economic decline, depopulation, war, famine, and disease formed a backdrop for a series of intellectual triumphs unparalleled since the Golden Age of Athens. Art and architecture concretely illustrated the self-confidence of elites and their intoxication with power. The governing form of aristic expression was called baroque. It derived from the Italian Renaissance, took hold around 1620, became an international style at midcentury, and influenced painting, sculpture, and architecture to the 1750s. It was soaring, dynamic, and passionately intense. It stressed curves and shadow, avoiding clear lines and sharp contrasts. Seeking to capture the fleeting moment, the act of revelation or climax, baroque enjoyed its greatest prestige in religious sculpture and building. Its most celebrated practitioner was Lorenzo Bernini (1598–1680), for a half-century the papacy's official artist. Bernini sought the heart of the viewer by dazzling his senses. The tombs for Popes Urban VIII and Alexander VII dramatically revealed subjects surprised by death, underscoring the inexorable fact of mortality, while his "Saint Theresa in Ecstasy," her heart pierced by the shaft of divine love, subtly intertwined the facts of spiritual and erotic rapture. In all three pieces, sensuality dominates. As an architect, Bernini built Roman churches that remain stellar attractions. His masterpiece was the staggering monumental square that faces Saint Peter's basilica in the Vatican, bordered by free-standing open colonnades, four deep, that embrace the beholder. Never before or since has an ellipse of columns been used with such daring and effectiveness.

Baroque's influence spread from Muscovy to South America. The Jesuits adopted it as the official form for their churches, and the reconstruction of central Europe after 1648 was largely the work of baroque-inspired architects. The Hapsburgs used the style as a visual means of linking together into a common civilization the diverse people of their empire. In the most southern Catholic regions, particularly Spain and Latin America, baroque churches assumed fantastic proportions. They were riotous and bombastic, flinging passion and eccentricity into the face of the beholder. They went far beyond Bernini's intentions and illustrated the degenerate form into which the style could fall. On the other hand, baroque was more restrained in the Protestant North. The Great Fire of London in 1666 necessitated the reconstruction of the English capital. Christopher Wren (1632–1723), mathematician, charter member of the Royal Society, and engineer as well as architect, proposed a whole new baroque city. However, Parliament commissioned him with the more modest task of rebuilding or restoring some fifty churches ruined by the fire. Chief of these was old Saint Paul's cathedral. Wren envisioned a new edifice, Protestantism's response to Saint Peter's. It took nearly forty years to complete the job. Wren worked empirically, modifying and changing details as the building went up. What emerged was not a clumsy hodgepodge but a masterful blending of earlier classical, Gothic, and Renaissance styles that gave a unique tone to English baroque.

French baroque assumed such distinctive national characteristics that it has been given its unique label: classicism. Obsessed by the achievements of the ancients, Louis XIV personally preferred rectilinear shapes, order, and harmony to the less disciplined sensous, soaring forms of Italian baroque. Yet the emergence of French classicism preceded Louis, as early seventeenth-century architects such as François Mansart and painters like Nicholas Poussin deviated from baroque forms. Under Louis, a rigorously defined court style established itself, and royal institutions were built to enforce a dictatorship of taste. Colbert managed this harnessing of art. In 1663, he awarded a constitution to the Academy of Painting and Sculpture, already fifteen years old. To be assured commissions in Louis XIV's France, an artist had to be in good standing with the academy and obey its aesthetic standards. Other academies regulated dance, music, and architecture. The painter Charles Lebrun operated the state-financed Gobelins tapestry works, controlling a multitude of sculptors, painters, weavers, and cabinet makers. The French Academy in Rome was founded to train young French artists in the heart of classical—and baroque—civilization. A great symbolic confrontation between Italian baroque and the French style occurred in 1665 when by invitation the sixty-seven-year-old Bernini arrived in Paris with his plans for rebuilding the Louvre palace. The passionate Italian was flabbergasted to find artists and critics forced to work within the confines of bureaucratically defined canons of taste. Unruffled, Bernini presented his flamboyant sketches to Louis and Colbert, who promptly rejected them for the more orthodox and less expensive designs of a French artist. Bernini cast the mold for his famous bust of the king and left Paris indignantly.

Classical architecture embodied reason, regularity, and conformity. To reflect seventeenth-century standards of palatial grandeur, it nevertheless had to borrow from Italian baroque. One building, the royal palace at Versailles, showed how baroque and classical might coexist in the most spectacular way imaginable. From the moment of its conception, Versailles was to be monumental as form and symbol, the costs of its construction unaffected by falling revenues and economic recession. Louis XIV detested Paris and longed for a country estate where he could live in the grand manner. His father had built a small hunting lodge fifteen miles southwest of the capital. Early in the 1660s, the lodge was modified into a place for official receptions. Then, in 1669, Louis decided to construct at Versailles his new residence, the playground for his court, and the central offices for his bureaucracy.

The architect Le Vau preserved Louis XIII's little hunting lodge but dwarfed it inside an enormous U-shaped edifice. The most active period of construction took place from 1669 to 1684. From 1679 to 1689, the formal gardens were laid out. Great open courtyards were carved from marble and stone in order to celebrate military conquests, marriages and births and to stage theatrical performances. The three-storied building and its enormous façade flanked by a pair of wings exuded baroque magnificance, while inside classicism reigned. Lebrun and his decorators filled the walls with vivid allegorical paintings comparing Louis XIV to the gods and heroes of antiquity. The statuary was noble and placid. A great canal was dug through the palace grounds, and the completed gardens were models of symmetry and order. Around the chateau, the town of Versailles was built. The ensemble represented man's total mastery of nature—a cold, ruthless, mechanically conceived power. Filled with pilgrims, St. Peter's square vibrated with life. On the other hand, the great courtyard at Versailles was a stage setting and the palace a monument to artificiality and ritual. Though housing a government, Versailles seemed divorced from the real world. As architecture it was Europe's most oppressive masterpiece.

Baroque painting was symbolic, allusive, and decorative. Its intention was to seize the fleeting moment. The picaresque studies of Caravaggio and the overflowing church walls and ceilings of Corregio were its sources. After 1648, church interiors in the Mediterranean, the Hapsburg empire, and South America literally swamped the beholder under heavy cloud formations, gesticulating figures, and flowing draperies. A pompous aristocratic society adored this sacrifice of spirituality for decoration. Once more, the French offered a classical variant, indeed an alternative, to the Italian style. Lebrun and the Academy of Painting stressed the notion that the ancients had perfected beauty through a balance of realism and ideal form. Chief among the French classical painters was Poussin, who spent forty years in Rome for inspiration. Paris merchants, *parlementaires*, and aristocrats bought Poussin's pastoral scenes and dignified mythological subjects bathed in cool, light colors. Claude Lorrain, another Frenchman in Roman exile, seconded Poussin with arcadias that greatly influenced west European landscape gardening. Poussin and Lorrain equated reason with nature and nature with virtue. Late baroque offered overripe magnificence as an alternative to war and uncertainty; classicism yielded escapist arcadias.

A second alternative to baroque painting was perfected in the Dutch landscapes of Jacob Van Ruysdael, domestic scenes of Jan Vermeer, and late portraits of Rembrandt. The Dutch artists were the first to work exclusively for an open market, not for a specific patron. No academy bound them to regulations governing subject matter or technique. They drew from tradition but also felt free to express individualized visions of humanity and the world, all the while experimenting with color, light, shadow, and technique. What resulted was a burst of creativity unmatched in the century.

Vermeer and Rembrandt were the greatest painters. Born in 1632 in Delft and dying forty-three years later, Vermeer painted no more than sixty canvasses in his lifetime. His subject matter was limited to domestic scenes in two small rooms in his modest provincial house. The furniture and people hardly ever change. Women working in the kitchen, making lace, or playing a musical instrument possess a disturbing air of silent mystery, and in their day, Vermeer's paintings did not sell very well. However, no painter has ever understood better than Vermeer the impact of light and space or the subtleties inherent in the most ordinary scenes of life. Vermeer's masterpiece was a landscape, the "View of Delft," an artistic victory for expression and understanding as complete as Newton's.

On the other hand, Rembrandt began his career as a baroque artist. Born to a Leyden miller's family in 1606, he studied art in Amsterdam and settled there in his midtwenties. In 1632, he skyrocketed to fame with his group portrait, "The Anatomy Lesson of Dr. Tulp," commissioned by the physicians represented in the painting. Then personal misfortune struck hard with financial difficulties and the early deaths of his beloved wife and several children. Wealthy burghers grew less interested in his portraits of them. Though Rembrandt painted "The Night Watch," perhaps the greatest of all baroque paintings, his ultimate fame was not to depend upon depicting the grandiose and elegant but rather upon depicting the tragedy and turmoil of the inner self. His last portraits and religious scenes brought out his true genius, a psychological perception softened by comprehension and tenderness, uncompromisingly honest evaluations of human existence.

In the late seventeenth century, art was expressed in mature and overripe baroque, academic classicism, and experimental realism. Literature pursued similar trends. By 1648, baroque writers created a common style that transcended differences in language, religious tradition, or social and political circumstance. The religious allegory provided an excellent framework for baroque expression. In *Paradise Lost*, John Milton depicted the rebellion of the angels and fall of man in a grandiose poem, a Protestant response to the *Divine Comedy*. Across the channel, the Dutch epic poet Joost van den Vondel, author of *Lucifer*, followed a path similar to Milton's. In *The Pilgrim's Progress*, the self-educated tinker-preacher John Bunyan brought the allegorical fantasy of the baroque to the lowest rung of literate English society. Bunyan's artistic recreations of abstract Christian principles derived straight from the medieval morality play; the passion, conflict, and digressive story line are indisputably baroque. Besides *The Pilgrim's Progress*, vulgarized courtly romances fascinated village audiences throughout England, the Netherlands, and France. A reader and his listeners would virtually memorize the dog-eared volumes, and oral tradition passed the stories on to the next generation.

Built mostly upon the 2,500 plays of Felix Lope de Vega, Tirso de Molina, and Pedro Calderón, Spain's literary Golden Age had peaked. However, the sacred dramas of these three, based upon allegorical representations of the Eucharist, Bible stories, and saints' lives, remained as popular as their secular plays emphasizing patriotism, chivalry, and virtue. The Spanish dramatists were more than mere moralists. A deeply religious spirit and sense of guilt over the vanity of the world etched their way into the Spanish baroque theater, perhaps the playwrights' reaction to the virtual collapse of their country after its brief moment of splendor. Spanish baroque theater influenced French literary life through the work of Pierre Corneille, whose characters were beset with excruciating choices between emotion and duty. However, in Corneille's plays the Spaniards' skepticism about life is missing. The Frenchman moreover leaned heavily upon classical subjects, since they were the only ones the rising academic arbiters of national taste considered dignified enough to be represented by tragedy. Convention also required Corneille to write in Alexandrine verse. He eschewed stage violence, limited stage action to twenty-four hours or less, and constructed his plots upon logic and argument as opposed to atmosphere and visual mood. Corneille's inspiration was baroque, but his universe was classical.

The modern literary tradition of central and eastern Europe was baroque seasoned with folk realism. Germany's most important writer was Hans Jakob Christoffel von Grimmelshausen, whose adventure novel *Simplicius Simplicissimus* (1669) owed much to the immensely popular extravagant romances of France and Spain. The setting of *Simplicissimus* is Germany of the Thirty Years' War, and its basic theme is survival in the jungle of the world. The protagonist is the obverse of the dignified Corneillian hero. His fantastic, vulgar, and shocking adventures are told in a style that is naturalistic and bitterly ironic. In its extravagance, *Simplicissimus* was baroque, but its exposé of war and concern for the common man's instinct to survive give it a very realistic turn.

While Corneille was a baroque writer constrained by a classical mold, his younger French contemporary Jean Racine revealed how elevated a literature might emerge from pure academism. Racine's most prolific periods coincided with Versailles's classical phase. However, the playwright's work gave a depth and substantiality to the classical style that formal gardens, placid statuary, and arcadian harmonies could not hope to match. Racine wished to analyze emotions rather than illustrate them. The individual confronted by a hopeless destiny fascinated Racine. The French academy limited his vocabulary, and like Corneille, he was restricted to the unities of time and space. He had to write in Alexandrine verse, and all his plots were derived from classical or biblical themes. The results were remarkable. The reasoned tone, intellectualized emotions, and obsession with dramatic unities reduce action to pure dialogue. Scarcely a playwright has written better poetry than Racine about the individual's hopeless struggle against fate. True to Jansenist theology all his life, Racine applied severe discipline and singular direction to his masterpieces of character analysis. He developed the classical literary style to its fullest bloom. Its very restrictiveness afforded him the opportunity to concentrate, analyze, and dissect.

In France, classicism produced a wealth of theoreticians for whom clear thinking and expert craftsmanship were the hallmarks of literary art. These attributes were particularly necessary to forms like the funeral oration, court sermon, maxim, and even personal letter, all of which were in vogue during Louis XIV's reign. Dramatist, poet, and theoretician, John Dryden was England's greatest exponent of classicism. Few were more skillful than Dryden in applying verse to heroic drama. Most other English classicists wrote formally correct works to combat what they believed to be Shakespeare's baroque excesses, but they lacked the incisiveness, depth, and subtlety of a Racine.

The greatest comic author of the century, Molière, wrote his plays while remaining true to the French academy's classic rules. Born Jean-Baptiste Poquelin to a family of merchant upholsterers, Molière left law school in 1659 to establish a theatrical company in Paris. He gained the favor of the young king. One of the few original spirits in Europe's most convention-bound court, Molière succeeded in picking apart miserliness, hypochondria, status seeking, religious hypocrisy, and the foolishness ingrained in the learned professions, such as law and medicine. Molière knew the limits of his freedom; he never touched politics. His comedies usually take place within the confines of the bourgeois family, so that king and court could join in the humor without embarrassment. As a professional actor, Molière knew firsthand what it meant to suffer outside the mainstream of society, and his plays penetrate deeply into the tragic ironies of human existence. Mocking excess, he exposed society to analysis and criticism. His most attractive character was the practical, quick-witted servant girl whose refreshing authenticity contrasts with the pedantry and floundering of her social masters.

Though baroque and classical remained the dominant forms of seventeenth-century European literature, a restless desire to break out of traditions and habits gave rise to experimental approaches that defy classification. At the century's close, the popularization of science itself had become literature. Bernard de Fontenelle's *Conversations on the Plurality of Worlds* (1686) tried to make the Cartesian universe intelligible to a nonscientist. The *Conversations* took the form of five dialogues in a moonlit garden between a beautiful marquise and her tutor. Never before had instruction been made so entertaining. Fontenelle also wrote about the possibility of life on other planets. His *History of Oracles* (1686) attacked religious charlatanism. His *Dialogues of the Dead* (1683) challenged French worship of classical antiquity by substituting the idea of civilization's progressive development for that of its inevitable decline. In a lifetime that spanned a century, 1657–1757, Fontenelle propagandized for exploring new cultural vistas. He spoke up for experience and common sense; he was skeptical about the past and optimistic about the future. He did more than anyone else of his time to increase public awareness of the unfolding scientific civilization. Along with increasing numbers of other writers on politics, society, and religion, Fontenelle merged a trenchant critique of existing institutions with a profound hope for discovering more reasonable, authentic, and happier alternatives. With Bayle, Locke, and Leibniz, Fontenelle's work helped lay the groundwork for the eighteenth-century Enlightenment.

Part Two

**An Age of Hope and
Revolution: 1715–1789/91**

The People, the Land, and the State

POPULATIONS: RURAL AND URBAN

By 1720 and especially after 1750, Europe's "long century" of nearly stagnant population growth was over. The 120 million alive at the beginning of
the eighteenth century left just under 200 million descendants at the end.
Only North America, enriched by both immigration and natural reproduc-
tion, and China, whose population tripled to over 300 million, exceeded
Europe's rate of increase. Though statistics for the period are only esti-
mates, and trends inside Europe varied widely, apparently most eighteenth-
century couples continued the reproductive habits of their ancestors. Peasant women still married in their middle or late twenties and averaged three
to five births. However, no longer did one-fourth of the infants born perish
in their first year. No longer were half of those born dead by twenty. During
the eighteenth century, the first-year mortality rate dropped below 15 percent, and the chances were seven to ten that a peasant infant would survive
adolescence. Thus, of the half-billion Europeans born, 40 million were
spared who would not have reached adulthood a century earlier. Those who
reached twenty-five could count on living ten years longer than their fathers
had. Half would reach sixty. For the first time in modern European history,
people began rejecting the presence of death. Death became a private,
family matter, not a public ceremony. It was shunted aside, hidden from
view, thrust out of the consciousness.

More elemental physiological reasons than medical progress lay behind
the increased life expectancy. Preventive medicine, such as widespread
inoculation against smallpox, still lay in the future, and curative medicine
was the privilege of the rich. Hospitals were places where one awaited the
end. The most elementary rules of personal hygiene, such as regular bathing
with soap, were largely ignored. Though the ravages of the plague passed
after the 1720s, crowd diseases such as influenza, smallpox, typhus, and
dysentery still struck hard. However, because they were better nourished,

Europeans born after 1720 resisted disease more successfully than had their seventeenth-century predecessors.

Earlier we noted how limited agricultural productivity restrained population growth from 1648 to 1715. Until the 1690s, Europe's farming frontier receded from what it had been in the sixteenth century. Except for England and the Dutch Netherlands, regional dearth could easily grow into widespread famine, with weakened survivors easy prey for disease and epidemics. After 1700, however, opportunities increased for extending cultivation and settling new areas of Europe. The Russian Ukraine, Hapsburg Hungary, Swedish Finland, and East Prussia were such regions; and in the course of the eighteenth century, Europe's cultivatable space nearly doubled. Intensified methods of crop raising increased productivity in parts of western Europe. From Ireland to Russia, new crops such as potato, corn, and rice were introduced, diminishing consumer dependence upon other cereals. Improved roads and waterways, reduced or eliminated customs tolls, and more effective state intervention in times of regional dearth facilitated agricultural transports and saved countless thousands. While it is overly simple to see in the eighteenth century a steady, progressive increase in food supply, the fact remains that people were better-fed than their parents and grandparents had been. They survived, married, and reproduced.

The growth of central and eastern Europe is most striking. In 1700, the population of Hungary, liberated from the Turks, was a million and a half. Germans and Slavs poured in. By 1800, the same region held over 6 million. Frontier areas such as Finland and eastern Germany saw populations triple. The same Russian lands that had 19 million in 1762 possessed nearly 30 million a generation later. Rulers thought they saw a link between extended or improved agriculture, expanding populations, and a strengthened state. The Hapsburg emperor Joseph II ennobled a propagandist for clover cultivation. Frederick II of Prussia and Catherine II of Russia encouraged immigration, paying the costs of displacement and promising new subjects religious freedom, fiscal exemptions, and even serf labor.

In western Europe, population increases were less dramatic than in the eastern frontier regions, but the social consequences proved more telling. England and Wales had under 6 million in 1700 and more than 9 million a century later. In the same period, the population of France rose from 19 million to 27 million. Neither country possessed virgin lands to accept additional people. In fact, after 1760, England's rural population declined markedly. While "improving" English landlords increased agricultural productivity with fewer hands, the dispossessed rural poor could secure passage to America or migrate either to London or the industrial boom towns. On the other hand, French peasants found emigration less possible or attractive than did their English counterparts, and there were fewer industrializing places to absorb them. Tenaciously, French men and women tried to stay on the land, but the competition for scarce plots drove up rents past what most could afford. By the 1780s, a French rural population of unprecedented size and in exceedingly difficult straits lay at the root of a profound social crisis. Never before had France experienced such a large population at the point of indigence—perhaps 10 million people. The coincidental merging of a political and constitutional crisis with a social-economic one stimulated a great revolution. Though revolution failed to occur in either the Italian states or Spain, growing populations of rural poor presaged mounting social tension. During the century, Italy's population rose from 13 to 18 million, Spain's from 6 to 11 million.

Relatively few observers pinpointed the inherent dangers of dramatic population growth until the English economist and social critic Thomas Malthus published his *Essay on Population* in 1798. Malthus was among the first to make a mathematical correlation between food supply and demographic expansion. He believed that from generation to generation the production of food might be described in arithmetical progression (1, 2, 4, 8, 16); at the same time, births occurred in geometrical progression (1, 2, 4, 16, 256). The major checks upon growth would be the familiar ones: war, famine, and epidemic. Nineteenth-century "progressive" theoreticians built their own implications on to Malthus's findings. They believed that the best way to avoid a future universal calamity was by keeping the poor at subsistence levels. Let nature take its course and seize the weak.

From 1715 to 1789, however, a few west European regions seemed to have avoided the Malthusian peril. The Dutch Netherlands was commercially rich and urban, while Denmark was agriculturally rich and rural. During the eighteenth century, the Dutch increased only from 1.9 million to 2.1 million, while the Danish population rose only from 750,000 to under 900,000. Prosperous Lombardy and Tuscany witnessed population increases that were proportionally smaller than the so-called backward areas of Sicily and Naples. Within larger states certain well-to-do provinces grew less rapidly than others. The reasons were neither high mortality nor fears of catastrophe. These regions had no agricultural frontier and were not industrializing rapidly. While opportunities were limited, residents lived well enough. They appear to have instituted family planning in order to keep things that way.

Poor country people often tried their luck in town, whether the town could absorb them or not. Urban growth was again becoming important in Europe west of the Elbe. London and Paris turned into metropolises. The English capital grew from 400,000 in 1700 to 900,000 a century later. Paris contained half a million in 1700 and 700,000 when the revolution of 1789 exploded. London was a royal capital, great international port, and hub of world finance. Paris was Europe's cultural center, an aristocratic residence, a lawyer's town. Both cities had great floating populations. Filth and overcrowding were endemic. Though deaths probably exceeded births in both cities, immigration from the countryside more than made up for losses.

In the 1770s, two of every three inhabitants had been born elsewhere.

Nor were London and Paris the only large cities. Istanbul rivaled London in size, and by 1800, Naples contained over 400,000. However, with insufficient commerce and neither culture nor industry, both of these places were baskets for the poor rather than cities comparable to the booming northern capitals. By 1800, fifteen additional cities had populations exceeding 100,000. In 1700, there had been seven. Berlin, Vienna, Warsaw, St. Petersburg, and to a lesser extent Moscow owed their growth to government. They were administrative centers or royal courts. On the other hand, after London and Paris, the most vigorous west European cities over 100,000 were ocean and river ports such as Barcelona in Spain, Marseilles and Lyons in France, Amsterdam in the Netherlands, and Dublin in Ireland. However, not even these cities were representative of eighteenth-century Europe. Most urban populations lived in towns under 100,000. During the seventeenth-century recession, these places in western Germany, France, Spain, Italy, Belgium, and the London basin had suffered the most noticeable decline. After 1740, many revived, largely as markets for grain and cattle, as centers for the administration of government and country estates, and as residences for entrepreneurs, craftsmen, and shopkeepers.

Around 1770, a new type of city was beginning to emerge in northwestern England, Belgium, and northern France. This was the industrial town, a place far different from the administrative-commercial agglomerations that Europe had known since the Middle Ages. These new towns were to become living embodiments of the most important displacement of population Europe had experienced since the fall of the Roman Empire. It is true that the industrial city was not the consequence of the Industrial Revolution. As late as 1800, most of the industrial population of Great Britain still clustered around textile mills or iron and coal mines in the countryside, whose source of power depended upon fast streams. Nevertheless, the rise of Manchester, from 20,000 to just under 100,000 in the course of a century, coincided with its emergence as a great textile producer. Between 1760 and 1800, Birmingham, Britain's major source of light metals, doubled in population, as did the shipbuilding city of Liverpool. Suburbs grew around factories. These "cities" were genuine boom towns, traps for the new industrial poor, lacking housing, sanitation, or breathing space. Well into the nineteenth century, deaths there outstripped births; but the countryside still fed them its surplus. The saying "Alcohol is the quickest way out of Manchester" stems from the 1850s. Already in the 1770s it was a fact.

A DECLINING PEASANTRY

Despite population shifts towards towns, eighteenth-century Europe remained overwhelmingly rural. Even in the highly urbanized Netherlands, half the people lived in the countryside. In England, seven in ten did, in France four of five. Eastern Europe was practically townless. In 1726, 97 percent of the Russians were on the land; seventy years later, 95 percent.

On the continent, land tenure systems consolidated in the seventeenth century were perpetuated in the eighteenth. East of the Elbe River, a largely unfree peasantry labored for noble landlords who enjoyed legal, economic, and judicial powers over their workers. Except in Prussia, the landlords might be immensely wealthy and powerful. Three noble families controlled all the land in the Polish Ukraine. One of them, the Potockis, had 3 million acres and 130,000 serfs. The Hungarian Esterhazy clan ran 7 million acres, and the properties of the Lithuanian Charles Radziwill absorbed six hundred villages. In Russia, 15 percent of the estate owners held 80 percent of the serfs. Law and custom kept the great properties intact, and heirs usually were prohibited from dividing estates for sale. Protected by the law, the landlord aristocracies institutionalized serfdom. In Poland, peasant males spent four days per week on the estate owner's domain. In Russia, the serf was constrained to work his own tiny garden plot by night. In Bohemia, if a peasant was half an hour late for work on the domain, the landlord's bailiff charged him with an additional seven hours free labor.

Social relationships fed upon a psychology of mutual distrust and fear. Masters suspected bailiffs, and bailiffs held villages collectively responsible for the misdeeds of individual peasants. Village chiefs, serfs themselves, were caught between the contempt of the bailiff and mistrust of their fellows. The favorite folk hero in eastern Europe was the bandit, who, beyond the realm of the law, was beyond the realm of subjugation. Runaway peasants joined the bands of those who attacked merchants and manor houses. East of the Elbe, poor harvests and the threat of famine easily ignited collective passions. From 1762 to 1772 alone, the Russian army confronted forty different regional uprisings.

Yet such revolts had little effect upon the static quality of east European rural life. Raising cereals for distant markets, the estate owner preferred to control production rather than parcel out plots for money rents. The serf's pitiful patch remained the legal fiction recognized by government and landlord in return for the labor services expected of him. Without even this pitiful patch, tens of thousands of serfs worked merely for a hovel and bread. The estate owner customarily denied peasants the right to acquire their own tools. Collecting taxes for the government, serving as magistrate and police chief, he remained an impenetrable wall between regimes and the most numerous body of their subjects. Serf agriculture was as wasteful as it was degrading. Eighteenth-century domains might expand in space, but their per-acre yields remained as limited as they had been in the Middle Ages. The open field system left one-third of the strips fallow every year. The active strips alternated between spring-sown barley and oats and autumn-sown wheat and rye. The permanent pasture provided insufficient fodder, and mechanized improvements were virtually unknown. An innovation like manuring the soil was considered an act against nature or crime against God.

Midway into the eighteenth century, some central and east European governments attempted to improve agricultural productivity. The Hapsburgs brought clover from their Belgian possessions and planted it in their German ones. Frederick II of Prussia virtually had to shove the potato down the throats of his Prussian peasants, but by 1770, its cultivation assured the conquest of absolute famine. Genuine social and economic reform was a far thornier issue than the introduction of fertilizing agents and foods. Governments had considerable self-interest in modifying or eliminating serfdom. Peasants able to sell crops on the open market would have cash for state taxes. Free from threats of eviction or sale, with additional time to till their own plots, peasants might become more efficient, trustworthy, and intelligent cultivators. All of this worked toward a prosperous state, but it also worked against social custom and the privileged status of rural aristocracies.

The Austrian Hapsburgs took the lead in chipping away at the foundations of serfdom. They began in Hungary, where vast immigrations of Germans and Rumanians had created an unprecedented ethnic diversity. This new settlement invited Vienna to reassess landlord-peasant relations. The old arrangement had been the classic east European formula: enserfed cultivators tilled tiny plots leased by the peasant village. For their land, peasants gave the estate owner free labor services, certain stipulated dues, and a share of the crop. They also contributed state taxes, which the landlord was exempt from paying, and a tithe to the Church. Landlord justice controlled peasant life, sales of individuals were possible, and the scale of dues and services varied according to what the individual landowner believed he could get.

Following an investigation of rural conditions that genuinely shocked her, Maria Theresa published an edict in 1769 guaranteeing the Hungarian peasant the right to leave his holding upon expiration of the contract with his landlord. Peasant labor on the landlord's domain was limited to two days per week and four in emergency situations. Imperial officials, not the landlords or their bailiffs, were to enforce the edict. Though not yet a free tenant, the Hungarian peasant at least was released from the bonds of landlord arbitrariness. From 1771 to 1775, the Hapsburgs extended regulatory decrees to their German territories. As in Hungary, the spirit of the legislation had not been to abolish peasant dues and services but to regulate and possibly reduce them. In 1781, Maria Theresa's successor, Joseph II, moved a step toward genuine emancipation. A serf no longer would need landlord approval in his choice of occupation or spouse. At length, in 1789, peasants whose plots were inheritable and who paid a yearly state tax of two *gulden* or more were relieved of labor obligations on the domain. In place of free services and multifarious dues, they were to pay the landlord a flat sum of around 18 percent of their annual income. In addition, the state was guaranteed 12 percent. Though peasants covered by the reform were a minority of the total, the law represented the most important step taken in eighteenth-century Europe to free a servile work force through means short of political revolution.

Shortly after publishing the Edict of 1789, Joseph II died. Estate owners persuaded the emperor's successor to restore most peasant labor services. Nevertheless, they were rigorously defined and scrupulously observed. The role of the state as arbiter of landlord-peasant relations was now an accepted fact. The reformist example of the Hapsburgs influenced legislation elsewhere. Denmark and the German state of Baden abolished serfdom. Though Frederick II of Prussia and Catherine II of Russia limited their activity to the realm of good intentions, public opinion in their countries considered serfdom as a problem rather than an institution. In Poland, where forced rural labor was more deeply entrenched than anywhere else in Europe and where the central government was thoroughly incapable of defending the most elementary rights of the peasantry, a reformer wrote: "We have imposed upon our serfs the intolerable burden of an enslavement that has no counterpart elsewhere in Christendom." Humanitarian motives joined pragmatic ones to question and modify timeworn practice.

Peasant-landlord relations west of the Elbe were more complex than in eastern Europe. In parts of Germany, Italy, and France, serfdom still existed, but not more than 10 percent of western Europe's peasantry was subjected to its restrictions. Tenancy arrangements varied from country to country and region to region. In southern Italy, Sicily, Spain, and Portugal, sharecroppers and landless migrants were the rule. Though technically free to move, they nevertheless were so poor and dependent upon estate owners that their misery could not be distinguished from that of the most downtrodden Polish serf. West European governments rarely intervened in peasant-landlord relations. Tenants tried to defend their holdings in law courts. However, what satisfaction could they obtain from judges who themselves were landlords? Moreover, rural populations were expanding. Larger peasant families meant split inheritances, and split inheritances meant smaller, less productive plots. By the tens of thousands, peasant tenants had to sell out, wealth was concentrated in fewer hands, and the number of landless rose. The latter comprised a particularly embittered group, relatively young in age, increasingly poverty-stricken, conscious of deteriorating social-economic conditions, and as consumers hard hit by mounting prices.

France offers the classic case of the declining eighteenth-century tenant farmer. In 1789, more than 22 of 27 million people lived on the land. The French peasant was highly sensitive to his place in society. Though details of his obligations varied from place to place, he knew that he bore the overwhelming share of his country's taxes. He alone paid the *taille*, the state's tax on possessions and agricultural production. While other social groups had won exemption, for the peasant, Louis XIV's "revolutionary" contributions had become additions to the *taille.* Along with others, the peasant paid consumer taxes for his salt, shoe leather, playing cards, drinks, tobacco, and iron implements. He was aware that the state did not take these taxes directly but rather farmed them out to wealthy individuals who kept the major share of them in return for a fixed contribution to the government. The peasant paid a tithe to the bishop of his diocese, knowing that only a tiny fraction of his contribution would ever return to his parish to pay the priest and provide relief for the destitute. Most of the tithe supported the bishop himself, his episcopal administration, and wealthy abbeys. If the peasant was a sharecropper, he paid half or more of his crop in rents to the estate owner, plus sums for seed, tools, and the use of animal power. If he was a long-lease tenant, he paid not only his rents but also a welter of dues for use of the estate owner's mill, oven, and wine press. He had to perform a stipulated amount of road maintenance on the estate. It is true that these latter dues and services, the product of an age when the estate was a self-contained, self-sufficient community, were not a very great economic burden. Yet it was all the more galling to see greedy landlords charge legal experts to hunt down neglected dues in musty charters and then demand back payment for ten, twenty, or even fifty years. In good times and bad, the peasant bore a threefold burden to state, Church, and landlord. He might see his entire income seized by grasping hands.

After 1740, French tenancies declined in both number and size, and tenant farmers who sold out were reduced to sharecropping or migratory labor. Landlords tried to take over pastures administered in common by the peasant village. Consumer pressures caused the price of agricultural products to rise, and the large-scale exploiter derived the biggest profits. Until 1775, he lived in a golden age. Rents were up, prices were good, and even enclosures were increasing. From 1776 to 1789, however, a series of poor harvests in most parts of the country ended the period of agricultural prosperity, and estate owners tried to make up for underproduction with an even more vigorous assault upon long-term tenancies. They increased rents and dues at a time when the small cultivator had less to sell. As scarcity-provoked high prices forced consumers to spend a disproportionate share of their incomes on bread, they could not afford clothes. The textile entrepreneur sent out less material to be spun and woven in peasant cottages, and another source of rural income was cut. Nevertheless, peasant obligations to state, Church, and landlord remained as high as ever.

The cultivator's bitterness was directed at those who demanded payments from him. He believed that a conspiracy of government officers, tax farmers, *intendants,* high churchmen, and landlords was intent upon securing his destruction. He tried to fight back. The social climate of the 1780s illustrates not only an unprecedented rise in peasant-landlord lawsuits but also an increase in rural violence, brigandage, and simple peasant "usurpations" of pieces of the domain, seigneurial hunting grounds, and contested pastures. Late in 1788, the government admitted the rapidly deteriorating climate in the countryside and called upon each parish in France to list and collect specific grievances. But the time for discussion was past. With thousands of one-time tenants taking to the road monthly, those still on the land reacted in spontaneous and violent desperation. During the summer of 1789, a widespread peasant revolt destroyed the remnants of the feudal regime.

In eighteenth-century England, the communal patterns of rural life changed more dramatically than was the case in France, and the period has been called an age of agricultural revolution. In 1700, some English estate owners farmed directly with hired labor, but the overwhelming number leased plots to tenants residing in country villages. Like their west European counterparts, the most privileged members of village society in England claimed immunity from arbitrary eviction and willed plots to heirs and widows. On taking over a new plot, they were exempt from the irritating dues and services that continental landlords customarily milked from their tenants. English freeholders did not have to pay any annual rent, and they had the right to vote in county elections.

Beneath this cream of English peasant society were less privileged tenants, sharecroppers, and landless villagers. Despite distinctions in material wealth and social rank, all peasants derived a sense of communal security from the village. The village was responsible for seeing that no member suffered from excessive need. As on the continent, in the Midlands and most of southern England, open strips of land surrounded the village. While tenants considered themselves individual owners of stipulated strips, the village government controlled the sale of crops and distribution of livestock. Moreover, the village represented the peasant in disputes with the estate owner or his steward. The field strips belonging to a peasant were irregular in shape and size and seldom contiguous. Their patchwork distribution and small size precluded individual initiative and experiment. Landlords grumbled over the wastefulness of open fields and anachronism of village controls. England's population was growing; the continent was crying for grain and bread. Already in the 1730s, Lord Townshend showed how turnip cultivation could improve yields when rotated properly with barley, clover, and wheat. Jethro Tull described how a mechanical drill made possible more regular sowing and breaking up of the soil. For these innovations to work, however, scattered strips had to be consolidated into single plots, and the owner himself had to have the final say in cropping and stocking. Most important of all, a psychological mood had to develop that emphasized intensive exploitation and profits as opposed to the maintenance of collective village security.

In the eighteenth century, this mood became overwhelming. Six million acres of common lands were enclosed and developed. Furthermore, estate holders took advantage of a right to obtain enclosures through individual acts of Parliament. From 1700 to 1750, 115 enclosure acts were passed. In the 1760s, there were 424; in the 1770s, 642; from 1800 to 1810, 906. In the redistribution of enclosed fields and common lands, tenants were entitled to their plots, but the disposition of land involved expensive litigation, and construction of fences and roads involved costs that most village governments could ill-afford. Tenants therefore sold out to landlords or an enterprising peasant. The small tenant became an anachronism in the dawning world of capitalistic agriculture, and the enclosure movement destroyed the village community in England. Landless farmhands now, the majority of its inhabitants were thrown upon the parish, which found itself engulfed by victims. Several parishes might combine to establish workhouses, and industrialists took advantage of available labor in return for keeping the inmates alive. To prevent their running away, workhouse children were manacled and ringed by the neck. Still, inmates and prospective inmates fled to towns, wholly unprepared for the world they were to find.

Those able to profit from enclosures were the big winners. Free to experiment, "improving landlords" often increased productivity in ways unimaginable a generation earlier. Thomas William Coke of Holkham made marginal lands so profitable that in forty years he was able to increase rents nearly ten times over. He gave his renters long leases and insisted that they follow his prescribed model of cultivation. In Leicestershire, Robert Bakewell crossbred stock for superior traits and kept them alive through the winter on grass and root crops. His methods spread, and within a short time, England was raising animals for food whose size flabbergasted Europe. At the Smithfield market, oxen that had averaged 370 pounds in 1710 were averaging 800 pounds in 1795. Calves went from 50 to 150 pounds, sheep from 38 to 80 pounds.

The agricultural revolution had created a paradoxical situation in England. The destruction of the village dislocated society. Thousands were dumped into workhouses; tens of thousands drifted to the misery of towns. Yet practically no one was starving. Absolute famine was considered an unacceptable scandal, the sign of a barbaric past age. People were eating white bread, not rye. Cottagers and laborers alike knew the taste of roast beef and beer.

THE VICTORIOUS ARISTOCRACIES

Serfs and small tenants, the core of Europe's peasantry, might well have regarded the eighteenth century as a new iron age. They were the losers in a time of relative prosperity. For other groups, however, the three generations between 1715 and 1789 represented a moment when landed wealth had created a sense of incomparable refinement and luxury.

The primary beneficiaries were the aristocracies. In most of eastern Europe, the greatest landlords comprised the aristocracy. Members enjoyed an inherited superior social position that they translated into political power. Through their nominees, they controlled regional political assemblies, and where a national diet existed, they sat in it themselves. The sovereign awarded them the best posts in the army, civil administration, and Church. They had controlling interest in whatever rural industry existed. Fifteen magnatial families comprised the aristocracy of Poland. Around them, seeking favors, gifts, and appointments, swarmed their clients, a country nobility 700,000 strong. Many of these petty nobles were threadbare; half were without land. Parting from its rebellious traditions, the eighteenth-century Hungarian aristocracy constructed fantastic residences in and around Vienna and began priding itself upon service to the Hapsburgs. Meanwhile, the Magyar gentry stayed home, took the reins of district government, and criticized the assimilation of its natural leadership. In Russia, a similar aristocrat–country noble breach widened in the eighteenth century. Provincial landlords technically served the czar by collecting his taxes, administering his justice, and running his regiments. They considered the St. Petersburg court, however, as distant, decadent, and foreign. With its French manners, German music, and self-conscious cosmopolitanism, it indeed was. Of the European rulers east of the Elbe, only the king of Prussia appeared to merge both great aristocrats and country nobles successfully into the civil and military service of the state. Regional assemblies were shorn of their independence and transformed into functioning units of the bureaucracy. Old Junker families and petty nobles alike came to share a mentality based upon loyalty, duty, and service to the state.

In western Europe, distinctions between powerful aristocrats and mere nobles were more subtle and complex than in eastern Europe. Estates in the west rarely reached proportions that set apart magnates from everyone else. Few aristocrats could count on their landed wealth to draw swarms of noble clients to their side. Furthermore, unlike the east, the west was filled with towns and cities whose patricians, while not technically noble, possessed an inherited political power marking them as aristocrats. Great Britain had a titled nobility of only 200, but its ruling aristocracy of 75,000 controlled local politics and sent representatives to govern the country through Parliament. In the west, neither excessive propertied wealth nor a title guaranteed aristocratic status. Unlike the east Elbian regions, a wealthy bourgeois in France or west Germany might purchase a landed estate, call himself marquis, or add "von" to his surname. In time, king or prince might even confirm him in his nobility. However, only an important army commission, government post, seat in a provincial Estate, or judgeship in a law court brought him aristocracy.

After 1740, the aristocratically controlled society of western Europe grew more exclusive than ever. Those seated at its peak noted an ever-increasing number of young, literate, nonprivileged individuals beginning to question the foundations upon which the structure itself was composed. Rulers called upon aristocracies to increase their financial responsibilities to the state; some princes challenged aristocracies in their political privileges. The predictable reaction was for aristocrats to underscore the exclusiveness of their station, frustrate reform whenever possible, and unleash a counteroffensive of their own.

The aristocratic reaction can be measured in many ways. One was to make longevity of noble pedigree the ultimate requirement for public office. For example, after 1760, the parlements of France were demanding four generations of nobility for new members. Half the best administrative posts and most of the top military officerships were reserved for families possessing noble status for at least two hundred years. Under Louis XVI (1774–92), neither a prerevolutionary bishop nor *intendant* emerged from the bourgeoisie.

Elsewhere in western Europe, parallels could be found. After 1720, Sweden reverted back to the rule of the great families. The constitution was aristocratized, and only the existence of a strong civil service prevented slippage into a political climate resembling Poland's. The English House of Commons spoke for the aristocratic country gentry. The latter and their most prosperous tenants comprised the majority of the electorate of 250,000, and in 1776, it was estimated that 5,723 voters, nearly all gentry, chose half the members of Commons. Technically, English merchants could purchase country estates and adopt the ways and habits of the aristocracy. Conversely, the country gentry might invest in trade. For generations, this interchange of city-country, middle-class–aristocratic wealth contributed to the fluidity of English society. After the 1740s, however, the gentry began obstructing the lines between the moneyed and landed interests. Merchants and industrialists found it more difficult to acquire country estates. Rural gentlemen grew reluctant to send their sons to town to learn about business. Instead, they went straight into Parliament, where they distinguished their interests from those of the older, numerically fewer men of commerce. In the English counties, the aristocratized society was just as noticeable. After 1750, engaging in commerce or manufacturing disqualified an aspirant for the post of justice of the peace.

In England, the aristocracy was the government. This was also true in the continental republics, such as Geneva, Venice, or Berne. On the other hand, the assimilation of aristocracies into absolute monarchies was fraught with tensions. On March 3, 1766, King Louis XV of France, a ruler who disliked political confrontation, addressed the Parlement of Paris:

> Sovereign power resides in my person alone . . . I alone possess the independent and indivisible power to legislate. By my sole authority the officers of my courts proceed, not to form the law, but to register, publish, and execute it. . . . All public order emanates from me; and the rights and interests of the nation, that some dare

to separate from the monarch, are necessarily united with my own, and reside wholly in my hands.[1]

This berating of France's most prestigious corporate-aristocratic group ushered in a lingering constitutional crisis that would contribute a quarter century later to the dissolution of the ancien régime. The king's position was unadulterated absolutism, such as his great-grandfather, Louis XIV, was fond of representing. Louis XIV had forced parlementary aristocrats, the so-called robe, into accepting royal dominance. He had converted the great country aristocracy, the so-called sword, into dependent courtiers at Versailles. Even prior to the Sun King's death, however, suppressed aristocrats begin stirring against the absolutist ideal. After 1715, robe and sword aristocrats mingled socially, intermarried, and resurrected some of the political ideology of the Fronde. In eighteenth-century dress, its message was a sovereignty shared by the king on one hand and parlements, provincial Estates, high clergy, and important officers on the other. The Parlement of Paris took the lead in demanding the right not only to verify legislation but also to participate in its formation.

However, the *parlementaires* had no intention of extending either legislative privilege beyond their own corporate body or their antiabsolutist ideology into a movement for political and social reform. They blocked reform as vigorously as they blocked attempts by nonaristocrats for membership in their body. Responding to a royal attempt in 1776 to improve the tax structure, abolish the guilds, and do away with compulsory peasant labor in building roads, the speaker for the Parlement of Paris read:

> Any system which, in the guise of humanitarianism or improvement, causes a well-ordered monarchy to establish an equality of duties among men, thereby destroying necessary distinctions, will lead to anarchy. . . . The lower orders of the nation, unable to render the state distinguished service, acquit themselves through their tribute, industry, and corporal labor.[2]

Thus, after 1740, a lingering constitutional crisis existed in many parts of Europe, pitting kings and their reform-minded ministers against lay and clerical aristocracies. Though the major source of conflict was constitutional, the need of rulers for money played a large role as well. From 1715 to 1740, most sovereigns refrained from costly wars. For the next half-century, however, international rivalries erupted into terrific military struggles. The Anglo-French competition for empire revived, an aggressive Prussia upset the equilibrium in central Europe, and both the Hapsburg and Russian empires extended into the Balkans and Poland. Great armies and fleets had

---

[1]Quoted in J. Flammermont and M. Tourneux, *Remontrances du Parlement de Paris au xviiie siècle* (Paris, 1895), Vol. II, pp. 557–58. (Author's translation.)

[2]Solonelle remontrance du Parlement de Paris, 4 March 1776. Quoted in *Documents d'histoire vivante de l'antiquité à nos jours* (Paris, 1968), Vol. IV, p. 27. (Author's translation.)

to be built and maintained. Governments demanded that aristocrats yield needed revenue, and the privileged groups resisted with equal firmness. In England, for example, the gentry-controlled Parliament refused to reassess the value of land for tax purposes, even though no adjustments in value had been made since 1692. Consequently, the government had to seek other means of revenue, like tax stamps on articles of general consumption. This infuriated nonaristocratic Englishmen and helped drive colonists into rebellion.

In France, the crown wished to correct obvious inequities in the *taille*, the tax paid by peasants. It also wished to establish a general property tax that everyone would pay. The Parlement of Paris, provincial parlements, and officer corporations united in resisting any major fiscal reform, and in 1788, an "assembly of notables" declared that only an Estates General possessed the authority to resolve the government's financial predicament. The crown yielded, and the convocation of the body inaugurated the French Revolution.

In the Hapsburg lands, virtually the entire nobility was exempt from direct taxation in 1740. From peasants and townsmen, regional aristocracies collected what they thought the government needed to support a court, maintain defense, and pay officials. By 1790, however, the crown had made significant gains. It was collecting its own revenues, and under Joseph II (1780–90), state income rose by 70 percent. Noble land was duly registered as taxable and at the same rate as inheritable peasant properties. It is not surprising that uprisings in Hapsburg Hungary and Belgium in 1789–90 were led by disgruntled aristocrats and country gentry.

Elsewhere in Europe, governments intent upon economic reform faced inevitable aristocratic opposition, but even aristocratized Churches felt the sovereign's demands. The king of Naples began taxing his clergy; Joseph II of Austria and Catherine II of Russia seized monastic lands that they termed useless and then sold or redistributed them to the laity.

Aristocrats resisted rulers, but they also served them. Participation in government was the ultimate mark of social leadership, and most members of a diet, parlement, or estate would protest loudly if one likened their protection of privilege to acts of political obstructionism, much less disloyalty. Venal officers, whose fiscal, judicial, or administrative posts provided income in fees and bribes, insisted that they were devoted servants of their sovereigns. More worthy of the name, however, were those officials whose posts were not owned as inheritable property but rather were revocable and conditional upon the administrative effectiveness of their occupiers. This alternative bureaucracy of royal commissioners and secretaries had blossomed in France and Prussia in the late seventeenth century and became the lifeblood of royal administration in the eighteenth. Rulers in the Hapsburg empire, myriad states of Germany, Italian principalities, Spain, and Russia established their commissioner corps.

As the king's superior agent in each of thirty-four administrative districts within the country, the French *intendant* was the prototype commissioner —overseeing military recruitment, apportionment of the *taille*, the manner in which officers collected direct taxes, and the regulation of trade, industry, and agriculture. Under Louis XV (1715–74), the post of *intendant* grew exceptionally prestigious, and the robe aristocracy trained its brightest young members to serve. Often blood relatives of parlementary elites, French *intendants* displayed a spirit of initiative and independence in their work, and the king often selected his chief ministers from among their ranks. Thus, the great constitutional-political struggles of eighteenth-century France involved aristocratic personalities serving different sides. As ministers, commissioners, and courtiers, one group banked its future on the side of royal authority. As *parlementaires* and officers, the other group sought to moderate absolutism through oligarchic means. Ideology divided families, and individuals themselves changed sides. Yet to an extent unmatched in modern French history, the *function* of high administrative, judicial, and military service had become the monopoly of the aristocracy.

Unlike the time of Louis XIV, the eighteenth-century French bureaucracy failed to welcome earnest, ambitious nonaristocrats to high posts. The Prussian bureaucracy never did. Many Prussian noble families were quite poor, and the country possessed no magnatial landowning class around which clients could hover. Once William of Brandenburg and his two successors had tamed the regional diets and assemblies, state and military service offered the sole avenue to prestigious careers. The administration of districts, towns, and royal lands, as well as the responsibility for tax collection, the fostering of industry, and internal colonization, necessitated the labors of at least five hundred senior and several thousand junior officials. The central government in Berlin and the military administration needed expert personnel. Landowning nobles monopolized the important posts. Their commissions could be revoked, and little scope for individual initiative was permitted. Regulations from Berlin were explicit; commissioners were poorly paid and trained to spy on one another. The Junkers called into the civil service of Frederick the Great took pride in knowing that their bureaucracy was the least corrupt and most efficient in Europe. The king repaid them by acknowledging their mastery over the peasants on their manors and by fitting society around their needs and code. Moreover, he possessed the security of reigning over a docile, well-integrated, working aristocracy. On the entire continent, only the esprit de corps of the Prussian military rivaled that of the Prussian bureaucracy.

Peter the Great had also wished to convert the Russian nobility into a state-serving aristocracy. He destroyed the old boyar councils, reorganized administrative and military structures, and created the Table of Ranks of obligatory service. No ancient charters of privilege protected Russia's aristocrats. They were creatures of the czar and his needs. During the forty years after Peter's death, however, a period largely marked by palace coups and political instability, aristocrats succeeded in evading the compulsory aspects of state service; and in 1762, Czar Peter III granted them the privilege of leaving state service at any time they wished. Twenty-three years later, Czarina Catherine II conceded additional privileges to the Russian noblesse that erased its dependence upon the sovereign and turned it into a caste that was the envy of west European aristocracies. Nobles ran their provincial and district assemblies, controlled the military, and filled the inner councils of the Czarina's government. Only they could acquire or own lands with serfs and build factories. They were exempt from taxes and corporal punishment. If accused of a crime, they were tried by their peers alone.

In Spain, aristocratic officeholders labored at preventing the development of a professional civil service. In their hereditary German lands, the eighteenth-century Hapsburgs tried to create the nucleus of one, its members either chosen from the older nobility or else raised to noble status, and these district officials took over public welfare responsibilities resembling those of the French *intendants*. Urged by the Hapsburgs to submit to the will of Vienna, the Hungarian gentry resisted and considered enviously the justices of the peace of the distant English countryside. In the latter place, no central government imposed orders upon the justices. No monarch threatened them with armed intervention. As unpaid country gentlemen serving for life, their idea of administration was to fulfill duties as described by common or statute law. They knew that the law, made and interpreted by Parliament, was the work of those who shared their interests and rank.

Therefore, while eighteenth-century aristocracies consolidated their position as the dominant force in society, their role in government was ambivalent. In England and Poland, they were the government. In Prussia, they served willingly, and under Catherine II, they helped convert the Russian empire into an aristocratized state. In France, Spain, and the Hapsburg empire, they proclaimed devotion to monarchical principle while alternately serving and challenging absolutism. Not necessarily the wealthiest individuals in European society, aristocrats were indisputably the most privileged. In most Catholic countries, they dominated the high clergy. Their social and economic strengths were engraved in the land they controlled or owned and in the day-to-day power this afforded them over the lives of those who worked the soil.

THE EMERGING BOURGEOISIE

While eighteenth-century aristocracies consolidated their social leadership, in Europe's north Atlantic states, individuals were establishing lucrative careers in trade, the professions, and ultimately industry. In constructing their bureaucracies, the rulers of France, Prussia, Austria, and the smaller German states needed trained and educated lower-echelon officials, secretaries, and clerks which traditional aristocratic or noble sources were unable to supply. Of course, the social, economic, and political importance of the bourgeoisie was nothing new. Medieval Flanders and north Italy had prospered upon middle-class commerce and preindustrial manufactures. Merchants and guildsmen had built the civilization of the south German communes. The roots of France's parlementary aristocracy were bourgeois, as was a considerable segment of England's landed gentry. In 1726, Daniel Defoe reminded English aristocrats all too willing to forget their origins that "the tradesman's children, or at least their grandchildren, come to be as good gentlemen, statesmen, Parliament men, privy councillors, judges, bishops, and noblemen, as those of highest birth and the most ancient families."

Certainly the topmost layer of the eighteenth-century bourgeoisie possessed a material lifestyle that, family pedigree and noble quarterings aside, was similar to that of wealthy aristocrats. The regents of the Dutch Republic and men who filled the council seats of the urban republics in the Holy Roman Empire, Switzerland, and north Italy, were nonnoble aristocrats. In France, bourgeois individuals might purchase certain stipulated offices, especially municipal ones, and thus acquire limited prestige in government service. They also might purchase rural estates and beleaguer unfortunate tenants with rent hikes or long-forgotten dues responsibilities. A group of bankers and financiers distinguishable as "bourgeois living nobly" constituted the dominant economic element in French society. Its members had reaped fortunes by supplying Louis XIV with loans and provisioning his troops. In return, they were permitted to keep the lion's share of the state's "indirect" taxes, customs receipts and sales taxes that everyone paid on salt, tobacco, wine, liquor, leather, iron, paper, and cloth. With their private administrations of receivers, controllers, clerks, and troops, these financiers, the Farmers General, formed a state within the state. Eighteenth-century Frenchmen of all social groups detested them, but their wealth brought them large landed properties. Nobles took their daughters as wives, and Louis XV took their daughters as mistresses.

Municipal regents and Farmers General comprised a nonnoble crust that was aristocratic, privileged, and well-entrenched. Just beneath this level, among the shipbuilders, arms makers, international traders, and important textile manufacturers of the north Atlantic states, the temptation of an aristocratic lifestyle and hope of entering the charmed circle itself remained powerful. However, in a world governed by aristocratic values, where an industrialist or merchant was held in general contempt by those above him, to attain aristocracy meant rejecting bourgeois occupations. In France, whenever reformers tried to establish a noblesse of great international traders, they were repulsed by aristocrats. Numerous businessmen accepted this fact of life and therefore invested their hard-earned capital in aristocratically acceptable enterprises, such as country property or office. Others, however, challenged the contempt of social superiors with a scorn of their own, with what has been termed a "kind of moral-consciousness, a contrasting of solid qualities of character against the idleness and superficiality of one's social superiors."[3] Furthermore, tension between social orders was aggravated by increasing numbers of both aristocratic and nonaristocratic males surviving adolescence and receiving good educations. They expected jobs commensurate with their training and abilities, but first-class opportunities in government, military, and Church failed to keep pace with the numbers seeking them. Attractive posts became virtual preserves of the aristocracy, thus contributing to both the status anxiety and moral class consciousness of the ambitious bourgeoisie.

However, the overwhelming majority of Europe's bourgeois did not live opulent, comfortable lives as shipbuilders, speculators in sugar, or traffickers in slaves. They did not have their solemn portraits made for posterity, nor did they build stately town houses. Their lives and interests were parochial, and their dealings rarely extended beyond their town or street. It is very difficult to depict the average burgher, whose place on the social ladder of the Third Estate had as many rungs above as below him. From country to country, particular conditions defined him. In England, he might be a small merchant manufacturer of cotton cloth, distributing and collecting goods from fifty peasant weavers scattered round his town. In Spain, he was much poorer, living out a dull, rhythmical existence mapped out by guild, Church, and king. In Germany, small merchants and master craftsmen mingled traits of sobriety with grudging deference to superiors and haughty authoritarianism towards inferiors. A Leipzig bookseller worked regularly from seven in the morning until eight at night, shunned card games, and never set foot in a tavern. On Sundays, he went to church, read a newspaper, and strolled around his town. In the summer, he would treat his family to a few trips into the countryside, where they would drink a bottle of wine. Once per year he would take his apprentices for a two-mile drive in his carriage. Moving eastward toward the serf societies of Poland and Russia, burghers became rarer in number and were even considered alien. Polish petty commerce was in the hands of Germans and Jews; in Hungary, Germans and Greeks were the tradesmen.

The eighteenth century witnessed the evolution of two categories of bourgeois, distinguishable in wealth and lifestyles from the topmost ranks of middle-class society and differing as well from the merchants and master craftsmen who had formed the nucleus of Europe's urban life since the Middle Ages. The first category, intimately linked to the growth of govern-

---

[3]R. R. Palmer, "Social and Psychological Foundations of the Revolutionary Era," *The New Cambridge Modern History*, Vol. VIII (Cambridge, England, 1965), p. 435.

mental bureaucracies in central Europe, contained lawyers, clerks, treasury agents, and other trained officials who served as subordinate members of the departments and boards established by the Prussian Hohenzollerns, Austrian Hapsburgs, and German territorial princes. Aristocratic commissioners, weaned away from diets and estates in order to serve sovereigns more directly, needed expert advisers and administrators. Princes trained them in new schools and universities. The three-hundred-odd independent German states, each with a specific jurisdiction, necessitated civil services that contained far more officials in proportion to the general population than at any other time in the region's history. Prussia expected honorable service from its middle- and lower-rank civil servants, who were given tax exemptions and privileges. They were trained to follow orders and perform their tasks meticulously. Yet they were not dull automatons. Throughout central Europe in the eighteenth century, bureaucrats founded reading rooms and reading societies. They patronized the theater and opera. Their culture was more political and more cosmopolitan than that of the older mercantile–master craftsman bourgeoisie. By learning French and copying French fashions in furniture, dress, and eating habits, they perhaps aped their aristocratic superiors. Still, after 1750, this newly educated, "official" bourgeoisie responded most positively to the German literary revival, and this same group proved most receptive to extending religious, civil, and political liberties.

The second category of evolving bourgeois emerged from industry. A major goal of government in eighteenth-century England was to increase private profit and insure economic development. Indeed, an argument for the enclosure acts was that the acts made it possible to accumulate excess capital for investment outside agriculture. Traditionally, the chief area of investment had been overseas trade. By 1700, European demand for Indian cotton goods had persuaded investors to subsidize the cotton industry elsewhere. Money was channeled into West Indian plantations and the American South; Africa provided the slave labor for planting and picking. Most important, the raw goods then would be shipped to England for processing and manufacturing. Peasant and, later, factory labor created Britain's new textile industry. In the late eighteenth century, the cheap cotton clothes manufactured in the regions of Liverpool and Manchester were intended to cover the backs of the English and, even more importantly, were to be exported to Europe and America. From 1750 to 1770, the export of British-made cottons grew tenfold. Inventions greatly accelerated the pace of spinning and weaving: among the first came the flying shuttle (1733), waterframe, and spinning jenny (1769–70); and a decade later, the spinning mule and power loom.

Even before the 1780s, the decade of England's celebrated "takeoff" into industrial revolution, adventurous entrepreneurs in textiles could become rich very quickly. Not much capital was needed to start. Market demand brought profits, and there was no shortage of labor. Manufacturers sent out the goods to be spun to peasant cottages. Once mechanized weaving permitted the realization of maximum profits by concentrating equipment and workers in one place, the modern factory was born. Industrial capitalists assumed responsibility for housing workers, paving roads, and providing a modicum of law and order, thus creating the factory town. The rising bourgeois industrialist spread from England to northern France and Belgium. In addition to textile plants, collieries and ironworks developed. Here, too, England took the lead, and invention stimulated production. Newcomen's steam pump permitted deeper reaches into the mines without flooding them; the Darbies learned to smelt iron with coke instead of forest-denuding wood for charcoal. In the second half of the eighteenth century, England bounded into first place in iron production, and after 1781, Watt's rotary steam engine assured the industrialist the power with which he was to supply the world.

A bourgeois culture accompanied the evolution of bourgeois social groups and transcended national frontiers, occupations, and at times even the barriers between Estates. A Prussian civil servant or Manchester cotton manufacturer might share aspects of this culture with a French notary, book publisher, "philosophic" *abbé,* "liberal" nobleman, or even "enlightened" yeoman. Lacking a precise ideology, the culture must be defined as an evolving consciousness. It fed upon several seventeenth-century sources, chiefly the skeptical tradition of Descartes and Bayle, the empirical psychology and political liberalism of Locke, and faith in the great scientific discoveries. Nourishing it further were the works of eighteenth-century writers who tempered trenchant criticisms of mankind's present lot with poignant hopes concerning his future possibilities. It is foolhardy to envision armies of bureaucrats, businessmen, and professionals joyously leaping into their Spinoza, Newton, or Locke every time their occupational cares afforded them a moment's respite. Nonetheless, during the eighteenth century, a mental attitude was shared by many middle-class people who rejected a culture directed by the conservative forces of Church and guild and who were growing impatient with the preeminence of aristocratic values and aristocratic social-political leadership. The new mentality possessed many inner contradictions, but in general it called for freer trade and manufacture, religious toleration, the thawing of barriers to upward social mobility, and the opening of political life to more widespread participation.

In France this critical spirit grew most forceful and bitter, reaching upward into segments of the noblesse and downward into segments of the peasantry. In the 1740s, the aristocratic marquis d'Argenson termed as worthless those grand seigneurs who based social status and political power upon their "dignities, wealth, titles, offices, and functions. . . . If you listen to these individuals, . . . you will hear that they are the foundation of the state. . . . I understand that a good race of hunting dogs should be preserved;

but when they degenerate, we drown them."[4] The peasant father of the writer Restif de la Bretonne added: "My son, we are non-noble and proud of it. The non-noble [*roturier*] is the man *par excellence*. It is he who pays the taxes, works, sows, harvests, trades, builds, and manufactures. The right to be useless is a poor right indeed!"[5]

However disenchanted they might have been with a world governed by aristocratic privilege and rank, few eighteenth-century bourgeois dreamed of leveling society altogether. Their envy of land, the traditionally aristocratic source of wealth, was strong, and the aristocracy's reluctance to allow their social and political advance turned them against that order. Moreover, a bourgeois sense of corporate virtue made members of the middle class suspicious of the peasant or artisan, distinguished scornfully as "the people." Voltaire, one of the most important formulators of the bourgeois consciousness, wrote: "The people will remain ignorant and weak-minded, always needing to be led by a small number of enlightened men." It nevertheless remains true that bourgeois discontents from the 1750s to 1789 were directed against aristocratic leadership rather than the lower social orders. In North America, the discontents merged into a colonial revolt. In England, Ireland, the Dutch Netherlands, and Geneva, the discontents hardened into political movements against the political status quo. In France, they were the necessary catalyst for a great revolution that became international in scope during the last decade of the century.

THE WORKING CLASSES

The great social dramas of the eighteenth century concerned the crisis of the peasantry, the offensive of the aristocracy, and the disaffection of the bourgeoisie. Seemingly overshadowed by these movements, Europe's artisans and laborers found their lives changing rapidly. From Yorkshire to the Urals, the worker in traditional rural industry was customarily a peasant who supplemented his income or kept himself alive in the slack season by producing objects destined for sale. In a corner of his cottage was a primitive loom or spinning wheel. Wives and daughters sewed. Those who descended into coal mines or iron pits were customarily peasants or rural serfs, as were those who labored in glassworks, forges, and paper mills that dotted the countryside. Even skilled artisans, such as cutlers round Sheffield and Solingen or the linen weavers of Silesia, were through most of the century part-time workers from the fields.

In those towns of western and central Europe where guild control was

---

[4]Marquis d'Argenson, *Journal* (Paris, 1867), ed. E. J. B. Rathery, Vol. I, p. xv. (Author's translation.)

[5]Restif de la Bretonne, *Vie de mon père*. Quoted in *Documents d'histoire vivante de l'antiquité à nos jours* (Paris, 1968), Vol. IV, p. 27. (Author's translation.)

strong, a clear-cut hierarchy of labor existed. Fiscal and judicial privileges protected certain trades, contract and statute dictated the terms of apprenticeships, and mutual-assistance organizations served journeymen. The craft guild represented labor's aristocracy and was most highly developed in the oligarchy-controlled towns of southern Germany, northern Italy, Switzerland, and the Netherlands. The French guilds, on the other hand, formed the channel through which royal government exercised its surveillance over industry. Clannish rather than competitive, with masters fixing both prices and production, with style and quality rigidly adhered to, guilds stood for the economic order of the past. During the eighteenth century, relations between master and worker degenerated. At the same time, barriers between them heightened. Masterships became hereditary, and except through a fortuitous marriage, journeymen found it nearly impossible to rise to top ranks in their trades. Consequently, worker class consciousness increased, and journeymen began imposing a militant character upon the traditionally benevolent one of their protective associations. In France, master craftsmen had the government suppress these primitive trade unions, and in the Holy Roman Empire an edict in 1731 deprived them of their legality. The peculiarly German tradition of journeymen traveling from town to town with their skills continued, though imperial governments became highly suspicious of these rootless, contentious young individuals. Journeymen became the first people in Germany to endure having to report to police when arriving in or departing from a town.

By 1715 in England and the larger German states, guild-dominated industry had deteriorated markedly. East of the Elbe, it had never existed. After 1750, the French government turned against the guilds and in 1776 dissolved most of them. All regimes saw guilds as weights chained to the neck of industrial development, their production methods and corporate structures incapable of meeting the consumer needs of growing populations. Moreover, they shielded masters from the state's judge or tax collector. In offering subsidies to individual manufacturers or industrialists, governments bypassed the guilds. Capitalists were encouraged to hire wage labor, and in eastern Europe, the state gave them serfs.

Throughout the eighteenth century, the factory replaced both the guild workshop and cottage industry. The effects can be seen in urban development. The growth of innumerable eighteenth-century towns was identical with the influx of working-class populations. In northern France, the laboring population of Sedan comprised 800 in 1683; in 1789, it was 14,000. In present-day Belgium, the textile and metallurgy complex round Verviers and Liège employ 100,000 people. Cotton finishing brought similar numbers respectively to Barcelona and Manchester. On the eve of the revolution of 1789, 2 million French workers were devoting more than half their laboring time to industry, and nearly half the adult population of England was producing goods that others sold. The nomadism of unskilled and semiskilled laborers overwhelmed the journeyman wanderings of previous ages. In England, the movement was from south to north. In France, it was towards Lille, Lyons, and the Île de France. In Spain, the pull was eastward, and in Germany, it was toward Dresden and Breslau. Not even the borders between states stopped these human migrations. Saxons, Styrians, Piedmontese, and Carinthians went wherever there were mines. Swiss cotton workers moved to France, Belgium, Saxony, and Silesia.

The immigrant to town or mine had to develop different work habits from those he had known in the countryside. A small-time entrepreneur employing a few peasants in a backyard shed was bound to be close to his workers. The workweek was long but flexible. Employer and employee might well leave for half a day to see an itinerant circus or attend a cockfight. Later they would make up for lost time with three or four feverish eighteen-hour workdays. The factory's claims to efficiency changed all that. The impersonal engagement between worker and foreman meant 7:00 A.M. to 8:00 P.M., Monday through Saturday, with an hour of unpaid time for meals. In the factory and mine, women and children endured equality of toil, though at a fraction of the man's salary. Pay might be based upon the worker's productivity, it might be a weekly/monthly wage, or else it might take the form of an indemnity against housing, food, and tools which the owner supplied, thus reducing the worker to a state of perpetual indebtedness. Fines for alleged worker negligence, absenteeism, or defective products cut further into wages.

Salaries varied from region to region and from industry to industry. By 1780, French engravers, watchmakers, and cutlers were earning six to eight times more than spinners and weavers in country districts. At the same time, English day workers in textiles earned five to six shillings per week, skilled weavers in Leeds earned eight to ten, and Newcastle coal miners, fifteen. Throughout the course of the century, salaries rose but at a rate half that of prices and one-fourth that of agricultural rents. In Spain from 1740 to 1790, the purchasing power of workers dropped by nearly a third. In the industrializing regions of France, the loss was rarely less than 25 percent. The indices of precarious existence, while not so murderous as in the seventeenth century, nevertheless had not disappeared. A poor harvest meant skyrocketing bread prices, and this meant low demand for textiles and industrial goods. Widespread layoffs followed, and hunger returned as a haunting fact of life. In 1789, workers in Paris were spending up to 90 percent of their salaries for bread. In normal times, the average was 50 to 60 percent.

Hunger was not the sole oppressor of the new factory hand. Throughout Europe, aristocratic governments and bourgeois industrialists agreed that no distinction seemed to exist between laboring classes and dangerous classes. Legislation was intended to ensure docility. French workers could not quit their factory jobs without the consent of their employers. When they changed residence, they had to present certificates of good conduct to the police. They could neither assemble nor strike. They had to be off the streets by 10:00 P.M. England, the German and Italian states, and Spain had similar laws. Nevertheless, illegal worker organization took place. Englishmen in textiles, hatmaking, paper manufacturing, and small metallurgy took the lead, but what they formed were in themselves corporate elites, intended for the most specialized and best-paid workers and excluding the laboring masses. In most of Europe, workers were weak and unorganized. Their class consciousness was mounting, but it was less than employers and governments thought. Journeyman associations still fought street battles with each other. The semiskilled in factories scorned newcomers from the countryside. A skilled cutler had nothing but contempt for the humble domestic spinner. Worker unrest before 1789 took the form of bread riots and vague mob action. Only rarely did it demand amelioration of actual labor conditions. It took the French Revolution and its aftermath to instill in the working poor a conviction that organization, collective action, was necessary to establish genuine programs that carried over into demands for political power.

Chapter Eight
The Enlightenment

THE RELIGIOUS CULTURE

From 1715 to 1789, religion remained the dominant cultural force for most Europeans. The majority of books printed were devotional works, evangelization was active, and Churches tried to purge folk religion of pagan elements. Governments served the faith by enforcing respect for the Sabbath and punishing transgressors vigorously. In Germany and Scandinavia, Pietists kept alive the flame of Protestant revivalism, and in England, Methodist preachers carried the religion of the heart to thousands of villagers, the lost souls of the coal pits, and the slum dwellers of the teeming new industrial towns. In Italy and France, Catholic Jansenism revived. Monastic and priestly scholarship thrived. At their abbey at Saint Germain des Prés in Paris, the Benedictines of Saint Maur produced meticulous critical editions of the Church Fathers and medieval history. The history of the Roman emperors by the French Jansenist Le Nain de Tillemont inspired Edward Gibbon to write his *Decline and Fall of the Roman Empire*, and the Italian priest Ludovico Muratori made an unsurpassed collection of the antiquities of medieval Italy.

Nevertheless, the period was not a religious age. Established Churches lacked independent leadership. Eighteenth-century popes were especially weak and ineffective and were chosen mainly because they were aristocrats. Bishops in France, Spain, Portugal, and the Hapsburg empire found it more efficacious to bend to the wishes of their rulers when the sovereigns' orders contradicted those of the pope. In Protestant countries such as England, Prussia, Sweden, and Denmark, the Church was an agency of government, and such subservience continued to sap organized religion of its spiritual vigor.

As a comfortable, harmless, drifting institution, Anglicanism offered the most notorious example of an organized Church that had lost its sense of mission. Most English bishops were politicians, using their places in the

House of Lords to advance to more lucrative sees. The king reserved the best sees for favored aristocrats, but no village curacy escaped the patronage and favor seeking that marked political life. Anglican clerics had relatively little to do and did not even need to reside in the parish that they ostensibly served. Neglecting the issues of evil, sin, and redemption, eighteenth-century Anglican leaders made a religious virtue of political or economic success. They weren't alone. Even the Protestant Dissenters fell under the spell of Deism and worldly wisdom. Denied full civil rights by law and excluded from the universities, they attended their own academies, and many turned their immense energies from religion to business, scholarship, and science.

The failure of Anglican leadership and secularization of Dissenter ideals left a spiritual vacuum in eighteenth-century English Protestantism, one that was greatly aggravated by the social dislocations of the agricultural revolution and beginnings of industrialization. With its stress upon worldly virtues, the established Church hardly addressed the needs of the miserable workers moving to mine and town. A few sensitive spirits founded charity schools for the poor or devoted themselves to missionary work, and others, like John Wesley, rediscovered sin and portrayed it with a realism that was comprehensible to the poor.

The children of an Anglican priest and his iron-willed wife, John Wesley and his brother Charles attended Oxford University in the 1720s. Their acts of self-mortification and penance made them curiosities, and in the following decade they left to do missionary work in Georgia. However, they discovered that devotion to the formal rites of Anglicanism was out of place in a rough frontier society, and they returned to England with a sense of failure. In May 1738, John underwent a mystical experience based upon total submission to Christ that transformed his life. His zeal drew followers, and the distinctive organizational lines upon which Wesley constructed his movement provoked the hostility of Anglican leaders. Thus Methodism evolved into a Protestant sect with its own habits and practices. Wesley himself ordained a clergy. Between the day of his mystical experience and that of his death in 1791, he traveled 224,000 miles and delivered over 40,000 sermons. He went to the darkest slum and remotest village, preaching a basic message of salvation and rebirth and urging upon his listeners a morality of thrift, abstinence, and work. Methodism's political and social message was profoundly reactionary. Under Wesley's leadership, the movement was hostile to education and receptive to child labor. It was fundamentalist and intolerant of non-Protestants. Because it channeled the material misery of the poor and weak into otherworldly hope rather than worldly change, Methodism unwittingly served the forces of economic expansion and the political status quo.

For eighteenth-century Protestantism, the great event was the rise of the Wesleyites; for eighteenth-century Catholicism, it was the fall of the Jesuits. Both events derived from the weakness of venerable religious institutions.

After 1715, rulers in Catholic Europe waged an unrelenting campaign against papal influence in national affairs. They expropriated monasteries and convents, nominated bishops and abbots, and their theorists on Church-state relations might call the pope an Italian politician, the Roman Curia his Fifth Column, and the Jesuits his shock troops. By the 1740s, the problem of the Jesuits had become the most serious matter of all. Their hold upon secondary-school education was firm. They knew too much about the molding of young minds and had enemies everywhere. Memories of the Chinese and Malabar rites remained fresh, and even the pope's esteem for them had fallen. Following a long period of official harassment, in 1759 the king of Portugal expelled them from his country and colonial possessions. Five years later, after an examination of the Jesuits' constitution found it to be subservient to a foreign power, Louis XV removed the order from France. In 1767, the rulers of Naples and Spain followed suit. Finally, in 1773, Pope Clement XIV, submitting to the bullying of princes, Dominicans, and Franciscans alike, suppressed the Jesuits entirely.

Eighteenth-century Churches had to endure much more than princely incursions into their spiritual authority and organizational structure. During this period, skepticism about the claims of orthodox doctrine became a central feature of Europe's intellectual heritage. While the overwhelming majority of Europeans remained attached to their fathers' beliefs and prejudices, for numbers of comfortable, literate individuals, indifference or hostility to Christian tenets was increasing. In Protestant countries, natural religion permeated official orthodoxies. The disappearance and decline of official censorship in the Protestant states led to publication of deistic writings. Influenced by Newtonian physics and astronomy, these works established God as a providential watchmaker who had set the universe running for the best and invited individuals to revere Him by adhering to a very brief and reasonable set of rules for human conduct. Old credal distinctions were to be abandoned; people were to be socially useful and charitable toward one another. As the poet Alexander Pope wrote in 1733, "For Modes of Faith let graceless zealots fight; he can't be wrong whose life is in the right."

Deism penetrated Catholic Europe also. In France, the young baron de Montesquieu wrote in his *Persian Letters* (1721) that the most certain way of pleasing God was "to observe the rules of society and the duties of humanity." Voltaire added that the meaning of religion is "to be a good husband, good father, good neighbor, good subject, and good gardener." The *abbé* Pluche's best-selling *Spectacle of Nature* held that Divine Providence's only demand upon humanity was contentment with one's lot. Such dismissal of dogma in favor of a complacent, optimistic ethic touched the beliefs of the rising body of civil servants in Prussia, north Italy, and the Hapsburg empire. In France, however, early eighteenth-century Deism evolved into an aggressive anti-Catholic movement because official French

Catholicism resisted deistic principles, especially the practice of religious toleration, as threats to the social order. Seeing their pleas for toleration and natural religion treated as heresy, Deists exposed clerical institutions and practices before the bar of Reason. Materialists and atheists joined, and the Church was thrown on the defensive.

Timeworn Christian attitudes and practices were forced to confront "philosophic" alternatives supposedly derived from common sense and social utility. Critics called original sin morally reprehensible and the Trinity an affront to principles of logic. Biblical explanations of natural phenomena were accused of retarding scientific progress, and those poor souls who took seriously the vows of poverty, chastity, and obedience and who practiced the contemplative life were accused of denying their genuine humanity. Eighteenth-century *philosophes* confronted Christian teachings by stressing the legitimacy of earthly happiness without guilt. The French *Encyclopédie*, an immense collaborative effort of more than two hundred contributors, observed: "Who can deny that the arts, industry, the taste for fashion—all those things which are beneficial to commerce—are not a genuine boon for countries? However, Christianity, which condemns luxury, weakens and destroys those things that are dependent upon it. Through its renunciation of vanity, it introduces laziness, poverty, the abandonment of everything—and in short destroys the arts."

Sporadic attacks by rulers on clerical wealth and religious societies, critiques by the encyclopedists and their allies of ecclesiastical institutions and Christian values, the advance of deistic ideas in literate society, and the emergence of a respectable materialism grievously weakened the underpinnings of traditional religious life. The advance of Methodism notwithstanding, society was turning toward the secular, especially in the fashionable reaches of western and central Europe. The same critical turn of mind that questioned king worship and acceptance of social immobility approached religious dogma and practice. The great revolution at the century's end transformed belief nearly as profoundly as it changed the social structure and political forms.

THE SCIENTIFIC CULTURE

The progress of science most accurately exemplified the eighteenth century's concern for a rational, socially useful approach toward life. The scientist had won his struggle to achieve cultural parity with the theologian and university professor and even became a new kind of folk hero. Because inquiry had not yet diverged into esoteric specialties, curious amateurs still could understand what scientists were doing. Scientific societies arose all over Europe and the Americas to explain technique and discovery through magazine articles, public lectures, demonstrations, and courses. In Paris, the *abbé* Nollet passed electrical charges through companies of royal troops and volunteer monks while onlookers gasped in delight. Electricity became a fashionable toy. Private parties offered occasions for charging up. However, public obsession with science led to misrepresentations of science as magic for modern man, far more certain in its results than medieval incantations. Charlatans used elaborate contraptions to commune with the dead or other worlds; they pretended to cure ancient diseases through magnetism or electricity, and the gullible paid handsomely for their services.

Writings on pure science formed a branch of literature. Joseph Priestley's *History and Present State of Electricity* (1767) set the tone, and with unparalleled verve a generation of remarkable Frenchmen described their findings in the vernacular rather than Latin. In 1796, Pierre-Simon Laplace proposed science as humanity's next religion. To Laplace, the successful mission of science was to have "dissipated the fears of celestial phenomena and to have destroyed the errors born of being ignorant of our genuine rapports with nature, errors and fears which will revive promptly if the flame of science is ever extinguished."

Eighteenth-century science was directed toward the concrete and empirically derived, and the passion for measurement and calculation markedly affected chemistry. In 1750, earth, air, fire, and water still were considered elements. The "phlogiston theory," first expounded in 1697, held that all combustible bodies expelled an inflammable substance on burning. For a metal to be reduced to elemental earth, its "phlogiston" had to be released. The theory dominated much of eighteenth-century chemistry, and the isolation of gases such as chlorine and manganese occurred virtually as fortuitous accidents. Though Priestley successfully isolated oxygen in 1774, he remained chained to the phlogiston theory. He called oxygen "new air." Though Priestley isolated nine gases, his discoveries lacked plan, coming as accidents or surprises.

On the other hand, Antoine Lavoisier, indisputably the century's greatest chemist, removed the last vestiges of magic from his chosen branch of science, isolated oxygen from both air and water, underscored the active role of the gas in calcination and respiration, and destroyed the phlogiston theory. Lavoisier proved that matter is indestructible and gave to chemistry its nomenclature, the list of elements, and its means of expression, the equation. The forty memoirs that Lavoisier wrote for the Paris Academy of Science tightly coordinated his work into a systematized whole. His *Elementary Treatise on Chemistry* (1789) remains a landmark in the history of science. A Farmer General and director of the state's saltpeter works, Lavoisier was a part-time experimenter. He wished to convey his view of the larger perspectives of science to lay people. His basic tool was the scale, and he was guided from start to finish by the hypothesis that matter might change form but would neither augment nor diminish.

Genius applied to painstaking observation and experiment permitted

Lavoisier to grant scientific respectability to chemistry. Similarly, the patient laboratory work of the Dutchman van Musschenbroek, Frenchman Coulomb, and Italian Galvani turned electricity away from being a fashionable toy and paved the way for Alessandro Volta's discovery in 1800 of current and his invention of the electric battery. Meanwhile, processes of heat fascinated both the public and experimenters, even though precise and universally accepted measures of temperature eluded scientists. A professor of chemistry and anatomy at Glasgow University, Joseph Black, was puzzled by the extraordinary time it took ice to melt or boiling water to evaporate into steam. Black observed that a "capacity for heat" caused mercury to heat and cool much more rapidly than water. He was particularly astonished to find that capacity for heat had nothing to do with the weight or density of the substance involved, and he discovered how to measure the specific heat of a substance by comparing it to the heat of water. Black's work turned the study of heat into a careful, exact science. Specific heats were worked out for liquids, solids, and gases, and instruments were devised for measuring thermal expansion. In a rare case of theoretical and technological interdependence, James Watt used Black's researches in his invention of the separate condenser for the steam engine.

"Collect experimental evidence and shun the spirit of system-building." Despite this advice by the French naturalist George-Louis Leclerc, count de Buffon, the passion for collecting objects and facts and for determining the age of fossils, rocks, and the earth itself continued to challenge heretofore sacrosanct systems, including Genesis. Under an obligation to offer up alternatives, in 1778 Buffon himself published the *Epochs of Nature*, which proposed an authoritative and thoroughly naturalistic history of the earth and life upon it. According to Buffon, more than 60,000 years ago, a comet crashed into the sun, spewing forth a piece of molten matter which formed our planet. Seven historical stages followed, each cooler than its predecessor. The process was continuous and unalterable, and Buffon volunteered the gloomy conclusion that in 88,000 years the earth would grow too cold to sustain life. Divine intervention had no role in Buffon's story, and he earned the condemnation of the Sorbonne's theologians. Though government censors prohibited the *Epochs*, clandestine editions flooded France and translations flooded Europe.

Eighteenth-century Europeans were introduced to a concept of geological evolution that challenged not only Genesis but also the concept of a static Newtonian world machine. Buffon's exciting hypothesis of the earth's development stimulated thinking on species development. As early as the 1750s, the French mathematician Maupertuis proposed that climate and opportunities for nourishment determined the variety of animal life. Poorly constructed types degenerated or perished; the fortunate survived. Maupertuis suggested a common ancestor for both the horse and donkey, and

Buffon held that the same might be true for humans and monkeys. However, he advanced no further. Already the earth had been reduced to a speck located in a cosmically remote solar system, its birth and history attributed to impersonal, natural causes. However consonant with the spirit of empiricism, eighteenth-century scientists were reluctant to apply similar causes to human development.

As a pragmatic branch of scientific inquiry constructed on the foundation of observation and experiment, therapeutic medicine also could have been well-served by empiricism. Though medical students at the Sorbonne still spent two years listening to the syllogistic debates of professors, anatomy, chemistry, and botany were nevertheless introduced into the curriculum. So were visits to the sick in Parisian charity hospitals. Europe's first university-sponsored medical clinic was established in Vienna in 1754; Paris followed suit in 1770. The French specialized in studying childbirth, and thanks to their pragmatic approaches, the lives of tens of thousands were spared. As outlets for publishing research, medical journals were founded. Surgeons escaped the sign of the barbershop, obtaining corporate recognition that appreciated their services to the healing arts.

Despite the evolution of diagnostics and the symptomatic observation of heart disease, diabetes, typhoid fever, and some forms of tuberculosis, eighteenth-century therapeutic medicine was not yet fully enlightened. Physicians still believed that the illness itself was purgative, ridding the body of unwanted elements, and that high fever was an unmistakable sign of release. They were reluctant to attack symptoms too quickly or to suppress fever through artificial means. The most common therapy was either to allow nature to take its course or else assist it moderately in the purging process through bleedings, diets, and thermal cures. Though priestly confessors might still advise the gravely ill to swallow neck crucifixes, such bizarre remedies sank into the realm of folk medicine; pearls and viper's skin lost their miraculous powers.

In this period, modern preventive medicine was born. Physicians advised the public powers on quarantining inhabitants to ward off the ravages of epidemic, and governments began removing responsibility for public health from religious bodies. Travelers were required to carry certificates of good health, and doctors wrote treatises on hygiene that schoolmasters and priests disseminated. As the eighteenth century witnessed the world's first massive campaign of disease prevention, the struggle against smallpox, individuals sensible to the curative powers of medicine started expecting better treatment. By the 1770s, it was considered a public scandal for four sick persons to occupy the same bed in Paris's Hôtel Dieu hospital. A generation earlier, this would have been accepted practice. English private philanthropy constructed clinics in London and the new urban centers. In Hapsburg Austria, Emperor Joseph II commanded the construction of state hospitals in larger towns and decreed compulsory hygiene lessons for the poor. Even the imprisoned and insane won medical treatment as a basic human right.

The eighteenth century also witnessed the initial signs of flirtation between science and technology. Customarily, technology had been oriented toward warfare. By 1715, the rapid-fire rifle dethroned the musket, and the invention of the cartridge permitted a soldier to fire three rounds per minute. A generation later, however, industrial demands for sources of power and methods of production drew the factory and laboratory closer. The relationships between empirical scientists and inventors customarily had been strained. The maker of machines was considered either a tinker or grubby profit seeker, supposedly lacking the patience for painstaking research into the underlying processes of nature. Ironically enough, such a view helps explain why the eighteenth-century chemical industry was so far in advance of chemical theory. Chlorine was used as a bleaching agent before laboratory scientists understood just why it was effective.

Nevertheless, attempts were made to bring technology to a wider audience. Denis Diderot, editor of the great French *Encyclopédie*, was the son of a master cutler. Diderot had a passion for technology and invention and devoted large sections of the *Encyclopédie's* eleven volumes of plates to illustrating industrial and mechanical processes. His collaborator d'Alembert wrote that "it most likely is among artisans that we can find genuine proofs of the wisdom of the human mind." Even as the publication of the *Encyclopédie* got underway, the Paris Academy of Science undertook its own *Descriptions of Arts and Trades.* By 1788, the latter venture had reached eighty-eight folio volumes.

Europe's economic advance, and not her scientific progress, explains her technological breakthrough in the eighteenth century. Foreseeing the use of a great reservoir of raw cotton in America if mechanization could assist hand labor, English investors encouraged invention in unprecedented fashion. From John Kay's perfected "flying shuttle" of 1733 through Samuel Crompton's spinning mule forty years later, technology revolutionized England's textile industry. Spinners learned to produce yarns nearly as fine as hand-crafted Indian cottons. The thread makers were in advance of the weavers. In 1800, however, the Pastor Edmund Cartright put together a mechanical weaving machine to which he eventually applied steam power. The development of his machine was rendered possible by the perfection of malleable iron for its construction.

The quest for power sources preoccupied inventors throughout the century, and in this fortunate instance, science came to technology's aid. James Watt worked as an instrument maker at the University of Glasgow. One day in 1763, while repairing a model of Newcomen's steam engine, the young Watt was appalled by the heat wasted as a result of the need to cool the hot cylinder with a jet of cold water discharged inside it. After consulting with

Joseph Black, Watt was able to condense the steam outside the cylinder. Then he fitted a jacket round the cylinder and employed steam instead of atmospheric pressure to force the piston downward. Armed with a patent, Watt began building steam engines for Matthew Boulton, a Birmingham industrialist. In 1782, he patented a double-acting engine which obtained twice the power. In 1788, the rotary steam engine was standardized, and by 1800, the Watt-Boulton partnership had created more than five hundred machines.

Even before Watt's remarkable discoveries, visionaries dreamed of steam-powered transportation. In 1763, the French military engineer Cugnot built a three-wheeled cannon bearer upon which he placed a modified version of Newcomen's engine. The contraption moved at less than three miles per hour, and it was necessary to stop it every fifteen minutes to feed its furnace. Steam-powered land transport made little headway, but by 1780, several experimental ships were plying French rivers. Nor was steam power the sole means of propulsion that caught imaginations. On August 27, 1783, before a delirious Paris crowd of a quarter-million, the French physician Charles launched a hydrogen-filled balloon into the atmosphere. It reached three thousand feet, then tore apart, and dropped to earth fifteen miles from the capital, astonishing peasants who thought the moon was falling. Three weeks later, before King Louis XVI and his court at Versailles, Étienne de Montgolfier launched and landed a balloon containing some caged animals. On November 21 of the same year, Pilâtre de Rozier and his friend the marquis d'Arlandes entered a balloon basket in Paris, spent half an hour in the air, and landed six miles from their starting point. Two years later, victim of a torn balloon, de Rozier became aviation's first martyr. By this time, however, humans had flown across the English Channel, and in 1794, the armies of revolutionary France were using air transport for reconnaissance missions.

The overwhelming number of mechanical and industrial inventions were English or French. In central, eastern, and southern Europe, capital investment was missing, and the agrarian states in these regions participated minimally in world commerce. Bohemian and Silesian textiles, Solingen cutlery, Russian draperies, and the small manufacture of lace, clocks, mirrors, and glassware depended upon the dispersed labor force and traditional manufacturing methods of the cottage industry. Prussian soldiers spun cotton in their barracks, prisoners at Spandau prison in Berlin worked with wool, and orphans in the asylum at Potsdam made lace. Except for England, where faith in consumption flourished, entrepreneurs lacked confidence in an international market and depended upon traditional village handicraft to work their raw materials. In England, entrepreneur inventors timidly consulted scientists and persuaded wealthy individuals to be bold. Capital was invested. Occasionally, disaster struck, as in the oversupplied cotton industry in 1792, but in the long run, the gamble paid handsomely. Early in the nineteenth century, England's industrial power prevailed by defeating Napoleon. In subsequent years, it created an empire of unprecedented proportions.

THE SPIRIT OF THE *PHILOSOPHES*

For a literate west European public, Reason had become autonomous. Neither theology nor metaphysics needed to sustain it, since the techniques of eighteenth-century science, experiment and observation, were established firmly as the means for acquiring knowledge. Ideally, whatever hypotheses failed to submit to their test were suspended or rejected as unworkable. It is, of course, nonsense to suppose that the *philosophes* had rid themselves of phlogiston theories of the mind. Even with untrammeled Reason as their guide, their prejudices ran deep. They failed to understand the emotional needs that attracted civilized people to Jansenism, Methodism, or Pietism, and with the sweep of a facile generalization they could condemn an entire epoch such as the Middle Ages. Though the *philosophes* never established a formal school of thought, for the first time since Rome's fall, secular and secular-minded intellectuals demanded responsibility for Europe's cultural guardianship. They defined the boundaries of knowledge and the means for attaining truth. Committed to liberty of thought and expression, they expressed their opinions in epic poetry, satire, the essay, novel, and even the dictionary. For what did the *philosophes* stand? In 1715, at the very dawn of the Enlightenment, Madame de Lambert, a Paris bluestocking who afforded advanced thinkers the protection of her home, stated that the *philosophes* intended "to clothe Reason in all its dignity and to restore it in its rights by shaking off the bonds of tradition and authority."

West European in character, the Enlightenment fed on English sources, namely the empiricism of Locke and scientism of Newton; and it took deepest root in France. Nevertheless, there was an American Enlightenment and a Scottish one. Sympathetic German and Italian intellectuals were in regular communication with French colleagues. Progressive nobles in Poland and Russia lined their shelves with volumes of liberal thought. Following the example of their king, Frederick the Great, Prussian bureaucrats became familiar with the new ideas, and despite the warnings of their empress, Maria Theresa, Austrian civil servants did as well. Frederick and Catherine II of Russia offered subsidies to *philosophes* and made them welcome at court. Despite the fact that several thinkers, like Montesquieu, Condillac, and Turgot, were nobles and might gather and debate in aristocratic salons, the Enlightenment was a bourgeois movement. Its chief audience was a skeptical, literate, reform-minded middle class possessing faith in science and technology and in the power of human Reason to better the world. It could afford the luxury of books and had sufficient leisure time to read them. In general, this audience belonged to scientific and cultural clubs and to Masonic lodges which grew rapidly after the 1730s. It was stimulated not only through social intercourse and books but through a periodical literature as well. In England, *The Spectator*, founded in 1711 by Joseph Addison and Richard Steele to popularize science, literature, and ideas, attained a circulation of nearly 30,000. Its French counterpart, the *Mercure*, was sold in fifty-five towns by 1774. Elsewhere in Europe, circulation figures for literary journalism dropped as one headed eastward, an accurate gauge of the spread and depth of Enlightenment thought and controversy.

Not merely representing the supreme intellectual effort of *ancien régime* society, the Enlightenment also underscored the inner contradictions of that society. The *philosophes* chipped away at both Church and aristocracy, the two most important institutional pillars of the eighteenth-century world. The intent of most critics was not revolutionary. Rather, the *philosophes* called for social and political reform, so that science and Reason might develop untrammeled and individuals like themselves might achieve recognition for their usefulness. "It is not a question of pleasing the people, but of doing what is good for them," wrote Condorcet, one of the most vigorous of the thinkers. Most *philosophes* supported strong government, even absolute government, if regimes would attack privilege and social abuse as vigorously as they would protect civil liberties. Most *philosophes* despised war as a crime against Reason and humanity, though they courted favors and protection from warring sovereigns. While sharing their readership's contempt and pity for the "lower orders," the *philosophes* indignantly denied that they addressed themselves to bourgeois prejudices and ambitions. They proclaimed that they were addressing mankind.

Charles de Secondat, baron de Montesquieu, was born near Bordeaux in southwestern France in 1689. His family belonged to the robe aristocracy, and he was educated by Oratorian priests, the rivals of the Jesuits. Then he studied law. At twenty-five, he replaced his late father as a councillor in the Parlement of Bordeaux, and three years later he obtained a late uncle's parlementary office as *président*. Though tempted by the delightful obscurity of a comfortable judicial life on his beloved native soil, Montesquieu also yearned for a literary career, the salons of Paris, and travel to Italy, Germany, and England. He therefore resigned from Parlement and composed the *Persian Letters*, an irreverent political and social satire. At thirty-five, he was elected to the French Academy, but because of the *Persian Letters*, Louis XV refused to sign the warrant of admission. Eventually received, Montesquieu passed the remainder of his life alternating between his travels, town house in Paris, and the family chateau at La Brède. In 1748, his masterpiece, the *Spirit of the Laws*, appeared. He wrote the article "Taste" for the *Encyclopédie* and in 1755 died in Paris—in Christian sanctity, said one witness; as a true *philosophe*, retorted Voltaire.

In the *Persian Letters*, Montesquieu exploited the Oriental tale to describe the "enlightened" reactions of a group of Persians confronted by the brutalities, inconsistencies, and irrationalities of life in eighteenth-century

Europe. The device was entertaining and allowed Montesquieu to escape personal responsibility for the ideas expressed by his characters. Montesquieu's Persians envisioned the pope as "an old idol who is doused with incense out of habit ... but who no longer is feared." As for the king of France: he "is a great magician. He exercises an empire over the minds of his subjects. He has them think whatever he wishes. If he possesses only a million *écus* in his treasury and needs two millions, he simply persuades them that one *écu* is worth two and they believe him." The *Persian Letters* stood out as a bold pamphlet against despotism, papal claims to temporal authority, the arbitrariness that passed for justice in France, and the worst features of financial speculation. Behind the *Persian Letters* lay a belief that identifiable and defined causes, not blind chance, form our institutions and habits. In his *Considerations on the Causes of the Grandeur and Decline of the Romans* (1734), Montesquieu applied his ideas to a single historical circumstance, and in his *Spirit of the Laws* (1748) he wrote that the institutions of a people are the exterior manifestations of specific circumstance and habit, such as climate, quality and size of land, popular occupations, religion, wealth, population, and social customs. By noting that in some countries there may be "natural" reasons for slavery or polygamy, Montesquieu denied any intention of *justifying* institutions. Rather, he was merely seeking out the reasons for them. A man of the Enlightenment nevertheless, Montesquieu was also a moralist, with a clear sense of what *ought* to be. In the *Spirit of the Laws*, he devoted considerable space to evaluating the nature of political constitutions and the effect they ought to have upon a people's laws.

In judging any society, political liberty stands out as Montesquieu's ultimate moral criterion. Eschewing determinism, he wrote that liberty can survive only through a conscious effort at balancing the ambitions of contending political forces. If one force goes unchecked, despotism threatens. Montesquieu thought he saw such a balance being practiced in the government of eighteenth-century England, where he found function and power divided among Parliament, king, and judiciary, each making certain that none of the others should overstep bounds of authority. Idealizing the English constitution, Montesquieu accepted the political compromise, horsetrading, and corruption that played such a significant part in daily government as merely the consequence of Britain's constitutional balance. When he found the so-called intermediary powers in France—the high clergy, great nobility, and parlements—to possess sufficient constitutional responsibility to check the despotic tendencies of absolute monarchy, Montesquieu's aristocratic prejudices got the best of him. Except for small republics, he opposed democracy nearly as vigorously as he hated despotism. Nor did he say much about forswearing social privilege. Nonetheless, modern sociology and political science are in Montesquieu's debt. With the precision of a physical scientist, he ingeniously employed empirical data, and he perceptively analyzed the spirit which lay behind laws and institutions. His lasting heritage was the priority he awarded to civil liberties. In this respect, Montesquieu was not only a worthy descendant of Locke but also an inspiration to those who followed him.

No eighteenth-century figure tried more forcefully than Voltaire to implement Montesquieu's principles on civil liberties. Born François-Marie Arouet to a comfortable Paris lawyer and a woman descended from the petty nobility, Voltaire became the Enlightenment's best pamphleteer and most tireless warrior against institutionalized injustice. While in his teens, he gained the reputation of a quick-witted, acid-tongued man-about-town. For allegedly insulting the regent of France, he spent most of 1716 in the Bastille. He became well known as a writer of classical tragedies, but his penchant for wrangling with the powerful earned him two years (1726–28) of forced exile in England. The English impressed him, as they would impress Montesquieu several years later. Back in France, Voltaire published an adulatory essay on their customs, *The Philosophical Letters* (1734). However, his acknowledged writings, anonymous pieces, and spoken comments continued to anger important officials of Church and state, and at the age of forty, Voltaire withdrew from Paris to the countryside with his companion Madame du Châtelet. For a time, the pair entertained an array of guests and studied Newtonian science, history, and philosophy.

However, envying the limelight, Voltaire abandoned country life, and for nearly a quarter-century served as unofficial roving ambassador for the republic of letters. Sovereigns and aristocrats fought for his favors. His international reputation reached its height. In 1760, aged sixty-five, he announced he would settle on his property at Ferney in southeastern France, close to the Swiss border. There he supervised a permanent community of around sixty, which grew its own crops and had its own handicrafts, library, and theater. Visitors, supplicants, and guests poured in; pamphlets and letters poured out; Ferney became a literal clearinghouse for causes. Voltaire concentrated upon rehabilitating the reputations of victims of intolerance, such as Jean Calas, a Protestant merchant executed for having allegedly murdered a son who contemplated conversion to Catholicism, and General Lally, scapegoat for the loss of India to the British. In warring for the individual, Voltaire hoped to reform the system. His efforts helped reduce secret trials and vindictive judicial punishment. Just prior to the revolution of 1789, Protestant civil liberties were restored in France. Persuaded to visit Paris in 1778, he was universally acclaimed with banquets, receptions, concerts, and plays held in his honor. The trip was his last. Utterly exhausted and crowned with an aureole of glory, he bade farewell to a life he had so cherished. His remains were placed in the Pantheon, resting place for France's great.

The intellectual development of Voltaire is attested to by his fifty volumes of published writings and a hundred of correspondence. His religious views became more radical as he grew older. Through the 1730s, he consoled himself with faith in "Newton's God"; but even during his years of scientific experiment with Madame du Châtelet, he suspected that the universe was something less than a playground built for humanity's understanding and enjoyment. Too many innocents suffered without apparent cause; there was too much confirmation of the reality of evil. Following the premature death of Madame du Châtelet and a catastrophic earthquake in Lisbon which took 50,000 lives, Voltaire fell into a period of profound pessimism. He found some solace in scholarship, and wrote his great histories, *The Century of Louis XIV* and *Essay on the Habits and Customs of Nations.* Incapable of escapism or passivity, however, the old man recovered. His brief novel *Candide* (1759) counseled the active, useful life, and for nearly two more decades he launched his most spirited attacks upon the cruelties of religious fanaticism. Clinging to the straw of a skeptic's vague, ill-defined God, he assumed fanaticism to be far more dangerous than atheism and at seventy-four wrote: "I only preach the adoration of God, good will, and indulgence. Armed with these sentiments I challenge the Devil, who doesn't exist, and the real devils, who exist only too well." Even Voltaire's religious position was subordinated to his defense of individual liberties. Still, he was no democrat. Enlightened, absolute, tolerant princes were necessary to check the passions of priests and people alike.

For all of Voltaire's destructive wit and irony, Denis Diderot outstripped him as the boldest thinker of the French Enlightenment. Diderot came from a provincial artisan family. As a child he was precocious, and his parents sent him to a Jesuit school for training as a priest. Diderot continued his studies in Paris but lost his religious faith, dropped out of the university, and took to a bohemian existence in the capital. Earning his living as a translator and anonymous author of soft-core pornography, from 1746 to 1749 Diderot also wrote some essays that spoke lightly of Christianity and suggested that practical morality had little to do with divine law. For his writings, Diderot found himself in trouble. One work was publicly burned, and its author was thrown into Vincennes prison. Upon his release, Diderot continued to write "dangerous" books, but other facets of his immensely creative personality surfaced. The bohemian *philosophe* wrote sentimental art criticism and plays that sought to replace the classic formalism of the French tradition with a style underscoring the bourgeois virtues. He made friends with bankers and Farmers General and welcomed a pension provided by Russia's Catherine II.

Most significant of all, for more than twenty-five years (1747–72) Diderot edited the most important literary monument of the century with a scholar's dedication, the French *Encyclopédie.* This twenty-eight volume work was not only a superb compilation of current scientific and technological data, but in the hands of Diderot and his coeditor for several years, the mathematician d'Alembert, it was also an attempt to place all human creativity in the service of what Diderot and approximately two hundred other collaborators perceived to be untrammeled Reason. Most articles reflect upon facts. Cropping up periodically are criticisms of Christianity, divine right monarchy, metaphysics, and other "un-Reasonable" institutions or attitudes of mind. Diderot did not impose ideological or theoretical limitations upon his contributors, but the immense *Encyclopédie* clearly illustrated that a common attitude of mind indeed had swept over a broad section of Europe's intelligentsia. Virtually all the contributors, French and non-French, were moralists and teachers, believing in the virtues of literacy and proper education. The majority shared a faith in the workings of science and technology. For them, Reason was no cold abstraction. They exalted the pleasures and passions of life. Above all, they addressed themselves to the concept of universal brotherhood, to the idea of a humanity undivided by superior national, religious, or racial attitudes, drawn together by proofs of natural equality, natural rights, and natural law.

For Diderot, the *Encyclopédie* proved to be a hornet's nest of trouble as well as a monument to truth. Clerics, politicians, and jealous rivals made for enemies everywhere. Twice the project was stopped by government order. The French Royal Council revoked the publication permit in 1759, accusing the *Encyclopédie* of having caused "irreparable damage to morality and religion." The Church denounced the work and threatened to excommunicate all who possessed or even read it. Anxious contributors, as well as d'Alembert, defected. Nevertheless, Diderot labored on, collecting materials, writing dozens of articles himself, setting up pages, and preparing plates in semisecrecy. The first edition of text was surreptitiously printed in 1765, and the plates were finished seven years later. The publishing event of the century took twenty-five years to complete. Sets and pirated editions subsequently found their way into private libraries all across Europe. For those unable to afford their own sets, the periodical press freely lifted excerpts and printed them.

During the years of editing the *Encyclopédie*, Diderot composed radical and materialistic personal writings. Rather than risk scandal by publishing them, he left most in manuscript form where they remain testamentary evidence of his evolving thought. Whether advocating a "natural" morality in relations between the sexes, suggesting biological evolution based upon natural selection, or wrestling between amoral cynicism and sentimental conformity as guides for life, Diderot argued with earnestness and utmost sincerity until the end of his life. Built upon facts, his *Encyclopédie* was a monument to combative Reason, passionately espoused. So perfectly did Diderot represent the Enlightenment that his colleagues addressed him alone as "*the* Philosopher."

By the 1760s, due largely to the *philosophes*, most of Europe's literate public believed that enlightened self-interest might provide an adequate basis for private morals. Complementing this was a conviction that legislation and education might indeed reform the worst evils in Church, state, and society. Claude-Adrien Helvétius urged not only the extension of educational benefits but also the reformation of the curriculum. For Helvétius, it was obligatory to scrap the old catechisms of priest and schoolmaster. More reading, more arithmetic, and less religion were what the child needed. Such ideas bore fruit. Academies that emphasized science, history, and modern languages sprouted in Germany. Prussia and Austria began regulating elementary education and added "useful" subjects. In England's Dissenting academies, where non-Anglican Protestants denied access to traditional schools and universities obtained educations, the teaching of scientific subjects made enormous headway. Wealthy Nonconformists in trade and industry generously supported the academies.

The promise of state-directed educational reform led Enlightenment theorists to hope that political authorities would experiment with other ideas as well. The preoccupation of the French government with the "peasant question" was due largely to the influence of a body of economic thinkers called physiocrats. The spiritual father of physiocracy was Louis XV's court physician, François Quesnay; and another prominent physiocrat Anne-Robert Turgot rose from *intendant* of Limoges to controller-general of finance in 1776. The French reformers linked the problems of stagnant agriculture to the government's chronic need for money. They also proposed capitalist land development as was practiced in Britain and the free internal movement and export of grain. They insisted upon the elimination or at least reduction of seigneurial privileges and the imposition of a single tax based upon landed rents. The physiocrats hated tax farmers and the guilds. To them, mercantilism, which still defined the course of French economic life, was outmoded and detrimental to progress. Turgot's twenty-month stint as controller-general, from 1774 to 1776, gave physiocrats the chance to begin working on what they called the "natural order" of economic development. In the end, however, the force of corporate, guild, and seigneurial privilege brought down Turgot and defeated French physiocracy.

Economic reform in central Europe proved more successful. In the Hapsburg empire, where professors of economics doubled as ministers of state, the task was to increase agricultural production that was meager and based on serf labor. The reformers in the Hapsburg lands were more pragmatic and less ideological than the French physiocrats. They were more insistent upon state involvement and administrative efficiency than upon free trade and laissez-faire production methods. Emperor Joseph II (1780–90) encouraged his experts because he wished to destroy the social barriers to economic growth, and the abolition of serfdom in 1789 was the culmination of Hapsburg economic reform.

However, Adam Smith, unlike the Hapsburg reformers, was neither a neomercantilist nor a politician but a professor of philosophy at the University of Glasgow, and his epic *Wealth of Nations* (1776) became a primer for the emerging industrial civilization. Like the French physiocrats, Smith illustrated how a highly regulated economy might frustrate agricultural development. Unlike most physiocrats, however, Smith was friendly toward commerce, and to his followers laissez faire became a byword. A humanitarian, Smith predicted exploitation of industrial workers and saw government as needing to protect them. Moreover, for Smith, the state was essential not merely to prevent monopolists from getting a stranglehold over a nation's economy but even more fundamentally to put laissez faire on an operating basis. Old laws restricting the sale of land had to be abrogated, restrictions upon grain exports had to be removed, and duties on imports abandoned. Subsequently, government was to mediate benevolently, encouraging industrial growth and free trade and eradicating special interests when necessary, but never again concerning itself with minute mercantilist regulations. Adam Smith's economics were those of unqualified optimism concerning mankind's material future.

Secular humanitarianism permeated the century's most celebrated analysis of criminal law and procedure, *On Crimes and Punishments*, published in 1764 by a twenty-six year old Milanese, Cesare Beccaria. Within Europe, judicial torture still was being used to extract confessions, punishments hardly ever conformed to the crimes, and trials commonly were secret judgments based upon circumstantial evidence and unreliable witnesses. Influenced by Montesquieu and Voltaire, Beccaria held that punishment ought to serve as a deterrent, not an act of vengeance. It therefore must be suitable, prompt, and certain. Penal codes, he contended, must be defined clearly, so that would-be criminals were aware of the risks involved. Beccaria had no use whatsoever for torture. Fearing prosecution for his work, Beccaria published it anonymously. The French translation, however, skyrocketed the obscure young Italian to renown, and he was feted by *philosophes* and enlightened rulers alike. His most outstanding legacy lay in the development of criminal codes by most European states, the growth of procedural reform in courtrooms, and the abolition of judicial torture.

Penal reform and code building wedded Enlightenment humanitarianism to the government desire to intensify command over the institutions of the eighteenth-century state and the lives of its citizens. Religious toleration fulfilled a similar dual purpose. In their quest for useful, obedient subjects, eighteenth-century sovereigns had no use for Louis XIV's bigotry, and literate public opinion began accepting criticisms of civil disabilities based on religion and forced conversions. After 1778, British Catholics began to regain their civil rights, and in central Europe, German princelings imitated Frederick the Great's avowed indifference to the religious practices of his subjects. By 1787, French Protestantism once more was recognized by the crown.

The Hapsburg empire, cradle of the Counter-Reformation, offered the century's most spectacular example of toleration. The empire, of course, was religiously pluralist, containing along with the Catholic majority pockets of Orthodox, Protestants, Moslems, and Jews. Almost as soon as Joseph II succeeded to his mother's titles and lands, and despite his timid advisers, he issued a sweeping Edict of Toleration (1781). Freedom of public worship, the right to hold land, the right to schooling, and free entry into the professions, public office, and the military were offered to members of all religious groups in the empire, Christian or not. At the same time, Joseph ensured the subservience of Catholicism to the state. The clergy was prohibited from writing to the pope without government permission. Bishops had to swear an oath of allegiance to the regime. Pious lay brotherhoods and contemplative monastic orders were suppressed. State seminaries were established to educate priests; religious processions and church services were regulated, sermons censored, and civil marriage validated. Joseph was no Voltairean; his Catholicism was sincere, and he warned Protestant pastors lest their diluted zeal degenerate into "rational paganism." In his own time, Joseph was accused of using religion to further the aims of the omnipotent state, and his Belgian subjects greeted his reforms with armed revolt. However arrogant his regulations must have seemed to contemporaries, in historical perspective the Edict of Toleration stands as the most noble testament of the ancien régime to the Enlightenment program of idealistic zeal and pragmatic vision. It was government's way of fulfilling the promise of the *philosophes.*

Viewing Reason as a weapon rather than a process, reformers hoped not only to correct and modify institutions but also to rewrite history in the service of their perceptions of truth. Scholars of course had long used the past to justify the present, and from St. Augustine to Bossuet, historians served Christian revelation. Following Bayle's footsteps, the "philosophical historians" of the eighteenth century laid claim to objectivity and roundly denounced fable masquerading as fact. They held that human records alone were historical material, and they widened the scope of these records to include sociological, economic, geographical, literary, and psychological sources. If their appreciation of sources permitted them to study non-European civilizations more objectively than predecessors had ever done, their preconceived skepticism of Christianity forced them to downgrade the epochs of the Old Testament and Middle Ages. They also believed that history must tell a lively story. Therefore, they rejected fact-grubbing. They loved pagan antiquity and initiated the serious study of the recent past. Voltaire was their pioneer. In his *Century of Louis XIV* (1752) and *Essay on the Habits and Customs of Nations* (1757), he emphasized the contribution of the arts, sciences, and secular institutions. Postulating the universality of human nature, Voltaire categorized heroes and villains according to his own system of values and misapplications of human psychology. His British successors, David Hume and Edward Gibbon, were more flexible in attributing motive and cause. In his *History of England* (1754–62), Hume even doubted whether the historian could decipher any spiritual or secular plan in the development of humanity. On the other hand, in Gibbon's *Decline and Fall of the Roman Empire* (1776–78), he did not shrink from generalization and, in fact, leveled a sharp indictment at Christianity for contributing to the collapse of classical civilization. The greatest of the eighteenth-century historians, Gibbon was more subtle and more skeptical than Voltaire. He wished to instruct and explain but was less certain whether he was going to reform anyone. Alone, neither Christianity nor the Germans had destroyed Rome. Montesquieu taught Gibbon that climate, geographical factors, size of the empire, exhaustion of economic resources, and human folly had done their share as well.

THE LATE ENLIGHTENMENT AND ROMANTIC REACTION

As a state of mind based upon the application of empirical techniques to life's questions, the Enlightenment was not all-conquering. The success of Methodism and Pietism illustrates the liveliness of religious sentiment throughout the century. In England, a work of popular mysticism, William Law's *Serious Call*, remained a best-seller from 1728 to the 1770s, and Fredrich Klopstock's *Messiah*, which heralded Germany's literary awakening in the eighteenth century, was a poem of pure religiosity. In artistic expression the cultural strengths of religion were obvious. Painting and sculpture were less dependent upon biblical expression than previously, but music was another story. The chorales of Bach, oratorios of Handel, and masses of Mozart represent the peaks; and nearly every composer of the century tried to attain the sublime through means that spoke to the religious impulses of Christian listeners.

Reaction to the Enlightenment was not confined to the religious responses. Voltaire himself doubted whether in the long run mankind would be beholden to Reason, but he kept right on fighting injustice. Hume called "pure reasoning" as much the result of custom and habit as religion. In the mid-1760s, the Paris salon of a self-declared German noble, Paul-H. Holbach, believed that despite all human effort, blind determinism of matter in regular, aimless motion controlled the universe and dictated our destinies. This fatalism notwithstanding, Holbach emphasized that the individual must enjoy total moral and political liberty. With unprecedented directness, he attacked the restrictive institutions of his day, and though falling short of a call for total revolution, his *System of Nature* (1770) is replete with "what *ought* to be's." This hunger for a new kind of society characterizes late Enlightenment thought. Some, like the French *abbé* Mably or Englishman Richard Price, found inspiration for change in the successful American Revolution. As early as the 1750s, Mably had written: "Choose between revolution and slavery; there is no middle course." Others, like the English-man Jeremy Bentham, rejected the Enlightenment's cherished Natural Law in favor of an ethic based upon untrammeled individualism, while the early marquis de Sade pushed preoccupation with moral liberty to a demand for unbridled personal sexual fulfillment.

Yet neither skepticism, materialism, nor sadism offered an adequate syn-thetic alternative to the Enlightenment's passionate attack upon traditional value systems and its attempt to reconstruct the universe upon the supposi-tions of the intellect. Prior to Jean-Jacques Rousseau's formal challenge to the moral legitimacy of Reason, artists questioned whether the faculties of mind could accurately explore human experience. For example, the heroine of Pierre Marivaux's novel, *The Life of Marianne* (1736–41), declared: "As far as I am concerned, only feeling can give us reliable information about ourselves, and we must not put too much trust in what our minds twist to their convenience." The French moralist Vauvenargues added: "Reason betrays us more often than Nature does." Diderot defended the passions as inspiring a desire for happiness, and Edmund Burke added that no reasoned balance sheet of pros and cons could ever hope to provide a more sincere guide to human conduct than feelings. Though Rousseau himself never completely rejected Reason as a means of tempering the wishes of the heart, for him neither empirical observations of society nor utilitarian approaches to conduct could resolve the truly basic dilemmas of human existence. These dilemmas are moral ones, and only a spontaneous inner voice, unco-erced by either Church or state, can resolve them. Natural feelings are therefore infallible guides to moral action. Through the 1760s and 1770s, Jean-Jacques Rousseau dominated the cult of sensibility. It took root in France, deeply affected England, and inspired Germany's cultural awaken-ing. It influenced court fashions at Versailles, became the basis for the poetry and art of romanticism, and lay at the source of Immanuel Kant's philosophy.

In 1749, Rousseau first set down his personal challenge to Enlightenment assumptions. His irregular, adventurous life had brought him from an aban-doned childhood in Geneva to the bohemian quarters of Paris, where he associated with Diderot and other representatives of the high Enlighten-ment. Along the way he had composed operas, poetry, and plays, taught music to the children of the wealthy, served as secretary to the French ambassador at Venice, and developed a liking for the amenities of civiliza-tion. On a morning in October 1749, he walked from Paris to Vincennes to visit Diderot, who had been imprisoned for "dangerous writings." The journey was long and the day was hot, so Rousseau brought along a maga-zine to read. In it he noticed an essay contest inviting contributors to respond to the question: "Has the restoration of the arts and sciences contributed to the improvement of mankind's morals?" As Rousseau wrote twenty years later, his mind "was dazzled by a thousand lights," his head swam, and he sank down beneath a tree to regain his composure. "If I had ever been able to write a quarter of what I saw and felt under that tree, how clearly would I have explained all the contradictions of the social system! With what power I would have exposed all the abuses of our institutions, how simply I would have shown that man is good by nature, and that only institutions have made men evil!"

Rousseau wrote his essay, won first prize, and broke with polite society. He dressed plainly and soberly, rejecting friends, sinecures, and gifts. To support his mistress and himself, he copied music. Taking up a solitary, wandering life, from 1755 to 1762 he published the four works that made him a household word among literate Europeans and marked him as a singular watershed in the history of modern thought: the *Discourse Upon the Origins of Inequality* (1755), *Nouvelle Héloise* (1761), *Émile* (1762), and *Social Contract* (1762). The first three had an immediate effect upon his generation, while the fourth became a bible for revolutionaries thirty years later. Rousseau's thematic message is clear: mankind emerges from Nature a creature unspoiled, virtuous, and noble. The individual is not stained by Original Sin, but sins consciously when he creates civil society; for he constructs something that is artificial, built upon pretense, prospering upon lies. Obviously, humanity cannot simply return to the woods. It is within humanity's power, however, to remodel the world in a manner conforming to mankind's original psychological state, where feeling and conscience rather than intellect guided human action. Rousseau removed moral direction from the hands of priest and king, but unlike his encyclopedist contemporaries, he refused to delegate it to the care of an intelligentsia. Each individual was at liberty to construct a moral vision, conforming to what was best within himself.

In the *Discourse Upon the Origins of Inequality*, Rousseau held that once humanity renounced a casual, wandering, propertyless existence, social interdependence produced social problems unknown in the state of Nature. Chief among these problems concerned property. Rival claims to what is "mine" stifled the sentiment of natural compassion and made individuals "avaricious, ambitious, and evil." Conflict and bloodshed ensued between the first occupier and the strong. Thus for Rousseau, Hobbes's anarchic state of Nature in fact becomes the first stage of human society. It is impermanent, however, because the wealthiest persuade the poor that it is the interest of all to recognize the legality of property and establish government to protect it. This sounds like the reasonable Lockean contract, but Rousseau claims to know better. In his ringing style, he wrote that the law now "converted clever usurpation into an irrevocable right, and for the advantage of a few ambitious individuals, henceforth subjected all of humanity to labor, slavery, and wretchedness."

This was no longer injustice coolly analyzed by Montesquieu or subjected to the satirical wit of Voltaire. This was fire. Though the *Discourse Upon the Origins of Inequality* concluded grimly as to humanity's current state, it left some hope of redemption—a moral and political rededication of the individual to his community. Later, in the *Social Contract*, Rousseau illustrated what he meant by this rededication. Meanwhile, from 1758 to 1760, he wrote two novels leading directly to his great political testament. The first, the *Nouvelle Héloise*, was a love story that affirmed morality as an innate rather than a calculated principle. It also rediscovered the countryside and underscored the links between the individual's physical and spiritual environment. Tens of thousands drank in the potion of the *Nouvelle Héloise* with its elevation of virtue, emotion, and nature. In France alone between 1761 and 1789, it went through seventy editions. Rousseau's second novel in this period was *Émile*, essentially a treatise on education. He agreed with the *philosophes* that formal schooling ought to be more than fact-grubbing and the catechism. For them as for him, education must bring about the moral elevation of the individual and hence the renovation of society. However, in his description of the teacher's function, Rousseau broke with his contemporaries. Rather than a master conditioning the child's social and intellectual environment, Émile's tutor was to permit his charge to grow autonomously, uncorrupted by the forces of conventional society. Free the child and let him explore nature and express his imagination. To be sure, Rousseau was referring to male children. Little girls were to be trained to please men and serve their vanity by learning domesticity and docility. Feminine subjugation notwithstanding, for progressive upperclass families, *Émile* stood for a new freedom, and many tried to adopt its principles.

A section in *Émile* which appeared to avow a Spinozalike pantheism brought Rousseau grief at the hands of religious authorities, and he found little sympathy among his old *philosophe* acquaintances. Personally and ideologically he had broken with them. They had placed Reason on a pedestal; he seemed to be giving all to sentiment. They held that human nature did not change; he considered it historically mutable. They spoke for the virtues of urban civilization, social intercourse, technological improvements, and a world controlled by scientists and philosophers. He advocated a return to nature, solitude, introspection, and the simple life. Misunderstanding and personal clashes widened the gulf. Most important, it was becoming evident that two diametrically opposed views of the world confronted each other. To Rousseau, the Voltaireans, however they denounced the injustices of the ancien régime, still profited from the system. They visited and lectured royalty, invested in land and industry, and hoped for the triumph of a bourgeois order. By 1762, Jean-Jacques considered the system unreformable. The sole option lay in complete moral revolution.

The *Social Contract* represents Rousseau's vision of the new world. Of all his works it had received the least notice prior to 1789; but in the revolutionary 1790s, Rousseau's name became indissolubly associated with his political theory. As the crowning achievement of the school of Natural Law, the *Social Contract* forged an original conception of society and politics. In it Rousseau wrote: "[The] passage from the State of Nature to the civil state produces in man a very remarkable change, substituting in his conduct justice for instinct, giving to his actions the morality which was largely lacking in them hitherto." As instinct becomes a social force, the individual finds his spirit emancipated and his conscience absorbed into the general will of his community. Because Rousseau saw in the social-political world of the eighteenth century a congeries of petty, warring pressure groups, the general will cannot be merely the sum of the desires of society's members. On the contrary, in Rousseau's new society, privilege had to be eliminated, economic differences reduced, luxury abandoned, and every member guaranteed equality before the law. Rousseau coined the apparent paradox that the individual who gives himself to the community really gives himself to no one. He hoped that the communitarian spirit would guide the actions of all of society's members and believed that it would guide the actions of the majority. The genuine social contract took the form of a pledge to pursue the general will. The general will is sovereign; governments are not. Once regimes start claiming sovereignty, they tend towards illegal despotism. At this point, the people should replace the rascals. With Rousseau, government has no sacrosanct character. It becomes a necessary evil.

The *Social Contract* concerns the reconciliation of authority and liberty. To Rousseau, the general will did not enslave society. On the contrary, individual freedom perishes when one person is subjected to another. In the eighteenth-century world, this was everywhere present; in Rousseau's utopia, this was impossible. There a common law to which people voluntarily consent binds them to a common social life. Rousseau is not gentle to those who refuse to respect the legislation deriving from the general will. Those who find it impossible to accept the deistic assertions and beliefs implicit in the civic religion of the state are to be banished. Those who accept and later reject the civic religion are to be put to death. Moreover, the device of an all-wise lawgiver who divines and then implements the principles of the general will is as troubling as is Rousseau's quest for moral absolutes and perfection in politics.

What led Rousseau to sanctify the general will was his unquestioned faith in the moral sense of the individual, and true freedom is legal obedience which the individual voluntarily imposes upon himself. Because apostates to the civic religion have transgressed the law Rousseau treats them harshly. Their subversive activity places the entire community in mortal danger. We cannot blame Rousseau for subsequent totalitarian perversions of his thought. On the contrary, he was the first modern political thinker to underscore the absolute legal and moral equality of all citizens—*male* citizens, that is. His most impassioned indignation was reserved for those who would degrade others for reasons of birth, religion, or race.

Rousseau spent his last years, from 1770 to 1778, in Paris and in a small house on a friend's estate in the countryside. He wrote his *Confessions*, an autobiography seeking to justify his life and vilify false friends, and he had few visitors. By this time, however, the two *Discourses, Émile*, and the *Nouvelle Héloise* had turned him into a living legend. His influence extended into rivulets all over Europe. English Methodism borrowed his claims to the heart and reverence for nature. The so-called preromantics found a vigor and honesty in the deeds of primitive peoples and medieval ancestors that rationalists would have derided. A Highland Scotsman, James Macpherson, took advantage of the cult for the "wild and coarse" by supposedly rediscovering the bardic songs of pre-Roman Britain. They proved to be forgeries, Macpherson's own creation, but no matter. The "Ossianic Poems" became the rage of the English-speaking world. Translations of Rousseau, the novels of Samuel Richardson, and the poetry of Edward Young and Thomas Gray created an amalgam of emotion, sensibility, and quest for the mysterious that rejected neoclassical formulas.

In 1768, the German Justus Möser began publishing his *History of Osnabrück* in which he revered the small, primitive, uncorrupted folk society. The Osnabrückers did not represent the historic reality of the social contract, but Möser's idealization of their society stood in marked contrast to the existing imitation French courts of aristocratic Germany or her dull, socially frozen towns. Möser himself remained personally respectable, but certain of his youthful contemporaries who achieved maturity in the 1770s literally went wild with emotion. These were the poets of *Sturm und Drang*, who rejected the powdered wigs of conventional society, wore their hair long, and cried out their suffering in terms more pantheist than Christian. Frustrated by a stratified society and aristocratic politics, Germans like the young Goethe and Schiller turned to pure literature, especially the novel and theater. Their tragic heroes feel spontaneous inner needs, but a cold, mannered world frustrates and eventually kills them. To the preromantics, the genuine problems of life were moral, not lending themselves to empirical observation. Alone, an inner voice showed the way to moral judgment, and neither state, Church, nor *philosophe* could impose a will on the conscience of the individual.

At the close of the century, the East Prussian philosopher Immanuel Kant grappled with the issues unleashed by Rousseau, defined the frontiers of empirical knowledge, and achieved a metaphysical synthesis for thought and action. Kant established realms for pure Reason and ethics. Knowledge of the external world had to do with phenomena, and the body's organs of perception conveyed no direct knowledge of the essence of a perceived object. Thus the external world is reduced to what is measurable, and the human observer conducts his measurements through the imposition of subjective dimensions of space and time. Though objective reality may lie outside the scope of human intellect, the mind still possesses a vast power of intuitive awareness, and duty is a consequence of this awareness. A "categorical imperative" derived from within ourselves spurs us to moral action. For Kant as for Rousseau, only conscience can sanction moral law. The individual is a morally autonomous creature with self-imposed obligations. This is the essence of true freedom.

With its stress upon the unchanging quality of human nature and the influence of environment, Enlightenment thought was highly cosmopolitan. Voltaire, Helvétius, and the encyclopedists prided themselves on serving no specific nation. Their avowed intention was to liberate mankind. In reality, of course, they embodied an emerging bourgeois consciousness that wished to submit tradition-based value systems to the test of Reason and social utility. Furthermore, with Paris as its capital and the salon as its workshop, the Enlightenment seemed definitely French. "I have passed half my life wishing to see Paris," wrote Prince Henry of Prussia, brother of Frederick the Great, "and I pass the other half wishing to return." By midcentury, however, European opinion was becoming less flattering. What Louis XIV had failed to accomplish by force of arms, namely the French conquest of Europe, Voltaireans and encyclopedists were doing with the pen.

In Germany, the preromantic reaction to the Enlightenment became particularly anti-French. The *Sturm und Drang* Germans exaggerated the contrasts between Reason and sensibility as though they alone had discovered passion, and they emphasized a new kind of moral liberty—the liberty of genius to rise above the natural rights the *philosophes* ascribed to everyone. Even German extollers of Reason and realism, like the dramatist Gotthold Ephraim Lessing, denounced French intellectual hegemony. Lessing pitted the raw genius of his native language against rule-laden French classicism, and German poets and scholars alike glorified a distant medieval past when the national culture seemed both whole and untainted.

Though the most vociferous preromantics were Germans expressing hostility to the *French* Enlightenment, the new movement should not be identified as simply the first modern case of cultural nationalism. More than that, it restored to intellectual respectability the nonrational aspects of human nature. Nevertheless, with the German philosopher Johann Gottfried Herder, one of the founders of the *Sturm und Drang* movement, preromanticism rejected the cosmopolitan and empirical claims of the Enlightenment in favor of an organic view of cultural development. Though appreciating the influence of environment, Herder refused to believe that savages could be civilized through the mere application of will. Human nature, he felt, is not so malleable. The individual is not an atom in the world but rather the product of a historic community from which he never can be completely divorced. For Herder, cultural forces, particularly language, are what determine the individual's relationship to community. Language is not merely a vehicle for expression but rather the very repository of a nation's culture, joining together those who share it and keeping out those who do not. In each language, Herder believed, there exists a kind of mystique that conditions the thought and action of a people. He wrote: "Each nation speaks in the manner it thinks and thinks in the manner it speaks." The *Volk* share a common language, transmitting fable, folklore, and traditions to future generations. The case for Germany particularly saddened Herder because political barriers and social cleavages divided the authentic *Volk*. On the other hand, a multinational, multilingual state such as the Hapsburg empire was an aberration to him. Herder himself was no racist, nor did he believe in the superiority of one *Volk* over another. In stressing human diversity and laying such emphasis upon the uniqueness of national traditions and characteristics, however, Herder broke with Enlightenment cosmopolitanism. His exclusion of the Frenchified aristocracy and the wandering rabble from the authentic German *Volk* surely supplied future racists with a good supply of poison. Yet Herder had enough of the Enlightenment within him to state the belief that each distinct nation contributed to human brotherhood if only through its distinct gift of culture.

THE ART OF LIVING AND THE LIFE OF ART

For many aristocrats and urban bourgeois, the eighteenth century witnessed improvement in the quality of life, and the *philosophes* defended one's right to comfort. In domestic habits, the quest for graciousness gave birth to both the dining room and the art of French cooking. Because urban life placed a premium upon space, rooms were toned down in size, heated properly, and given specific functions. The spectacular marble staircases and open galleries of the baroque age yielded to tasteful and intimate salons intended for the art of polite conversation. Blended woods replaced stone interiors, mirrors and bookcases became standard items of furniture, and cushioned Louis XV chairs supplanted the stylized, comfortless seventeenth-century models. Exotic items such as Chinese cabinetry, Persian carpeting, and Turkish sofas penetrated town houses and country estates.

Fashion extended to the provincial towns of western and central Europe. On the continent, urban elegance emerged as the new standard, while in England the pleasures of country life created a new art of living. Though the poor knew only necessity, not style, for the upper tiers of the west European peasantry, comfort definitely had become a consideration in housing, and in French, Belgian, and German villages, the solid stone and brick cottages of the eighteenth century still stand. They possessed large windows, and at least half the rooms could be heated; each room had a specific function and contained sturdy, homemade utilitarian furniture and household wares, genuine beds and chairs, tables and tools differentiated for use either in eating or working. It would be too easy to exaggerate. For the overwhelming majority of Europeans, eighteenth-century housing was substandard. Yet, of the houses standing in 1800, 60 to 70 percent had been built within the previous half-century. They were larger and better made than those they had replaced. They became genuine centers of family life, fulfilling an elemental need for shelter and just comfortable enough to serve as places for conversation and work, where the generations might gather and, in the complete sense of the term, live.

Just as functionalism found its way into the humble peasant cottage, it also contributed to the growth of the eighteenth-century town. The tasks of postwar reconstruction, the creation of princely residences and administrative centers, and the growth of town populations gave rise to government-sponsored urban planning. A capital created out of swampland, St. Petersburg was the most spectacular example. Czar Peter had dreamed of a Baltic Amsterdam, a place independent of Russia's half-oriental architectural past. Under Carlo Rastrelli, chief architect for Catherine II, baroque and the neoclassical revival found a receptive home in St. Petersburg. The czarina demanded a summer and winter palace. The Tsarskoe Selo, Nevski Prospect, and dozens of other gems turned the Russian capital into the Enlightenment's architectural crown, which by 1800 was a living, vibrant city of 200,000. In the image of Versailles, the princely court cities of Germany witnessed an orgy of construction, while older capitals such as Paris, Nancy, Copenhagen, and Brussels were refurbished with government buildings and roomy squares crowned by the equestrian statues of the reigning sovereign. For the aristocratic elite and bureaucracy, vast new residential quarters arose. Eighteenth-century Vienna would have been unrecognizable to a resident of the little polygon that had been besieged by the Turks in 1683. Lisbon's Commercial Square, reconstructed after the earthquake of 1755 and surrounded by ministerial palaces, had nothing in common with what had existed before. In the New World, Rio de Janeiro was built according to Lisbon's model, and of course, the new American capital at Washington was based upon the planning of a French designer, L'Enfant, himself inspired by the regularities of classicism.

Baroque survived in the early eighteenth-century residential and church architecture of Austria, Bohemia, and southern Germany, where the style literally exploded in testimony to the revived grandeur of the Hapsburg empire. The summer palace of Prince Eugene of Savoy, the Belvedere of Vienna, consisted of magnificent pavilions ending in sharp-ridged corner towers crowned with cupolas. Surrounded by stately formal gardens and an artificial lake, the place was a fairyland for triumphal entries, feasts, and receptions, a fabulous escape hatch from the frightening and squalid real world beyond its gates. As for religious architecture, the Karlskirche of Vienna, or even more graphically the fortresslike Melk monastic church sealed on a ridge high above the Danube, evoked Hapsburg religious militancy—"Arise, arise ye Christians!"—the battle song of 1683. Inside Melk, however, was a paradise of music-making cherubs, an orgy of angelic decorativeness. Profuse statuary and gilded busts added to the emotional impact.

Though the Hapsburgs proved that baroque could prosper in the eighteenth century, it was not the Enlightenment's style. English aristocrats felt more comfortable emulating the dignified domestic habits of ancient Roman senators than playing baroque heroes, and their architects pored over volumes written by sixteenth-century Italian predecessors who had studied ruins firsthand. One of these Italians, Andrea Palladio, became the authoritative word for English country-house architecture. Façades came to resemble antique temple fronts, and sense of order and simplicity became the primary canon of good taste. A new kind of garden, which tried to reflect the beauties of nature rather than represent the architect's mastery over her, surrounded these noble residences.

Eventually, neoclassicism became the Enlightenment's artistic response to baroque ostentation. In southern Europe, parts of Germany, and Latin America, baroque itself degenerated into spiritless tinsel and flash, a style called rococo, which by 1750 was regarded as frivolous and decadent. In reaction to rococo, architects sought the purest lines imaginable, and their quest led to an unparalleled interest in ancient Greek art, the older the better. Purity meant simplicity and sincerity, an art freed from unreasoned aberration or academic rules. During the 1750s and 1760s, Pompeii and Herculaneum were uncovered. Interest extended to the Doric ruins in southern Italy and Sicily, and the great German archeologist Johann J. Winckelmann formulated an aesthetic code based on the ancient Greek masterpieces, which found wide acceptance throughout the remainder of the century.

Until the 1750s, the tastes of aristocratic patrons and purchasers largely dictated the evolution of painting styles. Owners of manors and town houses wished to decorate their walls with pastoral fairylands where ladies were forever beautiful, lovers always graceful, and life itself a minuet performed by sensuous shepherds and shepherdesses. Demand for frivolity eclipsed the sober requests of the great old patron, the Church. Clever technicians profited from the rococo fad, but very few painters were sufficiently talented to turn the make-believe into timeless art. One exception was Antoine Watteau, who died in Paris in 1721 before he was forty. Watteau's universe is an earthly paradise of idle young dreamers, but it possesses sufficient melancholia and mystery to make the place appear interesting. With Watteau's successor, François Boucher, sex moved into the gardens and parks, and the jaded Louis XV admired Boucher's nudes of teen-aged royal mistresses idealized as Aphrodites. Perhaps the greatest of the rococo painters was J.-H. Fragonard (1732–1806). Fragonard lived in the twilight period of the style, and when it no longer was popular, he adapted his talents to portraiture and landscapes. He was the unquestioned master of rococo painting, imparting to its innate delicacy vibrancy and even robustness.

Rococo painting outlasted rococo architecture, but by the 1750s, the intellectuals of the Enlightenment concluded that its fanciful characteristics could never express their practical concerns. In England, the dignified portraiture of Sir Joshua Reynolds and his school made rococo superfluous, and in Italy, under the brushes of the Venetians Canaletto, Guardi, and Tiepolo, baroque monumentality never conceded to rococo grace. Increasingly popular as an architectural style, neoclassicism also found expression in painting in the second half of the century. The Frenchman Jacques-Louis David espoused stoic virtues so convincingly that after 1790 the revolutionary regime adopted neoclassicism as a weapon of visual propaganda. Nothing could contrast more vividly with rococo frivolity than David's manifesto, the "Oath of the Horatii" (1785), where the stern, sober lesson of patriotism overwhelms all other human sentiments, even filial love.

Between rococo make-believe and neoclassical heroics, however, stood the middle ground of realism. Commonplace scenes of contemporary life, teaching a moral lesson, appealed to *philosophes* worshipping the common-sense virtues. The greatest English realist of the century, William Hogarth, was an unashamed moralist best known for his serial engravings that taught the rewards of virtue and consequences of sin. The most important French realist, Jean-Simon Chardin, was subtler than Hogarth. An artisan's son who preferred painting to a craftsman's trade, Chardin rejected Watteau's dream world, first for the realism of still life and subsequently for scenes of ordinary people engaged in ordinary tasks. Mastering texture, light, and color to evoke emotions through understatement, Chardin can be compared favorably to Vermeer. His "Saying Grace" transposes a humble dinner rite into pure poetry; the "Return from Market" turns a tired young housewife into a timeless embodiment of domestic virtue. Chardin's portraits of little boys building card houses or spinning tops represent acts of intense mental concentration. They conform to the Enlightenment's adulation of intelligence and to its concern for the concrete.

Neoclassicism in architecture and realism in painting became the visual aesthetic standards of the Enlightenment, standards that were consistent with the clarity of a Voltairean tale or *Encyclopédie* article. But we must not oversimplify. Side-by-side with Montesquieu, Gibbon, and Lessing there existed an extraordinary popular longing for literary sadism that antedated the unhappy marquis by a full half-century. In the visual arts, pornographers had no shortage of aristocratic and bourgeois patrons. An underground book trade with illustrations flourished everywhere in Europe. Nevertheless, for most of the eighteenth century, socially sanctioned art rested upon a commonly accepted theory. The artist must study nature and classical antiquity; "style" was a quality handed down through the generations.

Rulebooks like Palladio's were acceptable guides for beauty. In all countries, annual art exhibitions encouraged conformity. Until the 1790s, relatively few disputed the accepted bases, and those who did spoke to later generations, not to contemporaries.

Around 1770, an English gentleman, Horace Walpole, built a country manor with Gothic spires and medieval turrets; his fellow aristocrats, schooled in classicism and convinced that Gothic was synonymous with poor taste, considered Walpole an eccentric. Yet a generation later, the Gothic revival was in full swing. Still, in the eighteenth century, the Spaniard Francisco Goya and the Englishman William Blake began working on their etchings of horror, nightmare, and fantasy; and a few landscape painters turned from arcadian and pastoral scenes to depict nature in all its power and violence. Some painters ceased relying upon traditional rules of craftsmanship and insisted that their imagination and inner eye sufficed; a few theoreticians even questioned the old regulations. For example, as early as 1757, Edmund Burke wrote that the sublime, as distinguished from the pretty, might well use terror and awe in imparting visual pleasure. Gradually, a new spirit, later identified as romantic, was seeping into the realm of aesthetics. With the French Revolution, the artistic assumptions of the past three hundred years were challenged from all sides.

Curiously enough, just as general agreement upon what constituted beauty in the visual arts began to break down, music internationalized. Borrowing from folk and classical traditions, a body of German composers led by Bach, Gluck, Handel, Haydn, and Mozart injected sufficient genius into their work that earlier theoretical struggles among national schools were overwhelmed. Technological development was important too. Orchestras were enlarged; the organ, harpsichord, and clavichord were perfected. Musical forms such as the oratorio and fugue matured. Above all, the century witnessed the triumph of opera. Born in baroque Italy during the early 1600s, opera originally had been conceived as court entertainment to celebrate marriages, baptisms, and military triumphs. By the 1670s, however, public opera houses were built in the larger Italian towns, and Italian troupes carried this secular liturgy to northern capitals. Wherever performances were open to all elements of society, the opera houses were veritable arenas where audiences mingled loudly, played cards, drank wine, and made love. The bustle ceased only at the moment when grand arias were sung. Tied down by convention, the Italian-inspired opera was made for singers. Dramatic action and psychological characterization were secondary, and production managers loved to stage diversionary extravaganzas, such as ballets, fireworks, or aquatic spectacles within performances.

What eighteenth-century composers accomplished was to make opera into genuine musical drama, in effect the theater of the Enlightenment. In England, John Gay derived his inspiration from popular culture and invented the ballad opera. In Italy and France, the simple, melodious, realistic *opera buffa* succeeded baroque's ornate *opera seria*. In 1762, when the Bohemian Gluck proclaimed that the aim of his new opera, *Orfeo*, was to strive for aesthetic truth rather than simply compose set arias, he made a revolution. Gluck blended choral singing and instrumental music into his operas, and most fortunately of all, Gluck was succeeded by the century's most complete musical genius, Mozart.

No previous century was more an age of music. Bach transposed the musical culture of the German people and Lutheran church service into magnificent universal statements; Handel perfected vocal music, particularly the oratorio, and placed his adopted England on the musical map; Haydn did more than any other of his contemporaries in converting the string quartet and symphony into the forms we know today. But the most representative musical spokesman for the Enlightenment was Mozart. He was born at the height of the movement—in 1756—and he died in its twilight, in 1791. As virtuoso and composer, Mozart was history's archetypal prodigy, his early life a ceaseless round of voyages and concerts. Before he was eight, he had performed before the elector of Bavaria and Empress Maria Theresa. At Christmas, 1763, he played before the court at Versailles, and the following Easter, he astounded the English court. Between the ages of six and twenty-one, he had written half his repertoire. Mozart's reception by aristocratic Europe ought to have awarded him a life of ease and patronage, of a kind enjoyed by far less gifted artists. Indeed, in 1771, after hearing Mozart's organ performance at the funeral of his predecessor, the new archbishop of Salzburg offered the seventeen year old the post of concertmaster. Though his patron proved to be a tyrant, Mozart behaved as the dependent artist in an aristocratic world.

However, in 1781, he quit his post, bade farewell to Salzburg, and left for Vienna, where he hoped to live exclusively off his talent. It proved to be a fatal mistake. He matured so rapidly that his work was a decade ahead of his time. Audiences accepted it but as often were puzzled by it. Rejecting the aid of would-be benefactors, insisting that genius must be free to survive, and exhausted by his perpetual struggle against poverty, Mozart died prematurely in 1791. He was thirty-five.

The most versatile composer of his century, Mozart also was its most accomplished dramatist. From *The Abduction from the Seraglio* (1782), through *The Marriage of Figaro* (1786), *Don Giovanni* (1787), and *The Magic Flute* (1791), his uncanny ability at penetrating and contrasting character through the most beautiful melodies ever written mark him as a singular phenomenon in the history of creativity. He was no political revolutionary, but the social message in his operas was unquestionably dissatisfaction with the status quo. Moreover, his greatness does not rest exclusively with the operas. We must add his chorales, so melodious that sober clerics were reluctant about admitting them into churches, and his forty-one symphonies, keyboard concerti, string quartets and quintets. Every line that

Mozart wrote betrayed a confidence in human transcendence and moral perfectibility, a faith that links him not only to the *philosophes* but also to Rousseau and Kant. Unlike the Romantics who came after him, Mozart did not employ music to confess the personal longings and torments of the artist. (Two of his most jubilant works, the *Jupiter Symphony* and *Requiem Mass*, were written in the shadow of a miserable death.) Rather, Mozart used music to reconcile the spiritual dilemmas of life and death, mystery and Reason, laughter and tears. His vision was the Enlightenment's vision, suffused with grace, vigor, passion, and, above all else, with a confidence in humanity's ability to transcend the darkness of its soul. More profoundly than any of his contemporaries, Mozart expressed the aspirations and affirmations of the age. He was the Enlightenment's last spokesman and its most soaring voice.

Chapter Nine

The Ancien Régime Triumphant (1715–63)

GREAT BRITAIN: THE AGE OF WALPOLE AND RISE OF PITT

The British aristocracy gathered the harvest of the Glorious Revolution, establishing economic expansion and maintenance of a political and social status quo as national goals. However, to view eighteenth-century Britain solely in terms of capitalist development and political management would ignore the civil rights won under the Stuarts, William and Mary, and Queen Anne. All Englishwomen and men, not merely privileged groups, were free from arbitrary arrest and imprisonment. Provided that their words did not breach the peace, they were guaranteed the right to speak or write what they pleased. An independent judiciary and local self-government were the two benchmarks of public life. While civil freedoms did not exist for the Irish Catholics and while in England itself the death penalty for more than two hundred offenses was the chief means of keeping property safe, the English were nevertheless loath to raise the necessary police force or army to track down potential offenders. Nor did the king possess a network of officials resembling continental *intendants*. There were neither regional bureaucracies tied to a central core nor a civil service. Anything that smacked of direct royal control was suspect.

An independent judiciary and lively system of aristocratic self-government comprised one side of public life in eighteenth-century Britain; the world of patronage, management, and graft comprised the other. The king himself had to pay a royal fish-bearer for bringing him a carp caught in the royal pond. A bishop who changed sees was expected to donate sums of money to a regiment of courtiers. Contractors who supplied uniforms and weapons to the military had to pay off government clerks and ministers. The mentality of graft for services rendered was etched deeply into public life. Nor was Parliament immune. In order to obtain desired revenue and laws, the king's ministers needed parliamentary allies. To get themselves elected,

M.P.'s needed a pliable electorate. It was at the highest levels of government that the system of patronage and management became a fine art.

The source of revenue and legislation was an unreformed Parliament. Each of England's forty ancient counties sent two representatives to the House of Commons, and the twelve Welsh counties sent one apiece. Fifty additional M.P.'s sat for cities. The remainder, an overwhelming majority, sat for the boroughs, towns, and villages of widely varying size and population. Except for excluding females, no nationwide standard defined or restricted suffrage in the boroughs. In some, voter residence was obligatory, while in others, nonresidents outvoted residents. Some borough electorates were in the pocket of a great family. Others were up for sale regularly. Southern and southwestern England were overrepresented, while the newly settled regions in the Midlands and Yorkshire had little representation. A borough might contain a thousand voters or, as was the case, a single one. Since political power was essential for attaining social influence and since control over legislation and state finance determined the nation's future, the English aristocracy worked hard and long to control borough representation in the House of Commons. Local squires and nobles flattered, browbeat, and bribed voters. Until the 1730s, the rivalries for borough seats were keen. Afterwards, money began to tell its tale. The wealthiest patrons secured their strongholds and selected both friends and relatives for Commons. It was not difficult to win and hold a borough with a small electorate. In 1715, sixty seats were contested in boroughs with fewer than four hundred voters. In 1761, only fifteen were.

The system invited collusion between the king's ministers and most members of the House of Commons. At the borough level, a squire or magnate desired jobs and favors for his clients that only the court, chief dispenser of patronage, could supply. In return, the court and ministry needed the laws and funds that the borough M.P.'s could deliver. The parliamentary votes of representatives from the controlled boroughs thus became the fulcrum upon which rested the stability of eighteenth-century English political life. Meanwhile, the most important magnates found their way into court and the royal ministry. As secretary of state for nearly forty years, the duke of Newcastle dispensed favors with an uncanny eye for detail. He cemented the alliance between the government and borough patrons. Though individual ministers and country magnates might have disagreements, the court-country alliance worked so well that during the eighteenth century no general election ever went against a sitting ministry.

Some independent voices remained outside the control of patrons and prevented the House of Commons from becoming a complete agency of the executive. Among borough M.P.'s, there always were some courageous and independent men. Furthermore, the ninety-two representatives from the counties of England and Wales, the knights of the shire, took special pride in the exercise of independent political judgment, and county elections were customarily more honest than borough elections. The knights distrusted magnates and political operators, inveighed against borough mongering, and opposed both standing armies and continental entanglements. Because their own friends, relatives, and constituents expected jobs and rewards, the independents tolerated much of the system, remaining in both the Whig and Tory parties. Nevertheless, during most of the eighteenth century, it was they who, as critics and watchdogs of executive power, assumed a role that in earlier times had been that of Parliament as a whole.

The executive power was far from negligible. Most of the 220 members of the House of Lords were pliable, and both Commons and Lords were technically the king's high courts. The courts of law interpreted the king's justice, and the court of exchequer collected the king's revenue. Selecting his own advisers and delegating authority to those he trusted, the king alone made political decisions. In point of fact, of course, England was no continental absolutism. The king's advisers had to cooperate with Parliament in order to work within a framework of what was politically possible. If a series of parliamentary defeats over individual bills informed a royal ministry that it no longer commanded a majority in Commons, either the ministry had to steer a new course or else several of its members had to resign. On the other hand, very few M.P.'s made careers of overturning ministries, and even fewer were so bold as to prescribe advisers for the king. Regular, continuous opposition to the ministry still smelled like treason.

When people spoke of the government, they customarily meant the king and his ministers. Because the old councils of nobles had become too large to function effectively in matters of diplomacy and national security, early in the eighteenth century, King George II and his trusted confidant, the Whig politician Robert Walpole, began leaning heavily upon a small group of eight to ten men. This inner cabinet gained control over most royal patronage and formulated important domestic and foreign policy positions. Its members met informally, often at dinner, and had access to secret papers. In time, cabinet ministers developed the principle of consensus and collective responsibility. If a single member disagreed with his colleagues over an important matter, he had to resign. Once agreement was reached, the cabinet member possessing most influence with the king requested the sovereign's assent, though this was not always easy to obtain. Once royal approval was won, cabinet, courtiers, and allies in the House of Lords started guiding the proposal through Commons, where the regime of patronage and management was put to the test. As long as Walpole commanded the confidence of both king and Commons, he successfully manipulated cabinet government. Policy lines he considered essential became those for Britain. He wished to conciliate the landed gentry, keep taxes low, foster trade and commerce, and avoid war. Speaking for the oligarchs, neither Walpole nor his immediate successors intended to establish a ministerial despotism but rather contented themselves with manipulating the king's influence in Parliament and the country. In the end, they were answerable to the nation's elected officials.

When Queen Anne died in 1714, the fifty-four-year-old elector of Hanover became George I of England. Most Whigs accepted this and considered a Protestant succession an act of faith. Newly rich and newly powerful, the Whigs had a healthy respect for Britain's commercial expansion. They wanted a limited monarchy and saw a need to protect the civil liberties obtained in the seventeenth century. On the other hand, the Tories mistrusted the new Hanoverian dynasty. They were attracted to James II's young son in continental exile and drank toasts to "the king across the waters." However, the Pretender's refusal to abandon Catholicism disqualified him from the throne. The 1715 election brought a large Whig majority into Commons, and an uprising led by a pair of misguided Tory leaders in the name of the Pretender failed miserably. With Toryism thus discredited, in control of Parliament and emerging as defenders of the Glorious Revolution, the Whigs considered the future to lie in their hands.

By 1719, however, storm clouds appeared. As chief guardian of the Utrecht settlement, Britain incurred expensive military commitments, and the Whig leadership was searching for a way to reduce the national debt. A group of merchant investors, consolidated as the South Sea Company, proposed a fantastic scheme. The group offered to pay the debt if government securities would be transferred into South Sea Company shares. Transfixed by the vision of turning a huge debt into an outlet for credit, Parliament approved the idea. When shares in the company were placed on the open market, a speculative frenzy swept across England. By June 1720, shares in the South Sea Company were selling at ten times their face value. Then the bubble burst. The company intended to invest in Latin America, but shareholders themselves began to doubt whether the plan ever would bear fruit. They started selling, first to make a profit, then frantically to salvage what they could. Ruined investors called for the heads of culprits. It became clear that members of the royal household had initiated the selling wave. The Whig leader Sunderland, the chancellor of the exchequer, and two royal mistresses were implicated. King George had to reconstruct his ministry. He asked Walpole, who was unstained by the scandal, to form a government and salvage a situation dangerous enough to threaten the Hanoverian succession itself.

Walpole removed the court from the stench of scandal and returned the country to stable financial moorings. Instead of depending upon unlimited credit, Walpole reduced the national debt through a reserve fund fed with regular infusions of tax revenue. This restored investor confidence. Out to make England safe for country gentlemen, Walpole also helped her tradesmen and manufacturers by abolishing most export duties and instituting tariffs on imports that competed with home production. Walpole's pet scheme, developed in the 1720s and proposed in 1731, was to abolish the land tax, an idea warmly supported by most of his fellow gentry, and replace it with a series of sales taxes on consumer articles. The idea itself was not new, for France and Prussia depended heavily upon excise revenue. Moreover, the English gentry basked in the hope that it might be moving towards a privileged fiscal position heretofore reserved for continental aristocracies.

Supported by the king and most of Parliament, Walpole, however, underestimated the fury of nonaristocratic resistance. Opposition was most vocal in the press. After 1688, licensing acts and other forms of censorship had become dead letters. Literacy increased, and coffee houses and taverns became locations where franchised and unenfranchised might gather to discuss public affairs. To many, "excise" meant a new tyranny, with paid thugs inspecting warehouses and shops in search of contraband. London's merchants led the opposition of townspeople. Some spoke of armed resistance. Walpole knew he had crossed the line and withdrew his proposal. For the remainder of his tenure in office, he refrained from introducing legislation that threatened to extend government. He was content to live by his motto: "Let sleeping dogs lie."

Walpole's belief that England could live without a land tax was based upon his vision of its place in the world. An advocate of conquest through trade and a supporter of the Navigation Acts, Walpole also wished to preserve the Peace of Utrecht. He asked France to join him. For a dozen years after 1713, Austro-Spanish enmity threatened to plunge Europe into new wars. The Hapsburgs were not reconciled to their failure to secure the Spanish throne, and the Spaniards resented the partition of a once-great empire. Concerted efforts by Britain and France kept the peace, but in 1725 Spain turned its wrath upon England. In defiance of Spanish navigation laws, English merchant ships were smuggling slaves and merchandise into Latin America. The Spaniards stopped them and also demanded Gibraltar's return. Despite Walpole's desire for peace, by the 1730s, Anglo-Spanish relations degenerated into what amounted to undeclared war.

As long as England and France pursued common goals, however, Walpole considered matters manageable. Above all, he hoped to avoid committing British troops to any continental adventure. Since George I and II remained electors of their ancestral German principality of Hanover, the possibility of intervention existed. In 1733, an international dispute over the Polish succession brought Austria, Russia, and Prussia into a coalition against France. The Spanish Bourbons now supported their French relatives. Though Walpole kept England aloof, at the conclusion of the Polish succession war, the friendship of Spain and France held firm. As the Bourbon monarchies recognized a common need to contain England's growing colonial power in Asia and America, Walpole had to face the prospect of major new wars.

The Spaniards kept up the pressure. Meanwhile, a new generation of Whig politicians surfaced, critical of Walpole's pacific diplomacy and fed up with management's stranglehold over domestic affairs. Calling themselves the "Patriots," the aggressive young Whigs believed that war with France and Spain was inevitable, and Britain could best protect its commercial interests through strikes on the high seas and seizures of its enemies' colonial outposts. William Pitt, whose family had reaped a fortune in India, was the most impassioned parliamentary spokesman for the Patriot cause. Never warm to Walpole, London's merchants and English West Indian planters adopted Pitt as their own. In 1738, a British naval captain named Jenkins testified before a House of Commons committee that several years earlier a Spanish boarding party had taken control of his merchant ship, tortured his crew, and lopped off his own right ear. Throughout the period, similar incidents had occurred, with Walpole insisting that they were the price of the dangerous game of smuggling, not a cause for war. The Patriots seized the affair of Jenkins' ear as symptomatic of freedom of the seas and the struggle for empire. Cries of "Protect the flag!" overwhelmed the first minister's pleas for moderation. The old, safe parliamentary majorities evaporated. Country gentlemen and even old cronies deserted Walpole. King George commanded him to have the Spaniards stop searching English ships on the high seas, or else he would support the war party. Put to the test, the great political strategist was unable to bring off his most crucial victory. In 1739, open warfare flared up between England and Spain.

What was to be a quick and glorious naval-colonial war merged with a bitter struggle on the European continent, and England became bogged down in a series of costly, inconclusive conflicts. French armies threatened Hanover, and George II had to beg for the electorate's neutrality. The Patriots bristled at Walpole's halfhearted prosecution of the sea war, and in 1742, his ministry resigned. England's continental entanglements grew more complex than ever, and in 1745, its army was defeated by the French at Fontenoy in the Austrian Netherlands. At the same time, a revolt in the name of the Stuart Pretender erupted in Scotland. However, public dissatisfaction did not reach the point of repudiating the Hanoverian dynastic settlement, and the "revolt of the '45" disappeared into the annals of lost hopes and romance. In the end, the individual who profited most from the nation's troubles was not Bonnie Prince Charlie but rather William Pitt.

Pitt complained that the government's miscalculation had been to fight both a continental and sea war at the same time. In Pitt's imperial vision, Britain must confront Spain and France for colonial and maritime supremacy. Reluctantly, George II took Pitt into his government, and from 1746 to 1755, Pitt's vision was transformed into a national crusade. Country aristocrats and city tradesmen alike became convinced that Britain's imperial destiny and commercial power were indissoluble. Pitt allowed other politicians to bring off an empty-handed peace in 1748. In 1755, he even left the government, but he knew he would return. That very year, fighting broke out between English and French colonists in North America, and shortly thereafter Frederick II of Prussia again plunged Europe into a continental war. On this occasion, Britain knew where its priorities lay, and the moment was ripe for Pitt to make good his claim: "I know that I can save the country and that I alone can!" George II asked him to form a government. Both London and the aristocracy accepted Pitt's promise that an age of grandeur lay at hand.

FRANCE: FROM THE REGENCY TO THE EMERGENCE OF LOUIS XV

Because Louis XIV had brought the country to the brink of military and financial disaster, his last years were universally hated. The death of the old king in 1715, after a personal reign of fifty-four years, represented the opportunity for a fresh start. Smallpox had removed all of Louis's adult heirs from the scene, and the new king in 1715 was a five-year-old child. Those who had been shunted aside in favor of Louis's bureaucratic absolutism drew hope that their voices would be heard once again: courtiers resentful of having been reduced to gilded housekeeping at Versailles, parlement members itching to have their rights of protest restored, important clerics dreaming of the day the French Church would cease to be servile to the government. Other groups, such as regional Estates, financiers, writers, artists, and intellectuals, were aware that an era had passed, and lacking the imposing presence of the Sun King, the façade of conformity and absolutism might well collapse.

Louis had designated a forty-one-year-old nephew, Philip of Orléans, to serve as regent during the minority of Louis XV. A council of princes, headed by two illegitimate sons of the old king, was to join Orléans in making executive decisions. However, Orléans refused to take orders from the grave. To solidify his own future and outface the royal bastards, his major rivals for the throne in case of Louis XV's death, Orléans invited the Parlement of Paris and leading courtiers at Versailles to share in his government. Out went Louis's two sons, along with most of his veteran ministers of state. In came the *Polysynodie*, a system of advisory councils for the regent, manned by courtiers and including a few parlementary magistrates and former royal secretaries. Unfortunately, Orléans was incapable of making the *Polysynodie* function. Cliques formed, personalities clashed, and the courtiers proved incapable of sustained work. The only councils to work efficiently were those few run by former secretaries. In 1718, four councils were dissolved. Five years later, the *Polysynodie* was abandoned and the old ministerial system restored.

The major problem of government was financial. In 1715, the national debt stood at 3.5 billion *livres*, and the anticipated tax revenues for the next two years had already been spent. The government could neither meet its interest on loans nor pay officeholders their stipends. Worthless paper money circulated. If holders demanded payment in specie, the government would have had to declare national bankruptcy. The Council of Finances therefore embarked on a policy of retrenchment, monetary devaluations, attacks upon speculators and Farmers General, and the recall of notes at a fraction of their face value. By 1717, the debt had fallen by a third, but it still was an astronomical 2 billion *livres*. The traditional expedients exhausted, the regent sought advice from individuals who considered themselves experts in state finances, particularly the use of credit. Thus he discovered John Law.

Law was a Scottish banker's son who had settled in Paris late in Louis XIV's reign. Some shady schemes led to his expulsion, but in 1715 he returned to the capital and gained access to the regent. He proposed an economic program that was both bold and archaic, combining appeals to individual greed with a systematized monetary and banking system for the country. Unlike the Netherlands and England, France possessed no national bank. Wealth was fragmented and controlled by corporate groups. Law suspected that while the state was poor, the country was rich. The key to reform therefore lay in the stimulation of credit possibilities. A central bank was necessary to control gold reserves and invigorate investment in colonial commerce. Then the public debt itself could be converted into shares in a state-underwritten trading company, and the company in turn might become the sole creditor of the state. Law's schemes carried into fiscal policy too. He desired a single land tax, which would eliminate the need for tax farming, painful excises, and the exemptions enjoyed by individuals, social groups, and geographic regions.

The regent permitted Law to establish a bank. By 1717, it was emitting bills of exchange which the state accepted as payment for taxes. Next, Law established the Company of the Occident with a monopoly over the commerce of Louisiana. Rival financiers protested, but the regime conspired to have the Company of the Occident absorb all other international trading companies in France. Law's organization dominated the state's colonial commerce. In 1719, the regent removed from the Farmers General the right to collect the state's indirect taxes. He passed on this right to Law. Converting to Catholicism, the Scotsman was named controller-general of finance and minister of state. Thus, within four years, the entire economic life of France had fallen into the hands of a single individual.

The success of the experiment now depended on the will of investors. At first, matters looked promising, as sellers of estates and lands threw their resources into Law's bank and company. Caught up in the spirit of optimism, Law planned canals, roads, and new projects for commerce and industry. However, in the late spring of 1720, just as English investors were becoming wary of their own South Sea Bubble, the bottom fell out. Investors demanded quick development of the Company of the Occident. Exploiting a virgin colony like Louisiana, however, could not occur overnight. Settlers had to be found, lands peopled, and ports built. Law counseled patience, but nervous shareholders began selling out. Throughout the summer of 1720, investors rioted in the capital. Desperately, Law tried to save his system by pouring everything he owned into the bank and company. The regent abandoned him, and the state stopped honoring his bank notes. Shares in the company became worthless. Ruined and stripped of authority, Law fled France. By 1729, he was dead.

Law's system had reduced the state debt by one-fourth but at the ruin of hundreds of investors. It left bitter memories. Throughout the eighteenth century, potential investors mistrusted state credit institutions and shuddered at thoughts of a national bank. They returned to the tradition of placing their funds in land, buildings, and offices, or they engaged in shipbuilding and overseas commerce. While wars and economic expansion contributed to inflationary spirals and mounting government deficits, the state's income failed to rise proportionately. Nonetheless, there were a few positive signs. The government enacted Law's plans for road construction and canal building, so that by 1789, France had Europe's best network of internal communications. Restored, the Company of the Indies gave a vigorous impulsion to overseas commerce. While many were left with worthless shares in the Company of the Occident, those who had bought and sold early enough found themselves rich; and the top layers of society received doses of new wealth and new blood.

Though the failure of the *Polysynodie* and John Law's system did not destroy the regency, the adventurous spirit of the regency disappeared. Worn out by physical excess, Philip of Orléans died in 1723, leaving a poorly governed, half-bankrupt state. Louis XV was still a minor, and the country desperately needed a no-nonsense regime that would finally meet the state's financial obligations. In 1726, Cardinal Hercule de Fleury, the king's former tutor and at seventy-two the most powerful voice in the Royal Council, assumed control over the government. Like Walpole, Fleury wished to avoid adventure abroad and maintain social peace at home. Selecting political associates with views as conservative as his own, Fleury restored collection of the indirect taxes to the Farmers General, and the currency was stabilized according to the gold standard. No revolutionary schemes were tried for increasing government income—just tight controls over private loans, royal lotteries, and the clergy's "gift." In the tradition of France's great minister-churchmen, Fleury was ruthless toward his enemies. He had Jansenist priests silenced, exiled unfriendly members of the Paris Parlement, and closed the celebrated Club d'Entresol, meeting place of "advanced" political thinkers who were overly critical of the regime.

Unlike Walpole, Fleury had no parliament to cajole and no electorate to pacify. He was secure as long as he enjoyed the young king's confidence. He had luck too—an agreement with England to keep local conflicts from erupting into generalized warfare, a series of good harvests until 1738, and the growth of state-directed coal and textile industries. State budgets were balanced. Paris glittered, and in reviving provincial towns like Rennes, Lyons, Bordeaux, and Dijon, construction boomed. Trading in West African blacks and West Indian sugar, France emerged as a great colonial power. Its Atlantic ports thrived, and under the skillful governors Lenoir and Dumas, important advances were made in India.

However, by 1740, Fleury was eighty-seven, and Louis XV was thirty. The death of the Hapsburg emperor Charles VI provoked an international crisis, worsened by the deepening naval war between England and Spain. Several years earlier, France had played a halfhearted role in the War of the Polish Succession, and now young, bellicose courtiers around Louis XV urged the king to be rid of his aged preceptor lest the country suffer a new diplomatic or military defeat. Like his great-grandfather, Louis had strong personal loyalties, and Fleury died in office in 1743. However, by this time, genuine power had fallen to hawks at the French court, led by the count of Belle-Isle. Belle-Isle dragged the country into an anti-Austrian coalition with Prussia, Spain, Sardinia, and Bavaria. French troops were committed to fighting in Germany, and in both America and Asia, French and British forces confronted one another. After twenty years of relative success, the post-Utrecht settlement built upon the foundation of Anglo-French cooperation cracked. Cries of national honor overwhelmed the work of both Fleury and his friend Robert Walpole.

When Fleury died in 1743, Louis XV wished to direct the government in fact as in name. Lacking his great-grandfather's sustained drive at neutralizing factions and dominating advisers, Louis XV quickly fell victim to ambitious counselors. He submitted to courtiers, ministers, and royal mistresses alike and followed conflicting lines of policy at the same time. Consequently, Louis was mistrusted, and his government became weak; for an absolutism, this invited disaster. French diplomacy reacted in confused fashion to the initiatives taken by other states. The corporate elements in French society, particularly the clergy and parlements, reasserted themselves. Declining military leadership, new financial difficulties, revived regionalism, and a near civil war inside the French Church produced many unforeseen problems. Because of weakness at the top, nearly all remained unresolved. Lazy and vain, thoroughly spoiled since infancy, Louis XV found solace from responsibility in childish pleasures and sexual adventures. Inherently timid, on occasion he might conjure up a majestic attitude and play the part of a determined statesman. But he disliked being king and would have been happier as an intriguing, cynical courtier. Unfortunately, neither Louis nor France possessed this option.

During the War of the Austrian Succession (1740–48), France's ally Frederick II of Prussia, who started the conflict by seizing the Hapsburg province of Silesia, held on to his acquisition and converted his small, scattered kingdom into a contending power. Though French armies held their own in the European theater, at the peace conference of Aix-la-Chapelle, French diplomats gained nothing. In 1748, some of Louis XV's advisers recommended reviving the English alliance. Across the channel, however, Pitt and the Patriots constantly stirred up anti-French public opinion, for they knew there was an empire to win.

At the conclusion of the war, France's main problems were internal. Because the indifferent king would appoint no prime minister, strong-minded department chiefs tried to fill the vacuum. The war had produced a new fiscal deficit, and Machault d'Arnouville, controller-general of finances from 1745 to 1754, attacked the problem in a spirit of reform. As Machault correctly saw it, the difficulty lay in distribution of the tax burden. Residents of certain towns, all aristocrats, all clerics, and many officeholders were exempt from paying the main tax, the *taille*. The *taille* was inefficiently collected, and the burden for paying it fell upon the countryside peasants, particularly those living in the regions of France known as the *pays d'élection*. Farmers General were adept at raking in indirect taxes on salt, customs receipts, and articles of consumption. But as private collectors, the tax farmers, not the state, derived major profit from receipts. Machault understood that only a major tax reform, converting heretofore exempt groups into contributors and loosening the stranglehold of the tax farmers, could cope with the fiscal problem. He also wanted the Church and regions where provincial Estates still met to increase payments to the state. In May 1749, the controller-general of finances therefore proposed to the king the *vingtième*, a 5 percent tax on revenues acquired from real estate and office ownership. The controller-general insisted that no region and no social group would be exempt from payment. Once Louis XV approved the plan, a storm of protest erupted among privileged groups. The Parlement of Paris declared its unqualified opposition; the Estates of Artois, Brittany, and Languedoc rejected the new tax out of hand; and so did the leadership in the French clergy. The royal court was divided. The influential royal mistress, Madame de Pompadour, supported Machault, as did most of the *philosophes*. On the other hand, Louis XV's family, led by his daughters, supported the clergy and Estates.

The king wavered and then sank under pressures. In December 1751, he declared ecclesiastical properties exempt from the *vingtième*, and eventually the Estates escaped too. Thus the teeth were removed from Machault's scheme. For the remainder of the ancien régime, the monarchy contented itself with tinkering and momentary expedients. No further attempt was made to confront ancient privileges in the name of fiscal justice, and the crown's timidity ensured the government's poverty.

The failure of the *vingtième* epitomized the regime's lack of nerve. So did a crisis over the Parlement of Paris. As magistrates of the leading law court in the realm, *parlementaires* restored the idea, popular in the Fronde, that they should participate in legislative and executive decision making. Provincial parliaments eagerly supported this position. In the 1740s and 1750s, a constitutional issue in religious disguise set parlements against the government. In 1713, Louis XIV had had the pope condemn Jansenism as a heresy, but the declaration failed to clear the land of individuals attracted to Jansenist theology. Moreover, in the first half of the eighteenth century, Jansenism became politicized. Large numbers of the lower clergy, hostile to the wealth, moral laxity, and religious indifference of their superiors, found Jansenism attractive and called for wider participation in church affairs. They added that the papal Bull Unigenitus of 1713, which had condemned Jansenism, compromised the independence of the Church of France and strengthened the hand of untrustworthy Jesuits.

Eighteenth-century Jansenism split the French Church. Anti-Jansenist bishops hounded suspected Jansenist priests and ordered the clergy to refuse last rites to communicants harboring Jansenist ideas. Meanwhile, the Parlement of Paris took the side of the Jansenists and, in April 1753, merged support for the heretics with a claim as repository and defender of the kingdom's fundamental laws. A "Grand Remonstrance" declared that in pursuit of its duty, the Parlement of Paris might legitimately countenance resistance to the crown. Angrily, Louis XV exiled the parlementary leadership from Paris. In retaliation, judges throughout France went on strike. The nation's courts were paralyzed, and the mood of the country suggested a new Fronde in the making. As popular opinion supported the Parlement of Paris and Jansenism, the government backed down. Exiled *parlementaires* returned to Paris, and the crown agreed to stop the Jansenist witch hunt. Dismayed, Louis XV wrote that the *parlementaires* would not be satisfied until they "led me by the nose. . . . They will wind up wrecking the state." He had a point. Composed of selfish, proud, and venal aristocrats, France's parlements had little interest in deep-seated reform. Nevertheless, they sowed the seeds of resistance to royal authority and desanctified the absolutist pretensions of the crown.

By the mid-1750s, all the elements of an explosive situation were present in France. The country remained divided religiously, the government's fiscal problems were unresolved, the regime itself had exposed the social injustice of the tax system, and the parlements were questioning the very authority of the absolute monarchy. An indecisive king headed a weak, drifting government. Soon military defeat would add to France's other woes.

CENTRAL EUROPE: THE HAPSBURG EMPIRE AND PRUSSIAN KINGDOM (1713–56)

In 1713 the House of Hapsburg reestablished itself as a great power. It had scored victories over Louis XIV on the western front and defeated the Turks decisively in the Balkans. With 24 million subjects, the empire of Charles VI (1711–40) comprised four basic segments: the hereditary Hapsburg German lands of the center; Bohemia with its dependencies of Moravia and Silesia; Hungary with its outlying regions of Slavonia, Croatia, and Transylvania; and the exterior dependencies ranging from Belgium in the northwest to Milan, Naples, and Sardinia in Italy. The Belgian and Italian lands represented compensation for the loss of the Spanish inheritance; the Treaties of Carlowitz (1699) and Passarowitz (1718) stabilized the southeastern frontier at the expense of the Turks.

Economically, the far-flung empire possessed vast potential for commerce and industry. In the style of high baroque, the imperial capital of Vienna offered an imposing façade of strength and power, and the court of Charles VI was focal point for an aristocratic and cosmopolitan culture that outdistanced even Versailles in many respects. Revenues collected from self-worked estates built great aristocratic residences near the capital for magnates called to Vienna to serve in the imperial chancelleries.

The drawing of talent and wealth to the center of government suggested that the time was ripe for the Hapsburgs to construct an apparatus for their empire, but by personality and inclination, Charles VI refused to establish a bureaucracy. The tastes of the emperor were aristocratic, and he took for granted the feudal, ethnic, and constitutional division of his lands and people. For Charles, central government meant the existence of separate departments for the various regions, each department responsible for maintaining the district concerned. Though the departments might work at cross-purposes, Charles made no effort to create institutions common to all the regions. Nor did he invigorate the few that already existed. He left the Estates and Diets intact. He allowed the army to sink to 80,000 ill-trained, ill-equipped troops. The quest for revenues was unaggressive, and a disproportionate amount of state income went into maintaining the court. A halfhearted attempt to establish a state-financed trading company working out of Belgian ports came to nothing, Spanish aggression in Italy resulted in the loss of Naples, the king of Savoy won Sardinia, and even the great triumphs over the Turks seemed in jeopardy. During a Hapsburg-Ottoman war from 1735 to 1739, the Austrian army was trapped in Belgrade. To win its release, Charles had to relinquish what he had gained at the Treaty of Passarowitz twenty years earlier.

The paradox of Charles VI's reign was that the weakened condition of his empire was directly attributable to his obsession with maintaining its integrity. He sought agreements from his family, from the imperial Estates, and from the powers of Europe that would guarantee the Hapsburg succession to his direct heirs. The roots of the emperor's obsession went back to 1703, when his father, Leopold I, had designated a line of succession in case neither Charles nor his elder brother Joseph sired male children. Leopold designated the daughters of Joseph as having imperial priority over whatever daughters Charles might sire. Ruling from 1706 until his death in 1711, Joseph had two daughters and no sons. According to the line of succession, Charles replaced his brother as emperor. He was at the time childless but determined to have a say in his own succession. This meant, of course, disregarding his late father's will. In the Austrian and Bohemian lands, it was taken for granted that a reigning monarch could name his successor, previous wills notwithstanding. On the other hand, the Hungarian Diet claimed the right to select its sovereign should the male Hapsburg line die out. To guarantee his own line and avert a possible civil war over the succession, on April 19, 1713, Charles replaced the Leopoldine declaration with his famous Pragmatic Sanction. The lands of the Hapsburg empire were declared indivisible. Should Charles sire only daughters, the eldest would succeed as legitimately as a male to all possessions. Only a failure to produce an heir would be sufficient reason for the Hapsburg heritage to pass on to others.

In 1717 a son recently born to Charles died in infancy. Shortly thereafter, two daughters were born, and there were no further offspring. The emperor passed the remainder of his life seeking assurance of his daughters' heritage. No female had ever headed the house of Hapsburg. To many, the possibility was a sign of divine displeasure and an invitation to political disaster. Therefore, Charles went after written guarantees. Since the Pragmatic Sanction was, in the first place, a family compact, the emperor had to secure the assent of Joseph I's two daughters and their husbands. One husband was king of Bavaria and the second, king of Saxony. Both would benefit from their wives' claims, and both coveted the title of Holy Roman Emperor. Nevertheless, Charles won family agreement not to challenge his selection of heir. Next, Charles got the regional Estates to accept the Pragmatic Sanction as a law of his empire. Before accepting, the Hungarians extracted concessions. Charles agreed to convoke their Diet regularly, to rule Hungary according to the nation's own law, and to permit the Hungarian Diet to apportion its own war contributions. By 1725, the Pragmatic Sanction had become part of the Hapsburg imperial constitution.

In persuading the European powers to recognize the document, the price greatly outweighed the result. For the assent of Saxony and Russia, Charles had to enter two costly and fruitless wars, the first over the Polish Succession (1733–38) and the second against the Turks (1735–39). To obtain the agreement of England and the Dutch, Charles sacrificed the commercial company projected for Belgium. For France to sign, Charles had to persuade his son-in-law to surrender the duchy of Lorraine and accept, as compensation, the Italian province of Tuscany. Nevertheless, on the eve of his death in November 1740, Charles VI considered his diplomacy a success. His eldest daughter, Maria Theresa, a young woman of twenty-three, succeeded to her father's lands and titles.

The peaceful accession of the princess was illusory. The collapse of the

Hapsburg army in the Turkish war proved how the emperor had neglected his military responsibilities for what an embittered Eugene of Savoy had called worthless scraps of paper. Moreover, the state's treasury was empty, the government demoralized, and Austria's rivals eager to repudiate their agreement. In France, Belle-Isle's war party was pressuring Louis XV to lead an anti-Hapsburg coalition; the king of Bavaria, Maria Theresa's uncle by marriage, laid claim to headship of the Holy Roman Empire; the Spanish Bourbons prepared to clear the Hapsburgs out of Italy; and the king of Prussia demanded the cession of Austrian Silesia.

Before all the pressures, the new empress held firm, but in December 1740, the first blow fell. Frederick II of Prussia, himself on the throne but a few months, invaded Silesia, quickly occupying its capital, Breslau. As the king of Saxony repudiated his wife's signature to the Pragmatic Sanction, France and Bavaria signed an offensive alliance against Austria. Soon Spain and Saxony joined. The allies agreed to partition among themselves all the Hapsburg possessions, except Austria proper and Hungary. On July 31, 1741, the French and Bavarians marched off to war. In Bohemia, Prague and Linz fell to the invaders. The Bavarian king, Charles-Albert, cowed the Bohemian Estates into deposing Maria Theresa and declaring him sovereign. In February 1742, the majority of Germany's electoral princes chose Charles-Albert as Holy Roman Emperor. Observers believed that if she could salvage as much as Spain had saved in 1713, Maria Theresa would be fortunate.

The major ally of the empress was England, both distant and untrustworthy. Fearful of losing Hanover, George II threw his support to Charles-Albert as Holy Roman Emperor. Meanwhile, Maria Theresa tried desperately to raise an army. Summoning the Hungarian Diet, she made a dramatic personal appeal to the Magyars. Raising her infant son Joseph high above her head, she cried that her throne and the child's rightful heritage lay in Hungarian hands. The dignity, honesty, and beauty of the empress proved irresistible. The Magyars vowed to defend her with their life and blood. Far fewer than the 100,000 troops promised Maria Theresa ever arrived, but those who came fought well. Moreover, the gesture of solidarity on the part of the Hungarian Diet raised the prestige of the empress in her beleaguered domains and on the international scene. The Austrian crown Estates sent troops. Public opinion in England rallied to her favor. The War of the Austrian Succession went through several stages before the conclusion of peace in 1748. Reluctantly, Maria Theresa had to concede Silesia to the Prussians, though this was all she lost. Her lands were cleared of invaders, and her empire was saved. After the death of Charles-Albert of Bavaria in 1744, her own husband Francis was elected Holy Roman Emperor.

The near collapse of the Hapsburg empire was a lesson not lost upon Maria Theresa, and the postwar period was the crucial watershed of her long reign. She needed to break with the complacency of her father's time, reduce regional loyalties, and translate mere affection for the dynasty into centralized state policies. Therefore, she began building a national army and centralized bureaucracy, both of which were essential if she were to regain Silesia. A national military academy was founded, regular camps and maneuvers established, and officer training systematized. In place of the voluntary contributions sent to Vienna by the regional Estates, which paid for but a fraction of the 100,000 troops needed to defend the borders, the government proposed a military maintenance tax on all property owners. Though the regional Estates were permitted to make the property assessments on their own, the central government was to be guaranteed ten years of stipulated income. Property owners growled. Those in Hungary even won exemption from the scheme. However, the other regions of the empire submitted; funds were guaranteed the army, and a new beginning was made in welding together the disparate heritage of the empress.

The need for allies was as essential as military preparedness. Back in 1740, Britain was the Hapsburgs' sole friend. However, the island kingdom was concerned primarily with trade and colonies, not with Austrian interests in central Europe. At the Treaty of Aix-la-Chapelle, the British advised Maria Theresa to accept the loss of Silesia. To Hapsburg diplomats, Austria was useful to Britain only as long as it kept France bogged down in a continental war. Therefore, after 1749 Hapsburg policy was to construct a new bloc of alliances replacing the pact with Britain. For her part, Maria Theresa unequivocally demanded the restoration of Silesia and destruction of Prussia.

A brilliant, egotistical, and eccentric statesman, Count Wenzel von Kaunitz-Rietberg, was entrusted with the empress's hopes. Kaunitz's scheme was to wean France away from its alliance with Prussia and use French power to destroy Frederick II. Because France had been the traditional enemy of the Hapsburgs for more than two centuries, winning it over would represent not merely a revolution in diplomacy but a revolution in ideas. As ambassador to Versailles, Kaunitz worked on getting support at the French court. In 1753, he returned to Vienna to head the Hapsburg foreign office. For several years, France's continental diplomacy had been directed at barring Russia's westward expansion, and in this endeavor, Prussia was a useful ally. In 1755, however, Britain offered to subsidize the Russian army in return for Russian guarantees to defend Hanover. Though George II was afraid that Frederick II might seize Hanover as he had seized Silesia, the Prussian king himself was consumed with fears. Aware of Austrian plans for revenge and the hatred of the Russian empress Elizabeth for him, Frederick envisioned Austro-Russian armies overrunning his poor, scattered domains. Therefore, he went to great lengths to convince the British that he had no hostile intentions toward Hanover and offered to defend the electorate against France. Britain accepted, and the resulting agreement was the Convention of Westminster (January 1756). In America and India, a new Anglo-French war had already erupted. Frederick promised to do what he could to keep Germany neutral.

Defensive though it was, the Anglo-Prussian convention played into the hands of Kaunitz. He redoubled efforts at courting France, dangling vague promises of Belgium and the Polish throne before the eyes of Louis XV's son-in-law and brother-in-law. News of the Convention of Westminster reached Versailles. France and England were already fighting overseas. By signing an accord with France's archenemy, Frederick II seemed to be flaunting before the world his contempt for his old ally. His pride assailed, Louis XV grew angry and denounced the Prussian king. Kaunitz proposed balancing the Convention of Westminster, and in May 1756, France and Austria signed their own defensive alliance. It guaranteed mutual assistance of twenty-four thousand troops or a money equivalent should one of the parties be attacked by a third power. On the surface, this First Treaty of Versailles was innocuous enough. It still did not commit French aid to the destruction of Prussia. Nevertheless, it marked a turning point in European diplomacy.

Thus the celebrated "diplomatic revolution" of the eighteenth century took effect. Two traditional enemies, France and Austria, now were allies. The Hapsburgs wanted the recovery of Silesia and an end to Prussia. On the other hand, France had little to gain from the alliance. She already had her hands full in a murderous colonial war with the English, and a costly diversion in Germany would not serve its interests. However, the Prussian king tended to infuriate fellow sovereigns to the point of conflict. Maria Theresa and Elizabeth of Russia loathed him. Now Louis XV did, too. Suddenly Frederick saw the dismemberment of Prussia as a certainty. Since striking first had worked back in 1740, he gambled again. To reach the Austrian border, in August 1756, the Prussian army invaded Saxony. Frederick's strategy was to knock out the Hapsburgs immediately. This time, however, the Austrians were prepared, and the Prussian king's move ushered in the Seven Years' War, the most destructive conflict eighteenth-century Europe had heretofore experienced.

How could Prussia, considered no more than the scattered domains of the Hohenzollern family, unleash the eighteenth century's two most titanic wars? In 1713 Frederick William I had become king of East Prussia, but the proliferation of titles he held elsewhere in his domains suggested that regional political bodies still set limits upon his governing authority. However, Frederick William I was less subservient to provincial Estates than were his neighboring sovereigns in Poland, Saxony, or the Hapsburg empire. His grandfather, the Great Elector, had stifled the political independence of the regions, leaving successors free to levy consumer taxes and war subsidies. Moreover, he had superimposed a loyal bureaucracy upon the old official-dom, and a devoted army supported his authority. Military strength, bureaucratic efficiency, and tight control over economic resources turned the Hohenzollern domains into an administratively sound absolutism. Aristocrats and ambitious commoners banked their futures upon serving the sovereign; the clergy, merchants, and peasants had no other choice.

Frederick William I deserves enormous personal credit for fulfilling the work of his grandfather. A combatant in the war of the Spanish succession, he was the "Sergeant King," accustomed to giving orders and being obeyed. He expressed himself coarsely and opted for simple manners and plain tastes. A pious Calvinist, he hoped to serve his God by performing human duties as faithfully as possible, all the while governing his domains and subjects as a harsh taskmaster. The king was seen in the streets of Berlin, swooping down upon loiterers, beggars, and prostitutes, striking them with his cane and urging them to take up honorable tasks. "Salvation is God's business," Frederick William said, "but all else is mine."

Frederick William was aware that more sophisticated contemporaries sniggered at his boorish personality. Mistrusting those around him, the king preferred to work at daily business alone in his study. From childhood to young manhood, Frederick William had seen his state tied to a pair of great European conflicts. As a member of the coalition against Louis XIV, it had joined Russia against Charles XII. Prussian troops fought well, but their continued use nearly always depended upon foreign subsidies. Convinced that the state's own resources must be capable of supporting its defense, Frederick William constructed his regime upon the twin pillars of military strength and economic self-sufficiency.

Building the army was a labor of love. Frederick William was one of Europe's first rulers to wear an army uniform regularly, and he was most at ease carousing with career officers over beer and tobacco. The army of forty thousand that he had inherited in 1713 contained too many foreign mercenaries for his liking. Private contractors raised and paid troops, and local district responsibility for levying stipulated numbers of soldiers had fallen into disuse. Frederick William went to work on military reform. Prussian nobles were prohibited from serving in foreign armies, a cadet school was opened in Berlin, and the relationship between the Junker landowners and officer corps became a seamless web in the social fabric of the state. In 1733, the military recruitment was reformed. Most of the domains were divided into districts of approximately five thousand households. Every district was responsible for replenishing the manpower of a regiment stationed within or near it. Once sufficiently trained, peasant or artisan recruits were released to perform their civilian tasks. Even at work they wore a piece of uniform, a constant reminder of their soldierly duties. Every fall and spring, they returned to their military units.

By no means was this a system of universal military service. Burghers, university graduates, and workers in high-priority industries had exemptions. Certain geographical regions escaped the cantonal system, too. The lowest ranks of society filled the regiments, and the highest ranks led them.

As a group, the Prussian aristocracy was relatively poor. For younger sons unable to survive on the land, military service for foreign princes had long provided an occupational outlet. When Frederick William I closed off this channel, established his cadet school, and favored a military state, it became obvious to Junkers that army service had become enshrined as a social obligation and mark of rank. The Prussian officer corps developed its distinctive characteristics as the elite corporation rooted in social privilege and joined to the political aims of the monarchy. Prussia's industrial development was aligned also to her military growth. Powder and ironworks arose to supply the army, while the textile industry clothed it. Five-sevenths of the government's revenues were channeled back into the military machine. By 1740, over eighty thousand precision-trained troops were afoot. A state that ranked thirteenth in Europe's population contained the continent's fourth-largest standing army. This military force no longer depended upon foreign subsidies. It was self-sustaining.

Despite scorn for those whom he called "ink-splashers," Frederick William understood that only a well-oiled government machine tended by an efficient bureaucracy could harness the resources needed to maintain his beloved army. Thus, the king pursued financial and administrative reforms, sought to increase agricultural and industrial production, and stimulated both immigration and internal colonization. The Hohenzollerns were Prussia's greatest landowners by far, working one-third of the peasantry. Instead of leasing royal domains to Junkers on a long-term basis, as had been the case previously, Frederick William opted for short-term leases at high rents, or else he hired bailiffs to exploit the crown estates directly. As a consequence of the changes in land tenure practices, government income increased. An increase in tax revenue complemented it. The burden of the country tax, the so-called contribution, fell exclusively upon the peasantry. It averaged nearly 40 percent of the peasant's net yield of his small plot. A second tax, the excise, fell on townspeople. It was imposed on their food, drink, and goods. In 1713, only three of Frederick William's provinces were subjected to the excise. He subsequently extended it across all of the regions. During the king's reign, government revenues doubled, and they were sufficient to pay for the army.

Reduced expenses accompanied the increased income. By abolishing his father's lavish court, Frederick William set a personal example, and he saw that town commissioners collected the excise with a minimum of graft and expense. Believing that centralized and controlled administrative practices could best pull revenues into government, the king established a single all-encompassing board of control for the kingdom, the General Directory. Meanwhile, different town and country administrations were fused into provincial departments, one for each of the kingdom's seventeen provinces. Everywhere civil servants were subjected to group discipline and collective responsibility. Individual initiative was discouraged; the common purpose was to raise revenue for military needs. Not even a senior official of the General Directory could act without the consent of his three colleagues on the board and, of course, the king. Unless an arch-bureaucrat sat upon the throne, the government was doomed. Fortunately, no eighteenth-century monarchs took their absolutism more seriously than did the Hohenzollerns. They nurtured a state for which military discipline, subordination, and centralization became bywords. The feudal, agrarian regions east of the Elbe River yielded easily. Like his predecessors and successors, Frederick William had some difficulty coercing the more urban populations of the Rhine Valley, but he succeeded.

A feared and demanding father to his subjects, Frederick William was a timid diplomat, suspecting that cunning foreigners might use his beloved army for their own ends. Respecting hierarchy, as elector of Brandenburg he maintained a correct relationship with Emperor Charles VI and signed the Pragmatic Sanction without conditions. The Hapsburgs miscalculated Frederick William's attitude as a sign of weakness and treated him with disdain. Other powers, however, were aware of the shifting balance of forces in central Europe. Seeking a protector for Hanover, Britain hoped to cement a tie by uniting the prince of Wales, heir to the throne, to Frederick William's daughter, and the Prussian crown prince to George II's daughter. Frederick William was fearful of the elegant amorality of English court life, and in 1730 he suspended the project. However, for eighteen-year-old crown prince Frederick, the king's decision was a crushing blow. From childhood, young Frederick had suffered from the brutality and ridicule of his boorish father, and now a brief moment of liberty was denied him. The prince tried to flee the kingdom, thus provoking the major crisis of his father's reign.

The personality conflict between Frederick William I and his son is one of the great dynastic dramas of modern European history. Nineteenth-century Prussian historians turned it into a moral fable for schoolchildren: the struggle between the duty-bound, tough, realistic father and the hypersensitive, intelligent, artistic prince, followed by the prince's desperate flight. But the flight fails. The boy is caught, chastised, and punished. He is forced to witness the execution of a coconspirator, his best friend. He is locked up as a common army deserter. Then, by stages, Frederick learns that his destiny to become Prussia's king must take precedence over his inclination to play music, write poetry, and read philosophy. His inner rebellion subsides, he takes his father's choice of a plain German princess as his wife, he learns about administration, and he becomes a soldier. Convinced that Frederick's change of heart is genuine, the king is reconciled with the crown prince. Knowing that the state is in safe hands, Frederick William can die in peace. Obedience and duty triumph.

The affair was more than a parable for children. Frequently, individuals and groups opposing the policies of a reigning sovereign might rally round an unhappy heir, forming a lair of malcontents bent on treason. Only a generation earlier, Peter the Great and the aged Louis XIV had suspected this. In England, Leicester House, where the prince of Wales lived, was a hotbed of opposition to Walpole. Frederick William feared that dangerous cliques might use the crown prince to destroy his own accomplishments, and as the king's apprehension mounted, he became more abusive. The attempted flight was the climax.

Whether the crown prince's repentance was as genuine as nationalist Prussian historians depict it is irrelevant. He never became a carbon copy of his father and may well have continued hating him. But he did learn how to rule. Settling down on a country estate in 1737, he delved deeply into both the classics and writings of the Enlightenment. He corresponded with Voltaire and even wrote a piece of political philosophy refuting Machiavelli. The hope of his father, Frederick, probably the most intelligent crown prince in modern European history, became the hope of the *philosophes*. They asked whether, once on the throne of Prussia, he might combine reason, humanity, and absolutism to enlightened ends. What intellectuals missed, unfortunately, was Frederick's profound cynicism, which provided a cutting edge to his belief in duty. Even as he wrote of his ideals in the *Anti-Machiavel*, even as he poured out heart and hopes to Voltaire, Frederick developed the contrasting principle of the state as a moral end in itself. As Prussia's first servant, the king must not only encourage trade and industry, maintain the state's social fabric, and protect the country from rapacious neighbors but he must also be prepared to add to the state's resources by any means he deems justified.

Frederick knew that his father would leave him a large army and full treasury. While the *philosophes* naively cheered him as one of their own, the crown prince spent long hours analyzing the weaknesses and strengths of the other European powers. He noted the Anglo-French *entente* and its unraveling, the tensions between England and Spain, the feebleness of Poland, and especially the insecurity of Hapsburg Austria. He sensed that a generation of relative stability was ending, and that boldness would pay dividends. On May 31, 1740, Frederick William I died. A few months later, Emperor Charles VI was dead as well. Turning a minor territorial dispute with Austria into a pretext for aggression, King Frederick seized the Hapsburg province of Silesia. Though few European sovereigns took Charles VI's Pragmatic Sanction seriously, the suddenness of the Prussian descent was stunning. A secondary, upstart power had attacked Europe's most prestigious empire. Charles VI left Austria weaker than it had been in a century, Silesia possessed mineral and industrial wealth exceeding all of Prussia's, and the strategic location of the region permitted future expansion to the south and east. An opportunity beckoned. In December 1740, the Prussian army marched. Six months later, the shock had worn off, and nearly everyone else was joining in for the spoils.

Frederick wanted a quick victory in a limited war. With Silesia in tow, he offered Maria Theresa money, a Prussian alliance, and his vote for her husband in the upcoming election for Holy Roman Emperor. But he would not yield a foot of conquered territory. The young empress scornfully rejected Frederick's entreaties, stating that to do so would betray the labor of her father's life, his Pragmatic Sanction. So she decided to fight. However, French and Bavarian plans to partition the Hapsburg empire sent events out of her control, and the empress was in no position to confront France, Bavaria, Saxony, and Spain—as well as Prussia. In 1742 she was forced to make peace with Frederick, thereby acknowledging the loss of Silesia. As ally of the French and Bavarians, Frederick later was forced back into the fray, and in 1745 Maria Theresa had to reconfirm Silesia's loss (Treaty of Dresden). Though Prussian diplomats did not even attend the peace conference at Aix-la-Chapelle in 1748, representatives of the other European powers recognized as an accomplished fact the event that had opened the War of the Austrian Succession.

After 1748 Maria Theresa was obsessed with recovering Silesia and destroying Prussia. She prepared for the next war by building an army and a system of alliances. Frederick II was aware of her fury, but even more he feared a hostile alliance in which France and Russia would be serving Austrian ends. From 1748 to 1755 he tried to persuade the great powers that he now was Germany's peacekeeper. But his past record was unconvincing. All through the War of the Austrian Succession, Frederick had been an untrustworthy ally, and to Louis XV, Prussia's Convention of Westminster (1756) with England, however defensive it looked, was an act of betrayal. It drove France into Austria's arms. Like Maria Theresa, Czarina Elizabeth of Russia despised Frederick and welcomed eradication of the Prussian state. In the Convention of Westminster, she saw British betrayal of her friendship. Russian diplomats spent the summer of 1756 conversing with Kaunitz. Horrified, Frederick witnessed the backfire of his diplomacy. If he waited for others to strike first, it would be the end. Therefore, in late August he attacked Saxony. Unlike the invasion of Silesia sixteen years earlier, his decision was born of desperation rather than self-confidence. The new war he unleashed represented Prussia's struggle for survival.

THE EVOLUTION OF RUSSIA (1725–55) AND THE SEVEN YEARS' WAR (1756–63)

A major element in the destruction of the post-Utrecht diplomatic settlement was the emergence of Russia. Peter the Great's western journey in 1697 had been largely symbolic, but the construction of his new capital and his triumphs in the Great Northern War from 1700 to 1721 meant that Russia was aiming due west. Russia now sent diplomats into Europe, and its commerce expanded with the English, Dutch, and French. Though the days were over when European sovereigns knew so little about Russia that they would write to czars long-dead, it still was a partially known quantity and thus feared. Some of the difficulty had to do with the country's bizarre political history after Peter's death. From 1725 to 1762, six czars or czarinas succeeded to the throne, often through murder and violence. Russia lacked a constitution or accepted system of dynastic succession. The fledgling bureaucracy built by Peter succumbed easily to clique and faction. While guards, regiments, and palace favorites made and unmade rulers, no administrative staff existed to keep government on an even keel. The French ambassador to St. Petersburg remarked: "The master here is the one who possesses bayonets, a cellar filled with *eau-de-vie*, and gold."

For fifteen years after Peter's death, it looked as though the czar's reforms were doomed. Favorites replaced the Senate, the aristocracy made important strides in escaping required state service, and for a time, 1727 to 1730, resurgent boyars even moved the capital back to Moscow. During the reign of Anna Ivanovna (1730–40), Peter's niece from the Baltic duchy of Courland, German adventurers poured into government and exploited Russia as a colonial conquest. Anna's death produced a year of immense political chaos, terminating in 1741 when a guards regiment established Peter's daughter, Elizabeth, as czarina. Elizabeth threw out the Germans, restored the Senate, and promised to restore the state to its moorings. As part of a cultural revival, the educator Ivan Shuvalov and humanist-scientist Michael Lomonosov founded the University of Moscow. Russian aristocrats were persuaded to start ironworks, distilleries, tanneries, and textile mills, and a government bank opened to loan funds to investors. A model of sensual excess and extravagance, Elizabeth thought of retaining the loyalty of the aristocracy by acceding to its desires—chief of which was freedom from state service. The social base of Russia remained serfdom, more hardened and ruthless than ever. In the recently settled fertile regions of the Ukraine, work service obligations were raised to six days per week. Where they could, landlords extracted cash dues from peasants. The recalcitrant were tried in makeshift courtrooms on estates and could be deported or imprisoned at the master's will.

Because of Russia's internal instability, until the 1740s European governments shied away from it, but the declining status of Poland, Sweden, and the Ottoman empire underscored Russia's growing importance. From 1725 until Elizabeth's accession in 1741, a Rhineland German baron, Andrew Ostermann, directed the country's foreign policy. Ostermann's aims were to preserve Russia's conquests along the Baltic, maintain its influence in Poland, and keep up pressures against the Turks. Since these ambitions coordinated with Austrian aims, the two powers kept on good terms. However, relations with France were very poor. Traditional enemies of the Hapsburgs, the French were friendly towards Sweden and the Ottomans.

In 1733, the death of Poland's king, Augustus II, provoked an international crisis. The crown was elective and the election open to bribery. France desired the restoration of Charles XII's former puppet, Stanislas Leczcynski, now father-in-law of Louis XV. Meanwhile, the Russians and Austrians supported the son of Augustus II. In a mood of national resurgence, the Polish Diet elected Stanislas, thus provoking the Russians to move an army toward Warsaw. Faced with a hopeless war, the Poles reversed themselves and named the Russian candidate as king. Nevertheless, Austrian and French forces already had clashed in Germany, and Russian regiments were sent to assist Charles VI. Never before had Russians fought so deeply in Europe, and the entire continent grew restive. Before a massive all-European struggle ensued, however, Stanislas withdrew his candidacy; Augustus III was crowned, and the crisis subsided.

Russia's participation in the War of the Polish Succession was the first step in becoming wholly enmeshed in European diplomacy. In 1735 Ostermann helped the Austrians against the Turks, but so dismayed were the Russians with the poor Hapsburg performance that in 1740 they made no move to save Maria Theresa's empire from partition. After Ostermann's fall during the succession crisis of 1740-41, Elizabeth behaved scrupulously. She promised the Hapsburgs aid in any subsequent conflict, but not the present one, and for seven of the eight years of European warfare between 1740 and 1748, Russia avoided involvement. It did not participate in the negotiations at Aix-la-Chapelle.

Nevertheless, Europeans respected the Russian army, and after 1748 the wooing of Russia became a preoccupation of diplomacy. While Kaunitz tried to maintain Austro-Russian friendship, in 1755 the English agreed to subsidize Elizabeth's army in return for Russian guarantees to protect Hanover. Much to the chagrin of Frederick II, this placed a Russian army on Prussia's frontier, and Russia's Baltic fleet was kept on constant alert.

In 1755, Britain already was at war with France in India and America and doubted whether its Russian alliance would hold Frederick in check in central Europe. Moreover, the British underestimated Frederick's morbid fears of a coordinated Austro-Russian attack on Prussia, with Britain unwittingly footing the bill. The Prussian king had to dissociate Britain from its old alliance with Austria and its new one with Russia. He believed he could not count on French help. Therefore, he proclaimed to Britain his unaggressive intentions in Germany and, to underscore his point, signed the Convention of Westminster (January 1756) with the British.

The immediate effect of the convention played into Frederick's hands. Prussia and Britain would protect central Europe from any would-be aggressor; George II saw Hanover's integrity guaranteed, reconfirming his Russian alliance. However, Czarina Elizabeth saw the British agreement with a king she despised as treachery. As Frederick hoped, she repudiated her pact with Britain, thus losing her army's paymaster. Then, however, disaster struck Frederick's diplomacy. Four months after the Convention of West-minster, France and Austria signed their treaty of friendship, and Russia quickly moved into the Franco-Austrian camp. Sensing a triple-pronged attack on Prussia, in August 1756 Frederick launched a preventive war against Austria. France stuck by its new ally, Austria, and in December, Russia joined the two powers in order "to reduce the king of Prussia within proper limits." Faced with the German war they did not want, the British reluctantly subsidized the Prussian army. Thus the mutual fears, distrust, and ambitions of the European powers thrust Russia directly into continental affairs. Despite long-standing apprehensions about the intrusion of this half-oriental, politically unstable, poverty-racked despotism whose existence was built upon the subjugation of countless millions, the die was cast. Russian armies now would fight across European battlefields, and just as Russia's presence helped precipitate the Seven Years' War, its premature withdrawal in 1762 turned out to be the key to ending the conflict.

Essentially, the Seven Years' War was Prussia's struggle for survival. Scattered in patches from the Niemen to Rhine rivers, the Prussian state was geographically artificial and insecure. It either had to extend or disintegrate. The coalition against Prussia had clear-cut territorial ambitions. The Austrians wanted Silesia, Russia coveted East Prussia, France desired Prussia's Rhineland regions, and on joining the coalition, Sweden went after Pomerania. The Second Treaty of Versailles (May 1757), committing 100,000 French troops to Germany, openly invited partition of the Prussian state. Frederick's attack on Saxony brought most of the German principalities into the war on the coalition's side, and England's George II considered Prussia's position as hopeless. To save his electorate of Hanover, George wanted to open immediate negotiations with Austria and France, but his chief minister, William Pitt, now committed to saving Prussia, counseled courage and patience.

With its unexpected twists of fortune, the Seven Years' War reads like melodrama. The allies fielded 450,000 troops to Frederick's 150,000, and in the first year of the war, the Prussians suffered nearly disastrous setbacks. They failed to help Hanover when an English-Hanoverian army was defeated by the French; the Russians occupied East Prussia; the Swedes debarked in Pomerania; and for a time, in October 1757, the Austrians took Berlin. In Prussia's darkest hour, however, Frederick's redoubtable army reorganized and under the direct command of the king scored a pair of victories that have become classics in the annals of land warfare. The first, on November 5, 1757, was at Rossbach, in Saxony, against a coalition of French and imperial forces; the second, a month later, was at Leuthen, in Silesia, against the Austrians. On each occasion, the discipline and courage of the outnumbered Prussians responded magnificently to the tactical skill of their commanding general.

Frederick's victories averted the immediate destruction of Prussia and turned the struggle into a war of attrition. The allied coalition revealed its cracks. Austrian military leadership was mediocre, the Russians never moved without receiving express orders from distant St. Petersburg, and the French generals were hindered both by divisive diplomacy at Versailles and a public opinion supportive of Frederick's cause. As early as 1758, a pro-Prussian faction in the French government began looking for a way out. The French reduced their financial commitment to Maria Theresa, and Russia and Austria became the major participants on the allied side. As long as Frederick could raise troops, England subsidized the Prussians. But Prussia was running out of soldiers. A costly defeat against the Russians at Kunersdorf in August 1759 erased the effects of previous victories, and by 1760 Frederick had fewer than 100,000 soldiers left. With his recruiters driving unwilling Saxon and Silesian peasants into battle, the Prussian king wrote despairingly: "To tell the truth, I believe all is lost. I shall not survive the ruin of my country." While Frederick contemplated suicide, only Austro-Russian disagreements over where to strike delayed the end. The Austrians insisted on liberating Silesia, but the Russians delayed in Saxony. Frederick held on, declaring that fortune alone "can deliver me from my present state."

This was precisely what occurred. On January 5, 1762, Czarina Elizabeth died. Her successor, Peter III, a fanatical admirer of the Prussian king, ordered his generals to cease hostilities. By May, Russia was out of the war. Sweden withdrew as well, and France was all but through. Lacking the resources to crush Prussia alone, Maria Theresa reluctantly opened talks with the Prussians late in 1762. In February 1763 at Hubertusburg, Maria Theresa was forced to confirm the territorial integrity of the Prussian state, including Silesia. Prussia was saved, but at a terrible price. One-tenth of her people perished in the war, and Frederick wondered whether the final chapter in his country's history had indeed been written. Shortly after 1763, Prussia's relations with England turned sour, France would not even accept its diplomatic mission, and both Saxony and Austria remained inveterate enemies. Desperately in need of an ally, Frederick turned to his old nemesis, Russia. He dangled a tempting prize, the impotent kingdom of Poland. For the next generation, the history of central and eastern Europe centered on schemes that resulted in the partition of that unhappy state.

THE ANGLO-FRENCH STRUGGLE FOR EMPIRE (1715–63)

A week before the signing of the Treaty of Hubertusburg, the Peace of Paris settled the colonial and maritime aspects of the Seven Years' War. What climaxed at Paris in February 1763 was a half-century rivalry for empire between England and France that since 1755 had degenerated into a death struggle. There were three chief geographic regions of conflict: North America, the Caribbean, and India. In North America, British acquisition of Nova Scotia and Newfoundland in 1713 was to have offered protection to New Englanders who felt threatened by French domination of Canada. However, the deep drives of French explorers into the Mississippi Valley and the threat of potential French settlement there rekindled the fears of hostile encirclement among English colonists along the Atlantic seaboard.

Meanwhile, in the Caribbean after 1713, the French were successful in developing sugar plantations. They controlled the large islands of Guadeloupe and Martinique, half of Santo Domingo, and a host of smaller possessions. Caribbean sugar represented one-third of French international commerce, and in mainland France nearly three million investors, traders, shipbuilders, and workers in ports and refineries owed their livelihoods to exploiting the Caribbean.

At the same time, English West Indian planters felt submerged by French initiative and called upon Parliament to stifle it. They demanded enforcement of the Navigation Acts and suppression of illicit commerce between New Englanders and the French islands.

India was the third major area of Anglo-French rivalry. As in North America and the Caribbean, recent French advances perpetuated crisis. The British East India Company was content to develop seaborne and inland trade around the company "counters" at Madras, Bombay, and Calcutta. On the other hand, the French, taking advantage of the power vacuum in India following the death of Shah Aurengzeb in 1707, made a series of military arrangements with semi-independent native princes and extended French influence across the entire middle belt of the peninsula. Commanded by French cadres, native auxiliary bands fought for India's warring nabobs and rajahs. Benoît Dumas, director of the French East India Company from 1735 to 1741, skillfully bartered military assistance for commercial privileges. Honored as a vassal by the Great Mogul himself, Dumas was named nabob of the Carnatic. He controlled a string of treaty ports, and native princes considered him an equal.

Though France was Europe's most aggressive colonial power, Spain remained its largest. The Spanish empire extended from the Philippines to Africa. Not only did it incorporate most of South and Central America, Mexico, and Florida, but it also penetrated deeply into the unexplored reaches of Texas, California, and Arizona. Cuba and Puerto Rico were the largest of Spain's Caribbean possessions.

Among the remaining European powers, only the Dutch and Portuguese still held overseas territories of significance. By adding coffee cultivation to spice production, the Dutch East India Company revived a slumping Indonesian economy. Holland retained footholds in Ceylon, South Africa, Curaçao in the Caribbean, and Guiana in South America. Portugal's future largely depended upon Brazilian gold, but the Portuguese also held Goa and Diu in western India, Macao on the South China Sea, and the African possessions of Mozambique and Angola as remnants of past glory.

Englishmen contrasted the political, economic, and social disunity of their twelve North American colonies with what appeared to be a well-integrated, militarily sound French administration in Canada. Moreover, the French built the New World's most powerful fortress, Louisbourg, on Cape Breton Island in the St. Lawrence, while their posts of Fort Niagara and Fort Pontchartrain on the Great Lakes guaranteed them command over the Ohio and Mississippi valleys. British strengths, however, were growing, too. There was no question of reducing the navy, which during the War of the Spanish Succession had more than doubled in size. The Bank of England advanced enormous sums to the government, invigorating investment in overseas commerce. From 1713 to 1740, London emerged as Europe's principal port of exchange for wheat, West Indian sugar, Indonesian spices, Indian textiles, and Virginia tobacco.

Despite the fiasco over the South Sea Company in 1720, the English continued to experiment with credit. They smuggled goods to Spanish colonials in the Caribbean and South America. This augmented the legal profits derived from the London-based South Sea Company's monopoly over African slave sales to the Creoles and the annual dropping of general cargo by a single British merchantman to the Spanish Americans. The Madrid government hated the latter concessions as reminders of the humiliations suffered in the Spanish succession war, and South Sea Company merchants smuggled into Latin American ports cargo besides the permitted blacks. The British government showed little inclination to investigate Spanish complaints of smuggling, its position being that if Spain was unable to supply its colonists, Madrid should not insist upon near-exclusive trade rights. So the Spaniards took matters into their own hands. Their coastal cutters stopped and searched merchant vessels, abusing British crews. Such a boarding party had provoked the incident of Captain Jenkins' ear.

All through the 1730s, British smuggler-planters in the Caribbean, South Sea Company traders, London merchants, and the Patriots of the House of Commons cried for retaliation against Spanish searches. Greed and appeals to national honor cost Walpole control of Parliament, and in 1739 Britain slipped into open war with Spain. The anticipated easy conquests never materialized, and Frederick II's unexpected invasion of Silesia late in 1740 embroiled Britain in both a continental and colonial struggle. British attacks on Spanish ports in the Caribbean proved futile. In India, the British trading counter of Madras fell to the French, while in North America an expedition of New England militiamen captured Louisbourg. Just as it appeared that Britain might prevail in North America, the peace congress opened at Aix-la-Chapelle. To the disgust of New Englanders, the British government restored Louisbourg to the French for Madras. In the treaty, neither French claims to the American hinterland nor the Spanish right to search at sea were mentioned.

For Britain and France the period 1748 to 1755 was no more than an interlude between colonial wars. In India it was not even that. While the Mogul empire fell to pieces, provoking civil wars on the subcontinent, the European commercial companies armed and fought alongside preferred clients. By 1751 the French East India Company controlled virtually the entire eastern coast of the subcontinent, from the Bengal station of Chandernagor to the Carnatic. Madras was isolated, and French influence penetrated deeply into the Deccan. Nevertheless, the British, too, were learning the techniques of alliance building and puppet forming. A former clerk in the East India Company office at Madras, Robert Clive, won a commission in a company regiment. He proved so successful fighting the French and their clients that the director of the French company, Joseph-François Dupleix, was recalled in disgrace. Dupleix's successor tried to work out a sphere-of-influence treaty with the British, but by the time the document was ready in December 1755, war between the French and English had erupted in America. The issue of European supremacy in India was left to force of arms.

The British colonists in North America felt betrayed in 1748 when Louisbourg was restored to France. With the St. Lawrence and Mississippi valleys still in French hands and the French laying claims to land along the Ohio River, the gates of settlement were closed to the colonials. The French built a military post at Fort Duquesne, just down the Ohio River from Lake Erie. Virginians and Marylanders considered it a dagger pointed at their hearts.

Individual English colonies challenged French claims to the Ohio Valley. In 1754 Virginia sent a force led by the young George Washington against Fort Duquesne itself, but it was beaten back. Jealous that Virginia's success might be achieved at their expense, other English colonists were not brokenhearted. Benjamin Franklin of Pennsylvania tried to overcome these mutual jealousies by proposing a pooled force of colonial militias, but his idea ran against the shoals of particularism, and the paralysis of the colonial assemblies abdicated the real decision making to London. At this juncture, the British government made its momentous decision for America.

When the duke of Newcastle said, "Let Americans fight Americans," he expressed the traditional viewpoint. While the colonists were supposed to defend themselves from local attack, the military responsibilities of Britain were limited to keeping sea lanes open. Above all, the homeland wanted to integrate America into an economic system described and defended by the Navigation Acts. Late in the 1740s, however, William Pitt had challenged this approach, calling it cowardly, shortsighted, and contrary to Britain's imperial destiny. Pitt considered this destiny and Britain's commercial interests to be inextricable. Both would profit immensely from a showdown colonial war with France. Shifting focus from Britain's traditional sphere of interest in the Caribbean, Pitt saw Canada as the key to the empire's future. The conquest of this unexplored wilderness would place North America's fish and fur trade in British hands; the French West Indies would lose their source of cheap lumber, and their sugar prices would mount accordingly; France would lose both a potential Canadian market for its manufactures and a source of material for building its ships. Finally, British North Americans might feel more secure.

Though Pitt himself was out of office in 1754, his Patriot supporters demanded that troops be sent across the Atlantic. When the news arrived of Washington's defeat at Fort Duquesne, even Newcastle came around to the position that America was in crisis. The mainland colonies were seen as the heart of Britain's entire colonial system, and their needs no longer could be shunted aside. Pitt took up his theme again: nearly two million British subjects considered themselves directly threatened. They deserved the crown's protection.

Early in 1755 General Edward Braddock led a small British expedition across the Atlantic; its assignment was to drive the French out of the Ohio Valley. Severe logistical problems and command disputes led to a humiliating defeat in which Braddock was killed. The French seized Fort Oswego on Lake Ontario, and New England felt engulfed by a French shadow. As war erupted in Europe in 1756, such fears proved unjustified. Tied down to a costly campaign in Germany, the French regime failed to summon resources and will for a colonial war. Defeated at the battle of Plassey in India (June 1757), France virtually abandoned the subcontinent and the great gains made there since 1713. Nor did it commit a royal army to North America. Returning to the ministry in 1757, Pitt urged a Canadian showdown. King, Parliament, and public opinion were behind him, and 35,000 troops were dispatched to America, the largest single trans-Atlantic military expedition that had ever been made. In 1758, Louisbourg and Fort Duquesne fell; the Ohio Valley was opened to English settlement. An abortive attempt to invade England in 1759 resulted in the destruction of the French Atlantic fleet, thus denying France's American possessions reinforcements and naval support. The French military commander in Canada, the marquis of Montcalm, tried to concentrate his outnumbered forces along the St. Lawrence River, and in late spring of 1759, the British made their major assault. A flotilla left Louisbourg and sailed up the St. Lawrence towards Quebec, capital of French Canada. For two months, the town was besieged. Because its citadel was located at the tip of a rocky peninsula whose cliffs jutted 300 feet into the St. Lawrence, the place was virtually impregnable. On September 12–13, however, the English commander, thirty-two-year-old James Wolfe, whom Pitt had selected over far more experienced officers, led a daring climb over the cliffs west of Quebec and attacked Montcalm's surprised forces just beyond the city walls. The Battle of the Plains of Abraham cost the lives of both Montcalm and Wolfe, but decided the fate of Canada. Quebec fell to the British; Montreal surrendered a year later. New Englanders might breathe more easily and the path to the West was secured.

By 1762, Britain's overwhelming sea power led to the fall of Martinique, Havana, and Manila. When the peace conference at Paris opened in 1763, the British held all the trumps. Earlier, Pitt had wished to crush the French and dictate terms, but in 1761 he resigned from office. A negotiated settlement surrendered Canada, Cape Breton Island, and France's smaller Caribbean possessions to the British. In Africa, France ceded the Atlantic slave station of Senegal. The British East India Company gained control over the Deccan and Carnatic. France's ally Spain yielded Florida to Britain, and the French compensated the Spaniards with the grant of Louisiana. Britain restored the sugar isles of Martinique and Guadeloupe to France and allowed French Canadian fishermen catch privileges in the Gulf of St. Lawrence. Five unfortified trading stations in India remained in French hands, and Spain was given back both Cuba and the Philippines.

The Peace of Paris was one of the great political settlements of the eighteenth century. Britain acquired an American empire stretching from the Atlantic seaboard to the Mississippi and from Hudson's Bay to the Florida keys. The British East India Company was Europe's major colonial force in Asia. Though Pitt's dream of empire had become reality, vast new problems were arising. Following the war, England's expenses continued to outdistance its income. A sense of national humiliation fed French pride, dictating plans for revenge. Moreover, with the French barricade to expansion gone, British North Americans gained a confidence and self-determination that was expressed in a chorus of criticism against the homeland's conception of empire.

Only thirteen years separated the Peace of Paris from the Declaration of Independence, but these were years of rapidly escalating bitterness and mutual recrimination. Pitt himself romanticized about the Americans and their bearing of British civilization into the wilderness. He had fought the French so that the Americans might feel secure; he wished the colonists well in their determination to make money, but he had no intention of going further. Just after the signing of the Peace of Paris, a contributor to the *London Chronicle* summed up the attitude of official Britain: "The colonies were acquired with no other view than to be a convenience to us, and therefore it can never be imagined that we are to consult their interest preferably to our own." This meant that America was to receive Britain's unemployables and supply the homeland with primary articles like tar, sugar, and tobacco. Americans were to purchase Britain's manufactures, especially its woollens. Parliament might impose indirect taxes upon the colonials. The ships that traversed the Atlantic were to be British built, manned, and owned, and future parliamentary legislation was to protect

Britain's interests. To the British government, the fruits of 1763 insured the integration of North America into a worldwide colonial system. Many Americans resisted this, abstracting into terms of freedom and tyranny what the British considered to be questions of profit. Furthermore, as Professor Palmer has noted, in all the colonies, but especially in New England, there was "no particular sympathy for the forces that had triumphed in English life since 1660, notably the aristocratic and Anglican governing class; nor did what they know of the realities of parliamentary politics inspire them with much confidence."[1]

At the same moment that the British Parliament insisted upon America as just another piece in the empire, the Americans realized that they did not wish to be governed by the British Parliament at all. Passions rose. A problem quickly degenerated into a quarrel, and the quarrel yielded a revolution.

---

[1] R. R. Palmer, *The Age of the Democratic Revolution*, vol. 1, *The Challenge* (Princeton, 1959), p. 159.

Chapter Ten

The Decline and Fall
of the Ancien Régime

ENLIGHTENED DESPOTISM

Disillusioned with what they considered to be the excesses of the French Revolution of 1789 to 1794, several nineteenth-century historians devoted scholarly careers to addressing the question: Did the ancien régime possess sufficient vigor and will to adapt to the needs of a peasantry seeking an end to personal servitude and the acquisition of genuine property rights, of a bourgeoisie anxious to expand individual commercial and industrial capacity while acquiring some political responsibility in the state, and of an aristocracy resenting the contraction of its power and privilege yet aware that certain compromises were necessary for its survival? The scholars concluded that, given a chance, late eighteenth-century monarchy might have reformed society without recourse to revolutionary bloodshed. They noted that most regimes of the time had a sense of moral purpose and public conscience that distinguished them from the despotic courts of their predecessors. The scholars coined a term for most late eighteenth-century monarchies. They called them enlightened despotisms.

Without doubt, the rulers from 1763 to 1789 included several remarkably intelligent women and men, supported by vigorous advisers and consultants. Reared in the Enlightenment's community of culture, rejecting pompous courts for intimate salons spiced with intellectuals, and taking a lively interest in literature, music, and the arts, the enlightened despots broke with a traditional aristocratic lifestyle that held intelligence in contempt. They applied reason to statecraft, and several equated the use of reason with programs for humanitarian reform. Believing that it is easier to persuade a prince than convince a nation the *philosophes* themselves struck up personal and epistolary acquaintances with sovereigns and urged rulers to consider the state a public trust, implement religious toleration, expand the educational system, improve and humanize legal procedure, centralize the administration, raise the peasantry to dignity, and better the economic situation of the country. Such a program, of course, was not particularly new, and it is tempting to disregard the *entente* between rulers and *philosophes* as a meaningless exchange of flatteries. Still, the Enlightenment gave rulers a vocabulary. They proclaimed themselves "citizens," "virtuous," and "sensible" to human needs and public welfare.

Nevertheless, at the same time rulers desanctified their own persons, encouraged individual economic initiative, and supported the equality of subjects before the law, they molded an institution that proved far more repressive to human liberties than any other previous agency of government had under the corporate-bound ancien régime. This of course is the modern bureaucratic state. The state was to assume political, social, and religious responsibilities formerly held by priest, village, town, landlord, province, guild, or corporation. The state would assure the health, wealth, wisdom, and security of its citizens. State intentions would be expressed lawfully to be sure. Experts and specialists, not an arbitrary tyrant, would draw up the regulations. The end would be the public good. As far as was socially safe, privilege would be attacked.

The spirit underlying enlightened despotism was paternalistic. To reforming sovereigns, the old corporations had never known what was good for the society at large. The individual needed direction and control. Therefore, enlightened despots gave more of a sense of urgency to the principle of sound administration than to civil liberties. As one of Joseph II's experts, von Justi, put it: "A properly constituted state must be exactly analogous to a machine, in which all the wheels and gears are precisely adjusted to one another; and the ruler must be the foreman, the mainspring, or the soul—if one may use the expression—which sets everything else in motion."

Enlightened despotism arose in the underdeveloped, agrarian regions of Europe, where landlord aristocracies had long been the fiscal, judicial, and legal intermediaries between the people and the state. Because of this, political reality limited the sphere of action from above. Though Frederick II believed that all private property in Prussia was held in trust to the state, he made no attempt to expropriate Junker lands or eliminate Junker privilege. On the contrary, Junkers headed Frederick's bureaus and departments, collected his country taxes, and led his armies. Frederick believed that in the reconstruction of Prussia after 1763, the aristocracy had to be welded tightly to the absolute structure. In reward for their diligence and loyalty, the Junkers ruled the peasantry and were trained in modern universities and military academies. For Prussia, enlightened despotism meant the well-ordered state, and the king was its first servant. The aristocracy was just beneath him.

The peasantry also served. Like his great-grandfather, Frederick welcomed rural immigration. After 1763, with state loans and gifts, tens of thousands of homesteads were staked, the potato and sugar beet cultivated, and both moors and swamps reclaimed. Frederick promised to keep new settlers from slipping into serfdom. In 1773, when he acquired the Polish province of West Prussia, a new wave of immigrants poured in. By the king's death in 1786, every fifth Prussian belonged to a family of colonists.

Still, this great invitation to settlement and pioneering failed to reform the social bases of rural life. The old alliance between the soil and military was too strong. On the land and in the army, serf remained beholden to Junker. Except in East Prussia and Silesia, the land tax fell exclusively on peasants. They gave three to four days of their workweek to landowners and built Prussia's roads. On private estates, Junkers were the law, and Frederick offered the peasants little more than promises that their tiny plots would not be added to the lord's domain. On crown lands Frederick assured serfs hereditary tenure rights, and their obligations at least were put into writing. Instinctively perhaps, Frederick might have liked to ease the peasant's lot. Reason told him, however, that this would have compromised the rights of the aristocracy, and in his view Prussia owed its survival to Junker landlords and Junker officers.

Burghers served as lower-rank bureaucratic personnel as well as tax payers. Though Frederick discouraged acquisitions of land and after 1763 dismissed faithful officers from the army because they were nonnoble, the king did appreciate skilled artisans and craftsmen. He kept them out of the army, but even in giving birth to Prussian industry, the king showed an aristocratic bias. Silesia, which had cost him so much, possessed a rich tradition of textile manufacturing. The province was the heartland of Prussia's wealth, and Frederick promised subsidies and manpower to Junkers if they would develop linen and woollens production there. But while granting capital, credit, and buildings, the state was careful to limit and control productivity. Mills, sawmills, distilleries, and brick factories were established on rural estates, but little individual initiative was encouraged in urban centers. Frederick was obsessed with certain luxury manufactures like silks and procelain. His inspiration was Colbertine France, not Hanoverian England. Heroic efforts at canal building, making the Oder River navigable, exploiting Upper Silesia's mineral deposits, and opening a state bank bore fruit. While a tariff wall surrounded Prussia, a new merchant fleet carried estate-produced grain to the west.

Frederick tried to use bureaucratic administration to perfect the authoritarian structures of his dynastic inheritance. The king dispatched orders through the General Directory, but in his haste to get things done he superimposed new functional departments of commerce (1741), war supplies (1746), excises and tolls (1766), mines (1768), and forests (1770) upon the regional competencies of the General Directory. To a greater degree than his father, Frederick worked alone. During the annual mid-June review of ministers, the king met with his department chiefs. Budgets were approvd and affairs discussed. As the ministers returned to their Berlin offices, Frederick withdrew to his own study at Potsdam. Until the following June, all transactions were communicated in writing.

Members of the General Directory and department chiefs sent the king reports and requests; Frederick sent out royal commands. Order and regularity defined procedure, and delays were not tolerated. Since Frederick was an impatient man and a very quick thinker, the system functioned efficiently. At Potsdam, Frederick's life was the model of controlled discipline. He lived there alone, with neither court nor etiquette, never observing a religious holiday. In the provinces, the "ink-splashers" were inured to the system. When no commands emerged from *Sans Souci* on August 17, 1786, and the couriers arrived in the provinces a few days later with empty bags, the officials knew the reason. The king was dead.

Ruler for nearly a half-century, Frederick imprinted his style upon Prussia. He fulfilled his father's program of instilling the values of duty, self-sacrifice, and obedience in his people. The army and bureaucracy remained the twin pillars of the state. In his old age, however, Frederick lost touch with French *philosophes* and cared little about his enlightened reputation. Cynicism engulfed the aged ruler, and he mistrusted everyone. He considered the army to have gone soft and worried whether Prussian institutions would long survive him. Later events justified his concern. Without Frederick's taskmaster spirit, the Prussian state of the next generation collapsed beneath French revolutionary and Napoleonic armies. What survived, curiously enough, were the legal code and the educational system, the two elements that parenthetically gave a humane tone to Prussian life.

Frederick intended these reforms to strengthen the autocratic state, and it was coincidental if such reform might at the same time benefit the majority of his subjects. From his father, he inherited an able minister of justice, Samuel von Cocceji, who had long recognized that justice in the Hohenzollern domains was a hodgepodge of local habit and custom, with cases piling up for years and procedure synonymous with graft, ceremony, and delay. From 1746 to 1755, Frederick and von Cocceji created an interlocking court system at local, provincial, and central levels. Judges became salaried officials and fee taking was prohibited. University education for judges became compulsory, and incompetents were dismissed. Thus, the judiciary ceased being a corporate guild.

Though he scolded and dismissed judges, Frederick wanted the law to be independent of the sovereign. Therefore, he did not intervene personally in court cases. The fact that Prussia had no unified body of law embarrassed the king, and he had a group of legal experts work on defining both criminal and civil law. In this way, Frederick believed absolutism might be given constitutional sanction. For example, for the past century, Prussian rulers had been collecting taxes without popular consent, and Frederick desired to see this practice confirmed by the laws. The laws also must define social rank and obligation. The aristocracy was to be enshrined as Prussia's First Estate, its landholdings protected by law and its members controlling the kingdom's chief civil and military posts. Burghers and peasants were to retain subordinate status. Such deference to absolutism and hierarchized social structure might seem a betrayal of the Enlightenment, but the Prussian law code, finally promulgated in 1794, at least humanized criminal procedures and recognized the individual's freedom of religious choice. Torture was abolished, penalties were intended to discourage future crimes rather than punish past ones, and the code affirmed Frederick's indifference to one's religious preference.

Frederick had a lively personal interest in educational reform, believing that proper education was imperative in training subjects for their calling. Disabled and retired soldiers were appointed as village schoolmasters, teachers' colleges were founded, and the state introduced a uniform inspection system for elementary schools. Frederick welcomed Jesuit refugees as teachers if they agreed not to proselytize for Catholicism. Prussia's universities received generous state grants for bright students, as well as funds for construction, books, laboratories, and professors' salaries. Nevertheless, political censorship limited the areas of genuine free inquiry, and the essential purpose of education in Prussia, as with so much else, was to provide human parts for the proper operations of a static, paternalistically directed civilization. Innovation remained suspect; duty was enshrined as a national virtue.

The *philosophes* gave Frederick a better press than he deserved, but Catherine II of Russia was their darling. The empress knew how to cater to intellectuals and invited several to her court at St. Petersburg. Born princess Sophie in the tiny German principality of Anhalt-Zerbst, at sixteen married to Peter the Great's grandson, she shed her name and Lutheran religion on arriving at Russian court in 1744. It was a court rife with brutality and intrigue. Since 1725, favorites and guards regiments had made or toppled five rulers. One of them, Ivan VI, was rotting in prison; three of the others were dead. Like Catherine, her adolescent groom, Peter, was raised in a German Protestant environment. He was duke of Holstein. Empress Elizabeth, his aunt, declared him her heir, and the court of the young couple became a den of political faction. Sharing a dislike for Russia's traditional friendship toward Austria, Catherine and Peter preferred an alliance with Prussia. Catherine admired Frederick II, and Peter worshipped him. However, Czarina Elizabeth loathed the Prussian king and the young court made little headway in efforts to influence Russia's political or diplomatic development.

Sympathy toward Frederick was the only element shared by Peter and Catherine. The crown prince hated Russia, despised its language, and mocked its religion. Stupid, half-mad, and perverted, he passed his days playing with toy soldiers and his nights in sexual encounters with masked servants and chambermaids. He abused Catherine, who found solace in the arms of lovers at court. She learned Russian, ostentatiously performed the Orthodox rites, and eventually decided to play on Elizabeth's heartstrings. In December 1761, Elizabeth died, and the throne passed calmly to Peter. On becoming czar, Peter withdrew from the Seven Years' War and, needing allies at court, exempted the Russian nobility from state service. This move had been building up over the years. In 1736, Czarina Anna had reduced the serving period to twenty-five years, and Elizabeth had contemplated rewarding war veterans with blanket exemptions. However, because he laid claim to Church income, brought Holsteiners to court, and publicly humiliated Catherine, Peter failed to win the Russian nobility. Late in June 1762, a guards regiment controlled by Gregory Orlov, Catherine's lover, led her to the Cathedral of Our Lady of Kazan, where she was proclaimed sole ruler. A week later, Peter died under mysterious circumstances, and in 1764 the imprisoned former czar, Ivan VI, was murdered.

Indebted to the soldiers who had placed her on the throne, Catherine II wished to build a firm base of support. For three years, she bided her time but in 1767 perceived an opportunity. What stood for a legal code in Russia was the document of 1649. Since that time, a chaotic mass of contradictory legislation had accumulated. Catherine saw the need for consolidating it, but with a novel twist. She herself would write the preamble to the new law code and then request both experts and representatives drawn from various segments of Russian society to draft, discuss, and ratify the document.

The czarina set to work on her preamble, called the "Instruction," the likes of which Russians had never before seen. Half the paragraphs were lifted from Montesquieu's *Spirit of the Laws* and Beccaria's *On Crimes and Punishments*. The "Instruction" blended reason, humanitarianism, and pragmatism. Because of Russia's size, the needs of impartial justice dictated absolute government. Citizens were to be equal before the law, torture and inhumane punishments eliminated, religious minorities tolerated. Catherine admitted that serfdom contradicted the spirit of liberty. Yet serfdom was so closely tied to the fortunes of state and society that the public good discouraged wholesale enfranchisement. The czarina wrote that the object of absolute government was not to "deprive individuals of their natural freedom, but to direct their efforts towards the highest degree of human happiness. . . . It is not possible that this will please flatterers who repeat daily to the sovereigns of the world that peoples are created for the sovereigns' sakes. On the contrary, we believe that we exist for our peoples, and are proud to say so."

The majority of the delegates who came to Moscow were elected by their peers. The Legislative Commission comprised 560 delegates, half of whom were townsmen (200) and peasants on crown lands (80). The landowning aristocracy was represented by 160 delegates and the government by 28 "experts." No privately owned serfs came and only one churchman. The commission sat for a year and a half but accomplished very little. A law code based upon principles of the west European Enlightenment was beyond its reach, and delegates droned on about personal or group concerns. In the minority, landowners nevertheless learned that theirs was not the sole interest group in Russia. Even without the voices of serf and priest, the commission unveiled a complex society steeped in tradition and inertia. It taught Catherine a great deal about her adopted country, and by having the deputies solemnly recognize her enthroned presence, she confirmed the coup d'état of 1762.

Once she dismissed the commission, Catherine decided that her authority, absolute in theory, needed to be confirmed by the privileged members of Russian society. Increasingly, she used the country nobles as the base of her power and in 1785 rewarded them with legal exemption from compulsory service, direct taxation, corporal punishment, and the billeting of troops on their estates. They could dispose freely of their lands, build estate industries, sell their products without government interference, and own property in towns. As in the west, nobility was hereditary and confirmed as a corporate body, and in each province, nobles were the state's key administrative personnel. Perhaps, as some have claimed, Catherine was merely replacing Peter the Great's iron fetters with silken cords. Nevertheless, by codifying aristocratic privilege in the Charter of 1785, Catherine assured herself of loyal administrators. Country nobles hereafter identified maintenance of their corporate liberties with maintenance of the empire.

Catherine accompanied the codification of noble status with an administrative restructuring of Russia into fifty provinces, each subdivided into districts. The extension of state control was provoked by Pugachev's rebellion, which inflamed Russia's eastern provinces in 1773. The rebellion was even more serious and widespread than Stenka Razin's had been in the seventeenth century. It began among the Cossacks of the Urals when Catherine revised the autonomous status of the free horsemen. The Cossack leadership submitted, but the rank and file refused. Instead, they began fighting government troops. Emilian Pugachev, an army deserter, organized the Cossacks by proclaiming that he was Peter III, not at all dead but back to regain his throne. He then urged serfs to destroy their landlords, promised non-Russian tribes an end to harassment, and told Old Believers that he would tolerate their faith.

By 1774, Pugachev had managed to appeal to every discontented element in Russian society, and he was welding together a revolutionary program. He maintained an imperial court, said he would abolish serfdom, end taxation and military conscription, and liquidate the gentry aristocracy. First, his motley forces moved northwest, toward the Volga, and Moscow primed for an attack. Estates were seized, manors burned, and owners lynched. The regular army had to be recalled from the front. Pugachev then retreated southward, toward his home country in the Don Valley. As desertions grew, he was betrayed and handed over to Catherine's generals. Transported to Moscow in an iron cage, he was displayed publicly, then hanged, quartered, and burned. His rebellion was the last major, organized rural uprising under the old Russian monarchy. Nevertheless, until the emancipation of the serfs in 1861, dozens of lesser revolts plagued governments, and for a century to come, the "peasant problem" was the overriding social issue in Russia.

Catherine herself deepened the problem. The Legislative Commission of 1767 had raised false hopes. Though its convocation endeared Catherine to west European intellectuals, under her reign, lords could imprison serfs at will, and serfs lost even the right to appeal mistreatment to the public authorities. The czarina extended serfdom into the newly cultivated Ukraine, and she awarded favorites and lovers great tracts of state-owned land with peasants. Nearly a million people were thus thrust into privately owned serfdom, where they could be torn from the land and sold as slaves. After Pugachev's revolt, Catherine suppressed whatever humanitarian instincts she might once have had and became a hardened reactionary. She persecuted the most celebrated spokesman for the Enlightenment in Russia, Nikolai Novikov, and she sent to Siberia the author Alexander Radischev, whose volume *A Journey from St. Petersburg to Moscow* (1790) reflected upon the injustices of serfdom and rapacity of local officials. She blamed the French Revolution upon Freemasonry, the *philosophes*, and royal weakness; she ordered Russian students abroad to return home, banned French newspapers and magazines, and increased the secret police. All her life, Catherine enjoyed the bric-a-brac of Enlightenment culture—the Sèvres china, English gardens, and imported French clothes—but the last years of her reign were etched in repression and fear.

Shrewd, opportunistic, and highly intelligent, Catherine was a consummate actress. By way of contrast, the Hapsburg empress, Maria Theresa, her contemporary until 1780, was authenticity incarnate. Reading no *philosophes* and abhorring most of them, the pious empress believed quite simply that the state had a moral obligation to protect its peasantry, and to accomplish this goal, it must tighten the reins of governmental authority upon regional landholding aristocracies. Maria Theresa's professional advisers could justify reform with appeals to natural law, economic doctrine, or natural sovereignty. For Maria Theresa, Christian humanitarianism was sufficient.

Maria Theresa's regime chipped away at the foundation of serfdom. If the state could not abolish peasant dues and services owed to aristocrats, at least it could regulate and reduce them. Fiscal reforms complemented social reforms. For the first time, the government at Vienna became aware of its resources and expenditures. In Church matters, the influence of the Jesuits was reduced and eventually abolished, forms of ostentatious piety discouraged, and underdeveloped monastic estates expropriated. With the establishment of a state ministry of education, Jesuit professors were expelled from colleges and universities, and the old classical curriculum was replaced by courses in political science, applied mathematics, and modern languages. The state removed from the Church the right to censor books and released for publication the literary monuments of the century. Maria Theresa's high officials, appropriately called "the Great Ones," were far more secular-minded than the empress herself and took charge of the expulsion of the Jesuits. Their seized properties formed the source of the state's education fund.

Maria Theresa died in 1780, never doubting the moral vision of her secular and religious policies. The eldest of her sixteen children, Joseph, succeeded her. Not quite forty, Joseph was experienced in the responsibilities of government. On his father's death in 1765, he had been elected Holy Roman Emperor. His mother named him coregent over her Hapsburg lands, and he commanded the Hapsburg army. A restless, unhappy prince, Joseph had urged his mother to attempt more extensive reforms than she dared. He hated the Magyar gentry, whose tax exemptions and control over the Hungarian countryside were extensive. He told Maria Theresa that peasants throughout the empire still possessed insecurity of tenure. For more than a decade, his impatience produced hostile scenes at court. At last in 1780, Joseph had his chance. With due respect, he buried his mother and set to work.

Joseph II was the most sincere and least understood of the so-called enlightened despots. Because he lacked Catherine's charm and Frederick's intelligence, the *philosophes* never were comfortable with him. Because he lacked his mother's pious warmth, his subjects feared him. Joseph's younger brother, Leopold of Tuscany, himself a progressive reformer, created the unflattering historical image of Joseph: an arrogant bad-tempered sovereign who "tolerates no contradiction and is imbued with arbitrary, brutal principles." More accurately perhaps, the Belgian aristocrat and man of letters, the prince de Ligne, thought that Joseph "desired the greatest authority so that others would be deprived of the right to do harm." Working incessantly, bitterly unhappy in his personal life, Joseph believed that the state might impress a humanitarian example uniformly on its subjects. His concern for human dignity was sincere, expressed symbolically when he commanded abolition of the practice of kneeling before one's social superiors or expressed ringingly through his decrees declaring religious toleration and an end to serfdom. (See pp. 156–57, 164, 191–92.) Too frequently, however, the need to make his authority known turned Joseph into a spiteful man. His insistence upon German as administrative language for the heterogeneous empire irritated Italians and Croats, the transfer of the Hungarian crown to Vienna angered Magyars, and the conversion of the unused imperial palace at Prague into an armory insulted Bohemians. The emperor lacked the gentle touch, and this proved his undoing.

Joseph's nine-year reign concluded with revolt in Belgium and unrest in Hungary. The Belgian uprising was led by a clergy resentful of Joseph's interference with Catholic liturgy and religious practice, such as "de-

Latinizing" the Mass, banning pilgrimages, and suppressing the monastic orders given to the contemplative life. Moreover, the Josephian state assumed responsibility for relief of the poor and hospital care and declared marriage a civil contract. Imperial decrees ordered Church hierarchies to take orders from the state, not the pope, and priests were told to sermonize on good citizenship rather than salvation of souls. The government started paying priests' salaries, assumed control over seminaries, and removed Catholic teaching from several universities. Far from Vienna and responsible to an intensely pious population, the Belgian clergy resisted the Josephian decrees. Privileged corporate groups in Belgium, such as provincial estates, guilds, and burgher fraternities, followed the bishops, and a popular insurrection in 1789 expelled the Austrians.

In Hungary the causes for unrest were political rather than religious. In the absence of a national diet which had not met since 1765, effective government in Hungary fell to local assemblies of country gentry. The emperor correctly accused these assemblies of representing only vested interests, of repressing the peasantry, and of having no concern for the general well-being of the empire. In 1785, Joseph started overhauling Hungarian institutions. He divided the country into ten new administrative districts, with attention paid neither to geography nor to historical tradition. German-speaking commissioners were sent into Hungary and bypassed the assemblies in preparing a proportional land tax project intended to sweep away the aristocracy's fiscal privilege and domination of the peasantry. At this point, the Magyar gentry considered their nation in danger, began arming, and asked Prussia for help. By 1788, matters were extremely grave. Bogged down in a new Turkish war, Joseph could scarcely cope with an insurrection. He might have appealed directly to the Hungarian peasantry, but he feared igniting the popular will. His goal was revolution from above. He therefore made a strategic retreat. Critically ill, he agreed to summon the national diet. In January 1790, he suspended most of his administrative reforms; by the end of the month, he was dead.

Clerical and aristocratic reaction defeated Joseph in Belgium and Hungary, but even in his German domains a shortage of crusading bureaucrats rendered it impossible to enforce the imperial decrees. The Hapsburg universities produced several brilliant, dedicated officials imbued with Josephian ideals, but these men were needed in Vienna's central bureaus. In the countryside, local landed aristocrats recruited from dormant regional Estates would not enforce orders abolishing serfdom, denying their own tax privileges, and inviting the settlement of religious and ethnic minorities. Lesser officials were as poorly paid as their Prussian counterparts and lacked Prussian devotion to either state, sovereign, or public welfare. Just before his death, Joseph lamented: "There is an absolute lack of men to conceive and will. Almost no one is animated by zeal for the good of the fatherland; there is no one to carry out my ideas."

Leopold II, Joseph's younger brother, reaped the bitter harvest. Grand duke of Tuscany since 1765, Leopold had himself earned a reputation as a progressive sovereign. He had attacked the corporate power of the guilds, clergy, and towns in Tuscany, eliminated tax farming, established an equitable fiscal system, and abolished internal tariffs. Leopold even proposed a consultative assembly for Tuscany elected by all taxpayers, but this gesture, the closest flirtation with constitutionalism attempted by a European autocrat prior to 1789, was discouraged by the grand duke's advisers. On becoming ruler of the entire Hapsburg empire in 1790, however, Leopold had to put aside many of his progressive ideas. Joseph's revolution from above had failed, and in France, the National Assembly was extorting a constitutional regime from Louis XVI. Leopold decided to bargain with the Diets and Estates in the traditional Hapsburg manner. Censorship and education were to remain state activities, most of the toleration decrees stood, and new owners kept most of the expropriated monasteries. However, the laws abolishing aristocratic privilege and peasant servitude, which lay at the heart of Joseph's program, were repealed. The Hapsburg peasantry had to wait until 1848 for the end to seigneurial dues and services, and the domination of provincial government and society by the aristocracy survived as long as the empire itself.

Leopold's relative success in Tuscany suggests that small states lacking the cumulative inertia and resistance of powerful aristocracies might respond better than large states to autocratic reform. With modest aims, extending from introduction to crop rotation methods to the granting of religious toleration, several princes in the Holy Roman Empire succeeded as enlightened despots. Only rarely did the princes tamper with the social order, and none sought to modify the aristocratic-absolutist political balance by experimenting with citizen participation in government.

In Scandinavia, however, eighteenth-century governments were more ambitious, and their encroachments upon noble privilege unwittingly laid the social foundation for the bourgeois regimes of the nineteenth century. In 1770 Danish absolutism had settled down to a cozy alliance between a royal administration of great landlords and an aristocracy of lesser property holders enjoying social and fiscal privileges. The Danish peasantry was enserfed. Then, a young Prussian physician, Johan Struensee, who had recently saved the king's life and become the queen's lover, skyrocketed to power. Despising aristocratic royal councillors, Struensee had them dismissed. For eighteen months, he became virtual dictator, mingling tightfisted political authority with an enlightened social program. Elegant, refined, and iron-willed, Struensee reduced the peasants' service obligations to their landlords and abolished commercial monopolies. In 1772, however, his enemies caught up with him. Convicted of high treason and illicit relations with the queen, who herself was exiled, Struensee was executed.

For a decade, the old order was restored. In 1784, however, another royal adviser, Count Andreas Bernstorff, progressive and more patient than Struensee, took up the reform program. By 1793, grain and cattle circulated freely throughout the kingdom, mercantile privileges and serfdom were abolished, and an effort was made to institute a proportional tax upon incomes. Absolutism and reform worked hand in glove until 1848, when the revolutionary movement of that year instituted constitutional government for the kingdom.

For a half-century after the death of Charles XII, a loose affiliation of influential landowners, military officers, and government administrators controlled Sweden. The two kings of the period, foreign-born nonentities, were elected by the four-chambered Diet, and the political life of the nation, like that of England, revolved around elections to the Diet. The characteristics of parliamentary government formed in coffeehouse rallies, political campaigning, party programs, and purchased votes. Foreign governments bribed Diet members, who called such awards healthy for the nation's economy. After 1763, however, the upper aristocracy, customarily identified with the Hat political party, tried to extend control over great military offices, seaborne commerce, and the Council of State. The gentry and clergy, belonging to the Cap party, resisted. The election of 1765 brought the Caps into power. They virtually abolished censorship, liberalized trade, and reduced military expenses. Unable to consolidate their political victory, the Caps encountered the resistance of the great aristocrats. Political and social conflict, complicated by Russian, Prussian, and Danish intervention in Swedish affairs, threatened to destroy the constitution. There was talk of partition. In the midst of the crisis, in 1771, King Adolphus Frederick died and was succeeded by his son, crown prince Gustav.

Gustav III was highly intelligent, inspired by the *philosophes*, and eager to end party wrangling with a royal power play. Hats and Caps could agree upon nothing. The Diet was paralyzed. In August 1772, the young king mounted his horse and, followed by a contingent of royal troops, rode into the streets of Stockholm exhorting the citizenry to help him deliver the country from calamity. The appeal worked. On royal order, the Diet threw out the constitution of 1720, and Gustav was given absolute powers. For the next fifteen years, he modified Swedish institutions, awarding a wide range of civil liberties to the populace, reducing the Council of State to an advisory capacity, and winning a share of taxation and legislative powers. Rather than destroy the old aristocracy, Gustav made it an embellishment to his court.

As long as the king enjoyed the backing of the burghers, freehold peasantry, and lesser aristocracy, his revolution was safe. Gustav had ambitious foreign policy, built upon memories of Swedish greatness and far too costly for current resources. Going to war against Russia with neither Diet support nor an adequate military budget, he faced an army mutiny and was fortunate to come away with an empty-handed peace in 1790. Meanwhile, the war emergency permitted Gustav to effect another coup d'état in 1789 against the Swedish aristocracy. Clearing the Diet of the noble Estate, Gustav offered religious toleration and civil equality to all subjects, permitted nearly anyone to acquire landed property, and centralized royal power. Aghast, the disestablished aristocracy opted for an extreme remedy against the royal revolutionary, and in 1792, a noble assassinated Gustav. The plot had little consequence, however. Gustav's successor kept the constitution of 1789. Burgher, clerical, and peasant Estates resisted an aristocratic reaction. The nobility remained a dangerous nuisance, though no longer a dominant power, in Swedish political life.

A Mediterranean version of enlightened despotism existed in south Italy, Spain, and Portugal, where the powerful Church and landed nobility enjoyed large rural properties and tax privileges. Though peasants were not legally enserfed, most either were landless sharecroppers or indebted tenants. Flights from rural poverty customarily brought them brief, miserable lives in the teeming slums of Mediterranean cities. King Charles IV of Naples-Sicily (1735–59) had attacked ecclesiastical privilege and made the clergy pay taxes on property. When he left Italy to become king of Spain in 1759, Charles left a reforming first minister in Naples, Bernardo Tanucci. For the next seventeen years, Tanucci waged an unrelenting political and economic struggle against the landlord oligarchs, finally freeing the peasantry from the arbitrary jurisdiction of seigneurial courts, though the economic domination of the great estate owners remained intact.

As king of Naples-Sicily, Charles IV understood the difficulties in bearing reform to an ignorant, economically retrograde region where the Church was too wealthy, the aristocracy too lazy, and the people underemployed and poverty-stricken. On becoming Carlos III of Spain, he faced familiar circumstances. Under the new Bourbon dynasty, early eighteenth-century Spain had revived as a Mediterranean power. The loss of lands in Flanders and Italy reduced state expenses, and highly productive Catalonia experienced a resurgence of textile manufacture. Strong-willed Bourbon ministers gained tight control over Catalonia, and a bureaucracy of commissioners built on the French model began to insinuate itself upon officeholders, local authorities, and cumbersome government councils.

With twenty years of experience behind him, Carlos III knew that he could not turn Spain upside down. Rather, he would modify institutions, gradually chip away at the Church, assume command over the Inquisition, reduce clerical privilege, and suppress the Jesuits, all of which he and his great ministers, Campomanes, Floridablanca, and Aranda, accomplished. The officer-dominated councils were reduced to routine chores, and government was speeded up. The source of Spain's problems, however, lay deeper than an overly ripe Church or a cumbersome administration. Land was scarce and expensive. Much of it was owned by the aristocracy and remained unexploited. Rents rose higher than prices. Short-term leases victimized tenured peasants, and the landless ones were even worse off. A dramatic population increase was creating a massive proletariat. How were these people to live? How were they to be fed?

Following severe riots in 1765–66 caused by food shortages and skyrocketing prices, Carlos developed an agrarian program of extending cultivation. Unused rural lands owned by towns were ordered enclosed and sold. The crown supervised reclamation projects in half-abandoned Castile, and proprietors whose estates were undeveloped because they lay in the path of the Mesta's sheepruns were granted enclosure rights. None of this greatly changed the social pattern of Spanish agriculture, for the beneficiaries were improving landlords, not small tenants. Moreover, the regime was fearful about tampering with seigneurial dues and existing property rights. Yet more land was put to use, and a reduction of the state's tax on business transactions liberated commerce. Ports besides Seville and Cadiz were permitted to trade with Spanish America. In the colonies, the introduction of *intendants* reduced corruption. After a century of humiliation at the hand of foreign competitors, Spain was supplying its people with home-produced goods—Catalonian cottons, Valencian silks, and Basque ironware. Industrial wages lagged behind prices, and manufacturers dictated labor terms. A bourgeois elite was forming that challenged the socioeconomic domination of Church and aristocracy. Such was the fruit of national recovery that Carlos III bequeathed to his heir in 1788.

Basking in the unearned wealth of Brazil, from 1759 to 1777 Portugal suddenly witnessed a frenzy of antiaristocratic, anticlerical terror masked as enlightened despotism. The Portuguese clergy owned two-thirds of the land and controlled the universities. Nearly half the adult population toiled on Church estates. The papacy was influential, the Jesuits powerful, and the Inquisition effective. Theoretically, Portugal was an absolute monarchy whose national Diet had not met since 1697. An aggressive king or first minister might still accomplish a good deal. The marquis of Pombal, skillful former director of Portugal's foreign affairs and supervisor of the reclamation work in Lisbon after the earthquake and tidal wave of 1755, obtained vast powers under King Jose I.

Under Pombal's guidance, Portugal became the first Catholic state to seize the property of the Jesuits and expel the order. Pombal then carried his program of terror to the great aristocracy, blaming several nobles for an assassination attempt upon the king and having them executed. Church and nobility fell into line. Pombal attempted economic reforms, awarding state monopolies and grants to those who would start woollens, linen, paper, and glass manufacture. The educational system was secularized. Though he burned the works of Hobbes, Locke, Voltaire, and Rousseau, Pombal possessed certain humanitarian ideals of the Enlightenment. He abolished the legal distinction between the "Old" and the "New" Christians, the latter descended from Moslems and Jews, and he freed children of slaves in

Portugal. Nevertheless, he left a heritage of fear. On the death of his k.
and protector, he resigned from office. When a general amnesty was d.
clared for Pombal's victims, hundreds poured out of obscure prisons.
Accused of despotism, he won a royal pardon and died in 1782 at the age
of eighty-three. Though shaken, the aristocratic-clerical alliance was restored.

Reviewing enlightened despotism, historians can describe the varieties of
the movement, but they have difficulty identifying its significance. Some
scholars hold that because it desanctified divine right rule by acknowledging
natural law as the basis of monarchy and stressed the sovereign's duties
rather than his privileges, enlightened despotism weakened absolutism and
perhaps even laid the foundation for popular sovereignty. The Scandinavian
experience seems to confirm this. On the other hand, few rulers and ministers disposed more freely of the lives and wealth of their subjects than
Catherine II, Joseph II, or Frederick II. In relinquishing the privileges of
divine right, these rulers also relinquished divine right's constraints of ad-
herence to immanent moral law, fear for one's soul, and respect for the
long-standing rights of corporate groups. The question of whether these
darlings of eighteenth-century progressives were also the ancestors of modern day totalitarians is worth pondering.

Approached from another angle, the movement institutionalized reform
from above and bolstered monarchical authority. Through appeals to social
contract theory and concern for general welfare, enlightened despots won
new revenues and exploited the state's power over society. But how far
could they go? All sovereigns had to weigh institutional and social tradition
against the price of public welfare. Where tradition was strong and protected by constitutional guarantees, as in the Hapsburg empire, an aggressive
form of enlightened despotism like Joseph II's would inevitably confront
violent opposition and result in tragedy. Frederick the Great was more
fortunate than Joseph. Frederick's predecessors already had incorporated
local aristocracies into state service, and the king consolidated the process.
Though conciliation of aristocracies compromised with privilege, few enlightened despots failed to submit in this way. Nevertheless, their customary purpose was to cajole the wealthiest elements in the state into
administrative service, land improvement, and industrial enterprise. The
enlightened despots ruled underdeveloped countries. They desperately
needed money and expertise. They found resources wherever they could.

Of course, they were not social revolutionaries. By 1791, faced with a
revolutionary menace that threatened to topple absolutisms and aristocracies alike, rulers reverted to conceding privileges to aristocrats in return for
political support. Leopold II restored serfdom to the Hapsburg empire,
Catherine's Charter for the Nobility sanctified the corporate personality of
the Russian aristocracy, and the Prussian Code of 1791 guaranteed aristocratic leadership over society and the state. The radicalization of the French

Revolution by 1792 assured the death knell for enlightened despotism. Monarchs and aristocrats alike recognized the common need for survival. Before outlining the popular challenge to the old order, however, we must observe the actions of enlightened despots in diplomacy and war. Here they greatly resembled unenlightened predecessors.

THE PARTITIONS OF POLAND AND THE EUROPEAN EQUILIBRIUM

War forced the enlightened despots to exploit the economic resources of their states, and the sovereigns also looked beyond their borders for cheap opportunities to add resources at the expense of others. Though Frederick the Great vowed never to repeat the bitter experience brought on by his seizure of Silesia, he recognized that a community of interest might tempt fellow sovereigns to cooperate with him in aggressive diplomacy. Eastern Europe contained highly ambitious states, such as Prussia, the Hapsburg empire, and Russia. It also contained weak ones, such as Poland, Sweden, and the Ottoman empire. Because Fredrick needed allies badly, he merged Prussia's interests with those of his strong neighbors at the expense of his helpless ones.

Poland represented Frederick's great diplomatic bauble, and he proposed formal partition to Austria and Russia. Dividing the possessions of a defeated power was nothing new. In 1713–14, the victors expropriated Spain's European colonies, and eight years later it was Sweden's turn. In 1741, half a dozen European states were prepared to devour Maria Theresa's inheritance, and twenty years later, Russia, Austria, and Saxony decided to make Prussia the victim. Overseas, it was accepted that colonies were the rightful spoils of war. The idea of partitioning Poland was unique, however, first because it was unrelated to war and second because predatory neighbors helped themselves to pieces of a sovereign European state in order to prevent the seizure of the whole by any one of them. Diplomats congratulated themselves that the balance of power would be maintained.

As early as 1752 Frederick had coveted the Polish province of West Prussia, standing between his own provinces of Pomerania and East Prussia. It offered him badly needed territorial unity and possible control of the lower Vistula, the heartland of Poland's grain-exporting economy. Following the Seven Years' War and the death in 1763 of Poland's king, Augustus III, events speeded up. Frederick and Catherine II bribed the Polish Diet into selecting as the country's next king Stanislas Poniatowski, a native prince who had once been Catherine's lover. Poniatowski, however, called on patriots to resist aggression by rapacious neighbors. Catherine warned Stanislas that he was playing with fire and stationed thirty thousand Russian troops inside Poland. The country became a virtual Russian protectorate.

Frederick became wary. Russia's traditional policy had been to keep Poland weak and dependent, but the Russian foreign minister, Panin, wished to place a strengthened, though servile, Poland into a northern alliance system against France, Austria, and above all the Turks. Panin hoped to draw the Scandinavian states, Britain, and Prussia into his scheme. Frederick wished no part of it. Therefore, to thwart building up Poland as a Russian satellite, he tried to move Catherine towards partition.

Though the czarina coveted eastern Poland, Frederick experienced little success until an uprising of religious minorities in Poland erupted in 1767. Nearly 250,000 Protestants lived in northwestern Poland, and over 600,000 Orthodox resided in the east. Both minorities felt themselves persecuted by the Catholic majority, as did the Jews scattered in ghettos throughout the country. Unlike the Jews, the minority Christians had powerful protectors. Prussia was to look after the interests of Protestants, Russia those of the Orthodox. This was a convenient pretext for interference in Poland's affairs. When Frederick and Catherine pressured the Polish government into extending freedom of worship and admission to public offices to Christian dissenters, Catholic magnates, gentry, and churchmen protested. Proclaiming national revival and demanding reinvigoration of Catholicism, deliverance from foreigners, and deposition of their puppet king, a resistance movement formed at the fortress town of Bar in southeastern Poland. Other movements established themselves, declared solidarity with the Bar patriots, and merged into a General Confederacy. The non-Catholic minorities feared a massacre, and since the General Confederacy was led by some of Poland's greatest magnates, a social factor was added to the religious tension. Orthodox peasants in the Ukraine rose up against their Catholic masters. Russian military commanders egged on the rebelling serfs, who crossed the Turkish border and burned manor houses. The Turks blamed the Russians and impetuously declared war upon Catherine. The czarina mobilized her army and asked Frederick to help put down the civil war which was spreading through Poland.

The Prussian king needed little urging. He worried about the Austrians, but Kaunitz and Joseph indicated interest in sharing some spoils. Meanwhile, Catherine's forces were scoring sensational victories over the Turks. The army took Moldavia and Wallachia and penetrated the Crimea. Russia's fleet sailed into the Baltic, down the English Channel and Atlantic coastline, veered eastward into the Mediterranean, and destroyed the Turkish navy off Asia Minor. Istanbul was threatened. Fearing that Russian triumphs might wed Catherine unalterably to the northern alliance, Frederick dispatched his brother Henry to St. Petersburg to plead for a Polish partition. Henry got nowhere at first. Suddenly, early in 1771, Catherine suggested that Russia and Prussia help themselves. The breakthrough thus made, a Russo-Prussian partition convention was signed, and Austria joined the discussions. "I am ashamed to show my face," Maria Theresa told

Kaunitz. But she went along. Before the armed might of the three great powers, the Polish Confederacy collapsed. In August 1772 the partition was sealed. Frederick obtained West Prussia, Russia took Poland's northeastern provinces, and Austria gained a large triangle in the southern part of the country. Poland lost 50,000 square miles and four million people, a third of the country.

One reason Russia agreed to the Polish partition was that since it was doing so well on its own against the Turks, no northern alliance seemed necessary. In June 1774 the Ottoman empire sued for peace at Kutchuk-Kainardji. The Crimea became independent, and Russia obtained the northern coastline of the Sea of Azov. Part of the Black Sea coastline between the Bug and Dnieper rivers, as well as the ports of Azov and Taganrog, became Russian. Russian ships plied the Black Sea and gained free entry to the Mediterranean. The Ukraine now was completely open to exploitation. For Catherine, this was but the beginning. In 1782 the czarina proposed to Joseph II a partition of the Turk's Balkan principalities. Catherine dreamed of taking Istanbul and reestablishing a dependent Byzantine empire. She would propose Egypt to the French. She planned to give something to Spain and England, too, should they resist this rearrangement of the eastern Mediterranean, labeled the "Greek Project."

Fanciful though the Greek Project might have been, Joseph took it seriously. In 1783 Russia occupied the Crimea and started exploiting it despite the sultan's objections. In September 1787, war between Russia and the Ottomans again erupted. Coveting prizes in the Balkans, Joseph joined Catherine, but the remainder of Europe, led by Britain and Prussia, protested vigorously. Catherine's anticipated entry into Istanbul did not materialize because, ill and preoccupied with rebellion in Belgium and unrest in Hungary, Joseph could offer very little help. In August 1791, Leopold II took Austria out of the war. A year later at Jassy, Catherine made peace with the Turks. The czarina contented herself with Crimea and Bug-Dniester coastline. The Greek Project was put aside for the moment. Nevertheless, Catherine had given birth to the Near Eastern problem, which would intrigue European statesmen for most of the nineteenth century.

Thus, for the third time since 1740, Frederick II's desire to secure Prussia's future had set off a string of developments that escaped his control. While Russia attempted to reconstruct the Near East, the Polish chapter was far from finished. The partition of 1772 gave rise to a movement of national revival that was remarkably different from either the desperate scapegoat hunting of the seventeenth century or the Confederacy of 1767. Every politically conscious Pole knew that constitutional weakness and magnatial jealousies had turned Poland into its neighbors' prey. History revealed how for two centuries the great powers had exploited the country's internal divisions, culminating in the disaster of 1772. The national Diet and King Stanislas went to work. The Diet restricted the authority of the provincial diets and strengthened central institutions. The king regained his right to mint money, and both hearth and import-export taxes were reintroduced. In 1788, sweeping economic reforms were enacted, and in 1790 the state's revenue doubled from what it had been two years earlier. In social reform beginnings were made. The gentry were permitted to engage in trade, and the landlord lost the privilege of executing a serf at will. The *liberum veto*, right of confederation, elective monarchy, and fifty regional assemblies were branded as banes to good government.

Certainly, powerful magnates had a vested interest in the old liberties, and some preferred the traditional anarchy to reform. A few, however, became convinced nationalists and concluded that hereditary monarchical government and a strong army were the country's only hope against continued foreign intervention. They had reason to fear the worst. Russian troops still were stationed in the country. Though preoccupied with her Greek Project, Catherine closely observed Polish developments. Particularly ominous for her was the fact that many Polish reformers in the Diet who had visited western Europe and read the works of the Enlightenment sympathized with the revolution that broke out in France in 1789. On May 3, 1791, the Polish Diet unfurled its crowning achievement, a totally new constitution. The government was made hereditary in the House of Saxony, and the king's job was to execute the Diet's laws. The traditional Estates of society were confirmed, but the landless portion of the gentry lost its political privileges. On the other hand, the landholding gentry joined magnates and bishops in the upper chamber of the newly constituted parliament. The *liberum veto*, confederacies, and confederation parliaments were abolished. Deputies to the new national legislature were no longer bound by the wishes of the provincial diets sending them there. The reforms were modest enough. They left Poland in the hands of her magnates and gentry; serfdom was left untouched. Catherine, however, grew furious. By 1792 the French Revolution had entered its radical phase, and the czarina was certain that its democratic spirit would infect Poland. As soon as she made peace with the Turks, she answered the appeals of unregenerate magnates and forcibly intervened in Polish affairs. Prussia joined the attack. The constitution of May 3 was abrogated, and a second partition followed. The Russians established a regime of magnatial puppets in what remained of Poland.

From 1763 until the French Revolution, the forefront of European diplomatic and military activity was in the east. Western powers refrained from coming to the aid of either the Poles or Turks. Britain was preoccupied with deteriorating conditions in America, and its difficulties there invited its old adversaries, France and Spain, to try to settle scores. Since the opportunity seemed ripe for the Bourbon powers to reduce Britain's maritime supremacy, France declared war on Britain in 1778, as did Spain a year later. In 1780 the Dutch joined the conflict against England and by declaring the League of Armed Neutrality, which was more a statement of anti-British principles than a true naval alliance of belligerents, Catherine herself posed as protectress of the seas. The European allies, however, were unable to take advantage of the American war and form a united front against the British. Their gains were modest. The French obtained a few trading stations in the West Indies (St. Lucia and Tobago) and west Africa (Senegal and Goree); Spain won Minorca and Florida, but not Gibraltar, its chief desire. Faced with its great imperial crisis from 1775 to 1783, Britain saw the loss of America as a defeat, but it might have been much worse.

In central Europe Joseph II tried to emulate Catherine by establishing a new equilibrium. His efforts, however, got nowhere. Aware that Silesia was irretrievably lost, Joseph picked other soft spots. For a century the Hapsburgs had coveted Bavaria, the acquisition of which would give them a territorially compact set of possessions along the Danube while increasing their influence in the Holy Roman Empire. In 1777, the Bavarian elector died. His successor agreed to cede one-third of the country to Austria in return for Hapsburg financial maintenance of his swarm of illegitimate children. Kaunitz and Joseph pushed the idea, but Maria Theresa considered it hare brained. She knew that Frederick II could not tolerate such an upset of the status quo in central Europe. As a warning, Frederick marched his army into Hapsburg Bohemia.

No one really wanted war, and France and Russia offered to mediate the dispute. Their proposal was forced on Joseph. The Hapsburgs obtained a tiny sliver of Bavarian territory, a symbolic gesture agreed to by Frederick, so that the emperor might avert total humiliation. Still desiring Bavaria, in 1784 Joseph offered its elector Belgium in exchange. From Joseph's point of view, it was a sound deal, ridding him of a distant, rambunctious set of towns and provinces that were hostile to his conception of reform. Once Frederick showed disfavor again, no other European power supported Joseph. The project fell through. On his deathbed in 1786, the Prussian king was determined to leave to posterity a check upon Joseph's ambitions. With Saxony, Hanover, and several smaller German states, Prussia signed a mutual defense pact. A secret clause specifically mentioned protection of Bavaria's integrity.

THE CHALLENGE: IRELAND, BRITAIN, AND AMERICA

The first partition of Poland, Greek Project, Anglo-Bourbon colonial rivalry, and Austrian schemes for Bavaria fit into the traditional pattern of international dynastic politics under the ancien régime. The motivations were territorial and economic. Except for Catherine's propaganda about liberating Balkan Christians from Islam's yoke or Catholics from Polish persecution, ideological factors were of little importance.

However, the *second* partition of Poland in 1793 was a different matter.

Catherine brutally destroyed the Constitution of May 3 because she was persuaded wrongly that the Polish reform movement was part of an international conspiracy to destroy the bases of a political and social order Europe had known for the past five hundred years. The czarina thought she saw a sinister new plant emerging in the traditional societies of Europe. The roots were widespread and difficult to locate, but the shoots were growing fast. They threatened to choke the older foliage that had flourished through aristocratic/royal tension and collaboration, thus giving the world of elites its distinctive character. From the mid-1760s, Catherine perceived attempts of subjects to enjoy greater liberty, equality, and a sense of participation in government than had previously been the case. Possibly experience with her own legislative commission of 1767 taught her this. Elsewhere, however, it was becoming clear that articulate individuals questioned the political and social norms of existence as defined by tradition and authority. Novels and, more discreetly, political tracts glorified the fulfillment of the autonomous personality unfettered by institutional shackles. In west and central European academies, reading clubs, salons, cafes, and Masonic lodges, individuals deprived of active political participation in affairs of their states, provinces, and towns were debating the legitimacy of privilege, basis for sovereignty, and notion of property. For Catherine, even worse were the few instances where debate exploded into action, as in the Polish national revival after 1773.

Though the American Revolution put Europe's aristocracies on notice that the age had become one of momentous change, as early as the 1760s political and social elites felt the first waves of challenge. In 1768, the better-born burghers of Geneva, heretofore excluded from aristocratic town councils, won access to them. In the next decade artisans and shopkeepers also lobbied for an active voice in government. At the same time, Dutch bankers, merchants, and intellectuals established the Patriot political group in opposition to the stadholder and aristocratized town councils that ran the Netherlands. Inspired by the Americans, the Patriots grew more numerous in the 1780s and even staged an abortive revolt in 1786, which Prussian intervention had to suppress.

From 1770 to 1778, Ireland was a volatile country. Though the Catholic majority, numbering 70 percent of the population, had no political and few civil rights, Anglican landlords, who were one-tenth of the people, owned five-sixths of the land. A third religious group, Presbyterian Protestants descended from Scottish immigrants, numbered around 20 percent of the population and were customarily farmers on short-term leases, artisans, and small traders. The Presbyterians believed that the Irish Parliament, meeting in Dublin, concerned itself exclusively with the interests of the great Anglican landlords; and they were correct. The Parliament was a rotten institution controlled by a hundred landlords. However, the landlords themselves complained that decision-making responsibility resided not with the Irish

Parliament at all but with the English House of Commons, whose trade laws were meant to protect British merchants and injure Irish interests. Thus in Ireland several tiers of dissatisfaction existed. The Anglican aristocracy desired autonomy for the Irish Parliament and freedom for trade; the Presbyterian minority desired to make the Irish Parliament more representative; and the Catholic majority suffered from its atrocious political and social subjection.

In 1778, crisis struck the country when the Americans, in revolt against Britain, ceased importing Irish linens and food products. Meanwhile, the British released troops for service in America, and Ireland was threatened by French attack. Native militiamen, largely Presbyterians, were recruited to defend Ireland. By 1782, there were eighty thousand armed Irish volunteers in the country. Under pressure of events in America, the British government offered the Irish Parliament autonomy. This satisfied the Anglo-Irish oligarchs, but the Presbyterian leaders among the Irish volunteers demanded more, namely reform of the Parliament in Dublin. The Presbyterians held a Grand National Convention to drive home the message to the aristocracy. Armed weavers, artisans, and small traders were demanding political representation. The convention threw some scraps to the Catholic majority, chiefly the right to buy land, but showed little genuine interest in ending the practice of Catholic subjugation. However, the Irish Parliament itself refused to become more representative because, as one insensitive landlord put it, the Irish constitution was "the admiration and envy of all nations and ages." Getting nowhere, the volunteers refused to disband after the American war. They continued to urge reform of the Dublin Parliament, and the crisis persisted. Meanwhile, among the Catholic majority, political consciousness began taking shape.

Before the American Revolution several efforts had been made to amend England's political institutions. One effort was the king's. A vigorous, authoritarian young man, George III assumed the throne in 1760. While he had been crown prince, courtiers unable to penetrate the curtain of Whig authority had gathered round him and were now royal advisers. Like George himself, this group wished to free the crown from what it believed to be the control of the Whig magnates and in doing so purify English political institutions. After forty years of placemaking out went Newcastle. Out went many others. Not even Pitt survived the royal housecleaning. The Whig idea of government held that control of patronage, social prominence, and party unity entitled political groups to royal favor.

On the other hand, George wished to use royal favor to award patronage and social prominence to parliamentary loyalists. Therefore, like Charles II, the king tried to construct his own party in Parliament, where dedicated servants would do the royal bidding. Time, however, was not on George's side. The unpopularity of the Peace of Paris in 1763 forced his prime minister, the earl of Bute, from office and a rapidly escalating crisis in America aggravated ministerial instability. George became enmeshed in aristocratic politics. The crown was victimized. Disgusted with the unedifying political struggle between George and the Whigs, newspapers and speakers demanded widened participation in politics. King and Parliament were suddenly called upon to respond to a critical question: Could England truly be a free country while maintaining a restrictive franchise, tolerating rotten boroughs, and accepting the politics of patronage?

If George proposed one way of changing status quo politics, John Wilkes offered another. A flamboyant, energetic adventurer who was elected to the House of Commons in 1757, Wilkes sat for Middlesex, a London suburb with a relatively wide franchise. He was an imperialist, eager to crush France in the Seven Years' War and bitterly disappointed when George III dropped Pitt. While in Commons, Wilkes founded the *North Briton*, a lively, importunate, immensely popular newspaper. It was patriotic and distrustful of George III, and in April 1763, it violently offended the king by accusing him of trying to establish a Stuart type of tyranny.

The government's reaction to Wilkes was remarkably inept and turned the journalist-M.P. into a martyr. To close down the *North Briton*, a "general warrant," naming no one personally, was issued. Wilkes was arrested, and his house was ransacked by searchers. He fought back in the courts. When the crown maintained that the *North Briton* had jeopardized national security, Wilkes responded that general warrants jeopardized individual liberty. In 1769 he was vindicated. General warrants were declared illegal, and Wilkes won damages.

While fighting his case, however, Wilkes widened the scope of the issues. He lectured and pamphleteered against the king, the king's friends in Parliament, and the unreformed constitution. For his troubles, Wilkes lost his parliamentary privilege, was wounded in a duel, survived an assassination attempt, fled to France, and was expelled from the House of Commons. Though Middlesex returned him to his seat in 1768, Wilkes's colleagues refused to admit him. The procedure occurred a second, then a third time, and finally Commons declared Wilkes's losing opponent from Middlesex the borough's legal representative. Wilkes himself was arrested for sedition and jailed for twenty-one months. He became a focus for discontent all over England and beyond. Workers protesting bread prices rioted in his name. Those demanding parliamentary reform and even Americans across the sea called themselves Wilkesites. In 1769 some of his English backers established the Supporters of the Bill of Rights, the first organized group to demand parliamentary reform. Petitions urged Wilkes's reinstatement. In the end, Wilkes became a national hero, lord mayor of London, a sitting M.P., and coauthor of the first, and unsuccessful, bill advocating parliamentary reform. His newspapers began reporting debates in the two Houses.

Prior to the 1790s, no figure in eighteenth-century Europe had done more than Wilkes to organize nonaristocratic public opinion and make it a factor in political life.

The various Wilkes affairs had given the lie to the benevolent reputation of the British constitution. Parliament's stands against Wilkes showed it to be unrepresentative of constituencies, dependent upon the crown, corrupt, prejudiced, and frightened. If Parliament had erred in promoting the government's vendetta against Wilkes, in the quarrel with the Americans its blunders were monumental. The great imperial crisis of 1764 to 1782 unveiled yet more symptoms of Britain's constitutional malaise.

In 1763, Bute's successor as prime minister, George Grenville, inherited a huge war debt. Furthermore, Grenville believed that the English country gentlemen were paying too much of it (around 15 percent of their income went to taxes), and the Americans were paying too little. For their part, the Americans were eager to settle the lands newly conquered from France. To Grenville, this meant expensive armed conflicts against Indians. Thus the minister declared a moratorium on westward expansion in America, moved to suppress smuggling in American ports, enforced the Navigation Acts, and in 1765 proposed a stamp duty on newspapers and legal documents for the colonies. Parliament passed the Stamp Act. Englishmen had been paying such taxes for three quarters of a century, but the Americans exploded in fury. To them, the Stamp Act was tyrannical, and they responded accordingly.

However much the colonies differed from each other in religion, culture, and social custom, however much the westward-looking pioneer scorned his coastal creditor or the Virginia planter misunderstood the Connecticut free farmer, Grenville's actions and Parliament's support underscored the solidarity of the New World and its distinctiveness from the Old. In no way was this more apparent than in political institutions. For Ireland a parliamentary act early in the eighteenth century had at least made clear Dublin's subservience to Westminster. For the American colonies, no such act existed. Colonists considered their right to representation in their elected colonial assemblies inherent to their rights as Englishmen. Westminster called upon colonists to acknowledge subjection to a British Parliament in which they were not directly represented. Very early in the game, therefore, the economic problem—parliamentary taxation of the colonists—veiled the deeper, political one: Parliament's *right* to tax them. Americans believed that raising revenue was their prerogative alone. As John Adams said in 1765: "A Parliament in Great Britain can have no more right to tax colonies than a Parliament in Paris."

In the colonial clamor against the Stamp Act, American merchants boycotted British goods, shopkeepers and workers intimidated stamp distributors, and rioters in Massachusetts destroyed the home of the royal lieutenant governor. Nine colonial legislatures collectively denied Parliament's right to tax Americans. Feeling the pinch of the American boycott, England's shippers called for repeal of the Stamp Act. Caught in an impasse, Grenville's ministry resigned. Its successor, led by the marquis of Rockingham, advised expediency, and the king personally asked Commons to repeal the act. Accomplished in March 1766, the repeal avoided an open break, but the question of political authority remained unresolved. In fact, Parliament explicitly underscored its authority "to make laws and statutes of sufficient force and validity to bind the colonies and people of America, subjects of the crown of Great Britain, in all cases whatsoever." In Britain, those who backed Wilkes and detested the unreformed nature of Parliament usually sympathized with the colonists. Pitt and his followers sought a compromise by calling duties that regulated trade legal and duties that raised revenue illegal.

As Britain's postwar debt grew, Parliament in 1767 voted a series of regulatory import tariffs for the Americans, the so-called Townshend duties. Addressing themselves to political theory and insisting upon the general illegality of taxation without representation, the Americans saw no distinction between Townshend's duties and Grenville's stamp tax. From 1768 to 1770, relations between the government and colonists deteriorated again. Boycotts against British goods produced more incidents. Political groups formed in America and talked of separation from Britain. In March 1770, British troops in Boston fired upon a crowd harassing them, and five citizens were killed. They became martyrs. Once more, the British tried conciliation. Another new ministry, Lord North's, withdrew the Townshend duties on all articles except tea.

Nevertheless, no atmosphere of mutual trust existed. Colonists accused the British of removing the Townshend duties in order to destroy American manufacturing with a flood of cheap articles. Nearly everywhere in America, politically radical "committees of correspondence" thrived. By 1773, Massachusetts alone had eighty of them. Incidents multiplied. A British revenue ship burned mysteriously in a colonial harbor; the British government dismissed the popular Benjamin Franklin as colonial postmaster. When the East India Company reduced its price of tea so drastically that American smugglers and middlemen alike were threatened with extinction, colonists in New York, Philadelphia, and Charleston refused to unload the product. In Boston they boarded the loaded tea ships in the harbor and threw £15,000 worth over the side. Conservative American merchants and political radicals were forging a common cause, and in Britain the government was exasperated. Early in 1774 the king wrote: "The die is now cast. The colonies must now submit or triumph." Parliament agreed. Orders from Britain closed the port of Boston. The colonial charter for Massachusetts was suspended, and the commander of royal troops in America was appointed governor of the colony. Parliament extended French civil law and toleration of Catholics into the region between the Ohio River and Great Lakes.

Americans in New York, Connecticut, Massachusetts, and Virginia interpreted this as a conscious attempt to discourage westward expansion.

In May 1774, the Virginia House of Burgesses called for representatives from all the colonial legislatures to attend a Continental Congress. Pennsylvania offered Philadelphia as the site. All but Georgia sent delegates. Moderates at the Congress asked for recommendations that would restore harmony to Anglo-American relations without sacrificing the "just rights and liberties" of the colonies. Delegates from Massachusetts and radicals from elsewhere pointed out that as a consequence of the recent "Intolerable Acts," Massachusetts had neither rights nor liberties left. The Congress condemned the Intolerable Acts and rejected the principle of parliamentary supremacy over the colonies. In England, Pitt (now Lord Chatham) and Whigs like Edmund Burke urged repeal of the Intolerable Acts. Lord North refused. The Continental Congress disbanded, and the colonial legislatures sanctioned its work. A new boycott of British goods occurred.

Large-scale violence broke out in America the following April when the Massachusetts governor, General Thomas Gage, lost 250 men (one-tenth of the entire royal detachment in the colony) during a fruitless quest for arms supposedly stored by the colonists at Concord. Lord North and Parliament now spoke openly of rebellion in America. In May 1775 a second Continental Congress meeting in Philadelphia disclaimed any intention of seceding from Britain and urged George III to intervene with Parliament on the Americans' behalf. However, these same sober conservatives also formed a "Continental Army" drawn from colonial militias and asked the Virginia planter George Washington to lead it. A series of uprisings drove out all the royal governors by fall 1775.

As the British withdrew their detachments from the colonies and tried to blockade the American coastal ports, most colonists clung to the hope that George III still might influence Parliament to recognize the legitimacy of their cause. However, by January 1776, they understood that confidence in the king was an idle dream, and the tremendous reception of the pamphlet *Common Sense* by the former exciseman Thomas Paine confirmed the new public mood. Paine called George a morally despicable fool, "the royal brute of Great Britain," and the British House of Commons an "aristocratized tyranny." Bitterly attacking monarchy in general, Paine demanded immediate separation from England. On June 28, 1776, Jefferson of Virginia, John Adams of Massachusetts, and Franklin of Pennsylvania submitted a draft declaration of independence to the Continental Congress. A week later, the declaration, with amendments, passed. The political theory of the document paraphrased Locke's philosophy of natural rights. The government of Great Britain had violated its compact with the governed, and the Americans had no recourse except to break their ties. The declaration enumerated a list of specific grievances. In essence, of course, the Americans were de facto independent long before July 4, 1776. The machinery of the old Whig government had existed to manage England's society, not build an empire. What George III and Parliament were trying to accomplish, first fitfully and now by force of arms, was to destroy that independence and rule America from London—in effect, reconquer the New World they had lost.

For six years, from 1775 until October 1781, reconquest eluded the British. Though Washington experienced troubles in raising an army and maintaining patriotic ardor among the Americans, Britain's difficulties proved insurmountable. It became diplomatically isolated. France, Spain, and Holland recognized American independence and went to war against Britain. Though the threat of a French invasion of England silenced colonial sympathizers in Parliament and business, and while fears of democracy at home moved churchmen and country squires to press the fight, the armies sent over the Atlantic lacked sufficient naval support to carry the day. After 1780 Lord North himself doubted Britain's capacity to win the war. When General Cornwallis and his force of seven thousand got themselves entrapped at Yorktown on the Virginia coast in October 1781, North lost heart completely. His ministry fell the following March, and George III instructed his new government to seek terms with the Americans. At the Peace of Paris (September 1783), Britain recognized the new nation. The distant Mississippi was set as its western boundary, the Great Lakes its northern one, Florida the southern. The Americans obtained the right to fish in Newfoundland's waters. France received Senegal and Tobago, and Spain obtained Minorca and Florida.

The Irish troubles, Wilkes, and the successful American Revolution made it clear that the halcyon days of the Whig oligarchy were no more. Nor had George III been able to supplant oligarchic rule with royal leadership. But how was Britain to be governed? The question now was more serious than ever. Edmund Burke, speaking for a new generation of Whig politicians, offered a dignified and aristocratic program he called "Economical Reform": reduce the influence and power of the throne, ensure honesty in Parliament, and allow its natural leaders to rule. Burke left room for the vision of a great British empire and for humanitarian treatment of Irish Catholics, but he could not accept electoral reform or the end to rotten boroughs. To do so, he claimed, would betray the prescriptive wisdom of the past. Burke mistrusted reason in politics, and he considered natural rights as illusions. His position was summed up in small gestures that would purify existing institutions, such as reduction of the number of sinecures in the royal household and prohibition of government contractors from sitting in Parliament.

On the other hand, the dissenting academies had already produced genuine radicals. Because of their non-Anglican Protestantism, graduates of the academies were excluded from both the universities and civil service. Influenced by Enlightenment thought, they believed in the inexorable advance of freedom and reason and equated virtue with one's value to society. Philip Doddridge, Joseph Priestley, and Richard Price, the leading Radical

Dissenters, spoke for economically successful and politically unenfranchised tradesmen, merchants, craftsmen, and freeholders. They were pro-Wilkes and pro-American; they wished to abolish pocket and rotten boroughs, end patronage and management, establish annual, responsible Parliaments, and give every male adult the vote. Throughout Lord North's ministry (1770–81), radicalism took root, and after 1778 it became dangerous. Unsuccessful in reforming institutions, radicals began thinking of replacing them. Some proposed an alternative to the unreformed Parliament, a grand national association of landowners, chosen by popularly elected county associations.

The "association movement," revolutionary because self-appointed leaders were addressing themselves as the people's will, climaxed during the darkest period of the American war. It attracted discontented M.P.'s and magnates, as well as the disenfranchised and opportunistic. From 1779 to mid-1780, dozens of meetings were held and many ideas posed. Though the influential Yorkshire leadership backed away from "associations" and instead proposed increasing the number of sturdy independent county M.P.'s in the House of Commons, old-fashioned borough politicians sensed that a world was ending. Suddenly, in June 1780, an outbreak of savage violence in London, the "Gordon Riots," frightened many moderates away from reform. Ironically, the riots had nothing to do with the reform movement. They were directed against recent parliamentary moves to assimilate English Catholics into civil society. Catholic neighborhoods were burned down, jails broken into, and two thousand prisoners set loose. Until the army restored order, John Wilkes himself led the militia to harness the mobs. The rioting cruelly hurt the associationists' cause. The people were viewed as incapable of political responsibility, and Burke's tinkering was accepted.

Unable to find a stable ministry, in December 1783 George III reluctantly asked Pitt's twenty-four-year-old son to form a government. The younger Pitt's youth, vigor, and idealism seemed to signify a new beginning, and the reformers thought they had found a second life. Previously, Pitt had backed parliamentary redistricting, elimination of the most rotten boroughs, a program of free trade, and an end to the slave trade. He understood that industrialization and empire demanded a redistribution of political and social power in Britain. However, Pitt was no revolutionary. His programs were not intended to democratize England but rather to release the country from aristocratic Whig control and give mercantile-industrial interests a larger voice in its future. Failing to get Parliament to eliminate either the rotten boroughs or slave trade, Pitt did persuade George III to pack the House of Lords with wealthy merchants. His India Act (1784) left patronage for the colony in the hands of the East India Company's directors, while granting overall administrative responsibility to the government. Pitt balanced government debts at last, simplified customs duties, and reduced consumer import charges. Negotiating a commercial treaty with France in 1786 based upon tariff reductions and liberal exchange, he buried British mercantilism. Enjoying the confidence of the king and keeping his distance from the Whig magnates, Pitt thus made England as safe for commerce and industry as it once had been for the landed gentry.

For the moment, the wave of material prosperity drowned out the radicals' cries for political reform, but the world beyond England was also changing. From 1789 to 1792, momentous events in France ended the ancien régime there, and English radicalism revived in support of the French Revolution. Pitt determined that political unrest must not undo his work. He therefore asked the landed gentry and great merchants to safeguard England's institutions and keep the country out of foreign entanglements. As late as February 1792, when the French had destroyed their aristocracy and their monarchy, Pitt predicted fifteen more years of peace for Europe. In April, however, Europe's kings declared war on the French Revolution, and in January 1793 the revolutionaries executed Louis XVI. England's great peacetime minister had no other choice than to plunge his country into a conflict that lasted twenty years, exceeding in scope anything that had preceded it.

THE COLLAPSE OF THE ANCIEN RÉGIME IN FRANCE

For the quarter-century between 1755 and 1780, France enjoyed good harvests and a commercial expansion based upon the judicious use of credit. Wholesale wheat and meat prices rose steadily, and large-scale agriculture became extremely profitable. As short-term rents skyrocketed, absentee landlords who made the most money invested in sumptuous town residences, mining, shipbuilding, overseas trade, and additional rural properties. Unable to keep up with inflation, however, agricultural tenants and urban workers were the victims of prosperity. Caught in a rent squeeze and unable to keep up their scattered plots before the onrushing domain of the landlord, peasants sold out to landlords and headed for towns. There they lost their sense of community and became helpless atoms, floating about in an unpoliced world of vagrants, prostitutes, and thieves.

Prosperity also victimized the French state. While the costs of government skyrocketed, the state's income stagnated. Finance ministers tried to raise sufficient taxes to meet expenses and increase the income of taxpayers so they could contribute more, but direct taxpaying in France was a mark of social inferiority. Great churchmen and the entire nobility, shipbuilders, the wealthiest merchants, and most officeholders possessed total or partial exemptions. Peasants and urban workers, victims of prosperity in the first place, were the chief source of the state's income, and their contributions were insufficient for the state's needs. After 1770 it was clear that France no longer could sustain fiscal privilege, but neither Church nor aristocracy would yield its privileges. As a matter of fact, to aristocrats mindful of their long night of humiliation under Louis XIV, the idea of a dependent, financially strapped monarchy was not unpleasant at all. Parliaments in particular appreciated the image of royal ministers coming to them, hat in hand, in desperate quest of funds. The magistrates would bargain hard in return for political concessions.

The financial desperation of the government helps explain why enlightened despotism failed in France. The incompetence of the king was another reason. Until 1770, Louis XV depended upon the duke of Choiseul, a brilliant soldier-diplomat who had guided France through the military disaster of the Seven Years' War and saved the Caribbean sugar isles at the Peace of Paris in 1763. In 1766, Choiseul managed the acquisition of Lorraine and in 1768, Corsica.

Concerning internal reform, however, Choiseul was a failure. By ridding France of the Jesuits in 1767, he hoped to ingratiate himself with the three thousand influential aristocratic magistrates sitting in the Parlement of Paris and twenty-eight other regional law and tax courts dispersed throughout the country. He hoped to convince the robe nobles of the need for fairly distributed taxation. By virtue of its extended judicial powers—the right to debate and register royal orders before they became law—the Parlement of Paris was a political power. With the regional parlements, it possessed vaguely defined powers over religion, law enforcement, corporations, public assistance, the press, road building, taxes, and education. The regional parlements controlled the politics of many provincial cities and subsidized culture through establishment of academies and funding of both literary and scientific contests. Their own culture was conservative, suspicious of the *philosophes*, hostile towards fiscal and administrative reform, and intensely patriotic. Because they considered the Jesuits to represent a fifth-column agency of the pope, they hated the order. Most importantly, by virtue of their landed and moneyed wealth, they were tied to the worlds of the old military aristocracy and the newer financial one—thus forming a powerful social element in France.

The Brittany affair illustrated the strength of the parlements and brought about Choisuel's downfall. Brittany was an isolated region whose parlement, provincial Estates, and rural nobility had always resisted the interference of Versailles in local matters. Early in the 1760s, the king's military commander in the province, the young duke d'Aiguillon, insisted that Brittany's fiscal charges were too light. Brittany's parlements told d'Aiguillon to mind his own business and then challenged the commander's contention that the government was authorized to build roads in Brittany. Choiseul supported d'Aiguillon, and in 1765, Brittany's parlements dissolved itself in protest. La Châlotais, his son, and four other *parlementaires* were arrested, but no judge could be found in Brittany to try the state's case. The Parlement of Paris backed La Châlotais, and at this point, on March 3, 1766, Louis XV reminded the magistrates of the absolute nature of the French monarchy. (See pp. 162–63.)

Characteristically, the king failed to follow through. The parlements in Brittany sat again and brought charges against d'Aiguillon, who was re-called. Other parlements converted the matter into a confrontation with the royal government. They corresponded with each other, challenged near-ly every prerogative Louis had claimed in his "Seance of Flagellation" of 1766, declared themselves the true spokesmen for the nation, and helped to force Choiseul's fall from office in 1770. Once more, the king tried to be firm. He now depended upon an able, ambitious lawyer, René-Nicolas Maupeou, and an iron-willed priest, abbé Terray. Maupeou knew the magis-trates well. Before casting his lot with the royal administration, he himself had served as an officer of the Parlement of Paris. He believed that behind the Brittany affair lay a basic political and constitutional question: who was to rule France—the king and his ministers or the parlementary magistrates? As controller-general of finances, Terray demanded a reform of the tax structure and predicted a long, bitter fight with the parlements. One way of averting such a struggle, however, was to abolish the parlements alto-gether.

Though it invited civil war, in January 1771, Louis let Maupeou maneu-ver the Paris *parlementaires* into another rejection of royal authority, and then the king exiled them to the provinces. A system of courts was estab-lished to assume most of the judicial functions of the old Parlement of Paris, and the tenure of newly chosen magistrates was revocable. Though the parlementary committee which had registered royal orders was retained and Louis refused to dissolve the provincial parlements immediatley, a beginning had been made. Maupeou believed that now the laws of France might be codified and unified, and Terray attacked the fiscal problem com-prehensively. He repudiated part of the national debt, suspended high inter-est payments on state loans, and forced new loans upon financiers. He revived the *vingtième* and renegotiated with the Farmers General their contract for indirect tax collection at terms favorable to the government. Terray's brutal retrenchment policies were even less popular with the privi-leged than Maupeou's political coup d'état. Commerce slowed down, and bankruptcies were blamed on him, but there was no violence.

Uninterested in public affairs, Louis allowed his reforming ministers free rein. They had three years. On April 29, 1774, court physicians observed an outbreak of small sores on the king's body. Two weeks later, he was dead of smallpox, leaving as successor a thoroughly unprepared twenty-year-old grandson. Louis XVI had spent nearly all of his days in suburban palaces outside Paris. He did not know the capital and was totally ignorant of the country. Governmental affairs had been kept from him. His queen, the Austrian princess Marie Antoinette, was an irresponsible, spoiled child interested in court intrigues. The time was critical for France and Europe. Maupeou and Terray were in midprogram. France had done nothing about the recent partition of Poland, the Austro-Russian alliance was poised to destroy the Ottoman empire, and Britain's North American colonies were at the edge of rebellion.

Inexperienced, well-intentioned, and stupid, the new king disliked the tyrannical ways of Maupeou and Terray. An aged courtier, the count of Maurepas, advised reconciliation with the aristocracy. Maupeou and Terray were dropped and the Parlement of Paris restored. The magistrates proclaimed victory over tyrants and looked forward to rebuilding their power. On the other hand, Maurepas gave Louis a gifted new ministry. The *inten- dant* of Limoges, A.-R.-J. Turgot, became controller-general of finances. A disciple of the physiocrats and friend of the *philosophes*, Turgot had abolished the *corvée*, compulsory nonremunerative road building by peasants. He also had improved canals and schools. Arriving at Versailles with many ideas, he reduced court expenses and removed collection of some taxes from control of the Farmers General. In September 1774 he organized free export of grain from one province to another, a necessity in the event of regional famine. He suppressed the *corvée* throughout the kingdom and recommended a special landholder's tax to pay for road upkeep. Considering the right to work to be dictated by the laws of supply and demand, Turgot abolished most of the merchant and craft guilds. Whenever he could, he removed monopolies from private contractors and foresaw wide landowner participation in both local and national affairs. He also showed himself firm in moments of crisis. Following the poor harvest of spring 1775, Paris mobs rioted at the flour markets because of a fear that provisions would be sent to other hard-pressed regions; Turgot ringed the capital with thirty thousand troops and hanged the riot leaders.

Other talented reformers entered Louis's first ministry: Malesherbes and Sartine, who as directors of the book trade had allowed the *philosophes'* works to circulate in France; the count of Vergennes, supporter of the American Revolution; the count of St. Germain, out to abolish favoritism and unmerited officerships in the army. As usual, court and parlementary opposition challenged innovation. By May 1776, the queen and Maurepas urged Louis to retreat. Turgot, Malesherbes, and St. Germain were dismissed. Saddened by the turn of events, the young king wrote: "Only Monsieur Turgot and I truly love our people." However, Louis XVI lacked courage to resist the pressures.

For the next eleven years, the financial crisis mounted, and in search of a solution the government stumbled from ministry to ministry. Once the crisis cojoined with a series of poor harvests, new revolts by the parlements and a general administrative paralysis, the ancien régime in France crumbled. Accelerating the financial catastrophe were the costs of the new war against Britain, from 1778 to 1783, which included the grant of supplies, loans, and troops to the American revolutionaries.

In October 1776, Maurepas restored the *corvée* and guilds. Then he awarded responsibility over state finances to a Geneva banker, Jacques Necker, who had made a fortune speculating in East Indian stocks. A technician rather than a social reformer, Necker believed in neither strict economies nor extended taxation. He intended to lighten the state's burden of debt through credit. His banking connections loaned the government huge sums at 8 to 10 percent interest, and half a billion *livres* quickly enriched the treasury. Believing that the *intendants* had too much power in the countryside, Necker proposed representative provincial assemblies to assume some of their responsibilities. As a test case, Louis acceded in two provinces but was reluctant to extend the experiment to all of France.

For a while, Necker's wizardry amazed all observers. France was financing a war without tax increases and without economies. By 1781, however, the loans began drying up, and Necker's critics predicted that the bubble would soon burst. The clergy and parlements rankled that the nation's fortunes lay in the hands of a Swiss Protestant, and the American war bill stood at two billion *livres*. Furthermore, an economic recession settled in. Wishing to justify his policies publicly, Necker printed an unprecedented accounting of state income and expenditures for 1780. He noted a 4 percent surplus of receipts over expenses and exposed the fact that one-tenth of government expenditures had gone to court aristocrats in the form of royal pensions. However, in challenging his critics, Necker was less than candid. As his successor illustrated, his figures covered up the greatest expense of all, the American war. Church, court and parlementary attacks on him continued, and in May 1781, he resigned in a huff.

Most of Necker's successors were intelligent men saddled with the impossible task of reestablishing the state's financial respectability within the framework of a fiscal system built upon widespread privilege. As controller-general of finance from 1783 to 1787, Charles-Alexandre Calonne at first depended upon borrowing. The debt rose accordingly and expenses exceeded income by 20 percent. Once the sources of loans dried up, Calonne turned reformer. To increase revenue and halt mounting deficits, he proposed a general tax on land, proportional to revenue, and without exemption. He urged the establishment of regional assemblies throughout France to supervise collection. Calonne knew that the parlements and provincial Estates would resist his reform and accuse him of reinstituting the Maupeou-Terray despotism. Therefore, the controller-general of finance tried a dangerous gamble. He asked the king to summon an "Assembly of Notables," including great clerics, aristocrats, and moneyed bourgeois. Calonne would propose his reforms to that group. If the Assembly, of Notables accepted them, perhaps the parlements and Estates might be neutralized. Courageous as it was, the move failed. Handpicked by Calonne himself, the Assembly of Notables met in February 1787 and rejected his reforms. Disgraced, the controller-general fell from power.

His successor, Lomenie de Brienne, archbishop of Toulouse, asked the Assembly to propose its own solution to the financial crisis, but the membership resisted, declaring that only the "authentic representatives of the nation" had the right to grant a new tax. By authentic representatives the notables clearly did not mean the king's ministers. A royal tax decree would invite a new parlementary revolt, and the parlements themselves were not authorized to initiate legislation. The Assembly of Notables therefore asked for the convocation of an elected Estates General, composed of representatives from the three social orders: clergy, nobility, and bourgeoisie. Such a body had met on occasion in the sixteenth century, but the hardening absolutism of the French monarchy had kept it out of political life for the past 170 years. Neither Louis nor his ministers desired to revive it. Thanking the Assembly of Notables for the suggestion, the king dissolved the group on May 25, 1787.

Even if the Assembly of Notables had sanctioned Calonne's reforms, it is doubtful whether the French Revolution would have been avoided. In fact, the reforms themselves—abandonment of fiscal privilege and establishment of representative local administration—were revolutionary. Moreover, the economic condition of France in 1787 was grave. The post-1763 production boom ceased in 1775, and three years later, the country slumped into a recession. Wheat and wine production declined, prices lagged, and several poor harvests, most notably one in 1785, contributed to hard times. Absolute famine and widescale mortality, supposedly relegated to the nightmarish seventeenth century, again seemed possible. Food shortages, rural unemployment, a lack of demand for textiles, layoffs in urban industry, and social unrest in the form of roaming bands of the hungry were ominous signs. Added to this, landlords sought compensation for declining production and sales, hiring lawyers to hunt down abandoned feudal dues and attempting to increase those in existence. Working a plot too small to support his family and saddled with rents already augmented during the boom of the 1760s, the tenant farmer viewed this seigneurial reaction with immense bitterness. Taken by themselves, the feudal dues were more an inconvenience than a crushing burden. In difficult times, however, the petty payments to use the lord's mill, oven, wine press, and bull and the services the peasant rendered to maintain manorial roads and manorial security not only symbolized the regime of authority and subjection but also contributed to genuine economic hardship. The tenant still had to pay the *taille* to the state, the tithe to the Church, and rents which had doubled over the past half-century. In the late 1770s, free tenants fell rapidly behind in their payments and slipped into sharecropping or migratory status. They blamed their misery on the seigneurial aristocracy, which controlled two-thirds of the country's rural property.

The Assembly of Notables dissolved, Brienne asked the Parlement of Paris to register as law most of Calonne's reform projects. The magistrates refused, declaring that only an Estates General could legally sanction a new tax. The feared constitutional crisis thus erupted. *Parlementaires* in the provinces supported the Parisians. Tracts proliferated, and royal ministers once more were denounced as tyrants. Though the magistrates were defending privilege and aristocratic selfishness, they veiled their position behind a shield of constitutional doctrine, just as they had done on countless occasions. Exasperated, in May 1788 the government resorted to a desperate act. It took the form of six edicts, largely the work of Lamoignon, a former *parlementaire* now serving Louis XVI as keeper of the seals. With royal troops ringing the Palais de Justice, home of the Parlement of Paris, the government compelled the magistrates to consent to a series of new royal courts that would assume many parlementary functions, including registration of royal orders. These May edicts would replace a considerable amount of seigneurial justice with royal justice and award certain prerogatives of the provincial Estates to royal courts. Two intransigent *parlementaires* were arrested.

The government underestimated the explosive consequences of the May edicts. From the courtiers at Versailles to the petty rural nobility, most of aristocratic France stood with the Parlement of Paris. The Assembly of the Clergy and the Orléans branch of the house of Bourbon protested formally. Publicists dependent upon the aristocracy for their livelihood printed tracts depicting the clergy and nobility as struggling for the people's liberties against rapacious ministers. Throughout the summer of 1788, public order was breaking down. In Rennes, capital of Brittany, the *intendant* was beaten up and had to flee. In Grenoble, rioting resulted in four deaths. In Pau, townspeople and mountaineers restored the parlement there to its customary functions while troops stood by idly. The country nobility was at the brink of revolt, and the king's army seemed untrustworthy. Brienne retreated. In late August, he suspended the May edicts, agreed to convoke an Estates General, and restored the parlements. He then resigned.

Seemingly supported by public opinion, the corporate aristocracy momentarily savored its triumph over the royal will. If tax reform was to come, an Estates General controlled by the high clergy and nobility would wrench political concessions from the government as compensation. However, the struggle between the parlements and government in the summer of 1788 was merely the prelude to wider and deeper unrest. For two centuries, rival elites within the aristocracy had uneasily shared political power. On one occasion, from 1648 to 1653, the rivalries among the elites had provoked a civil war. Under Louis XIV, the ministerial aristocracy appeared to win the upper hand over other factions, but in the eighteenth century, led by the Parlement of Paris, the antiministerial cliques regained strength.

Dizzy with their important victory in mid-1788, parlementary aristocrats failed to see how a generation of protracted struggle with the king's ministerial bureaucracy had awakened the political consciousness of social groups heretofore deprived of a decisive voice in national life. Yet there were recent signs of such an awakening. For example, in July 1788, a gathering of nearly five hundred nobles, clergy, and townspeople from the province of Dauphiny protested the May edicts and demanded both the restoration of the parlements and convocation of an Estates General. This accomplished, the nonaristocrats went further, proposing that the bourgeoisie in the anticipated Estates General have as many seats in the assembly as the clergy and nobles combined and that the vote in the Estates General be by head rather than order. This contradicted the old medieval system of balloting, where the combined will of clergy and nobility generally prevailed over that of the outvoted, underrepresented bourgeoisie.

In retrospect, it is a wonder that bourgeois political consciousness had lain dormant for so long. For two generations, urban professionals, shopkeepers, physicians, law clerks, merchants, artists, writers, low-rank military officers, and skilled artisans had been receptive to the Enlightenment and had followed the course of unrest in Great Britain and revolution in North America with excitement. To many, the latest wave of political infighting among France's elites, joining with an unprecedented economic crisis, suggested the crumbling of the ancien régime itself. As the nonaristocrats in Dauphiny made their revolutionary proposals, bourgeois political clubs formed throughout France. They aimed grievances and questions not merely at the government but at the aristocracy at large. Why had a bankrupt regime tolerated fiscal privilege for so long? When would corporate "liberties" be translated into civil equality? What was to be done about the abuses inherent in officeholding and arbitrary justice? What was to be done about corruption in the clergy? Why were landed seigneurs permitted to squeeze dry their tenants? Why were aristocratic parlements, provincial Estates, and guilds allowed to strangle the political life of the regions? An underground literature circulating in the 1780s had posed such questions, often in irreverent, pornographic, and violent form. Now the effects were taking hold. Readers who had absorbed the questions and criticisms were reciting them, boldly and openly.

Necker replaced Brienne. Given a second chance, the Swiss banker tried to pacify the aristocracy by recognizing the parlements and convoking a new Assembly of Notables. For the bourgeoisie's benefit, he let it be known that he favored an Estates General with increased representation for the Third Estate. Agreeing that the Estates General should propose the needed tax reforms, he would not commit himself on the procedural question of whether votes by order or head would count. However, the Parlement of

Paris and Assembly of Notables insisted that the forthcoming Estates General should be no different from the previous one, which had met in 1614–15. Each of the three orders should have an equal number of delegates, and the vote should be by order.

Bitterly disappointed by these positions, the bourgeoisie was no longer taken in by aristocratic propaganda. It was clear that the only liberties which interested the magistrates and notables were their own. They knew that some form of constitutional government and an end to fiscal privilege were in the offing, and they were determined to keep reform from degenerating into a democratization of political and social life. Above all, they wished to gain control over the king, protect seigneurial rights, and maintain officeholding. The public support held by the parlements in May 1788 disintegrated by year's end. At a rate of two dozen per week, pamphlets inundated France, most of them denouncing the privileged orders and calling for vote by head in an enlarged Estates General. Recognizing the new course that events had taken, in January 1789 the Swiss journalist Mallet Du Pan wrote: "The debate has changed aspect. The issue of the king, ministerial despotism, and the constitution have become secondary. Now it's war between the Third Estate and the other two Orders."

Mallet was prophetic. The Royal Council tried compromise. In the forthcoming Estates General, the number of bourgeois delegates equaled the number of clerics and nobles, but the vote remained according to order. Subjects in each order elected their delegates. Elections took place in open meetings, at which time memoranda of grievances called *cahiers de doléances* were drawn up. The meetings, over 40,000 of them, were held in late winter and early spring 1789. Nobles and clerics chose their delegates more or less directly. For the Third Estate, however, males of like occupation first gathered together to choose local deputies. These deputies then met to select a district's representative to the Estates General. As a result of the elimination process, men of speaking ability and with knowledge of public affairs were the ones ultimately selected to represent the Third Estate. Not a single peasant, not a single town laborer went to the great conclave at Versailles. In all, more than 1,100 delegates were elected: 291 for the clergy, of whom two-thirds were parish priests; 270 for the nobility, of whom one-third had expressed public sympathy for nonaristocrats; and 578 for the Third Estate, nearly half of whom were town lawyers and another hundred either merchants, industrialists, or bankers.

The delegates brought with them the distillations of more than 40,000 *cahiers*, grievances that revealed a nation in deep trouble. *Cahiers* from peasant villages bitterly denounced the universe of seigneurial privilege and exaction superimposed upon the burden of high rents, insufficient land, and the state's tax demands. The *cahiers* of townspeople reflected the conflicting aspirations of workers and employers, artisans and merchants. The *cahiers* of the nobility called for more constitutional government and accepted the end to tax privilege, but they also demanded maintenance of a hierarchized social order. Practically no *cahier* questioned the monarchical conception of the state, and there was large agreement for the need to enlarge civil liberties and establish representative political assemblies in all the provinces. Pamphleteers also cried out for change, and the country seethed with anticipation and excitement. The harvest of 1788–89 had been the worst in years, and scarcities resulted in very high grain and bread prices. In good times, the French town worker paid half his income for bread. Now 80 to 90 percent was required. Textile sales dropped sharply; the building trades braked to a halt. By April 1789, half the urban labor force was out of work, and in the countryside, bands of human misery clogged roads. Manor houses were sacked and town riots erupted.

In such a volatile atmosphere the Estates General gathered at Versailles on May 4, and the king opened the assembly the next day. Rigid seventeenth-century forms of procedure were in force. Members of the Third Estate had to dress in black, keep their heads bare in deference to the clergy and nobility, and even enter the meeting hall through a side door. Louis, Marie Antoinette, and the court attended the opening ceremonies, but the royal speech greatly disappointed Third Estaters, who hoped the king would make a dramatic recommendation for vote by head. Instead, Louis warned against excessive reforms, and the government speeches that followed were silent about both voting procedure and redistribution of the tax burden. By the next day it was clear that the regime had no program.

The Third Estate then took its revolutionary stand: the commoners would do nothing until the three orders met in a single assembly and delegates voted by head. Invitations were sent out to the clergy and nobles. In their separate meeting halls, the delegates of the Church voted against joining the commoners by 133–114; the nobles did the same, by 141–47. Thus, for the next six weeks, the great convocation was stalemated, and the Third Estaters organized their leadership. On June 17 the Third Estate formally declared the universe of orders to be null and void and announced that it alone stood for the French nation. This was not meant to be the nation in the traditional sense, composed of hierarchical corporate fragments, each with distinctive liberties, privileges, rights, and obligations. It was meant to be a community of citizens. The declaration of June 17 was an arrogation of power. Once again, clergy and nobles were invited to join. Three priests already had come, sixteen more arrived, and on June 19 the clerical Estate voted to join the commoners as the National Assembly. The delegates affirmed their demand to authorize taxation.

The gauntlet had been thrown down. By their own will, the commoners invalidated a constituted representative body, the Estates General, and they assumed powers over taxation. Deeply concerned, the king decided to address a joint session of the three orders and hurriedly scheduled it for the commoners' meeting hall. Carpenters were set to work to refurbish the room. Somehow, however, word failed to reach the commoners, and as they assembled on June 20, they found themselves locked out of their customary meeting place. While the carpenters worked within, troops guarded the building. Suspecting a plot, the delegates next were drenched by a sudden downpour. Nearby was an unused indoor tennis court. In a state of anxiety, anger, and determination, they rushed for the sports arena to hear some impassioned speeches. Next they swore an oath "never to separate and to gather wherever circumstances dictated until a constitution was written and solidified upon firm foundations."

The royal session took place on June 23. It was a stormy occasion. Inspired by the court and goaded by a Parlement suddenly committed to the cause of royal authority, Louis unequivocally declared that any program for change must emanate from the throne. Self-constituted political groups like the so-called National Assembly were illegal. The royal position was that seigneurial dues and all forms of privilege represented inviolable rights of property. The king promised decisions on taxation and constitutional reform. The government would introduce a system of provincial assemblies. Louis scolded the delegates for having accomplished nothing, reminded them that his explicit approval alone gave legal sanction to their recommendations, and commanded that they return to their different chambers to resume their sessions. Louis then left the hall, followed by his royal officials, most of the noble delegates, and a few of the clerical ones. All the other deputies remained in the chamber.

The event would not be forgotten. Faced with the choice, the king had forsaken the commoners for the aristocracy. He had insisted that the old orders must be preserved. Disappointed but not cowed, the deputies remaining in the chamber cheered wildly as the erstwhile aristocrat Mirabeau declared that bayonets alone would drive the National Assembly from its appointed task. On June 25 the Assembly met again. More clergy joined. So did nearly fifty noble delegates, including the king's cousin, the duke of Orléans. On June 27, the king made a sudden about-face. Exasperated, grieving over the recent death of his eldest son, and hearing of renewed violence in the countryside, he agreed to the conversion of the Estates General into the Constituent National Assembly. He ordered all the delegates to gather together at once. Observers considered the crisis surmounted. An Englishman in France at the time, the agrarian innovator Arthur Young, called the revolution "complete."

CONCLUSION

Of course, Young was wrong. It was only the beginning. One-third of the deputies to the National Assembly were there simply because their exasperated king had ordered them to attend, and they sullenly refused to participate in assembly deliberations. From this nucleus of aristocrats and clerics who believed that the constitutional legitimacy of the French monarchy was being torn asunder, the counterrevolution would emerge and influence the course of the nation's history for the next quarter-century. Already in the late spring of 1789, however, the mood of preservation was a defensive one. The monarchy's inability to cope with economic crisis, social injustice, and political mismanagement had created a contrary mood for fundamental change, and the recent boldness of the Third Estate gave the mood direction. The essential problem facing the National Assembly in June 1789 was not the consolidation of past victories, but how far the revolution would go.

It went very far, destroying the alliance of monarchy, aristocracy, and Church upon which the ancien régime had been built. Though the most radical changes would occur in France, where under Louis XIV the old alliance had been perfected and had served as example to the other states in Europe, the revolution internationalized. The Netherlands, Italy, Germany, Spain, the Caribbean, and Latin America would feel its shock waves; it would become an inspiration for millions. In the summer of 1789, the urban and rural poor of France would themselves become revolutionaries, pressing more prosperous and more reluctant political leaders into radical actions, and eventually bearing the ideology of change far beyond the nation's borders.

This book, however, is not about the revolution. It is about the long-term political, social, and intellectual conditions of Europe that concluded with a revolution. Curiously enough, revolts introduced our period. They illustrated that even in the mid-seventeenth century people responded violently to political mismanagement, social injustice, and economic crisis. For the century that followed, however, the elites who directed the ancien régime patched up the difficulties with administrative, ideological, and symbolic solutions that brought relative sense and order to western civilization. Absolutism and Enlightenment coexisted in a tense kind of harmony, while economic amelioration helped create more socially and intellectually articulate people than had been the case in previous centuries. Awareness produced both hope and expectation. Once the elites of the ancien régime revealed the limits to fulfilling them, the system was endangered. In 1789, it crashed down. Some say that a new, more chilling, and more exploitative order eventually succeeded the ancien régime. But that is another story.

Additional Reading: Selections

The following list contains a selection of books that students should find helpful in obtaining a firmer grasp of the historical issues for the period 1648–1789. Several of the works are scholarly syntheses; others have broken new ground. In their approaches nearly all the books listed are sensitive to developing techniques in social history. By no means do the lists exhaust the important recent literature. Valuable specialized studies appear regularly; series such as The New Cambridge Modern History have recently been completed; and others such as the Cambridge and Fontana economic histories of Europe (Great Britain) and "Nouvelle Clio" and "Vie quotidienne" volumes (France) are in course of publication. Moreover, several dozen scholarly articles published within the past decade have forced historians to re-examine many of their suppositions concerning the *ancien régime*. Students would do well to become familiar with articles and debates that receive publicity in major journals such as *The American Historical Review, Journal of Modern History, Past and Present*, and *Annales: E.S.C.* Until 1976 *The American Historical Review* published running bibliographies of articles appearing in professional journals throughout the world. Though the *Review* has ceased printing the lists, they can be obtained through subscription from the offices of the American Historical Association at Indiana University, Bloomington.

Ariès, Philippe. *L'Enfant et la vie familiale sous l'Ancien Régime*. Paris, 1960. (Translated as *Centuries of Childhood: A Social History of Family Life*. New York, 1962.)

Aston, Trevor ed. *Crisis in Europe: 1560–1660*. Garden City, 1967.

Baker, Keith Michael. *Condorcet: From Natural Philosophy to Social Mathematics*. Chicago, 1974.

Bernard, Paul P. *Jesuits and Jacobins: Enlightenment and Enlightened Despotism in Austria*. Urbana, 1971.

Boxer, C. R. *The Dutch Seaborne Empire: 1600–1800*. New York, 1965.

Braudel, Fernand. *Civilisation materielle et capitalism (XVᵉ-XVIIIᵉ siècles)*. Paris, 1967. (Translated as *Capitalism and Material Life: 1400–1800*. New York, 1973.)

Carswell, John. *From Revolution to Revolution: England 1688–1776.* New York, 1973.

Cambers, J. D. *Population, Economy, and Society in Pre-Industrial England.* New York, 1972.

Chaunu, Pierre. *La Civilisation de l'Europe classique.* Paris, 1966.

———. *La Civilisation de l'Europe des Lumières.* Paris, 1970.

Cobban, Alfred *et al. The Eighteenth Century: Europe in the Age of Enlightenment.* New York, 1969.

Davies, K. G. *The North-Atlantic World in the Seventeenth Century.* Minneapolis, 1974.

Davis, Ralph. *The Rise of the Atlantic Economies.* Ithaca, 1973.

Elliott, J. H. *Imperial Spain 1469–1716.* New York, 1963.

Forster, Robert and Jack P. Greene eds. *Preconditions of Revolution in Early Modern Europe.* Baltimore, 1970.

Gay, Peter. *The Enlightenment: An Interpretation.* 2 vols. New York, 1966, 1969.

Gibson, Charles. *Spain in America.* New York, 1966.

Gossman, Lionel. *French Society and Culture: Background for Eighteenth-Century Literature.* Englewood Cliffs, 1972.

Goubert, Pierre. *L'Ancien Régime.* 2 vols. Paris, 1969, 1973. (Vol. 1 translated as *The Ancien Regime: French Society 1600–1750.* New York, 1973.)

———. *Louis XIV et vingt millions de Francais.* Paris, 1966. (Translated as *Louis XIV and Twenty Million Frenchmen.* New York, 1970.)

Gutton, Jean-Pierre. *La Société et les pauvres en Europe (XVIᵉ-XVIIIᵉ siècles).* Paris, 1974.

Hahn, Roger. *The Anatomy of a Scientific Institution: The Paris Academy of Sciences, 1666–1803.* Berkeley and Los Angeles, 1971.

Hampson, Norman. *A Cultural History of the Enlightenment.* New York, 1968.

Hertzberg, Arthur. *The French Enlightenment and the Jews.* New York, 1968.

Hill, Christopher. *Change and Continuity in Seventeenth-Century England.* Cambridge, Mass., 1974.

Hufton, Olwen H. *The Poor of Eighteenth-Century France 1750–1789.* New York, 1974.

James, Francis G. *Ireland in the Empire, 1688–1770: A History of Ireland From the Williamite Wars to the Eve of the American Revolution.* Cambridge, Mass., 1973.

Jones, Robert E. *The Emancipation of the Russian Nobility, 1762–1785.* Princeton, 1973.

Kagan, Richard L. *Students and Society in Early Modern Spain.* Baltimore, 1975.

Kammen, Michael. *Empire and Interest: The American Colonies and the Politics of Mercantilism.* Philadelphia, 1970.

Kuhn, Thomas S. *The Structure of Scientific Revolutions.* 2 edition. Chicago, 1970.

Laslett, Peter. *The World We Have Lost.* New York, 1966.

Macpherson, C. B. *The Political Theory of Possessive Individualism: Hobbes to Locke.* Oxford, 1962.

Mingay, G. E. *English Landed Society in the Eighteenth Century.* Toronto, 1963.

Mousnier, Roland. *Fureurs paysannes: les paysans dans les reévoltes du XVIIᵉ siècle (France, Russie, Chine).* Paris, 1967. (Translated as *Peasant Uprisings in Seventeenth-Century France, Russia, and China.* New York, 1970.)

————. *Les Institutions de la France sous la monarchie absolue, 1598–1789.* Vol. 1, *Société et Etat.* Paris, 1974.

Palmer, Robert R. *The Age of the Democratic Revolutions: A Political History of Europe and America: 1760–1800.* 2 vols. Princeton, 1959, 1964.

Parry, J. H. *Trade and Dominion: The European Overseas Empires in the Eighteenth Century.* New York, 1971.

Paulson, Ronald. *Hogarth: His Life, Times, and Art.* Abridged edition. New Haven, 1974.

Plumb, J. H. *The Origins of Political Stability: England 1675–1725.* Boston, 1967.

Price, J. L. *Culture and Society in the Dutch Republic During the Seventeenth Century.* New York, 1974.

Raeff, Marc. *Origins of the Russian Intelligentsia: The Eighteenth-Century Nobility.* New York, 1966.

Ranum, Orest ed. *National Consciousness, History, and Political Culture in Early Modern Europe.* Baltimore, 1975.

Roberts, Michael ed. *Essays in Swedish History.* Minneapolis, 1968.

Rosen, Charles. *The Classical Style: Haydn, Mozart, Beethoven.* New York, 1971.

Rosenberg, Hans. *Bureaucracy, Aristocracy, and Autocracy: The Prussian Experience 1660–1815.* Cambridge, Mass., 1958.

Rudé, George. *Paris and London in the Eighteenth Century.* New York, 1972.

Sheridan, Richard B. *Sugar and Slavery: An Economic History of the British West Indies, 1623–1775.* Baltimore, 1974.

Shklar, Judith N. *Men and Citizens: A Study of Rousseau's Social Theory.* New York, 1969.

Spence, Jonathan D. *Emperor of China: A Self-Portrait of K'ang-hsi.* New York, 1974.

Thompson, Roger. *Women in Stuart England and America: A Comparative Study.* Boston, 1974.

Venturi, Franco. *Italy and the Enlightenment: Studies in a Cosmopolitan Century.* Translated by Susan Corsi. London, 1972.

Wade, Ira O. *The Intellectual Origins of the French Enlightenment.* Princeton, 1971.

Wilson, Arthur M. *Diderot.* New York, 1972.

Index